DANTE'S STYLE IN
HIS LYRIC POETRY

DANTE'S STYLE
IN HIS
LYRIC POETRY

PATRICK BOYDE

*Lecturer in Italian in the University of Cambridge
and Fellow of St John's College*

CAMBRIDGE
AT THE UNIVERSITY PRESS
1971

Published by the Syndics of the Cambridge University Press
Bentley House, 200 Euston Road, London N.W.1
American Branch: 32 East 57th Street, New York, N.Y.10022

© Cambridge University Press 1971

Library of Congress Catalogue Card Number: 74–130906

ISBN: 0 521 07918 7

Printed in Great Britain by
Alden & Mowbray Ltd at the Alden Press, Oxford

FOR KENELM FOSTER

AMICITIAE ERGO

CONTENTS

PREFACE

Work on this book occupied me, with intervals, for a period of eleven years. Most of the spade-work was completed in the years 1958–61, and the findings were presented in my doctoral thesis in 1963. Then began my collaboration with Kenelm Foster leading to our edition of Dante's poems which appeared in 1967. When that volume was ready for the press, I was able to read more widely in the field of stylistics and to gain new perspectives on the work I had done. Finally, during the years 1967 and 1968, I rewrote the 1963 thesis from beginning to end, modifying some of my original conclusions profoundly in the light of my deeper understanding of stylistics, of Dante's poetry, and of the literary context in which Dante worked. The original conception of the work, however, goes back to the 1950s, and in particular to my reading of E. R. Curtius's *European Literature and the Latin Middle Ages* in the summer of 1957.

I owe a great debt to past and present members of the Department of Italian at Cambridge University where I have been undergraduate, research student, and lecturer. The book could never have been completed without the encouragement of teachers and supervisors, the friendship and support of my colleagues, or the stimulus of our pupils. It is invidious to mention names in this context, but I feel that I have gained most from the example of Kenelm Foster, to whom this book is affectionately dedicated; and I have benefited greatly from many conversations on technical points with Joseph Cremona. I must also thank those friends who read and criticized the first draft of the introduction, and who thereby helped me to improve it in many respects: Linda Paterson, Allan Blunden, Frank Bott, Michael Caesar, David Frost and Michael Silk. It goes without saying that none of them is responsible for any errors of fact or judgement, and that none of them would support all my arguments as they stand.

My thanks are also due to the staff of the Cambridge University Press and, finally, to June Salmons and Vincent Moleta who helped me to read the proofs. P.B.

ABBREVIATIONS

The following abbreviations are employed:

For the text of Dante's works I have used the following editions: *Vita Nuova, Rime, Epistolae*, SDI edition; *Convivio*, ed. G. Busnelli and G. Vandelli (2 vols, 2nd ed., 'con appendice di aggiornamento a cura di A. E. Quaglio', Florence, 1964); *De vulgari eloquentia*, ed. A. Marigo (3rd ed., 'con appendice di aggiornamento a cura di P. G. Ricci', Florence, 1957); *Monarchia*, ed. P. G. Ricci (Milan, 1965); *Divina Commedia*, ed. G. Petrocchi (4 vols, Milan, 1966–7).

Abbreviations

Documentum	Geoffrey of Vinsauf (attrib.), *Documentum de modo et arte dictandi et versificandi* (ed. Faral)
Et.	Isidore of Seville, *Etymologiarum libri XX*
John of Garland	John of Garland, *Poetria*
Laborintus	Everard the German, *Laborintus* (ed. Faral)
Matthew of Vendôme	Matthew of Vendôme, *Ars versificatoria* (ed. Faral)
PN	Geoffrey of Vinsauf, *Poetria Nova* (ed. Faral)
Quintilian	Quintilian, *Institutio oratoria*

For the editions of the rhetorical works, see section II of the select bibliography.

PERIODICALS

AGI	*Archivio glottologico italiano*
AL	*Acta Linguistica*
AMAT	*Atti e Memorie dell'Accademia Toscana di scienze e lettere,* 'La Colombaria'
CN	*Cultura Neolatina*
DDJ	*Deutsches Dante Jahrbuch*
FR	*Filologia romanza*
GSLI	*Giornale storico della letteratura italiana*
RAL	*Rendiconti dell'Accademia Nazionale dei Lincei, classe di scienze morali, storiche e filologiche*
SMV	*Studi mediolatini e volgari*
ZRP	*Zeitschrift für Romanische Philologie*

INTRODUCTION

This book has two aspects. It is intended both as a contribution to the study of Dante's poetry, and as a contribution to the study of 'personal' or 'individual' style in any work of literature. These two aspects or aims are equal and complementary. The general theory must be put to the test in the analysis of particular texts; the analysis of particular texts should reveal its theoretical basis.

It is only in the introduction that a certain separation of these aims has seemed desirable. In the first and second sections, where I have outlined the method of description and its objectives, I have kept as far as possible to general principles and to those features which seem to me essential and universally valid. All discussion of the particular problems relating exclusively to Dante's lyrics has been held over until the third and last section of the introduction. In this way, readers whose main interests lie in the analysis of style should find what they require with the minimum of distraction.

On the other hand, since the book is written equally for the student of Dante, I have not assumed any special knowledge of stylistic theory or terminology, and the introduction is conceived more as an essay than as a treatise. It has also proved more convenient to present the method of description *before* discussing what it is designed to achieve, or what its limitations are. This is not without its drawbacks, but I hope it will be found that the second section provides an answer to any doubts and queries that may present themselves on reading the first.

I

It is a fact of common experience that many untrained but perceptive readers can at times distinguish the style of author X from author Y, or recognize the style of author Z, if they are given a passage of suffi-cient length. Please note the qualifications: I say 'many' and not 'all'; 'at times' and not 'always' nor even 'usually'; 'perceptive readers' and not simply 'readers'. The ability to recognize personal style presupposes intelligence, a good general education, and a fairly wide familiarity with the literature of one's native tongue. It is not innate. But it does not have to be taught systematically. And it is equally a fact of common experience that such a reader may subsequently be quite unable to justify or to explain in an analytical way his successful act of recognition or differentiation, which was made spontaneously and intuitively.

Our first observation, then, is that the purpose of studying personal style is not to discover something new, but to provide an adequate explanation of a familiar phenomenon. The questions we must answer are not: 'Does it exist?', or 'Does it work?'; but 'What is it made of?' and 'How does it work?'.

We could find further empirical support for these generalizations in the other arts, and especially in painting and music. There are many music lovers, for example, who have never received any formal training in the theory of music, but who can nevertheless identify an unfamiliar concerto as being by Mozart, or at least 'in his style', or definitely 'not in his style'. But I would prefer to develop a humbler and more everyday analogy.

Provided that exception is made for the case of identical twins, it is usually regarded as a truism that 'no two people look exactly alike'.[1] We may occasionally forget or make a mistake, but our normal assumption is that we shall recognize our acquaintances, and that we shall be able to distinguish one person from another by their appearance. We do this instantaneously and involuntarily, without any formal training, and certainly without any conscious analysis of the features which make possible this apparently infinite number of differentiations. And when we are asked to describe someone's appearance—even someone we know quite well—most of us make a wretched showing. At best our description consists of a few ill-assorted and ill-ordered adjectives, ranging from general impressions to unfounded assertions about height or the colour of hair and eyes.

Of course we could better our performance immediately if we were suitably prompted by a trained person. Let us take the case of an eyewitness to a robbery. No detective worth his salt would ask the witness simply 'What did the thief look like?' Instead he would put a series of particular questions: 'How tall was he? How old was he? Was

[1] '...nullo viso ad altro viso è simile', Dante, *Con.*, III, viii, 7.

2

he lightly or heavily built? What colour was his hair? Did you notice any-thing distinctive about his face, body or bearing?' And having conflated the answers of several witnesses to questions such as these, the police would subsequently issue a description of 'a man they wish to interview ...'

If it is well done, such a description can be extremely helpful. Boccaccio never saw Dante, but having collected, sifted and combined the impressions of those who had, he can tell us in his *Life* of the poet that Dante was of middle height and had a slight stoop; his complexion was dark, his hair and beard, even in middle life, were thick, black and curly; his face was oval ('lungo'), his eyes rather on the large side, his nose aquiline; he had a prominent jaw ('mascelle grandi'), and his lower lip protruded beyond the upper. In dress and bearing he was grave and dignified.[1]

Suppose for a moment that we were Florentine agents, hired to track down the notorious embezzler and traitor Dante Alighieri, known to be issuing treasonable propaganda in favour of the commune's enemies from some city in Northern Italy. We should be very glad of such a description. It would enable us to narrow our search immediately to some two per cent or less of the population in each town we came to. Nevertheless, we should probably be forced to recognize that the description still fitted quite a number of people. Assuming then, that we were forced to rely on such a verbal description—there being no one with us who could simply identify the culprit, and Dante having no known distinctive scars or birthmarks—what refinements would we require? Presumably we would want information about other variable features—the colour of his eyes perhaps, or his waist measure-ment, or his size in shoes: it would not really matter what features we chose, provided they are known to vary unpredictably from one person to another and can therefore serve to distinguish them. We would also require greater precision in the information we had. Thus it would be useful to know that Dante stood exactly 5 feet 5½ inches tall (as would appear from the measurements made of his skeleton in 1865[2]); and it would help if we could ascertain exactly how swarthy

---

[1] Boccaccio, *Vita di Dante*, xx, ed. D. Guerri, in *Giovanni Boccaccio, Il comento alla Divina Commedia e gli altri scritti intorno a Dante* (Bari, 1918), vol. 1, pp. 32–3.

[2] 'The length of the skeleton was 1·55 metres. Allowing for shrinkage through loss of cartilage etc., we may estimate that at fifty-six years Dante was about five feet five and one half inches tall (1·67 m.) when he stood erect'. R. T. Holbrook, *Portraits of Dante*, (London, 1911), p. 34.

his complexion was according to some reasonably objective scale of 'swarthiness'. What we are saying, then, is that if we had to identify a person on the basis of a purely verbal description, we should need reliable observations about a *large number* of features that vary from one human being to another, and that in each of these 'variables' we would want our information to be as *precise* as possible: linear measurements would have to be accurate to within a fraction of an inch; adjectives of colour, texture or shape would have to be closely defined, if possible by reference to a commonly accepted scale or standard.

Our pursuit of the analogy may seem to have led us far from our theme, but we may bridge the gap with ease if we now restate our tentative conclusions a little more forcefully. Thus: it is in fact possible to make a truly distinctive verbal description of an individual's appearance if we have sufficiently precise information about a sufficient range of significant variables. And, further: it is in fact just the kind of details which appear in such a description that collectively account for our ability to distinguish people. Differing dimensions subtend differing angles on our retinas; and the differing compositions of skin and hair reflect light at differing frequencies. The hypothesis which I shall try to demonstrate in the course of this book is that it is possible to make a truly distinctive description of an author's individual style by following similar principles, and that the details will be those which collectively account for our empirical and intuitive recognition of his personal style.

The description of style is inevitably far more abstract and far more complex than the description of appearance. There are many places, too, where the 'model' we have just set up will have to be modified, corrected, or even abandoned altogether. But however different the *techniques* of description may prove to be, this will not affect the *principles*. And the model can help us not only to grasp the simplicity of those principles, but to keep them steadily in view when the proliferation of detail may seem to obscure them. Let me repeat, then, that the essence of the proposed method of description is that one should study a *wide range* of significant variables, and that one should achieve the *greatest possible precision* in describing the alternatives possible under each head. The degree of precision and the kind of measurement will vary enormously from one variable to the next—just as they do in the case of height, weight, complexion—but the results should be verifiable. If another analyst repeats the experiment, using the same criteria, his findings should be the same. He might well disagree as to the presentation and interpretation of the facts, but there should be no dispute as to the facts themselves.

We shall return to the analogy from time to time, but it will not be exploited relentlessly nor wrung dry, and I shall not call attention to all the places where it does not hold good. There is one point, however, where the comparison between individual appearance and individual style could be so grossly misleading that we cannot let it pass in silence. It is this: if an author has written at sufficient length for us to be able to recognize his personal style, he will necessarily have written enough for there to be significant differences in style between one paragraph and another, one poem and another, one work and another. What we are seeking to describe, therefore, is not the single phenomenon of the author himself, but rather the family likeness shared by his spiritual children.[1] And so it is *not* assumed that where an author is felt to have a personal style it will be because in all his works, or in all sample passages of whatever length, he always uses each variable in the same way. That would be absurd. The hypothesis is, rather, that in those works where we recognize a personal style, the author has *tended fairly consistently* to prefer one mode of expression to another, to confine himself for the most part to one limited area of the range of alternatives possible in any given variable. (Of course the style will still not be individual, however constant the tendencies, unless the particular combination of preferences is peculiar to the author: but here the analogy still obtains.) To give one brief example: we shall not expect to find that every sentence written by Smith has neither more nor less than three dependent clauses. What we might conceivably find is that such sentences amounted to more than 50 per cent of the total in his works and that a further 30 per cent had four dependent clauses, whereas sentences composed of a main clause alone or a main clause with only one dependent formed a small minority. Such, at its very simplest, is the kind of description that will be required; and this not just for one variable but over the whole range of variables.

There are in effect two kinds of variable. There are those in which

---

[1] Cf. Dante, *Con.*, III, ix, 4: 'sì come sorella è detta quella femmina che da uno medesimo generante è generata, così puote l'uomo dire "sorella" de l'*opera* che da uno medesimo operante è operata; *ché la nostra operazione in alcuno modo è generazione*'.

the answer may be either positive or negative, for example, 'Is there a simile in this sentence?' And there are those in which the answer must be positive: the stylistic feature must belong to one or other of a set of alternatives. In each case the evidence we require is that of *relative frequency*. In the second case, as we have just seen in the hypothetical example concerning sentence structure, the answer to the multiple question ('is it Xa, Xb, Xc or Xd? etc.') will be expressed as a set of *percentages* ('Xa = 5%, Xb = 30%, etc.'). In the first case, the answer to the 'open or shut' kind of question will usually be expressed in a form such as this: 'There is 1 simile every 10 lines, or every 100 lines; or, if we choose a different unit of measurement, there is 1 simile every 100 words or every 500 words.' Thus, although the quantification of evidence concerning style is not quite such a straightforward matter as it is for height and weight, nevertheless only the most rudimentary mathematical skills are required in order to perform the analyses or interpret the findings. Note also that there are some variables —for example the tropes—in which the evidence cannot be presented quantitatively, because the alternatives are not sufficiently clear-cut for exact classification. In such cases, one should introduce such groupings as are possible and helpful, and present the evidence in the form of a complete list of examples for a stated unit of measurement.

Mention of the possible units of measurement—'words', the 'line of verse' or the 'printed page'—leads us to the next vital aspect of technique. Whether the text is long or short, whether it is in prose or in verse, it will always be necessary to hit upon a manageable standard unit for the purposes of the initial analysis. The text or texts will then be split up into these units; and one will carry out a whole series of self-contained analyses rather than a single, undifferentiated analysis of a whole work. In the first stages, the information must be compiled, processed and recorded separately for each unit. Other reasons apart, this is the only way of preventing errors of judgement or computation, or of detecting them when they have occurred. Ideally, these units should be complete as to their sense and equal in length: it is helpful to choose a number which is divisible by ten. Experience would suggest that the unit should not be shorter than 100 words or longer than 300 words. But this ideal could only be realized in a poem written in regular stanzas—in *ottava rima*, for example. In all other cases, compromise will be necessary. In a prose work, one would probably choose a fixed number of words, sacrificing completeness of the sense wherever necessary, in order to facilitate the arithmetical operations and make possible the direct comparison of all units. In the analysis of Dante's poems, however, I have taken the sonnet, or the stanza of a *canzone* or *ballata* as the standard unit. These are all complete in sense and alike in the principles governing their metrical structure, but the stanzas vary in length and may have fewer or more lines than the sonnet. Each case will obviously have to be resolved on its merits.

At a later stage in the analysis it will be necessary to collect these units into groups, so that one will eventually have information about the relative frequency of a given feature at three levels: the unit, the group, and the complete work. Once again, it would be analytically convenient to have an equal number of units in each group, and again the number 10, or a multiple of 10, has much to recommend it. But the economy of the work may demand a more flexible, *ad hoc* grouping, as again I have found necessary in this study.

The ideal size of these groups is determined by their *purpose*. They are introduced to test the validity of the hypothesis that an author who has a recognizable personal style 'tends fairly consistently to prefer one mode of expression to another and to confine himself for the most part to one limited area of the range of alternatives possible in any given variable'. No one would expect the average distribution of stylistic features found in the whole work to be matched consistently in each of the minimum standard units. At this level we should expect considerable fluctuations, especially if the units are nearer 100 than 300 words in length. But if the presumed consistency of style has any basis in fact, we should expect it to manifest itself in extracts of medium length. What we must establish, then, is just how long the extract has to be before its pattern of distribution will approximate to that of the whole work. Does it have to be 1,000, 2,000, or 5,000 words? In the ideally consistent work, the ideal group would represent the *shortest* extract to satisfy this requirement; and thus the distribution of features in any group would closely match that in any other group as well as that for the work as a whole. But there are no ideal works. And what we must never do is to take the consistency or uniformity for granted. We must do our best, as it were, to overthrow that comfortable working hypothesis. And the groups are therefore an indispensable control to the experiment.

7

The need for precision, for controls, and for a wide range of variables makes this kind of analysis a somewhat laborious undertaking. And it would be quite impracticable to carry out a complete description of a lengthy work. But this does not invalidate the method of description, because such completeness is not in the least necessary. The analysis of the lengthy work would be conducted on the same principles, using the same standard units and groups as cross-checks. The only difference would be that the series of standard units, instead of following one another without a break, would be selected so as to constitute an acceptable 'random sample'. (Nor is this in the least difficult or abstruse. Any handbook will provide a suitable random series of numbers, which can simply be taken to represent the page numbers in whatever edition of the work is used.) Errors in the method of sampling or inconsistencies in the work would be revealed by the checks and controls just as in a 'complete' analysis. And the evidence would be no less compelling.

For the sake of simplicity, I have so far presented the method of description as though it were limited in application to the study of those works in which a perceptive reader feels aware of a consistent and distinctive individual style. Now, it is equally the common experience of perceptive readers that many writers—probably the great majority—do *not* have a recognizable personal style. Either their style varies excessively and unpredictably from one poem or passage to another; or, more commonly, their works are too anonymous, too conventional, too deliberately impersonal. At first sight such works do not seem relevant to our inquiry. Nor would it appear that any useful purpose could be served by applying a method of analysis expressly designed to verify and explain our perception of personal style in certain works, in order to describe the style of other works from which we gain no such impression. But then we may reflect that if the one intuitive experience requires explanation so does the other; and that if the method of description proves unable to account for a *negative* impression—by demonstrating why two poems or works seem too *un*like to have a common author, or why works by several authors seem to have so much in common stylistically that they are all equally impersonal—then it cannot be used to confirm a *positive* impression. At some point, therefore, the method must be used to describe works which seem to lack any coherent individuality of style. And at the very least the information so obtained will be of value for the purposes of comparison, for which we shall see the necessity in due course.

If the method of description really can demonstrate both consistency and inconsistency of style, then it should be able to account for that mixed impression of continuity and discontinuity which we may experience on reading a number of successive works by one author, where it would seem that some features change more or less rapidly and decisively while others remain constant. In other words, the method should be ideally suited to a study of the *development* of an author's style. Conversely, such a series of works should constitute the ideal material with which to vindicate the method, since they would test it both negatively and positively at the same time. We shall see later that Dante's poems are precisely that kind of ideal material.

The problems of technique which we have examined up to this point all relate in some way to the need for quantification and precision in assembling the stylistic evidence. They have been given pride of place because quantification and precision are fundamental to the general theory of description which I am proposing, and because their central position in that theory constitutes its only claim to novelty. But we must now turn to the logically antecedent problem of the 'stylistic variables' themselves, and give some answer to the basic question: 'What are these variables?' Here the answer ought to be straightforward. No new variables will be proposed; and, in this respect at least, the book is intended simply as an 'applied study'—a work of *applied* stylistics rather than a work of 'theoretical' or 'pure' stylistics.

Now, in any such study, in any field of inquiry, that which is 'applied' is a body of general hypotheses and concepts formulated by earlier theorists. Where the branch of study is well established, and where the general hypotheses have stood the test of time (that is, where they have continued to provide a satisfactory explanation of particular phenomena), we speak of them as 'principles' or 'laws', and no longer think of them as the discovery of certain individuals. Generally, too, we assume that they form part of the common culture, or part of the specific preparation, which may be taken for granted in any reader of the applied work. Should the reader be ignorant of the meaning of any term, we expect him to find a definition in some standard work of reference. In newer branches of study, however, such as the social sciences or psychology, hypotheses are still hypotheses, constantly subject to attack and modification. There are rival approaches and rival bodies of theory. And so the author of an applied study will be required to indicate whose disciple he is, or from which schools of thought he has learnt, or to which books the reader may turn for a full statement of the theory followed, and an adequate definition of the terms used.

The student of style is in something of a quandary in this respect. On the one hand, many of his terms were coined by Greek and Latin rhetoricians over 2,000 years ago, and have been in continuous use ever since. They are to be found in any good dictionary. On the other hand, he knows that stylistics is a relatively new discipline, necessarily unstable and torn by jarring sects, and that its theorists and practitioners are united perhaps only in one thing—in their rejection of the assumptions, ideals and methods associated with the ancient rhetorical theory of style. Today we no longer study style with the exclusive aim of using the knowledge gained to teach the young to 'write well'—uniformly well! Even if we do try to teach them to write 'better', we have no one, absolute ideal of style to set before them, nor, indeed, any finite number of ideals. We shun the pedagogical methods which required students to imitate the style of admired authors, or to learn to apply in their work long lists of precepts and stylistic devices. And we do not confine our field of interest to public-speaking, to the writing of formal letters, or even to literature. Most important of all, we reject the traditional conception of style as something *added* to an idea, as an ornament to be put on or off.

Rhetoric, then, has been discredited, and it has long since disappeared from school curricula. As a result, the general reading public is no longer familiar with its teaching; and this, in turn, has brought it about that the rhetorical terms we continue to use are no longer stable. Severed from their original context and grafted on to new and developing theories of language, they take on new shades of meaning, or even entirely new meanings, as has happened with 'image' and 'trope'. Thus, in the case of stylistics, it is impossible to assert either that the concepts and terminology are all traditional, or, alternatively, that they are all new or 'renovated', and are to be understood only in the sense attributed to them by one particular school.

Perhaps the best course to pursue in these circumstances is one of a thoroughgoing eclecticism. And in many ways this is what I have done. I have taken something from nearly every book or article on stylistics that I have ever read; and it must be remembered that many of these—especially the applied studies—are also eclectic in point of theory. (The select bibliography at the end of this volume must stand as a grateful acknowledgement of a general indebtedness that is too complex to unravel.) I shall in fact explain and discuss all the variables as they are introduced chapter by chapter. But my eclecticism is not complete. There are general principles which have guided me in the selection of variables, quite apart from my subjective decisions that they were useful in the analysis of these particular poems. And since these same principles seem to me valid for the study of other works, they must be stated here. The discussion will take us back to traditional rhetoric. But this time rhetoric will interest us not merely in the abstract, for its merits and demerits as a system of stylistic analysis, but for the concrete, historical consequences of its teaching.

One of the most important scholarly achievements of the first half of this century has been the 'rediscovery' of rhetoric. Thanks to the work of such scholars as Norden, Curtius, Faral and Schiaffini—to mention only a few representative names—it has been shown that traditional rhetoric, itself deeply influenced in the formulation of its stylistic theory and ideals by the language of poetry, exerted a persistent and decisive influence on all aspects of the composition and study of literature throughout the central, learned, Latin tradition in Western European culture. It has been shown, indeed, that formal rhetoric, and the attitudes to literature which it fostered, are at the very heart of that tradition. And it has further been demonstrated that the tradition was never broken by a 'middle' age, or, as we should now say, by an 'intermediate' age: it survived without interruption from the Golden Age of Roman literature down to the threshold of the nineteenth century. If the character and style of medieval Latin or medieval vernacular verse differs from that of classical antiquity or the Renaissance, it is certainly not because the Middle Ages were innocent of rhetoric. It was rather because their knowledge of rhetoric derives not from the mature Cicero or Quintilian, but from more pedestrian treatises by the younger Cicero and the pseudo-Cicero, and from compilations made during the Late Empire; and also because they freely adapted the material they had inherited to meet their own scholastic needs. Since the publication in 1948 of Curtius's monumental *Europäische Literatur und lateinisches Mittelalter* all this has become common knowledge. And in what follows it has been assumed that the reader is not totally ignorant of the rhetorical conception of style, or the nature of the rhetorical influence on literature, and also, perhaps, that he has some awareness of the social and educational systems which made it possible for rhetoric to survive for so long, and to occupy such a dominant position in the minds of virtually all literate people.

It will be remembered that the first of the five branches of traditional rhetoric—*inventio*—taught the pupil *what* to say. Or, to be a little more exact, it taught him how to find what to say on any given occasion. This was not such a fearful undertaking as it may sound. At least, it was not necessarily so. It involved teaching the student how to analyse particular situations in the light of general principles and archetypal or recurrent patterns, and teaching him also enough about human nature, and human passions and prejudices, to be able to choose the kind of presentation and the kind of arguments that would seem convincing to a *particular* audience. At best, and when restricted to legal and political situations, such training could be, as it still can be, extremely valuable. But where the teacher was less than extraordinary, and where the pupils were less than brilliant, this approach to the *materia* fostered the belief that there were only a small and predetermined number of themes, whether for oratory or poetry. And it also led to those few themes being treated in a more or less predictable way. Again and again we meet the same topics, the same generalizations, the same commonplaces, all in the same uniformly abstract mode.

Another branch of rhetoric—*elocutio*—taught the pupil how best to express what he had found or been taught to say. The rhetoricians laid down certain conditions and principles for the achievement of good style, such as 'correctness', 'clarity' and 'appropriateness'. They provided models to exemplify these virtues. And this is all quite unexceptional. But they went further than this—much further! In their manuals they handed down a virtually invariable list of approved stylistic devices or 'figures'—culled originally, as the examples show, from the works of admired poets and orators. The pupil was taught to recognize these for himself in his reading of the prescribed school authors, and, also, to exploit them consciously in his compositions in order to lift his own expression out of the rut of the uncultured or the merely natural. And these compositions were in no way 'free', nor were the precepts merely hints. It is clear from the results alone that pupils were drilled until it became second nature for them to reproduce the well-defined stylistic features of the models set before them.

Such indoctrination would be dangerous enough if carried out today by English masters in English schools with a view to moulding the style and literary sensibility of English-speaking pupils. But these dangers—principally those of encouraging an excessive self-consciousness, precocity and uniformity in the style of the young, of reducing the distinctive element in literature to verbal style, and of reducing style itself to tricks that can be learnt—would all be limited and offset by the environment. The pupils would have learnt their linguistic medium in the first place by the natural process. They would thus have a sound basic knowledge of their language system, and would be sensitive and responsive to usage. And their knowledge and sensitivity would be constantly maintained, deepened and refined by daily contact with other native speakers in a wide range of linguistic situations. But the plight of most students of rhetoric in the first centuries of its predominance (for example, c. A.D. 300) would be more akin to that of twentieth-century English pupils who were forced to make their style conform to that of the Authorized Version of the Bible. And, in later centuries, when Latin as such was a dead language, their case would be like that of modern English schoolboys forced to model their French style on that of Racine, when their imperfect knowledge of French had been acquired artificially, and when virtually their only evidence for French usage was that of other literary texts from the seventeenth century.

By representing rhetorical influence as something confined to the schoolroom or to the pages of a textbook, and by confounding very different countries, centuries and cultures, I have oversimplified this account to the point of caricature. But caricature has its merits as a means to secure a limited end. And my present concern is simply to establish two related points. First, that *any* study of the style of a work belonging to this central literary tradition must take account of the influence of rhetoric, understood both as a code of specific precepts and as a general framework of attitudes towards literature and style. Second, that any quest for a 'personal' style in a work from this tradition is likely to prove a difficult undertaking, because the whole tendency of rhetorical teaching was to eliminate what is individual in its pursuit of a universal ideal. Rhetoric tended to produce an impersonal uniformity of style.

On the other hand, medieval literature—to which we may now limit the discussion—is obviously far from being perfectly uniform in point of style. Indeed, the rhetoricians themselves taught that the level of style, that is, the degree of stylistic elaboration, must at all times be appropriate to the level of the theme, to the audience, the occasion, the speaker and his purpose. It is true that they immediately withdrew much of what they had conceded by proclaiming that there were only three levels of style—*grandis*, *mediocris* and *humilis*. But these labels no more do justice to the real variety of style that we find in practice, than the labels Conservative, Liberal, Labour account for all shades of political opinion in Britain today (which is not to deny the validity of these labels, nor to ignore how their existence serves to simplify and stabilize the possible range of styles and political opinions respectively). Even where an author received a full, formal rhetorical education, this was no brain-washing. We must also reckon with conscious or unconscious resistance to the narrow doctrines of some of the *artes rhetoricae*, and with varying degrees of competence in the pupils. And if we find no uniformity even in works written in Latin during the Middle Ages, we naturally find much less in the vernacular literatures. There, even though the influence of Latin and Latin rhetoric was present, we have to take into account such factors as the different linguistic structure of the vernaculars and the writer's greater sensitivity to his mother tongue. Of course, this liberty must not be exaggerated either, for all the vernaculars rapidly formed their own literary conventions which equally tended to submerge individuality. Nevertheless, it is almost a matter of definition that the works of those whom we consider the greater authors transcend the narrowness and inflexibility of rhetorical teaching, or the stereotypes of the Latin and vernacular traditions.

In short, now that it has been accepted that the letter and the spirit of medieval literature were deeply influenced by rhetorical precepts, ideals and modes of thought—and, for the particular tradition to which Dante's poems belong this has been established and fully documented by the studies of Baehr and Dragonetti—what we now need to discover is exactly how far and in exactly what way each individual author was indebted to rhetoric and the literary tradition.

To demonstrate the influence of rhetoric in an author's work, then, is not to exclude altogether the possibility of its having a distinct, personal style. In fact, the individual stylistic characteristics of a work from this tradition, or the differences between one work and another may well be definable in rhetorical terms, within the framework of the rhetorical conception of style. And the study of an author's rhetoric might well be conducted on lines similar to those I have outlined for the description of personal style. So, the questions arise: would a description of style made in rhetorical terms be intelligible and usable within the framework of modern stylistics? Or are the ancient and modern approaches so diverse as to be quite incompatible? Can one in any sense combine a study of an author's rhetoric and a study of his personal style?

The ancient and modern approaches certainly are diverse—radically diverse, as was suggested above. Modern stylistic theory has been built up only after the demolition of traditional rhetoric: it has very different foundations and a very different structure. Nevertheless, many of the building-blocks, as it were, from the old ruin have been incorporated into the new edifice. And the fact that we still use so many of the ancient terms to describe the same stylistic phenomena ought to make us pause before dismissing rhetorical theory in its entirety as irrelevant or worthless. It is reasonable to point to the limitations of the work done by the earliest theorists and the creators of the 'art' of rhetoric; it is reasonable to object to the narrow, prescriptive use made of their work by later educators; and it is reasonable to deplore many aspects of the influence of school rhetoric on European letters. But we ought to recognize that, *within its own limits*, the original analysis of the constituents of literary or oratorical style was remarkably sensitive, coherent, logical and complete. The Greek grammarians and rhetoricians invented such names as trope, metaphor, synecdoche, anaphora, homoeoteleuton, hyperbaton, apostrophe, and prosopopoeia; but they did not invent the linguistic or stylistic features that these designate. They found these features in existing texts of a literary character, or, occasionally, even in popular speech. And their terminology was originally purely descriptive. Considerable tact and care will certainly be required to restore some of these terms to their descriptive status, and to put them back into working order. Some hints and passing remarks will have to be refined and expanded. But if the terms are refurbished with discretion, and if they are used only to make an empirical description of characteristic features in the style of works belonging to the central, learned and literary tradition, then I believe it will be found that the ancient rhetorical analysis need not be incompatible with modern theories of style. A description of 'personal rhetoric' could be compatible—although neither identical nor coextensive—with a description of 'personal style'.

The burden of my argument has been that, in works which are in any way related to the central learned tradition in Western European culture, it is not profitable to study either personal style or rhetoric in isolation from the other. The individuality of a personal style is limited by the influence of rhetoric; and rhetorical influence is always limited or diffracted by the individuality of personal styles. I am now urging that it is possible and necessary to kill the two birds with one stone. Personal style and rhetoric can and should be studied *simultaneously*. This can be achieved by rearranging and synthesizing material from the relevant rhetorical sources, and then taking that synthesis as the *nucleus* of the stylistic variables to be used in the description of personal style. The variables derived from rhetoric will have to be supplemented by others, drawn eclectically from modern studies, or suggested by the nature of the text under analysis. But these 'supplementary' variables will have to justify themselves in each case on grounds of utility. They will be worth incorporating only if they provide useful information about the particular text. The nucleus of rhetorical variables, on the other hand, have a quite separate justification, and the information they yield can never be irrelevant. For in the study of rhetorical influence the negative findings are no less important than the positive.

The general principle we have just enunciated allows considerable freedom for the exercise of judgement. One cannot legislate in the abstract concerning the nature or number of the 'supplementary' variables. In differing circumstances these might dominate the rhetorical nucleus or be dominated by it. Nor is the nucleus definable once and for all. The rhetorical tradition was unbroken; but there were variations and developments over the centuries. And these make it desirable that the terms and definitions should be drawn in each case from works known to be influential in the given period and culture, rather than from a modern synthesis of the whole corpus of rhetorical theory such as Lausberg's *Handbuch der literarischen Rhetorik*. There is no *one* way of arranging the material to meet the needs of a modern analysis. In the third section of this introduction I shall indicate the solutions I have adopted to the particular problems posed by Dante's poems. So, for the moment, let me simply reaffirm the general principle: in the description of the individual style of a work related to the central literary tradition, the nucleus of the stylistic variables should always be formed of the variables known to traditional rhetoric.

We turn now to the problems which arise at the second stage, when all the basic analyses of the text or texts have been completed, and the information must be interpreted and presented in an intelligible and accessible form. About presentation there is little one can say in general. In every case it must depend on the kind of interpretation to be put forward. But one condition must be satisfied, and it is so important that it must be stated immediately. If the interpretation is to be intelligible, the evidence will have to be presented in a selective and simplified form. But there must be no suppression of the evidence. Whether it is given in the text, in footnotes or in appendices, it must be given in full, for others to inspect and to use for whatever purpose they may think fit. The analyst himself will not have known any sharp, Baconian distinction between what I am calling the first and second 'stages' of his work. The process of analysis and compilation alternates and interacts with the process of interpretation. It is however highly desirable that the two 'stages' or 'processes' should be presented separately for the benefit of the reader, so that he may be in a position to say: 'the evidence has been gathered on the basis of faulty criteria'; or, 'the criteria are sound but the information is inaccurate'; or, 'the evidence is acceptable for what it is, but it cannot support that kind of interpretation'; or, 'the interpretation does not make sense of the evidence'.

What do we mean by 'interpretation' in this context? Clearly there is no simple or complete answer. But we can make some necessary progress in the right direction if we lay down some guiding principles and then go on to explain them and to explore their more important consequences.

Let us agree, first, to reduce the many possible levels or degrees of understanding to *three*. There is a level at which a mere fact about style becomes a *significant fact*. Then there is a level at which a significant fact can be seen as a *distinctive feature*, distinguishing either the individual from a group, or one group from another. Thirdly, there is the level at which one can perceive *distinctive combinations* of features.

Next, let us state the central proposition, that *any interpretation of stylistic phenomena depends on comparison and contrast*. The facts about an author's style are to be sought in his work. The meaning of those facts is to be sought in the work of other authors. To interpret the evidence means, first and foremost, to call attention to significant facts, distinctive features, or distinctive combinations of features. An interpretation may go further than this, but it ceases to be an interpretation of *style* when it is not founded on a comparison.

Comparison may be of many kinds, depending on whether individual is compared with individual, individual with group, or group with group. The kind of interpretation will vary accordingly. But we shall see that the 'higher' levels of interpretation depend on the recognition of 'groups', for example schools, coteries, movements, genres, or periods.

Finally, it must be made clear that there is no limit to the process of interpretation, because there is no limit to the number of possible comparisons. One decides to publish the evidence at a certain point, not because one has reached a 'final' or a 'correct' interpretation, but because the interpretation cannot be substantially improved until more work has been done on other authors, and because that work may be stimulated by making one's own evidence available.

Let us begin to clarify these propositions by returning to an earlier example. If one could establish that in Mr Smith's works, 50 per cent of the sentences had three dependent clauses, 30 per cent had four dependent clauses, whereas a mere 5 per cent had only a main clause, or a main clause with one dependent, the fact would, I suspect, be quite 'meaningless' to most readers. If we are told, however, that Mr Smith is 6 feet 6 inches tall, the fact is not only a fact that can be verified, but it is also immediately *significant*. We know that, with respect to other people in our society, he is exceptionally tall. If he were 7 feet 6 inches we would know him to be a freak; if 6 feet 0 inches, he would be merely 'tall'; if 5 feet 6 inches, he would be of average height. The fact would be immediately significant because it is expressed in the familiar scale of feet and inches, because we know our own height and that of some of our acquaintances, and, in all probability, because we know the average height of the members of our society. What we are doing, in effect, is to locate that measurement on another much cruder scale, something like this:

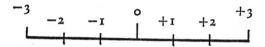

where o is the average, and −3 and +3 are the respective extremes we have met in normal experience. Note, however, that even where we have no evidence about the 'mean', and cannot refer to such a scale, the measurement can still be significant if it enables us to say that Smith is taller than Brown, but not so tall as Jones.

Reverting now to Mr Smith's syntax, we can see that the 'facts' would not really be meaningless. It would be more accurate to say that their meaning was 'latent', or that they were 'potentially meaningful'. The figures would begin to take on meaning as soon as we had made a comparable analysis of Brown's syntax. They would become more meaningful as we compared them with the facts established for Jones and Green. In fact, by this point they would quite definitely be *significant facts*. If we persevered in making these analyses until we had sufficient evidence to calculate the *average* distribution for the group to which Smith, Jones, Brown and Green all belong, then we should probably find that certain of the significant facts were *distinctive features*. In other words, we might be able to state that Smith's syntax was exceptionally and distinctively complex with respect to that group, and not simply that it was more complex than Brown's.

It must be emphasized, however, that this is still only the *second* level of understanding. From the outset it has been a central assumption that individuality, in style no less than in appearance, does not depend on the possession of a feature which is unique or distinctive in itself. One does not have to possess Cyrano de Bergerac's nose, one does not have to be 6 feet 6 inches tall; one can be 'near average' in every respect and still have an individual appearance. This was why we insisted on the need for a wide range of variables in making a proper description of personal style. And in fact we shall not reach the *third* level of understanding until we have made a series of comparisons over the whole range of variables. Then we shall be in a position to state which *combination* of features seems to constitute the common denominator of the group, and which more narrowly defined combination of features distinguishes a given individual in that group from all others.

Each level of understanding has its value, and each kind of interpretation would be desirable in some circumstances. But it will be as well to renew and enlarge upon the warning I have given with regard to the 'distinctive feature', because this is what the uninitiated tend to pursue as the ultimate goal, and because such a quest can so easily lead into error.

We have seen that our ability to recognize a feature as distinctive depends on our knowledge of the group to which the individual belongs. Change the group, and the meaning changes. In Northern Europe a man of 5 feet 2 inches in height would probably be considered 'short'; but in some Asian countries he would be of 'average height', and in a pygmy tribe he would be 'tall'. We must therefore turn our attention to the whole concept of the 'group' and of interrelated groups.

In trying to illustrate the 'levels' of understanding and the role of comparison, I deliberately kept to the simplest possible 'model', in which there is just *one* self-evident and self-contained group to which all the 'subjects' and indeed the analyst himself are deemed to belong. Let us now complicate the model slightly by assuming that there are just *two* groups, as distinct in every way as the Chinese and the English were in the fifteenth century. Let us further assume that a Chinese visits England for the first time ever, and that we ask an Englishman to describe his appearance. He would almost certainly concentrate on the stranger's 'distinctive features'—his slanting eyes and the yellow pigmentation of his skin. And in the hypothetical context we have suggested, such a description would be quite adequate for the purposes of identification; there would be no need to add anything more. But the 'distinctive feature' would of course be the common denominator of the group to which the 'subject' belonged. And if our English observer met the same Chinese amid a delegation of his fellow countrymen, his first reaction might well be that—truism or no truism—'they all *do* look alike'.

All this might well be recounted as a fable. For there is an important moral here for the student of literary style. It is this: whenever we read a work from a period or genre with which we are not familiar, the features of its style which first strike us as 'distinctive' will almost certainly be the common denominator of the 'group' to which the work belongs, and will thus be the least individual of all its attributes.

If our English observer were sent to live in China, he would soon become able to distinguish one individual from another. And eventually he might be able to describe that first Chinese in a way which would do justice to his individuality with respect not only to the English but to his own race. As an *external* observer, the description and the 'interpretation' would almost certainly be different from one made by an *internal* observer who was not familiar with any group beyond his own. In some ways it would be inferior, for the outsider will always remain less sensitive to nuances. But in other ways it could be superior, simply because he would be able to draw on a whole new set of comparisons—*comparisons between the two groups*. He would have a heightened sense of the possible variations and combinations. He would take into his account certain variables which the internal observer would overlook because to him they would seem universal and invariable. In a word, the outsider's different perspective could lend depth to his understanding at almost every point. If, finally, our Englishman returned to his own people and turned his critical attention to their appearance, their culture, or their literature, his detailed knowledge of the Chinese would almost certainly lead him to view familiar faces, institutions or books in a new light. And, in general, it seems safe to say that our understanding of any given group will deepen in proportion to the number of other relevant groups with which we are familiar, and from which we may draw comparisons and contrasts.

This second model, in which we have acknowledged the existence of two or more *distinct* groups, can demonstrate well enough why comparisons are necessary not only between individual and individual, or individual and group, but also between group and group. It shows that the first 'single-group' model was defective because we cannot in fact perceive the group to which the individual belongs *as a group*, unless we are aware of other groups extraneous to it. Any group is defined and delimited by the related groups on its frontiers. But in all this discussion I have evaded two central facts about groups which we must now consider. In the first place, many groupings are not so exclusive or distinct as those based on race or religion. Every one of us belongs simultaneously to many groups, some of which are concentric, some of which overlap, and some of which do not. We belong to these groups by virtue of certain features held in common with all other members of the group, whether this common denominator is family, nation, race, language, religion, politics, occupation, income, sex, age, intelligence, temperament, education, hobby or what you will. In the second place, we must remember that whenever we assign things to 'groups', 'classes', 'species', 'families', 'periods', 'societies', 'cultures', 'movements' or other '-isms', we are always dividing a *continuum* in a more or less arbitrary way. Any such concept is grounded as much in the nature of our minds and language as it is in the 'nature of things'. The class-labels are necessary, but the classes are unstable. Their boundaries alter, their relationships change; new classes appear and old ones disappear.

The individual belongs not to one but to many groups, then, and the groups are neither immutable nor finite in number. This means that the number of possible comparisons is infinite, and that we can never reach a 'complete' understanding of the individual. But this need not lead us into despair. Nor do we need to abandon the second model completely. Some categories are sufficiently well founded in the nature of things, or in the nature of the human mind and Western European languages, to have survived with relatively little change over the past 2,500 years. Some degree of understanding is always better than none, or better than a lower degree. Not all comparisons are equally illuminating, and one can set a limit to their number in practice by rejecting some as 'unprofitable'; there will come a point when the diminished returns no longer justify the expenditure of equal effort.

To sum up: in the interpretation of the evidence about an author's personal style, or the style of a given work, the first essential is to have a proper grasp of the concept of individuality and of the dialectical correlation of 'individual' and 'group'. Otherwise one will fall into the common errors of treating an individual work as something *sui generis* and existing in a vacuum, or, alternatively, of dismissing a work as though it were in some mysterious way merely representative of a genre or school or period, and had no individuality at all. The other essential requirement is that the analyst should remain critically aware of the kind or level of interpretation which he is putting forward at any given moment. He should always be able to specify the number, the kind and the quality of the comparisons on which conclusions are based. He must bear in mind, too, that his interpretation, his grasp of the author's individuality will never be 'complete', and that it will be liable to undergo *extensive* modifications, unless and until he has made proper comparisons drawn from works by the author's contemporaries and his immediate predecessors and successors, from works in the same genre and in other related and unrelated genres, from works in verse and from works in prose, from formal and informal works, and from works in related genres in related languages.

II

We have discussed in a general way how one might describe an author's personal style, how one should conduct the analysis, and how one should interpret the evidence. We must now try to answer the question: '*Why* should we describe personal style in this way?' 'What possible relevance can this kind of information have for the study of a literary work *as a work of literature?*' I must also fulfil my opening promise to indicate the limitations of the method and to resolve certain doubts and queries. Briefly, I will argue that the description is *ancillary* to literary criticism, or to that very small part of literary criticism which is concerned with verbal style. And that is its limitation. On the other hand, I will argue that it is an indispensable precondition for the proper study of many literary texts, from classical and medieval times down to the early nineteenth century. And that is why it *should* be made. Thirdly, I shall suggest that there is a kind of opposition between 'individual style', as I have been using the word over the last pages, and 'personal style', as this is normally understood—even though they were first introduced as synonyms. And this ambiguity is likely to have been the main cause of doubts and queries. It is in fact so important that we must take it as our point of departure. We must bring the opposition into the open, sharpen it, and defend it. Then we shall have to reconcile the terms again. For on that reconciliation all the other answers will depend.

With hindsight, it can be seen that the generalizations about 'personal style' with which we began satisfied two important conditions. First, the word 'style' was there used to denote something 'distinctive', something that made itself known by its *effect*. Second, the *study* of style was conceived as an inquiry into the causes—the linguistic causes

23

—of that effect. Latterly, however, my argument has tended to suggest that any work whatsoever has its individual style. If there cannot be an Englishman who is in some mysterious way purely English without being in any way individualized, then the analogy implies that there cannot be a Petrarchist *Canzoniere*, for example, in which the style is purely Petrarchist, without being in any way individualized. And with this approach to individuality, the *study* of style can be divorced from the study of its effects.

Is this second use of the word 'style' legitimate? Is it not equivalent to saying that what distinguishes one family of trees from another is 'style'; that what distinguishes any one species of that family from all its other species is equally 'style'; and that it is the 'individual style' of each representative of that species which makes it, in some minor details, different from all its fellows? There are many people who will say that the word 'style' could never be used in this way, that my use of the term 'individual style' is therefore illegitimate, and that this kind of study is misconceived. Their approach can be epitomized not unfairly in two propositions: 'no effect, no style'; 'no study of effects, no stylistics'.

Now, I certainly feel the force of this line of argument. But I still maintain that there is another valid approach to the concept of 'style' which also does justice to our normal use of the word. And if the validity of this approach is granted, then I believe that my extended use of the word is legitimate. Indeed, I will presently argue the case for a further and much more drastic extension.

The reason why we do not speak about the 'style' of trees is that we normally confine the word to human activities and human artefacts. And there is no sense in quarrelling with that kind of limitation by convention. But we cannot call a halt to legitimate extensions of a word's meaning within its proper field. It is the nature and the *virtue* of a word like 'style' that it is generic. Even if we confine ourselves to the uses of the word in the study of language and literature, we find that on the one hand it cannot be absolutely distinguished from such related notions as 'dialect', 'register' or 'specialist language', and on the other that it is not possible to draw clear, unwavering distinctions between the 'style of a poem', an author's 'personal style', the 'style of a coterie or school', the 'style of a genre', or the 'style of a period'. All the terms overlap. All are legitimate. And I would argue that all are perceived as 'style' when, consciously or unconsciously, we contrast *that* particular way of saying things with *other* possible ways. In each case we recognize that an utterance is *thus*, when it might have been *otherwise* while still conveying a substantially similar message. At each level we perceive and understand the *thus* in terms of the *otherwise*. Now if this is a correct explanation, if this is the justification for the use of the common term 'style' in all these different contexts, then we cannot escape the awkward consequence that virtually any utterance in a natural language has 'style', because there are always other words, other forms, other constructions, other arrangements which will convey substantially similar information. This is a vital and controversial point, and it will be as well to defend it and clarify it by glancing at a secondary system of signs in which there is no possibility of style, and establishing just what the differences are.

Let us take the international code for signalling by flags at sea. Ignoring the pennant-shaped flags which represent numerals, there are twenty-six flags in use, and each is designated by a letter in the Roman alphabet as it appears in written English. At times, obviously, the flags can *represent* those letters and be used—like semaphore or Morse—to spell out messages in any language with a Roman alphabet. But that is not our concern at the moment. Flown singly, the flag with vertical blue and yellow bars (G) means 'I require a pilot'. The pure yellow flag (Q) means 'My vessel is healthy and I request free pratique'; and so forth. Twenty-six flags, twenty-six messages. The flags may be hoisted in pairs: 650 combinations, 650 messages. Note, however, that GQ means 'How must I bring the buoy to bear?' while QG means 'You should send all available lifeboats'. They may also be flown in groups of three (15,600 combinations), four and even five, although relatively few of the thousands of possible combinations are in normal use. In the Royal Navy, signals were made with the same flags and under the same conditions, but the significance of some hoists would be changed from time to time for reasons of security. However, whether the flags are hoisted singly, in pairs or in multiple combinations, such a system would seem to differ in three main respects from living, naturally evolved languages; and it is these which individually and collectively rule out the possibility of style. In the first place, the number of messages is fixed, and each message has been unequivocally defined. No new message can be 'generated', and no modifications are possible save through a revision or a complete change for security reasons, both of which would be equivalent to founding the whole system anew. Secondly, there is a 'one-to-one' relationship between the sign and the message. The message cannot be conveyed by any other sign, and the sign cannot convey any other message. And thirdly, the elements in a multiple sign lose the meaning they would have as individual signs, and the order in which they appear is invariable: change the order and you change the meaning. It is because naturally evolved living languages seem to satisfy none of these conditions that 'style' is not only possible but *inevitable*. There is no one correct way of expressing any given 'message', even where this exists in a given determinable form, as, for example, when phrased in a foreign language. Each attempt, each utterance—or, better, every utterance accepted as meaningful by a native speaker—is merely one of many. And therefore every utterance has its own style.

By probing the tentative opposition between 'individual style' and 'personal style', we have uncovered not just an ambiguity but two sharply contrasted notions of what constitutes 'style' in language. One line of argument leads us to conclude that all works and all utterances have 'style'. The other insists that only certain works and certain utterances can be said to have 'style', and that the great majority do not. But, as I have already indicated, it is my belief that this opposition can and must be reconciled. On the one hand, we must recognize that no one would ever study variations in expression if all were felt to be of equal value. The study of style begins with the intuitive recognition that some of these variations are in some way 'distinctive'. It is therefore quite reasonable that the ultimate goal of the study should still be the proper understanding and definition of 'distinctiveness', whether the distinctive quality is held to be 'originality', 'beauty', 'perspicuity', 'persuasiveness', 'ornateness' or simply 'excellence'. And the most economical means to achieve that end is a dualist system, which enables one to dismiss the great, grey mass of irrelevant material as simply 'lacking in style'. On the other hand, it remains true that there is no such thing as a 'style-less' utterance or work. The difference between style and what we may agree to call 'non-style' will always be one of degree and not of kind. The opposition between 'style' and 'non-style' will always be highly precarious. It must never be taken for granted. And even if one achieves an acceptable definition of what is to be regarded as 'non-style' in one situation, this will not necessarily be valid for other situations. In fact, I would go so far as to say that *a general theory of 'style' can only be as good as its account of 'non-style'*.

This last point is absolutely vital to my argument, and I shall now attempt to illustrate and substantiate it by making a brief critique of the concept of 'non-style' in the three most important, fully elaborated systems of stylistic analysis yet devised—those of ancient rhetoric, the idealist school and the positivists. It will perhaps be as well to make it quite clear that none of the theorists use such a barbarous term as 'non-style'. Nor do they have their own terms for such a phenomenon. But my case is that all the theorists, in differing ways, build on the fundamental assumption that certain uses of language, certain texts are lacking in style; and that this assumption, while it permitted useful practical observations (just as pre-Copernican astronomy did), is quite inadequate in each case to sustain a valid comprehensive theory of style. Each successive 'model' proves itself inadequate, in fact, because the particular concept of 'non-style' is taken too readily for granted.

Within the framework of the seven liberal arts, the difference between rhetoric and grammar is that between the 'scientia *bene* loquendi' and the 'scientia *recte* loquendi'. And this opposition—still surviving in the French *bel usage* and *bon usage*—is the key to the whole rhetorical theory of style. Skilled, effective or pleasing speech was analysed and broken down into a number of stylistic devices, each of which was perceived and defined as *an artistic departure*—by substitution, addition, subtraction or rearrangement—*from a grammatically correct but style-less base*. Always the rhetoricians assumed that it is possible to express what one wishes to communicate in a form which is correct but has no other properties, a form which is as neutral as a message in international code or as a logician's propositions, a form which is 'pure information'. The characteristics of this base (which emerge only by implication) vary enormously from one context to another. In general, we can see that what the theorists have in mind is current, informal, unelaborated, 'natural' speech. At times, however, the base seems to be made up of elements which are common to educated and uneducated speakers alike; whilst at other times it is thought of specifically as uneducated speech. More narrowly, the base can be conceived as a logically un-exceptionable proposition; or as 'proper' words in their 'proper' order;

27

or as the simplest of several alternative syntactic structures; or as the shortest complete expression of an idea; or as 'unformed' discourse, that is, speech lacking any rhythmical organization.

Now, it is possible, as I have just done, to discern these shifting acceptations, and to pin them down with an acceptable paraphrase. And the distinctions and oppositions, taken one by one, are still sufficiently meaningful to enable one to use rhetorical categories in the analysis of certain texts—of those, at the very least, in which the authors were influenced by rhetorical doctrine and habits of thought. But frequency of occurrence, social status, brevity, simplicity, and logicality are all quite distinct criteria. A few utterances may seem to qualify as 'style-less' on all counts, but a great number will not. Popular speech, for example, is frequently longwinded, metaphorical and illogical; and legal documents testify that what is logically unexceptionable is usually far from simple or brief.

As a formative influence on literary style, rhetorical teaching went into decline for the same reasons that explain its long ascendancy: it was simple, its rules were hard and fast, and it promoted 'artificiality'. Unfortunately, flexibility was necessary for it to survive in the rapidly developing cultures of Western Europe; and 'artificial' became a term of abuse. I think it could be shown that the causes of its success, the causes of the perversions which it suffered at the hands of pedagogues, and the causes therefore of the extreme reaction against it, are all to be traced back to those original, 'self-evident' oppositions between civilization and barbarism, art and nature, *eloquentia* and *loquela*, 'style' and 'non-style'.

The twentieth-century school of idealist stylistics which we shall consider only in the person of its most brilliant and influential exponent, Leo Spitzer, clearly has its origins in the Romantic revolt against traditional literary values in general and traditional rhetoric in particular. And it will be necessary before discussing Spitzer, to indicate some of the more important features and consequences of this reaction.

Early nineteenth-century observations on style are radically different from the old. Not least in their form. They no longer appear in detailed textbooks on fine writing. Typically they are of a vague and evocative character, and are to be found scattered in gentlemanly essays on admired authors, or on literature in general. And by literature is increasingly meant lyric poetry, which now, and for the first time, is set quite apart from and high above epic or dramatic verse, narrative, oratory, or belles-lettres.[1] This complete change in form and character is no accident. For the Romantics would insist that good writing has no rules and cannot be taught. It is not the product of an *ars* (the systematization of past experience), nor yet, as Horace and Dante would have thought, of *ars* and *ingenium* combined, but of *ingenium* alone. The poet is no longer thought of as the 'maker', the craftsman fashioning existing materials with traditional tools in accordance with traditional techniques. He is the creator *ex nihilo*. Or, on a more humble view, since even the poet must await inspiration, he is the mouthpiece of a god, of a spiritual, more than human force. A poem is 'good' not because it is the superbly finished product of an assured craftsman, but because the poet is a man apart—original, exceptional, unique. And from this premiss it is easy to draw the consequence that the use of language, the style of a 'good' poem will also be original, exceptional and unique—'mental creativity immediately inscribes itself into the language'.[2] *Le style c'est l'homme même.* No other phrase expresses what is typical in the early nineteenth century more succinctly or pregnantly than this much-quoted tag. And its suggestiveness is only heightened when we discover that the originator of the phrase, the eighteenth-century philosopher Buffon, actually meant that 'it is clarity, lucidity and grace of expression which distinguish the man of culture and right reason'.[3] One and the same phrase can sum up two radically different attitudes to style only because the content of that word had been 'emptied out' and replaced.

Of course, this has been a crude and oversimplified account of some features in the revolution in concepts of style. And in any discussion of the work of a Vossler, a Croce or a Spitzer, it must be remembered that they were men of exceptional intelligence and culture whose

[1] For a brilliant and properly detailed account of the complex change in attitudes, the reader is referred to M. H. Abrams, *The Mirror and the Lamp: Romantic Theory and the Critical Tradition* (Oxford, 1953).

[2] 'Whoever has thought strongly and felt strongly has innovated in his language; *mental creativity immediately inscribes itself into the language,* where it becomes linguistic creativity; the trite and petrified in language is never sufficient for the needs of expression felt by a strong personality.' L. Spitzer, *Linguistics and Literary History* (Princeton, 1948), p. 15.

[3] Cf. R. G. Saisselin, 'Buffon, Style, and Gentlemen', *The Journal of Aesthetics and Art Criticism*, XVI (1957), 357–61.

thinking on literature was an integral part of a wider philosophy which we cannot discuss here. Moreover, they were reacting not against traditional rhetoric but against the materialism, positivism, and the cult of facts, which characterize philological and literary studies in the *later* nineteenth century. And yet it is important not to miss the simple fact that at the very heart of their thinking lies the equation of 'style' with uses of language that are original, inimitable and yet coherent, and which are felt to be the faithful record in language of the exceptional and unique personality of their author. Thus it was that Leo Spitzer, seeking a 'more rigorously scientific definition of an individual style, the definition of a linguist which should (*sic*) replace the casual impressionistic remarks of literary critics', tried to reach this goal through a study of 'individual stylistic deviation*s* from the general norm'.[1]

Spitzer's point of departure, as he explains in the essay from which I have just quoted, was always an unpremeditated, personal reaction to his reading of a particular text. He believed that any approach to a work of art with predetermined aims and categories was doomed to failure. His first 'breakthrough' would come when he felt he could see a common motivation for certain expressions which had struck him as 'aberrant from general usage' (p. 11). This first intuition would then be checked against *any* relevant evidence about the author or the work as a whole; and the process of verification would itself lead to further intuitions, and these in turn to further checking of hypotheses. Spitzer compared this stage in his thinking to a 'journeying to and fro' from the surface of the work to its centre. The 'journeying' would come to an end and the investigation would be complete when Spitzer felt that he could show that the author's 'deviations' in the use of language did indeed have a common denominator, which would be precisely the 'spiritual etymon', the 'life-giving centre' of the work. For Spitzer believed that 'the mind of an author is a kind of solar system, into whose orbit all categories of things are attracted: language, motivation, plot, are only satellites of this mythological entity' (p. 14).

Spitzer's method was thus professedly 'circular', and to many of his critics this circle seems 'vicious'. But this is not what I would regard as the weak part of his system. Indeed, when he adopts Schleiermacher's argument that 'cognizance in philology is reached not only by the gradual progression from one detail to another detail, but by the

[1] *Linguistics*, p. 11.

anticipation or divination of the whole, because "the detail can be understood only by the whole and any explanation of detail pre-supposes the understanding of the whole" ' (p. 19); and when he defends the 'circle' as the 'basic operation in the humanities' (ibid.), there would be many now who not only agree, but argue that it is basic in all forms of human thought whatsoever.

The weakness of the method—considered now as something distinct from its 'inventor', and as one which any qualified person might apply —seems to me to lie precisely in its claim to 'scientific rigour'. Spitzer insisted that his interpretations rested upon hard linguistic facts, which in this context ought to mean *definable* 'deviations' from a *definable* 'norm'. But he never attempted a definition of either. And although his own judgement may prove to be perfectly correct in some or all of his published studies, we still remain at the pre-experimental stage of the *ipse dixit*. Had he ever attempted to provide those defini-tions, he would of course have found that *both* concepts are relative, highly inconstant, and variable. At times he appears to have thought of the 'norm' as the whole language considered in its ideal existence at any point in time. But this is inadmissible even if one admits, *per impossibile*, that one could define the 'whole language'. There are always many over-lapping norms, all in process of change. And even where one is in a position to appeal to a representative sample of native-speakers—which is only possible within a short period after the composition of a given text—one would find disagreement as to which usages were normal and which aberrant. So that, even assuming one could agree as to the nature of the norm, one would find that there is not one recognizable class of deviations, but many degrees ranging from the 'nonce-word' at one extreme, to any complete utterance which has never been pronounced before at the other. All of which is to say that as a theory of style Spitzer's is inadequate precisely because he never paid adequate atten-tion to 'non-style', represented in his case by the 'norm'.

Charles Bally, pupil and successor of the great Swiss linguist de Saussure, made a number of important contributions to stylistics. First, he related the study of style to the larger problem of the study of language, which de Saussure had just liberated from the narrow con-fines of comparative, historical philology. Second, he treated style as an aspect of all forms of linguistic activity, spoken and written, instead of something confined to works of literature. Third, he defined style strictly as *affectivité*, that is, as comprising those aspects of the linguistic message which convey not information as such, but the speaker's attitude to that information, and which determine, wittingly or unwittingly, the kind of reaction which that message will produce in its hearers or readers. Bally thus set up a concept of style which is manifestly continuous with earlier usage of the term, but which is clinically distinct from 'persuasiveness', 'beauty', 'excellence', 'originality', 'individuality' or 'essence'. All these innovations are now commonplaces. His other major contribution is more specific, more important—and more debatable. Bally was the first man to make a comprehensive classification of stylistic effects which are achieved by 'evocation'. He argued that there are two kinds of stylistic effect, the 'natural' and the 'evocative'. Into the first category he would put phonetically motivated words, diminutive forms and certain syntactic structures—indeed, a great many of the so-called 'figures' of classical rhetoric. In the second category are all forms, words or expressions which are in some way 'restricted' in use. They may belong exclusively to one region (dialect), to one social class, to one profession, to one level of speech, or to one literary genre. But in each case they have the power to 'evoke' their normal context whenever they appear. This property may be exploited *congruously*, in order to establish that context (the method of the novelist or dramatist), or *incongruously*, in order to produce a wide range of shock-effects.

Now, as formulated by Bally, this account has one weakness; and once again the weakness arises from an oversimplified and inflexible opposition between 'style' and 'non-style'. In Bally's treatment of 'natural' effects—and it was with these sources of *affectivité* in everyday French that he himself was primarily concerned[1]—he tended to assume that certain forms, words, locutions or structures are *permanently* inexpressive, while others are *permanently* expressive. For example, a phrase like 'Mr Smith died suddenly' will never have style, whereas 'Old Smithy copped his lot all unexpected like' will always have style. But if the criterion for recognizing style is *affectivité* or expressiveness, then we shall have to admit that in certain contexts something like the latter phrase would be so common a mode of expression as to reveal nothing of the speaker's attitude to the deceased, and to produce no effect on its hearers. Whereas, in the same

[1] Ch. Bally, *Traité de stylistique française*, 3rd ed. (2 vols. Geneva–Paris, 1951).

context, the laconic, 'neutral' phrase could be intensely *affectif*, intensely moving. What we are saying then, is that with the criterion of *affectivité* there can be no permanent, inherent or natural properties. *There can never be a necessary connexion between a given device and a given effect. Affectivité*, expressiveness, or any other kind or degree of effect, can only be assessed in a particular *context*. This may seem the most elementary of points. Whenever we call a critic 'sensitive', we imply, among other things, that he has made proper allowance for the context. But theory almost inevitably lags behind practice, and it is only quite recently that it has become evident that a proper definition and understanding of context is essential to any theory of style. It is essential because it makes possible an adequate definition of 'non-style'.

We have examined three theories in which 'non-style' was assumed to be 'uncultivated speech', 'the norm', and 'inexpressive speech'. I now want to give an account of a fourth in which 'non-style' is defined as those elements which are predictable in a given context. When we have seen its strengths and weaknesses, we shall at last be in a position to reconcile the two conflicting approaches to style, and to grasp the relevance to literary studies of the kind of description of individual style which I outlined in the first section.

This fourth theory is the work of Michael Riffaterre and will be found in the introduction to his study of a novel by Gobineau, and in a series of articles which appeared in the late 1950s and early 1960s.[1] It must be borne in mind that, in his attempt to redefine style and context, Riffaterre has two general aims: he wants to harmonize the approaches of Bally and Spitzer, and he wants to establish stylistics firmly *within* the territory of modern linguistics, instead of leaving it in a 'no-man's land' between linguistics and literary criticism. It is from modern linguistic theory that he takes the root-metaphor by which our normal communication through language is spoken of in terms derived from communication by cipher: the 'message' is 'encoded' by the speaker, 'transmitted' and then 'decoded' by the percipient. And it is from linguistics that he takes the notions of the 'informant', of 'predictability', of the 'macrocontext' (the general situation in which a given utterance is pronounced, including our knowledge of the speaker) and

---

[1] *Le Style des 'Pléiades' de Gobineau* (Geneva–Paris, 1957). 'Criteria for Style Analysis', *Word*, xv (1959), 154–74. 'Stylistic Context', *Word*, xvi (1960), 207–18. 'Vers la définition linguistique du style', *Word*, xvii (1961), 318–44.

of the 'microcontext' (the immediate context of that utterance provided by the words and structures which surround it).

Anyone who has ever conversed against a background of extraneous noise or tried to follow a broadcast during atmospheric interference will know that—provided we are using our native tongue and are familiar with the general situation—we do not need to hear every component *sound* in a word before we can recognize it. Similarly, again with the same provisos, we do not need to catch every *word* in order to make out the sense of a sentence. And the same holds good for reading: we do not, if we are proficient, spell out every letter, nor do we register every word on the page. In all these cases we have in some way failed to receive parts of the incoming message, but we can understand the message because we are able to reconstruct the missing elements. *And we are able to reconstruct because we could have predicted.* This is the vital point. It is essential to recognize that a large part of normal discourse is highly predictable, and also that we exercise our power of prediction all the time, and not just in adverse circumstances such as those just exemplified. Nor is this undesirable. It is, on the contrary, absolutely necessary. And the proof of the ubiquity and necessity of our exercise of prediction is that we are so rarely troubled by the many possible meanings of one sign. The dictionary may tell us that *pound* can be a verb or a noun, and that in its latter capacity it may express a measure of weight or a measure of monetary value. But even though these substantival meanings will often occur in the same general context, we hardly ever confuse them, and more important, we are very rarely made aware that such confusion is possible. Our first conclusion then is this: when we are familiar with the general situation and when we understand the immediate context of an incoming 'message', we are able to predict, in some sense, a large part of it. The more familiar the context is, the more we can predict, and the more perfunctory our decoding of the message will become. And, for the moment, at this level of generalization, it does not matter whether the message is transmitted through the spoken or the written word.

This is Riffaterre's point of departure. He assumes that what he calls 'elliptic decoding' is normal. In other words, he argues that unless we are in some way *compelled* to pay more attention, we will always expend only the minimum amount of energy in decoding; which is to say, in effect, that we understand more or less only what we expected to hear or read. In what ways can the audience be compelled to pay more attention? To answer this, we must distinguish between speaking and writing. In conversation, the speaker can secure attention through his delivery: he can gesticulate, he can enunciate important words more distinctly than usual, he can vary his volume, pitch and speed. An author has none of these resources. Instead he must use 'style'. What does this mean? It means, in Riffaterre's view, that he must use language less predictably, he must frustrate the reader's expectations. For as soon as 'minimal decoding' yields no sense, the reader will become more alert, more cooperative, and therefore more receptive to the particular nuance or emphasis that the author wishes to convey. Thus, for Riffaterre, style is essentially 'an underscoring device', analogous in the simplest case to the resources of spoken delivery. 'Style is understood as an emphasis (expressive, affective or aesthetic) added to the information conveyed by the linguistic structure, without alteration of meaning. Which is to say that language expresses and that style stresses . . .'[1] Style is a 'control of the decoding . . . achieved through low predictability'.[2] And a stylistic device is any form, word, locution, structure or usage which is *of low predictability in a given context*. It follows that no stylistic device can be defined without reference to a context, and that style 'is not a string of stylistic devices, but of *binary oppositions* whose poles (context-stylistic device) cannot be separated'.[3] It also follows that there is no such thing as a permanent, or natural, or inherently expressive stylistic device. What is unpredictable in one context may be or may become highly predictable in another, thus becoming part of the context and liable to 'elliptic decoding'.

Riffaterre's reformulation of the concept of style (of which I have given only the barest outline) seems to me well-grounded in observable facts, simple, flexible, and remarkably comprehensive. It exposes the weaknesses of earlier theories, but incorporates all their valuable insights into its new framework. Of course, it is still very far from definitive. Analysis of poetic texts, especially from the past, will raise problems to which he gives no answer. For it is quite obvious—and entirely justifiable—that Riffaterre's thinking evolved in contact with contemporary texts in prose. Nevertheless his formulation is properly orientated; it points firmly in the right direction. He still retains a category of 'non-style', but this we may concede as inevitable in any

---

[1] 'Criteria for Style Analysis', p. 155.   [2] 'Stylistic Context', p. 207.   [3] Ibid.

study of stylistic effects. He allows no difference in kind between the features that constitute 'style' and those that are dismissed as 'non-style'. His 'non-style' is no longer something fixed or permanent, and it is no longer conceived in purely negative terms. It is seen to play an important part in determining the effect of the stylistic device. It is the background against which we perceive certain features as being in the foreground.

As it stands, though, his theory seems to have three serious weaknesses, two theoretical, the other practical. (a) His reduction of style to an 'underscoring device' is totally unacceptable, for it depends on an oversimplified view of meaning.[1] (In parenthesis, we may add that there will be no fully satisfactory, comprehensive account of style until there is a satisfactory account of meaning.) (b) His notion of 'context' has all the defects of the 'single-group' model which we discussed at the close of the first section, and it would have to be extended and refined along similar lines. And (c) at the level of practical analysis, it remains extremely difficult to establish objectively what is sufficiently unpredictable[2] in a given context to constitute a stylistic device and therefore to demand the analyst's attention. Riffaterre, to do him justice, does face this problem. He is not content to exercise the Spitzerian freedom that his system will accommodate. His solution entails the introduction of an 'average reader', whose relationship to the critic will be comparable to that of the 'informant' (that is, the linguistically untrained 'native speaker') to the professional linguist.[3] This reader

---

[1] It perpetuates a plain man's view of language which I should like to call the 'powder and shot' heresy. Here is a more attractive formulation of the doctrine from Captain Marryat's *Peter Simple* (published in 1834). The new midshipman asks the boatswain why he swears so much at the men. It is 'not gentlemanly', 'not requisite' and 'certainly sinful'. The boatswain, Mr Chucks, replies: 'Excuse me, my dear sir; it is absolutely requisite, and not at all sinful. There is one language for the pulpit, and another for on board ship, and, in either situation, a man must make use of those terms most likely to produce the necessary effect upon his listeners. Certain it is, that common parlancy won't do with a common seaman. It is not here as in the Scriptures, "Do this, and he doeth it" (by-the-by, that chap must have had his soldiers in tight order); but it is "Do this, d—n your eyes," and then it is done directly. The order to *do* just carries the weight of a cannon shot, but it wants the perpelling power—the d—n is the gunpowder which sets it flying in the execution of its duty. Do you comprehend me, Mr Simple?' (ch. 14)

[2] It is also important to stress that 'predictable' and 'predictability' must be understood in a very generic sense.

[3] 'Criteria for Style Analysis', pp. 162–6.

would be given a particular text to read, and wherever he felt moved to express an opinion about the style, there you would have a stylistic device. *What* the 'average reader' actually said (almost certainly a value-judgement) would be irrelevant. What matters is the reaction itself, which will have been provoked by some feature of low predictability; and this is the evidence the analyst requires. Now, this may be a recognizable description of what happens in a practical criticism class. It might even be methodologically sound in the analysis of passages drawn from contemporary journalism or popular novels. But in general it is so cumbersome, so staggeringly impractical as to be no solution at all.

However, it is just at this weakest point in Riffaterre's system, just where it seems to fall back on unverifiable subjective impressions, that I believe it can be saved if it is complemented by the kind of quantitative, broadly based description of style that I have outlined above. For what such descriptions can provide is precisely the kind of verifiable information about the context—or one of the contexts—which the critic needs in order to *confirm* his intuition that such and such a feature was 'unexpected' or of 'low predictability'. The information will not guarantee a correct interpretation of the effect of a device; but it will establish beyond doubt that a device—as Riffaterre defines it—is in fact present.

In the course of these four sketches of four different approaches to 'style' and 'non-style', I have in fact answered all the questions which were posed at the beginning of the second section. But since the answers were given only implicitly or in a fragmentary form, it will be as well to restate them catechistically here by way of conclusion.

Q. How can one reconcile the contradictory propositions: 'all utterances have style' and 'some utterances have style and some do not'?

A. The two propositions, and the two conflicting approaches to the study of style which they embody and express, can be reconciled if one adopts the model proposed by Riffaterre. The difference between 'style' and 'non-style'—where these categories are appropriate—will then be understood not as a permanent difference, or as a difference in kind, but as a matter of relative frequency, a matter of low or high predictability in a particular context. This formulation is perfectly compatible with the proposition that *all* utterances have style.

Q. Why is it necessary to reconcile the two conflicting approaches?

A. (i) Because the second approach ('style'—'non-style') facilitates the interpretation of evidence gathered in accordance with the first. It provides a touchstone of relevancy. It functions like Alexander's sword or Occam's razor. It permits and encourages a flexible and economical definition of the *goal* of one's study in any particular sector.

(ii) Because the second approach itself depends on an adequate definition of 'non-style'. And in certain texts the only way in which this can be determined satisfactorily is by the kind of neutral description which I have put forward, and which is the result of the first approach.

Q. What is the relevance of the method proposed for the description of an author's individual style *to the study of literature?*

A. (i) When a literary critic is making a close commentary on a short poem or an excerpt from a longer work, he ought to conduct his analysis with Riffaterre's model in mind. He must somehow make a proper discrimination between the relevant 'contexts' and the 'stylistic devices', between the background and the foreground. In many cases he will simply rely on his judgement and experience in making this discrimination. But his unaided judgement will be increasingly prone to error (a) if the text comes from a remote period; (b) if it is in a strict metrical form; (c) if it was subject in any way to the influence of traditional rhetoric; and (d) if it belongs to a homogeneous literary genre. (The more remote the period, the less evidence will survive about the author's language system as a whole. The other three factors all encourage a greater density of stylistic devices than one would find in ordinary speech, but they also encourage a greater uniformity in their use, so that the devices tend to become merely part of the special context. Beginners will see nothing but 'stylistic devices'; those with a little learning will see nothing but 'context'.) Thus, where the text is difficult on all four counts, one must first ascertain what is 'style' and what is 'non-style' by making the kind of neutral, broadly-based, quantitative description which I have advocated. And this is the relevance of the method at the level of 'practical criticism' or the *explication de texte.*

(ii) When the critic seeks to base his interpretation of an author's personality on an analysis of the author's stylistic characteristics, then not only must he have a proper grasp of the concept of individuality, but he must also be able to draw on *reliable* evidence about the author's style and about the style of other authors, both like and unlike in period, mode and genre. This evidence can be produced only by the method of description. And this is its relevance to stylistic criticism at a more general level.

I must not now invalidate the claims I am making on behalf of the proposed method of description by overstating them. For example, an author's individual style is certainly an important part of the stylistic 'context' in which to study an excerpt from his work: but it is only *part* of the context. Again, any categorical, quantitative description will always be far from complete, far from providing a satisfactory answer to every legitimate query about an author's usage. It can give precise information about the *classes* of words one would expect to find, but it does not reveal anything about the usage of *particular* words. Concordances and large-scale dictionaries on historical principles are no less indispensable auxiliaries. The polemics that flare up from time to time in the field of stylistics, and the coolness and suspicion with which the subject is often regarded in England today, all have their origin in exaggerated claims. The brash linguist with his 'science' and his 'objectivity', and his apparent claim that the act of criticism can be reduced to one of mensuration, either goads the literary critic into an angry counter-attack, or leads him to dismiss with contempt not only stylistics but linguistics as well. The wilder and more bizarre aspects of some stylistic criticism provoke corresponding reactions among linguists.

My own conception of stylistics and of the work I have done is more modest. I would suggest that the discipline is best regarded as a kind of buffer-state between linguistics and literary criticism. It is more than a 'no-man's land', but it can never be a major power. It must pursue policies which are acceptable to *both* its neighbours. If it does so, it will keep the major powers apart, and enable them to coexist in mutual respect. The literary critic will see that there is no threat to his experience, sensitivity and judgement, because the study of style itself requires these qualities, and because the hard evidence which stylistics can produce pertains only to the general context. It can disprove certain errors of fact, but it cannot prove anything. It is completely subservient to critical discussion, interpretation and evaluation, which must be concerned with the work *as a whole*. It is not a rival, but a 'guide'—and guides are only indispensable on the more arduous climbs. Conversely, the linguist need not fear that in the study of literary style all is anarchy, subjectivity and impressionism. He will see that the study is conducted with all the rigour that is possible, and that it rests on acceptable assumptions about the nature of language. Few people would wish to work permanently in this buffer-state. But there is no reason why they should. For the traveller and tourist it has many attractions. And, best of all, its existence can enable the two major powers to live in peace.

III

We come now to the particular problems posed by Dante's poems. I shall deal first with the choice of variables. Then I shall say a word about the presentation and interpretation of the evidence. And finally I shall discuss my selection and grouping of the poems themselves.

For reasons debated at some length in the first section of this introduction, the *nucleus* of the variables used in the description of Dante's style is drawn from traditional rhetoric. And so my task here is to indicate my choice of rhetorical 'authorities', rather than my choice of variables. Again for reasons given earlier, these 'authorities' are the works which we know to have been influential in Dante's period. They may be divided into three groups: (a) classical works, that is those composed before the end of the seventh century A.D.; (b) medieval *artes poeticae* composed in France during the twelfth and early thirteenth centuries; and (c) medieval *artes dictaminis* composed in Italy during the thirteenth century.

The main classical works are Horace's *Ars Poetica*;[1] the fourth book of the anonymous *Rhetorica ad Herennium*, a work which enjoyed enormous success in the Middle Ages, when it was attributed to Cicero; the fifth book of the *De nuptiis Mercurii et Philologiae* by Martianus Capella, and the first and second books of Isidore's *Etymologiae*: these last are compendia of the main tradition in the late Empire. Since they all derive ultimately from earlier Greek theoreticians, it is scarcely surprising that the contents of the *Rhetorica ad Herennium* on the one hand, and of Capella and Isidore on the other are substantially the same. They differ considerably, however, in point of arrangement,

---

[1] Details of the editions used will be found in the list of abbreviations and the select bibliography.

in the prominence given to certain figures, and in their terminology: the *ad Herennium* translates the original Greek terms, whereas the other tradition transliterates them. And they differ most of all in their examples. The author of the *ad Herennium* invented his own, as did the medieval writers who based their work on his. The other tradition, more subservient to the exposition and composition of literary works, drew its examples from the works of the school *auctores*, principally Virgil and Cicero.

From time to time, other classical works known in the Middle Ages are cited for the further elucidation or substantiation of particular points. And among these mention must be made of the following: the *Artes grammaticae* of Donatus and Priscian; St Augustine's *De doctrina christiana*; and Cassiodorus's *Institutiones*.

The medieval *artes poeticae* are those published in one volume in 1923 by E. Faral. The most important of these—both intrinsically and in point of influence—is the *Poetria Nova* by Geoffrey of Vinsauf (the 'original' *poetria* being Horace's *Ars Poetica*). But material has also been drawn from Geoffrey's *Documentum de modo et arte dictandi et versificandi*, the earlier *Ars versificatoria* by Matthew of Vendôme, the later *Laborintus* by Everard the German, and, finally, the *Poetria* of John of Garland (this last having been edited not by Faral but by G. Mari).

I have not incorporated much material from the *artes dictaminis* because the material they offer in places where they differ from other authorities is not usually relevant to the study of lyric poetry. It is worth recording, however, that the most important is the *Summa dictaminis* of Guido Faba, both because it is comprehensive, representative and influential, and because its author is one of the founders of artistic prose in Italian. I have also drawn on the *Rhetorica novissima* by the fiery and original Boncompagno of Signa, and on various compendia such as the *Microcosmo* of Tommasino d'Armannino and the *Ars arengandi* of Jacques de Dinant.

In addition to these three main groups I have of course drawn on Dante's own pronouncements on style, as set out in the second book of his *De vulgari eloquentia*, and scattered through virtually all his works. Occasionally too, reference will be made to the section devoted to rhetoric in Brunetto Latini's *Tresor*, which could well have been Dante's first introduction to formal rhetoric. But it will be seen that although comments of particular interest are quoted from Brunetto and

Dante, they do not rank as rhetorical 'authorities', nor have they been given particular prominence. Even if it were possible, it would not be desirable to ground the theory on their works. On the one hand, the theoretical framework of this method of analysis is intended to be equally valid for the study of any author writing in the thirteenth century, or, for that matter, in the later twelfth or early fourteenth centuries. And, on the other hand, it is no part of my purpose to show that Dante must have learnt such and such a technique or device from Brunetto,[1] or from a formal study of Latin rhetoric, rather than from the poems of earlier writers in Italian, Provençal or French. Nor is it my purpose to show that Dante's style does or does not satisfy his theoretical requirements. Others will perhaps take some of the material offered here as a point of departure for these or similar investigations. But the central aim of this book is to *describe* Dante's style in his lyrics, not to establish its sources.

Similarly, it is not my intention to show that Dante was influenced by certain *specifically medieval* aspects of rhetorical doctrine. And so I have not followed any one medieval *ars poetica* or *ars dictaminis* in its arrangement or order of presentation, as Baehr and Dragonetti have done, nor have I given preference, as a matter of policy, to the definitions and examples of any one medieval *ars*. For the actual wording of the definitions quoted, for example, it has seemed prudent to keep for the most part to the *Rhetorica ad Herennium* and Isidore or Capella, because these works would have retained their status as the true authorities in the Middle Ages, even though most students would then have learnt their rhetoric in a contemporary framework with contemporary definitions and examples. And the arrangement of the material, which is in fact closer to the order of the classical *artes*, is dictated largely by the needs of an analytical method. Had the original synthesis been made with a view to imparting to others the sum of medieval theory and expertise in the field of style, it would of course have assumed a different form.

---

1 Brunetto completely ignores the 'figures', and indeed he has very little to say about details of style (*elocutio*). *La rettorica italiana* is a commentary on the first seventeen chapters of Cicero's *De inventione*. The relevant section of his *Tresor* (ed. F. J. Carmody (Berkeley and Los Angeles, 1948), pp. 317–90) draws somewhat more on the *artes dictaminis* in its opening pages, and the eight sources of 'amplification' recommended by Geoffrey of Vinsauf and John of Garland are treated in full (pp. 330–2). But most of the material is derived from the *De inventione*.

In the second chapter, the analysis of vocabulary has led me to expand the rhetorical material considerably. And in the chapter on syntax and prosody, the majority of the variables do not have a rhetorical source: they have either been drawn from other modern studies of style, or they have been elaborated by me in the course of my work. Nevertheless, the nucleus of rhetorical variables is predominant in the book as a whole.

In the presentation of the evidence, I have given all the necessary information, in all the necessary detail, but I have striven to make the text readable, and intelligible to the non-specialist. Definitions of rhetorical terms are given in Latin, without translation. But they are given in the footnotes; and the text discusses and explains each variable and each term in such a way that even the reader who has no Latin at all should find no difficulty in following. In the text I confine myself to presenting and discussing the significant facts and the distinctive features. These are illustrated by a few unambiguous quotations, and by the relevant numerical evidence concerning frequency. The complete lists of examples and the full tables are given in the footnotes or at the end of a chapter. The footnotes are indispensable and are likely to prove the most durable part of the work. But in the first instance, many readers will be well advised to read the whole text through without consulting them.

It will be found that the interpretation varies considerably in kind and depth from one chapter to the next, and, indeed, from one variable to the next. This is because the interpretation depends on comparisons —and for comparisons I am dependent on the work of other scholars. Most of the necessary work still remains to be done; and some of what has been done may have escaped my attention, for studies of this kind appear in many languages and in many periodicals. For certain variables I have been able to compare Dante's poems with those by other *individual* poets, writing in Italian, in the same genre: for example, Dante's immediate predecessor Guittone d'Arezzo, his close contemporaries and friends, Guido Cavalcanti and Cino da Pistoia, or his greatest successor, Petrarch. In a few variables, I have information relating to what we today call the 'stilnovo' as a whole, that is, the *group* to which many of Dante's youthful poems belong. At times I have compared Dante's poems with other earlier poems, extending in language, period and range from the Sicilian school to the Provençal troubadours and the

French trouvères. In a few places, comparisons are made with a range of Latin works, both medieval and classical. In the chapter on syntax, I have been able to draw on studies of thirteenth-century Italian prose writers—including Dante—and on a study of thirteenth-century prose chronicles in French. In the second chapter, I have compared certain aspects of Dante's vocabulary with those of 200 English poets, from 1350 to the present day.

There are, however, three threads which run right through the book and which guarantee a certain consistency in the interpretation and a certain minimum level of meaningfulness. In most variables one can make comparisons of a sort between Dante's poems and the examples or models given in the rhetorical manuals. For many variables—although for fewer than one might have expected—there are studies in existence which permit comparisons with Dante's *Comedy*. And, most important of all, it is possible to make illuminating comparisons between the poems themselves. Let us now see why.

Michele Barbi, who edited Dante's poems for the 1921 edition of his works, recognized 88 poems[1] as genuine. And from a purely practical point of view, they present no difficulties. The poems comprise in all 2,720 lines of verse, which is a significant but not unmanageable total. The poems vary in length from 10 to 158 lines. But it is not difficult to find a standard unit for the purposes of analysis and comparison. This is because two-thirds of the poems are sonnets, whilst the longer poems— *ballate* and *canzoni*—are built up of stanzas, each complete in sense, which are broadly similar in point of length and construction to the sonnet. From other points of view, the poems present many problems but, as we shall see, it is *because* of them rather than *in spite* of them that the poems constitute an almost ideal subject for close description.

The difficulties arise in the first place from contradictory qualities in the poems. They are remarkable for their diversity in matter and treat-

---

[1] In the edition of the poems prepared by Kenelm Foster and myself (*Dante's Lyric Poetry:* vol. I, *Text and Translation*; vol. II, *Commentary* (Oxford, 1967)) there are 89 poems attributed to Dante. This was because we reversed the traditional attributions in a sonnet exchange between Dante Alighieri and Dante da Maiano (see vol. II, pp. 6–9). It does not affect the present study where I have followed Barbi's numbering as well as his text. Readers are, however, reminded that the poems are most easily consulted in our edition (the first volume is available separately in paper covers), because the poems scattered through the *Vita Nuova* and the *Convivio* are gathered accessibly in one book. A table for the conversion of Barbi's numbering to that used in our edition will be found there in vol. I, p. 213.

ment; and yet the reader will still feel some sense of unity. They are all conventional, and they all owe an enormous debt to the courtly tradition in Romance vernacular verse for their language, style and metrical form; and yet many of them are strikingly original. They are at once heterogeneous and homogeneous, conventional and unconventional. And this is why they are of a kind to challenge and vindicate the method of description. The method cannot provide a full and immediate answer to the question 'How far is the style of the poems personal and how far conventional?', but it must be able to demonstrate why and in what ways the poems differ from one another, and what it is they hold in common.

The complexity of the subject demands complex treatment. Only rarely will it be possible to make a relatively straightforward generalization about Dante's personal style, with respect to any one variable. In fact, it is the ever present need to consider not only the average frequency of any given device or feature, but also the differing patterns of distribution from poem to poem and group to group, that has called for a book of 350 pages instead of the mere 50 pages or so in which one could present the facts about a more unified body of poems. But it is this same complexity that justifies the existence of this study in book form as opposed to an article in a learned periodical. For the findings for one poem, or one group of poems, can be illuminated by comparison with the very different findings for another poem or group, or with the 'average' of all the poems. And so the book is, in a sense, 'self-pollinating'.

The last circumstance which makes Dante's poems so suitable for close description is that we have sufficient evidence about the chronology of roughly half the poems to establish with reasonable certainty the order and the approximate date of their composition. We know that the poems were composed over a period of about twenty-five years; and we have poems representative of all phases. As a result we are able to study the stylistic differences between the poems not just as the result of arbitrary factors, or of changes in genre or model—as we must in the work of most other medieval lyric poets—but also to some extent as *developments*. Our knowledge of the chronological sequence, sketchy as it is, provides a theme which enormously simplifies and clarifies the task of presenting the findings, and renders them more intelligible. In some ways, then, the book is more a chart of Dante's stylistic development than a description of his personal style. But, paradoxically, the chronological presentation will enable us to deepen our understanding of what is personal in Dante's style. We shall not see the personal element only as something static—locating it in those features which remain relatively constant throughout, or in others, more numerous, common to poems in several groups. We shall be able to see a dynamic pattern—a pattern of growth. We shall be able to plot the poems, both the earliest and the last, on a common line of development, and one moreover that points forward to the *Comedy*, which remains the ultimate goal of all studies on Dante.

The intelligibility and the limited 'self-sufficiency' of this study depends largely on its organization, on the coherent presentation of the complex facts about Dante's style. This organization in turn depends on our knowledge of the chronology of some of the poems. Chronology, then, is a decisive factor. It is in fact so important that about half of Dante's poems have been excluded from the main part of the study simply because their position in the sequence can only be inferred on internal evidence—that is, by their thematic and stylistic affinities with poems of known chronology. More will be said about the 'excluded' poems in a moment, but first it will be necessary to specify, characterize and group the chosen poems, and to indicate briefly the nature of the chronological evidence.

Numerically, the poems chosen for complete, detailed study represent just over half the total (45 out of 88); but in terms of length they amount to nearly 60 per cent (1,624 lines out of a total of 2,720).

They may be divided initially into two main sections—those written in the decade *c.* 1283–*c.* 1293, and those written in the decade *c.* 1294–*c.* 1304 (although three of the chosen sonnets were probably written after 1304). For the first decade, the chosen poems are those, *and only those*, included by Dante in the *Vita Nuova*, which, from one point of view, is the author's retrospective anthology and interpretation of his early work. These poems—31 in all, totalling 676 lines—will be referred to collectively as the '*VN* poems.' Those from the second decade (and later)—14 poems, totalling 948 lines—will be referred to as the 'later poems'.

The *Vita Nuova* itself provides the evidence for the chronology of the poems in the first section. Dante is purposely vague about the actual dates of composition (although we may deduce from the prose that no. I was written in 1283, no. xxv in 1290, no. xxx in 1291 and no. xxxvi in 1292), but he does present them, or profess to present them, in the order in which they were composed; and this is all we need to know.

For the purpose of this study, the *VN* poems are divided into eight groups designated by the letters A–H. Constant reference will be made to these groups by these letters and so, for the reader's convenience, the information to be given here is set out in tabular form on a pullout sheet at the end of the volume to permit easy consultation. Group A comprises the first six poems in the *Vita Nuova* (nos. I, and v–ix incl., *VN*, i–xiii), which are generally considered typical of Italian courtly verse in the period immediately before 1280. Group B contains the sonnets of lamentation (nos. x–xiii incl., *VN*, xiii–xvi), which show a strong influence from Dante's elder contemporary and closest friend, Guido Cavalcanti. In the next three groups the order of the *Vita Nuova* is slightly modified. The sonnets and the isolated *canzone*-stanza in praise of Beatrice, all showing a considerable debt to Guinizzelli, are in group C (nos. xvi–xvii, xxi–xxiv; *VN*, xx–xxi, xxiv, xxvi–xxvii). The interlude formed by the pair of sonnets in dramatic form (nos. xviii–xix; *VN*, xxii) and the *canzone*, *Donna pietosa* (no. xx; *VN*, xxiii) constitute group D, while in group E, I have taken together the two *canzoni*, *Donne ch'avete* (no. xiv) and *Li occhi dolenti* (no. xxv). This last coupling is perhaps a little questionable in view of the rather large gap between them in the *Vita Nuova* (chapters xix and xxxi respectively). The arguments in favour of the decision were that both are *canzoni*, that both are formal poems of praise (the lament being a species of encomium), and that the latter is modelled fairly closely on the former. The last three groups again follow the sequence of the *Vita Nuova*. Group F contains the remaining three laments for the death of Beatrice (nos. xxvi, xxvii, xxx; *VN*, xxxii–xxxiv); group G contains four sonnets tracing Dante's growing love for the 'gentile donna' (nos. xxxi–xxxiv; *VN*, xxxv–xxxviii); group H contains the last three sonnets in the work, written after Dante's return to the memory of Beatrice (nos. xxxv–xxxvii; *VN*, xxxix–xli).

The fourteen later poems have here been divided into five groups. The first, group I, comprises the two *canzoni* expounded by Dante in the second and third books of the *Convivio*, *Voi che 'ntendendo* (no.

LXXIX) and *Amor che ne la mente* (no. LXXXI), together with the *ballata*, *Voi che savete* (no. LXXX) which is intimately connected with them on the explicit testimony of *Con.*, III, ix, 1, 4. All three poems are written about the 'donna gentile' (cf. group G) and are in the manner of his earlier love poetry, but all of them are interpreted by Dante as allegories of his love for philosophy to which he had turned in order to seek consolation for the loss of Beatrice. The evidence in the *Convivio* (especially II, ii, xii) as to the actual date of their composition is extremely difficult to interpret,[1] but it is clear that all three were composed not long after the last of the *VN* poems.

The next group, group J, contains the two didactic poems, *Le dolci rime* (no. LXXXII) and *Poscia ch'Amor* (no. LXXXIII). These are compendious treatises in verse dealing with the courtly virtues of 'gentilezza' and 'leggiadria' respectively. The first of them is again expounded in the *Convivio* (book IV), and although no indication is there given as to the date of its composition, it is reasonable to suppose that both it and its companion were written in the years immediately after the allegorical poems we have just described: tentatively, then, we might ascribe them to the years 1295–6.

The next poems (group K) are very different again. They are the two regular *canzoni*, *Io son venuto* (no. C) and *Così nel mio parlar*, (no. CIII) from the group of four poems written to express a violent passion for a stonyhearted lady—a 'donna *petra*'—and, perhaps more important, written in emulation of the Provençal master, Arnaut Daniel. Here again the evidence regarding date is rather tenuous. For although the astronomical periphrasis which opens *Io son venuto* has been shown to indicate a date in December 1296, it remains true that the actual date is quite irrelevant to the 'timeless' poem, whereas every detail of the periphrasis is relevant. However, in view of Dante's precision in such matters elsewhere, it is commonly accepted that all the four very homogeneous poems written for the 'donna petra' were composed in late 1296 or in 1297.

Group L unites five late correspondence sonnets, all addressed to Cino da Pistoia but possibly composed at very different dates. *I' ho veduto già* and *Perch'io non trovo* (nos. XCV, XCVI) may well have been written, as Barbi believed, before Dante's exile in 1302, or, alternatively, they may belong to the first years of the exile. *Io sono stato* (no. CXI)

---

[1] See Foster–Boyde, *Dante's Lyric Poetry*, vol. II, pp. 341–62.

was accompanied by a Latin letter (*Epistle* III) which enables us to pin it down to the years 1303–6. The fact that no. CXIII, *Degno fa voi*, was written on behalf of the Marchese Malaspina enables us to place the poem in the years 1306–7, when Dante is known to have been his guest. *Io mi credea* (no. CXIV) could also belong to this period, or it could have been written much later—very late indeed, if it really contains an allusion to the *Paradiso*. All the poems in this group are probably later than those in group K however, and their common purpose and common stylistic interest can justify their being taken together.

The last group, group M, comprises the two *canzoni*, *Tre donne* (no. CIV) and *Doglia mi reca* (no. CVI), the twin peaks of Dante's poetic development before the *Comedy*. Both were written before the last sonnets to Cino. The former, with its closing plea for clemency addressed to the Black Guelph faction in Florence, must certainly belong to the early years of the exile: the most likely date seems to be late 1304 or early 1305. The latter is again to be ascribed on thematic grounds to the exile, and has a *terminus ad quem* not later than 1305, since it is mentioned in the *De vulgari eloquentia*: the most likely date is 1304.

Dante's remaining poems—those to which passing reference will be made, but which will not be analysed in detail—corroborate by and large the picture of Dante's style and its development that emerges from the close description of the chosen poems. Some of them simply confirm the evidence: in other words, they are related thematically to one group among the chosen poems, and they share the range of stylistic features common to that group. Others amplify the pattern in a perfectly coherent way. Thus, among the chosen poems there are none quite like *Non mi poriano* (for which we have a *terminus ad quem* in 1287) or *Guido, i' vorrei* or *Sonar bracchetti* (nos. LI, LII, LXI): but in genre and in style these agree well enough with the poems in group A. The style of the sonnets exchanged with Dante da Maiano (excluded because of doubts regarding the respective attribution of nos. LXI–XLV) is certainly more archaic than in any of the poems analysed, but this is precisely what we might have predicted in poems which, from every point of view, seem earlier than those in group A, and must be the earliest poems by Dante to survive. The three abusive sonnets addressed to Forese Donati (to be dated not later than 1296, the year of

Forese's death, and usually attributed to the years 1293–5) are the only examples of their genre in Dante, and in point of vocabulary at least they are very different from all his other poems: but they fit into that general pattern of restless experimentation which characterizes the other poems of the second decade.

There are in fact only half a dozen poems in which we can speak of some kind of 'conflict of evidence': poems, that is, with a certain combination of stylistic features which elsewhere seemed significantly discrete; or, alternatively, poems in which the style as a whole seems 'out of phase' with the subject matter and treatment. Thus *La dispietata mente* seems in general more mature than the poems in group A with which it seems to belong by genre and in the concept of love it reveals. Conversely, one of its closest relatives stylistically, the *canzone, Io sento sì d'Amor la gran possanza*, seems rather too stiffly archaic to have been written at the same time as the allegorical love poems in group I: nevertheless, that is the most likely period. More striking than these is the case of Dante's last *canzone, Amor, da che convien*. In view of the poem's *congedo* and of the accompanying Latin letter, *Epistle* IV, this can be assigned fairly securely to the years 1307–8. But thematically and stylistically it follows closely the modes of the pure Cavalcantian phase (group B, *c.* 1288 ?), the only clues to a later dating being the balanced energy of the syntax, and a small number of expressive words that one would not find in the earlier poems.

These 'contradictory' poems are not many, nor are they irreconcilably at odds with the majority. But they should be kept steadily in mind, for an awareness of their existence will help to maintain a proper caution when interpreting the facts derived from the chosen poems. In the first place, they can remind us of the axiom that 'all that changes is not development'. As is clearly shown in the *canzone, Amor da che convien*, in which the return to an earlier genre is accompanied by a return to the appropriate stylistic features, differences in style between successive groups of poems may owe little or nothing to the natural processes of maturation, and a very great deal to a change in genre, or in other words, to the imitation of different models. And secondly, they remind us that the chronological evidence is far from satisfactory: for the earlier period it is too much dependent on the selective, tendentious evidence of the *Vita Nuova*; for the later period it is altogether too vague. We may be sure, then, that the 'whole truth' about Dante's stylistic development was more complex, irregular and untidy than the 'truth' which will emerge from the evidence of the chosen poems. But on the other hand, if the findings are treated with the necessary circumspection, it is my contention that they do give a simplified but not otherwise distorted picture of Dante's style and its development in his lyric poetry as a whole.

'CONVERSIONES'

Logically, and by tradition, this first chapter should offer a description of Dante's vocabulary in his lyric poems. But I have chosen instead to give priority to a study of Dante's use of *conversiones*, that is of certain constructions involving abstract nouns. I do this because it is by no means undesirable to become familiar with the method of description in a very simple variable, and also because the *significance* of the findings is more fully apparent here than elsewhere, since, in this one case, the mere facts can be illuminated satisfactorily from each of the three vantage points distinguished in the introduction. Thus it will be possible to relate these constructions to what is specifically medieval in rhetorical theory (and, incidentally, to gain a particularly clear insight into the basis of that theory and the manner in which it was taught). Then, thanks to studies by Glasser, Heinimann and Corti[1] of the same constructions in Old French and in earlier Italian poets, we shall be able to compare Dante's work in this respect with that of his predecessors. And finally, it will become clear that Dante's use of the constructions is by no means constant, and that here, as in more complex ways in later variables, we shall not be studying Dante's personal style *tout court*, but describing the changes and developments in that style.

What then are *conversiones* ? No one can answer that question better than Geoffrey of Vinsauf, the first theorist to give them systematic

---

[1] R. Glasser, '*Abstractum agens* und Allegorie im älteren Französisch', *ZRP*, LXIX (1953), 43–122. S. Heinimann, *Das Abstraktum in der französischen Literatursprache des Mittelalters* (Berne, 1963); and 'Zur stilgeschichtlichen Stellung Chrétiens', in *Mélanges de linguistique et de littérature romanes à la mémoire d'István Frank* (University of the Saar, 1957), pp. 235–49. M. Corti, 'Studi sulla sintassi della lingua poetica avanti lo stilnovo', *AMAT*, XVIII, n.s. IV (1953), 263–365; 'Contributi al lessico predantesco. Il tipo "il turbato", "la perduta" ', *AGI*, XXXVIII (1953), 58–92; 'I suffissi dell'astratto "-or" e "-ura" nella lingua poetica delle origini', *RAL*, ser. VIII, (1953), 294–312. As the titles of these studies show, the authors have very different aims and emphases. From my point of view it is unfortunate that none of them give quantitative information about the frequency in different authors of the constructions we shall study.

treatment. But it may be helpful, just to demonstrate how simple the
constructions are, and to illustrate something of their effects and
associations, to preface Geoffrey's clear and circumstantial account with
a few unglossed examples from relevant sources outside Dante's lyrics.
The following are taken from poems by two of his more important
predecessors and from one of his own Latin letters:

> Poi no mi val merzé né ben servire
> inver' mia donna, in cui *tegno speranʒa*
> e amo lealmente,
> non so che cosa mi possa valere:
> se di me no le *prende pietanʒa,*
> ben morrò certamente.[1]

> Madonna, il fino *amor* ched *eo vo porto*
> mi *dona* sì gran *gioia ed allegranʒa*
> (ch'aver mi par d'Amore)
> che d'ogni parte *m'aduce conforto,*
> quando *mi membra* di voi *la 'ntendanʒa* ...[2]

> Dir Li porò: '*Tenne* d'angel *sembianʒa*
> che fosse del Tuo regno;
> non me fu fallo s'in lei *posi amanʒa.*'[3]

Neque ipsi *preheminentie vestre* congruum comperi magis quam Comedie
sublimem canticam que decoratur titulo Paradisi ... Illud quoque preterire
silentio simpliciter inardescens non *sinit affectus,* quod ... Sed *ʒelus gratie
vestre,* quam sitio vitam parvipendens, a primordio metam prefixam *urgebit*
ulterius.[4]

No mention of the *conversio* as such will be found in classical manuals
of rhetoric. But the constructions themselves had of course been
common—in certain contexts—for centuries. And Geoffrey's analysis
of them is entirely faithful to traditional principles. We have seen[5] that
traditional rhetoric conceived style as a series or combination of stylistic
devices, and that each device or figure was perceived and defined as a
departure from a neutral or 'style-less' mode of expression. Thus, to
analyse the style of a passage, one would first have to supply such a

---

[1] Giacomo da Lentini; text from *Poeti del Duecento*, ed. G. Contini (Milan–Naples,
   1960), vol. I, p. 64.
[2, 3] Guido Guinizzelli; texts ibid., vol. II, pp. 453, 464.
[4] Dante, *Epist.*, XIII, 11–12.   [5] Introduction, p. 27.

'styleless' paraphrase of its meaning (in language that would be modern, correct, complete, logical and simple etc.), and then compare the two modes of expression. Such paraphrases could be ruthlessly common-sensical. As an example of periphrasis, Isidore quotes Virgil's lines (*Aen.* IV, 584–5):

> Et iam prima novo spargebat lumine terras
> Tithoni croceum linquens Aurora cubile,

and comments: 'vult enim dicere "iam luciscebat", aut "dies ortus erat" '.[1] And Geoffrey, faced with the kind of substantival constructions exemplified above, would have said no doubt that *tegno speranʒa* means 'spero', or that *tenne d'angel sembianʒa* means 'somigliava a un angelo' or 'era simile a un angelo', or simply 'era come un angelo'. In other words he would regard the abstract noun (used in these cases as the object of a common, colourless verb) as a more elevated or ornate 'conversion' of a simple verb, or of an adjective used with 'to be'. Similarly, where the abstract noun appears as the active subject of a sentence—where an 'accidente' is treated as a 'sustanzia', as Dante puts it in *Vita Nuova*, xxv—Geoffrey would say that it has been 'converted' from an oblique case (for example in a prepositional phrase) into the nominative. And so when he comes to instruct his pupils how to express themselves with conscious elegance—*arte* not *casu*[2]—he assumes, as all rhetoricians did, that the pupil will already have his *thema*, that is something to say which already exists in a correct but styleless form. What Geoffrey will teach him is how to 'convert' his *thema*, as one way of rendering his expression more elevated and appropriate.

With this in mind, let us now examine his teaching as it is presented in the *Poetria Nova* (1,588–760) and in the prose *Documentum de modo et arte dictandi et versificandi* (II, 3, 103–31), which in what follows will be treated as if it were by Geoffrey, although Faral's attribution is not established conclusively. Conflating the two lengthy accounts, we can see that Geoffrey divides *conversiones* into four main categories, according to the original status of the converted word—verb, noun, adjective, or indeclinable part of speech. (In the *Documentum* he limits this last class to prepositions, but in the *Poetria Nova* he gives examples with prepositions, adverbs and even pronouns.) Here, in paraphrase, is how Geoffrey describes the process of 'converting' a verb.

---

[1] *Et.*, I, xxxvii, 15.   [2] Cf. *PN*, 1,589; *DVE*, II, iv, 1.

'Take the verb in your complete sentence and find the noun for the state or activity (*res*) to which the verb refers. Make this noun the subject of a new sentence, which you must then complete in an appropriate way. For example, in the sentence, "I see her", the verb is "see", and the relevant nouns are "looking", "sight", or "gaze". Make one of these your subject and then recast the sentence, e.g.: "my *sight* turns to her" or "my *gaze* rivets itself on her", or "the *looking* of my eyes encompasses her face".[1]

You need not keep the noun as your subject. You can put it into another case, always provided that you rewrite the new sentence so that it is roughly equivalent to your original. Suppose your *thema* is "ego scribo". The relevant noun is "scriptura" (or "scriptum"). It can be used in the nominative, "Sollicitat *scriptura* manum". But it could also be put into the genitive, "Stylus vel calamus meus fungitur officio *scripturae*"; or into the dative, "Manus mea invigilat *scripturae*"; or into the accusative, "Consilium manuum mearum res producit in *scriptum*"; or into the ablative, "Manus mea non desistit a *scripto*" '.[2]

Geoffrey is no less explicit in his description of how to convert an adjective. 'Albus' will become 'albedo' or 'candor'; 'pulcher' will become 'pulchritudo'. If we want to say 'facies est *alba*', we can say instead 'informat faciem *candor*'; 'iste est *pulcher*' becomes 'signavit faciem istius sigillum *pulchritudinis*'.[3]

---

[1] 'Secundum generale documentum est hoc: proposito verbo in quacumque perfecta locutione, sive aliud sequatur verbum, sive nihil, considera ad quam rem pertineat verbum et de illa re fiat sermo et ei quod suum est attribue.

   Verbi gratia ... in hac locutione perfecta: *Ego video illam*, ponitur verbum *video*, quod pertinet ad *visum*. Fiat ergo sermo de visu et ei quod suum est attribue sic: *Visus se flectit in illam*, vel sic: *In illam se meus defigit intuitus*, vel sic: *Faciem ipsius oculorum meorum comprehendit intuitus*' (*Documentum*, II, 3, 110).

[2] 'Vel aliter, cum verbum ponitur in perfecta locutione, converte illud in sustantivum quod pertinet ad rem verbi, et pone illud idem sustantivum in quocumque casu, et invenias sententiam accedentem sententiae illius perfectae locutionis quae proposita est. Verbi gratia, in hac locutione perfecta: *Ego scribo* ... ponitur hoc verbum *scribo*: convertatur ergo illud verbum in sustantivum quod pertinet ad rem verbi, scilicet in hoc verbum *scriptura*, et idem sustantivum ponatur in quocumque casu et inveniatur sententia quae accedat huic sententiae *Ego scribo*. Potest poni in nominativo et dici sic: *Sollicitat scriptura manum*. Potest poni in genetivo et dici sic ...' (etc., with the examples I have given in the text). *Documentum*, II, 3, 114, 116 corresponding to *PN*, 1,602–46.

[3] 'Sicut enim convertimus verbum in sustantivum quod significat rem illam ad quam pertinet verbum, ita debemus convertere adjectivum in sustantivum quod pertinet ad rem illius adjectivi. Verbi gratia, debemus convertere hoc adjectivum *albus* in hoc

A noun can be converted only in the more limited sense that if the *thema* has a noun in an oblique case, this noun can be made the subject of a new sentence and thus be 'converted' into the nominative case. Note, however, that it will not be a *conversio* if the original verb is retained and merely put into the passive voice. 'Video *rem illam*' must become something like 'Se *res illa* mihi praetendit *vel* offert se aspectui meo', or '*Res* oculis imminet *illa* meis'.[1]

When the converted word was an adjective the result may be identical with a species of metonymy—'ponere proprietatem pro subjecto'. And in this case the converted form will probably be briefer than any paraphrase. It may thus also qualify as an example of the figure *emphasis* (usually best translated with Faral as *sous-entendu*). Geoffrey does not make any of these equations, but his example of *emphasis* is identical with that given for the species of metonymy, which in turn has been adapted from the example given in the *Rhetorica ad Herennium* (IV, xxxii, 43) for the figure *circumitio* or periphrasis.

Emphasis enim est quaedam figura quae longam seriem verborum curtat eleganter, quae fit duobus modis: uno modo quando rem ipsam appellamus nomine suae proprietatis, uno modo quando locuturi de re loquimur de eius proprietate.

Exemplum *secundi*, ut, dicturi de Scipione quod ipse delevit Cartaginem per prudentiam suam, dicimus de prudentia sua quod ipsa hoc fecerit, sic scilicet: *Scipionis prudentia Cartaginem delevit* ...

Alius modus emphaseos quando, sicut diximus, rem appellamus nomine suae proprietatis, ut hic: *Medea est ipsum scelus.* Quod sic est exponendum: *Medea est ita scelerosa, quod in ea nihil invenitur nisi scelus.* Ecce per hunc

---

sustantivum *albedo,* hoc adjectivum *pulcher* in hoc sustantivum *pulchritudo* ... et sic de similibus. Verbi gratia, dicturi sumus: *Facies est alba,* dicamus ...' (etc., with the examples given in the text). *Documentum,* II, 3, 118–19, corresponding to *PN,* 1651–79.

1 'Ex praedictis generalibus unum tale est: convertere obliquum in nominativum. Istud ita generale est, quod non invenit instantiam; si enim locutione proposita verbum sequatur obliquus et illa junctura non fuerit elegans, converte obliquum in nominativum et sic reddes elegantem juncturam. Non dico ut obliquus convertatur in nominativum, et activum in passivum, quia hoc nihil est, immo, sive sit verbum activum, sive neutrum, sive alterius modi verbum et sequatur obliquus, converte obliquum in nominativum cum adjectione convenientis verbi et erit conveniens junctura.

Verbi gratia, *Video rem illam*: ponitur obliquus post verbum; mutetur obliquus in nominativum et adjungatur conveniens verbum, non dico ut activum convertatur in passivum, sed sic ...' (etc. with the examples given in the text). *Documentum,* II, 3, 107–8 corresponding to *PN,* 1,680–708.

modum emphaseos qualiter haec tota series per illud breviloquium compre-henditur.[1]

Geoffrey also notes that it is by no means necessary to form the substantive from the same root as the 'original' adjective or verb. One may take a synonym or, passing now into figurative usage, one may use a common metaphor (for example, 'nix' for 'candor'[2]); or again one may use yet another species of metonymy, 'ponere consequens pro antecedente'.[3] And in the phrases which the student composes to complete the sense, it is indeed preferable to use metaphorical rather than 'proper' terms. His example of these procedures is well worth study because of its close resemblance to the courtly lover's plaints in vernacular poetry (the *thema* is *ex hac re doleo*, and he has already given examples using *dolor* in all its cases).

> Vel item non sumes nomen ab illo,
> sed magis a simili verbo signante dolorem,
> qualia sunt *suspiro, queror, gemo, lacrimor*. Inde
> nomina sunt *lacrimae, gemitus, suspiria, questus*.
> Sic igitur sensum verborum nomina dicunt:
> *Ex animo veniunt 'suspiria', 'questus' ab ore;*
> *in faciem manant 'lacrimae', 'gemitusque' resumo*
> *continuos*. Sed dic festivius istud: *Ab imo*
> *pectoris erumpunt 'suspiria', 'questibus' aer*
> *exclamat, 'lacrimas' derivat fons oculorum*
> *et 'gemitus' rumpunt animum* ...
> In proprie sumptis satis est jocunda venustas,
> sed bene transsumptis magis est cognata voluptas.[4]

He also insists[5] that it is by no means necessary to be content with one conversion. One may go on to convert a verb or adjective which has been introduced into the converted phrase, or, using *duobus docu-mentis*, take a noun which had been introduced into the first conversion in an oblique case and convert it into the nominative. In short, one

---

[1] *Documentum*, II, 2, 32–4. For the species of metonymy, cf. ibid., II, 3, 28.

[2] *PN*, 1,666–7.

[3] *Documentum*, II, 3, 47; for example *'pallere pro timere'*. That Dante was aware of his own metonymic use of such words is shown by his gloss on a line in the last sonnet in the *VN*: 'passa 'l *sospiro* ch'esce del mio core' (XXXVII, 2). '... dico ove va lo mio *pensero, nominandolo per lo nome d'alcuno suo effetto*' (*VN*, xli, 3).

[4] *PN*, 1,633–43, 1,645–6.

[5] *Documentum*, II, 3, 121–31; cf. *PN*, 1,749–60.

should proceed with what we may call a 'chain of conversions' until one finds a structure which satisfies both the mind and the ear, 'quae bene respondeat animo et auri'.[1]

Now that we are familiar with the kinds of construction, it is time to say something about their stylistic significance and the reasons underlying their popularity. In rhetorical theory, and especially in medieval rhetorical theory, stylistic significance can be equated with stylistic level. And before we consider Geoffrey's answer to our questions, we can note that the constructions would have found favour if only because the resonant abstract noun, which they invariably introduce, was felt to be on a higher plane than the simple adjective or verb, just as these parts of speech were 'superior' to purely structural elements, such as prepositions, for which the medieval stylist displays a fine contempt. Geoffrey speaks of them as the 'common herd' or as 'villeins':

> Vocum quae flecti nequeunt *immobile vulgus*,
> in sermone licet tolerabile, tollitur apte:
> saepius et melius *plebs illa recedet ab aula*,
> sub quadam forma servanda.   *PN*, 1,709–12

And it is only grudgingly, in making his graded classification of words in *DVE*, II, vii, 6, that Dante concedes second-class status to 'necessary words that we cannot avoid'—'*necessaria* quidem appellamus *que campsare non possumus*, ut quedam monosillaba, ut *sì, no, me, te, sé, à, è, i', ò, u'*, interiectiones, et alia multa'.

Classical rhetoricians had been well aware that certain figures were appropriate only in certain contexts, but they avoided any systematic attempt to link each figure with a specific level of style. In fact they recognized *three* levels of style, whereas the figures were divided on a different principle into *two* classes—figures of 'thought' and figures of 'speech'. Geoffrey of Vinsauf and his successors sought to regularize this 'anomaly', and to do this they introduced a new distinction between 'easy' and 'difficult' modes of ornamentation. The *ornatus difficilis* or *difficultas ornata* is produced by using words in extended or transferred senses, that is by using the tropes, metaphor and metonymy. The *ornatus facilis* or *facilitas ornata*[2] results from the use of the re-

---

[1] *Documentum*, II, 3, 121.

[2] The first term in each pair is that used by John of Garland, *Poetria*, p. 898; the second that by Geoffrey, *Documentum*, II, 3–4, and 48.

maining figures of speech and the figures of thought. Now these two
modes might well have been allowed a conceptual existence quite
independent of the *tria genera dicendi*. But in fact there was a marked
tendency, made explicit in John of Garland,[1] to link the *ornatus
difficilis* with the highest level of style, and the *ornatus facilis* with the
middle level. And with this in mind we can see what Geoffrey means
when he asserts that the *conversiones*—which are not one of the traditional figures—are appropriate in either mode: 'sunt quaedam alia
documenta quae valent ad ornatum, *sive ornatus ille pertineat ad
facilitatem, sive ad difficultatem*'.[2] He means that the stylistic level of the
conversio is on the borderline between the middle and high styles.

Once again his account is endorsed, implicitly, by Dante in the
De vulgari eloquentia. In Dante's examples of the levels of style (*gradus
constructionum*), the lowest is distinguished only by its observance of
the prescribed rhythmic cadences or *cursus* in every phrase, and in
consequence by an unnatural word order:

Piget me cunctis pietate maiorem, quicunque in exilio tabescentes patriam
tantum sompniando revisunt.

The highest level is studded with tropes:

Eiecta maxima parte florum de sinu tuo, Florentia, necquicquam Trinacriam
Totila secundus adivit.

But the intermediate level is characterized—in addition to the *cursus*
and the irony at the expense of the miserly and hated Marquis of Este—
by the use of *conversiones:*

Laudabilis discretio marchionis Estensis, et sua magnificentia preparata,
cunctis illum facit esse dilectum.   *DVE*, II, vi, 5

And it was surely the *conversiones*, rather than the irony, which drew
from Dante the rather withering remark that this level was characteristic
of those who have only skimmed the surface of the spring of rhetoric—
'est quorundam superficietenus rethoricam [h]aurientium'.

One reason then for the popularity of these constructions was that
they were felt to provide, of themselves, a moderate elevation of style.
Another reason, not unconnected, was that they made it easier to find
suitable *cursus*. Indeed an abstract noun with its resonant suffix might
provide the *cursus* almost unaided. And it is clear that the ancient

---

[1] *Poetria*, p. 898.   [2] *Documentum*, II, 3, 103.

classroom drill[1] of putting a noun through all its cases, inserting it each time in a different meaningful phrase, all of which phrases might have to be roughly equivalent in sense, was intended to produce facility in the composition of verse or rhythmic prose. We may clinch this point and permit ourselves another glimpse of medieval pedagogy in action with two examples from the *Summa dictaminis* of Guido Faba. It will be noted that *conversiones* are introduced both at the first stage (*materia*) in the ornamentation of a *thema*, and at the second stage (*dispositio*).

Thema est factum in genere propositum; vel thema est brevis apertio dicendorum, per quam auditor loquentis intelligit voluntates. Exemplum: *Scias quod Bononienses contra Mutinenses exercitum iam fecerunt.* Restat videre quid sit materia. *Materia* est plena et artificiosa verborum ordinatio ex his que in themate assumuntur. Exemplum: *Sciatis quod Bononienses amicorum vocata multitudine copiosa, contra Mutinam iverunt cum suo carrocio tam magnifice quam potenter, et in obsidione castri Baçani diutius commorantes ad propria sani et incolumes sunt reversi, sed nec ipsum expugnare castrum, nec aliquam habere victoriam potuerunt.*[2]

postquam [materiam] invenerit, circa *dispositionem* laboret ut ordinetur sub verborum serie competenti, et postmodum ad colores procedat rethoricos quibus depingat eandem ornamento circumposito, quasi quodam pallio et florifero tegumento ... Exemplum. Aliquis vult scribere suo domino vel amico ut possit a curia litteras impetrare. Qualiter simpliciter diceret, si personaliter in presentia sua foret? *Ego rogo dominationem vestram de qua multum confido, ut dignemini mihi adiutorium vestrum dare, ita quod ...* Ecce, habes *materiam*: recurre igitur ad *dispositionem* ipsius hoc modo: *Dominationem vestram, de qua gero fiduciam pleniorem, humili prece rogito incessanter quod mihi vestre liberalitatis et gratie taliter dignemini subsidium impartiri, quod ...*[3]

It was this kind of language that satisfied the medieval 'mind and ear'. Are we then to attribute the abundance of *conversiones* in medieval

---

1 '*Quemlibet in casum sic mutes; cuilibet addas / structuram vocum similem quae competat ipsi / materiae*', *PN*, 1,631–3; '... idem sustantivum ponatur *in quocumque casu* et inveniatur sententia quae accedat huic sententiae ...' *Documentum*, II, 3, 116. For this exercise, certainly the ultimate source of Geoffrey's *conversio*, see H.I. Marrou, *Histoire de l'éducation dans l'antiquité*, 4th ed. (Paris, 1958), pp. 241–2, 379.

2 *Summa dictaminis*, ed. A. Gaudenzi, *Il Propugnatore*, n.s. III (1890), 334. There is an intriguing parallel between this and the example (quoted above) given by Dante for the highest style.

3 *Ibid.*, pp. 334–5.

writings of an elevated character solely or decisively to rhetorical indoctrination, to the influence of the *artes dictaminis* or *artes poeticae?* Certainly not. It must be emphasized that the epistolary style was in existence long before the use of *conversiones* was systematically taught. It will be found, fully-fledged, utterly unclassical, in such decisive influences on medieval literary taste as the allegorical framework of Martianus Capella's *De nuptiis* or in the letters of Sidonius Apollinaris or Cassiodorus. And the fondness for the abstract noun in that style must be seen in relation to the general increase in the number of abstract nouns in the vocabulary of post-classical Latin, especially in those formed with the suffixes *-atio, -itas, -itudo, -antia, entia.* Nor was this trend towards the abstract noun confined to Latin, or to the Latin of the late Empire. In many forms, and with many interruptions and resurgences, it has continued right down to the present day, and has brought about one of the most striking differences between classical Latin and its descendants or beneficiaries in modern Europe.

Quite why the current should have begun to flow in that direction in post-classical times will of course admit of many explanations. At a practical level, there was the need to come level and keep pace with Greek, which had long been rich in technical and philosophical terms of all kinds. One imagines, too, that the growth of bureaucracy, with the increasingly centralized administration of an expanding Empire, would not have been a hindrance to the development. At a quite different level of causality, many scholars are inclined to interpret the taste for abstractions as an indication of a changed view of the world— Christian Neoplatonism leading men to look beyond mere concrete particularity to the 'reality' of the unchanging, immortal 'form'.[1]

---

[1] See for example L. Malagoli, *Motivi e forme dello stile del Duecento* (Pisa, 1960). Glassner (*'Abstractum agens'*, p. 74), Heinimann (*Das Abstraktum*, p. 7) and Corti ('Studi', pp. 297, 339–40) all make a bow in this direction. Corti is perhaps most typical: 'Qual'è in definitiva la posizione da assumere di fronte a queste immagini di un pensiero perifrastico e astrattista? Cavarsela col motivo della comodità della rima, o del cumulo passivo di formule o del cattivo gusto enfatico di una corrente? Si potrebbe, ma è troppo semplicistico, e per così dire, malinconico, come lo sono i giudizi insufficienti. È più persuasivo comportarsi alla Spitzer; come lo Spitzer dallo studio del tipo *on va* per *nous allons* è risalito a una tendenza umana di subordinazione dell'individuale al generale, così è possibile dall'esame di queste strutture della lingua risalire alla disposizione di una cultura tesa a determinare, dietro l'attività degli uomini e delle cose, la staticità delle idee che li muovono' (pp. 339–40). At a different level, see also C. S. Lewis, *The Allegory of Love* (Oxford, 1936), ch. II.

Others will want to proceed more cautiously. And certainly before pursuing either a rhetorical, a psychological, a sociological, or a metaphysical explanation of the phenomenon, it is as well to recall that the free use of similar constructions is typical of the objective style of academic papers in the experimental sciences;[1] and that, in a different way, such constructions seem to be a constant temptation to administrators and civil servants. Again, a marked preference for substantival constructions by a particular author may be significant in a Spitzerian sense, and yet have nothing to do with rhetoric or the Middle Ages.[2] And finally it should be remembered that such constructions now belong among the many possible modes of expression in modern European languages which possess no particular significance at all.[3] All that we can safely say, then, about the influence of the schools is that the systematic inculcation of such constructions, whether by example alone, or by theory and example combined as in Geoffrey, would certainly have encouraged and stabilized their use, and have given them a very definite stylistic value.

Similarly, when I go on to list the *conversiones* in the *VN* poems under headings drawn from Geoffrey, it will not be my intention to suggest that Dante learnt to use them from his formal study of Latin rhetoric or that, when composing a poem, he went through the kind of procedures exemplified by Geoffrey. Such constructions had long been current in the Romance vernaculars, and their associations were as specific there as they were in Latin. In their studies of Old French and Provençal, Glasser and Heinimann show that there is a steady growth in the use of abstract nouns in translations from the Bible, in documents, in didactic poetry and even in the *chansons de geste*. But it is *only* in the poetry of the twelfth-century troubadours, and in all forms of courtly literature directly or indirectly influenced by them that they become both frequent and dominant, and that they are deployed in the constructions which are our concern.[4] It could be said, indeed, that

---

[1] Cf. R. Wells, 'Nominal and verbal style', in *Style in Language*, ed. T. A. Sebeok (Massachusetts, 1960), pp. 213–20.

[2] Cf. S. Ullmann, 'New patterns of sentence-structure in the Goncourts', in *Style in the French Novel* (Cambridge, 1957), pp. 121–45.

[3] Cf. A. Lombard, *Les constructions nominales dans le français moderne* (Uppsala, 1930). G. Herczeg, 'Stile nominale nella prosa italiana contemporanea', *AL*, IV (1954), 171–92.

[4] Cf. Heinimann, *Das Abstraktum*: ... 'die Lyrik zeigt eine ausgesprochene Neigung

troubadour poetry could not be what it is without those nouns and the constructions in which they appear. We may see them as essential to their very conception of love and its effects on the lover,[1] essential to their stress on the moral and social qualities which true love requires and brings to perfection, and essential to the aristocratic elevation of their style, through which alone they can give fitting expression to their refined ideal.

Maria Corti, too, has shown and documented that the type represented by *tegno speranza* or *posi amanza*, together with other periphrastic forms of the verb such as *sono perdente* or *sono perditore* (= 'perdo') —again of Provençal descent—are abundant and indeed stylistically dominant in the Sicilian court poets and their followers on the mainland. She writes:

Infine i poeti trovavano anche in questo caso dei modelli già pronti e insistentemente utilizzati nella poesia provenzale, di modo che tali perifrasi possiedono per essi *quel tono di ambiente linguistico poetico, di moda,* quell'accento evocatore di un'atmosfera poetica d'oltralpe ben nota; non a caso la maggior parte di queste perifrasi contiene sostantivi che terminano in *-anza* e in *-enza,* suffissi magari indigeni, ma che hanno tutte le carte in regola per appartenere al linguaggio della poesia provenzaleggiante.

Vengono così a formarsi, per il cumulo di tutti questi influssi, dei sintagmi fissi, delle *vere formule poetiche di dominio comune,* le quali perciò nella maggior parte dei casi *hanno perso quel valore stilistico che si potrebbe essere tentati di dare ai singoli casi, isolandoli dagli altri.*[2]

And as she implies in this passage, it was not just the constructions as a type that were imitated. What was taken over was an established phraseology, the linguistic structures together with the vocabulary. Thus the nouns and verbs most used in these constructions by early

---

zum nominalen Stil' (p. 44). 'In Frankreich wird der substantivierte Infinitiv zu einem der hervorstechenden Merkmale des höfischen oder höfisch beeinflussten Stils' (p. 56).

[1] Cf. Glasser, '*Abstractum agens*': 'Der Trobador unterscheidet sich von anderen Liebhabern und Liebesdichtern u.a. dadurch, dass er sein subjektives Gefühlsleben in eine Welt objektiver Beziehungen hineinstellt und sein Schicksal und Erleben als Resultante und Wirkung abstrakter Wesenheiten darstellt. Er sieht sich ganz als Objekt der Mächte, denen er ein persönliches Tun, eine Seele und Absicht andichtet' (p. 68).

[2] 'Studi', p. 335. She makes similar observations on the use of present participle + *essere* (ibid., p. 320), and she speaks of the free use of nouns with the suffixes *-anza, -enza, -ore, -aggio* as 'coerenza lirico-linguistica a una determinata poetica' ('I suffissi', p. 295).

'Italian' poets are precisely those which had been most used in Provençal and Old French. One could probably find a genuine parallel in the surviving literatures of those languages for almost every *conversio* in the *VN* poems.

To lay stress on this derivation is not to deny that an Italian poet may have favoured the constructions because they provided him with easy rhymes on common abstract suffixes such as *-anʒa*, *-enʒa* or *-ate*, or because they conferred on his style something of the dignity of artistic Latin, or, again, because the poet was an unconscious representative of certain deep-lying attitudes common to his whole culture. Nevertheless, those constructions articulating those words proclaim his proud allegiance to a well-defined literary genre and to a particular ideal of poetry, which is in some sense an ideal of the good life. And in early Italian poetry the *conversiones* have an extra range of effects and associations, which they could not have had in Provençal, simply because in Italy they were exotic. To assess their effect in Italian we ought to compare them not with similar passages in Provençal or French but with lines like the following:

> So hath myn herte caught in remembraunce
> your beaute hoole and stidefast governaunce,
> your vertues alle and your hie noblesse,
> that you to serve is set al my plesaunce.[1]

It is clear from the foregoing that among the influences on Dante's use of *conversiones* in his lyric poetry, we need attach only slight importance to the manuals of rhetoric. Formal rhetorical teaching, and even the example of rhetorically influenced Latin, are simply part of the general background. On the other hand, rhetorical doctrine and vernacular practice are in perfect harmony at this point, both in spirit and in letter. And the following list of the *conversiones* in the *VN* poems will demonstrate that Geoffrey's categories provide a framework which is analytically useful, and at the same time illuminating, in a way that no 'modern' categories would be.[2]

[1] *The Complete Works of Geoffrey Chaucer*, ed. F. N. Robinson, 2nd ed. (Oxford, 1957), p. 533.
[2] Heinimann (*Das Abstraktum*, p. 120) comes to the same conclusion: 'Die Lehre von der *conversio* oder *permutatio* ist die Theorie dessen, was Chrestien und vor ihm schon die Provenzalen mit Erfolg in der Vulgärsprache geübt haben.'

Conversio adjectivi in substantivum quod pertinet ad rem illius adjectivi.

adorna assai di *gentilezze* umane	XX, 2
e sua bieltate è di tanta *vertute*	XXIII, 5
la *qualità* de la mia vita oscura[1]	XXXI, 6
così mi trovo in amorosa *erranza*	X, 11
Amor, non già per mia poca *bontate*, ma per sua *nobiltate*	V, 7–8
e per la *ebrietà* del gran *tremore*	XII, 7
veggendo in lei tanta *umiltà* formata	XX, 72
dille: 'Madonna, lo suo core *è stato con sì fermata fede*	IX, 25–6
che donna fu *di sì gaia sembianza*	VI, 14
donna pietosa e di *novella etate*[2]	XX, 1

Conversio adjectivi vel verbi[3] in substantivum obliquum.

e dèi *aver pietate* e non *disdegno*	XX, 76
li occhi son vinti, e *non hanno valore* di riguardar persona che li miri	XXXV, 3–4
de li occhi, *c'hanno* di lor morte *voglia*	XII, 14
e *hanno* in lor sì gran *varietate*	X, 2
così *leggiadro* questi *lo core have*	V, 12
ed *avea* seco *umilità* verace	XX, 69
voi che *portate la sembianza* umile	XVIII, 1
or *ho perduta* tutta *mia baldanza*	V, 13
che s'io allora non *perdessi ardire*	XIV, 7
che per vergogna *celan lor mancanza*, di fuor *mostro allegranza*	V, 18–19
perché villana Morte in gentil core ha *miso* il suo *crudele adoperare*	VI, 5–6

[1] For the first three examples, compare respectively: 'una donna ... *gentile*' (*VN*, xxiii, 11 = Dante's prose paraphrase); 'ma dentro portan la dolze figura ... sì *vertuosa* ...' (LXXX, 9, 11); 'e *quale* è stata la mia vita, poscia' (xxv, 60).

[2] Cf. the prose paraphrase: 'una donna *giovane*' (*VN*, xxiii, 11).

[3] It is usually impossible to decide with any certainty whether the 'simple' form would have been an adjective or a verb.

prende baldanʒa e tanta *securtate*	XI, 8
poi *prende* Amore in me tanta *vertute*	XXIV, 9
io *presi* tanto *smarrimento* allora	XX, 35
altro sperando m'*apporta dolʒore*	X, 5
e se con tutti vòi *fare accordanʒa*	X, 12
audite quanto Amor le *fece orranʒa*	VI, 9
aiutatemi, donne, *farle onore*	XVII, 8 (see XXI, 5)
leggeramente ti *faria disnore*[1]	IX, 14

Conversio substantivi obliqui in nominativum; vel, *duobus documentis, conversio verbi in substantivum obliquum et huius obliqui in nominativum.*[2]

color d'amore e di *pietà sembianti*	
non *preser* mai così mirabilmente	
viso di donna . . .[3]	XXXII, 1–3
Spesse fïate *vegnonmi* a la mente	
le oscure *qualità* ch'Amor mi dona[3]	XIII, 1
Era *venuta* ne la mente mia	
quella *donna gentil* . . .	XXX, 1–2
sì che per voi *mi ven cosa* a la mente	XXXII, 7
nel cui cospetto *ven lo dir* presente	I, 2

---

[1] Cf. Heinimann, *Das Abstraktum*: 'Zahlreich sind in Chrestiens Romanen die mehr oder weniger festgefügten Verbindungen eines in seinem Bedeutungsgehalt verblassten Verbums mit einem Nomen actionis (seltener mit einem Nomen qualitatis), das die Funktion eines Akkusativobjekts oder einer adverbiellen Ergänzung hat. Das nominale Element bildet mit dem verbalen eine semantische Einheit. Es sind die Ausdrücke, vom Typus *faire penitance, metre en obli* . . .' (p. 87). He briefly traces the origins of the construction in Latin authors, and gives the following as the most common 'colourless' verbs used in the constructions in the works of Chrestien: *faire* (demorance, enor etc.); *avoir* (talant, vergogne, joie, an despit etc.); *tenir* (a desdaing); *doner* (congié); *randre* (merciz), *prandre; metre; mener, demener; porter* (enor, compaignie) (p. 88). The same vocabulary is found in early Italian poets; see Corti, 'Studi', pp. 333–40.

[2] Again I give a double heading because it is not usually possible to determine the hypothetical simple form. A clear example of the 'double conversion' would be v, 16, where we could reconstruct the imaginary stages somewhat as follows: 'I was afraid to . . .'; 'I felt fear about . . .'; 'Fear came upon me . . .'

[3] Compare the prose paraphrases of the first two examples: 'Avvenne poi che là ovunque *questa donna* mi vedea, sì *si facea d'una vista pietosa* e *d'un colore* palido quasi *come d'amore*' (*VN*, xxxvi, 1); '. . . quando la mia memoria movesse la fantasia ad imaginare *quale* Amore mi facea' (*VN*, xvi, 2).

e *venmene pietà*, sì che sovente	XIII, 3
che fai di te *pietà venire* altrui	XIX, 6
e spesse fiate pensando a la morte, *venemene un disio* tanto soave, che mi tramuta lo color nel viso	XXV, 46–8
e però no *li ven* di pianger *doglia*: ma *ven tristizia e voglia* di sospirare e di morir di pianto	XXV, 37–9
in guisa che di dir *mi ven dottanza*	V, 16
sì che *mi giunse* ne lo cor *paura*	XXXI, 7
sì che *dolce disire* *lo giunse* di chiamar tanta salute	XXV, 24–5
a lei si *volser* tutti i miei *disiri*	XXVII, 17
che da le genti *vergogna* mi *parte*	XXV, 53
che nulla *invidia* a l'altre ne *procede*	XXIII, 6
ciò che m'incontra ne la mente *more*	XII, 1
dannomi angoscia *li sospiri* forte	XXV, 43

It is of nouns in this category that Glasser uses the term *abstractum agens*, and it will be relevant here to summarize some of his points about their use in Old and Medieval French. He points out, first, that there is no need to assume a learned or literary origin for all these constructions. With nouns like 'pity', 'fear', 'desire', 'hunger', 'cold' the usage was almost certainly popular. And although one may detect a Christian, or more precisely a Biblical influence behind the 'active' use of such nouns as 'death', 'exile', 'sin', 'pride', 'confusion', 'anger' in the *chansons de geste*, he stresses that these nouns are very few in number and had probably been naturalized or assimilated into ordinary speech by that date. More important is the fact that in none of these cases is there anything to suggest that the nouns are truly personified. However, when, as happens in the twelfth century, other nouns are used as *agentia*, when the construction is used more freely, and when there is an element of personification, then the constructions are quite obviously of a literary character.

Glasser insists that literary *abstracta agentia* must be studied in relation to medieval allegory, understood not as a mode of interpreting scripture, but as the literary genre in which virtues, vices, dispositions, or branches of learning appear in human form and dress, are endowed with speech, and are in general treated as human characters in a dramatic or narrative action, in order to represent mental or spiritual activities or conflicts. Both he and Heinimann emphasize that the borderline between deliberate personification and mere recourse to a convenient linguistic structure is fluid and uncertain. To give just one practical example: only a very slight difference in the context justifies the modern editor in preferring *ira* in the first of these passages, but *Ira* in the second.

> Fugge dinanzi a lei superbia ed ira   XVII, 7
>
> e parve a me ch'ella menasse seco
> Dolore e Ira per sua compagnia.   LXXII, 3–4

We shall discuss Dante's use of personification later. For the moment, it is enough to say that the only abstract noun which is almost always treated by Dante as a 'sustanzia' and not an 'accidente' is precisely *Amore*, the word which occasioned his defence of the figure to which we have already referred. And although we may see Love laugh (XXI) or look dejected (VIII) or appear in travelling clothes (VIII) or wearing mourning (LXXII), on the great majority of occasions he is not described or in any way established as a being. It must also be said that there is no clear dividing line between the constructions exemplified in the list above and the use, as *agentia*, of nouns denoting parts of the body or mind, or, again, of words like 'sospiri' or 'pensieri'. But to these also, and to the 'psychologism' of which they are the consequence, we shall have to return at a later stage.

Conversio × *Metonymia* (*proprietas pro subjecto*).[1]

> quand'i' vegno a veder voi, bella *gioia*   XII, 2
>
> quando riguardo la vostra *beltate*   XI, 4

---

[1] Again it is worth documenting Dante's familiarity with the terms of our analysis: 'Ma però che, per alcuno fervore d'animo, talvolta *l'uno e l'altro termine* de li atti e de le passioni *si chiamano e per lo vocabulo de l'atto medesimo e de la passione* (sì come fa Virgilio nel secondo de lo Eneidos, che chiama Enea a Ettore: "O luce", ch'è atto, e "speranza de' Troiani", che è passione, *ché non era esso luce né speranza, ma era termine onde venia loro la luce del consiglio, ed era termine in che si posava tutta la speranza de la loro salute*; e sì come dice Stazio nel quinto del Thebaidos, quando Isifile dice ad Archimoro: "O consolazione de le cose e de la patria perduta, o onore del mio servigio"; *sì come cotidianamente dicemo*, mostrando l'amico, "vedi l'amistade mia", e 'l padre dice al figlio "amor mio")' (*Con.*, III, xi, 16).

l'una appresso de l'altra *maraviglia*	XXI, 11
e recolo a servir novo *piacere*	VIII, 12
abbandonata de la sua *salute*	XXVI, 14
lo giunse di chiamar tanta *salute*	XXV, 25
vede perfettamente onne *salute*	XXIII, 1
che vostra *spene* sia quanto me piace	XIV, 25
io vidi la *speranza* de' beati	XIV, 28
e se venite da tanta *pietate*	XVIII, 9
fu giunta da la sua *crudelitate*	XXVII, 19
perché 'l *piacere* de la *sua bieltate* partendo sé da la nostra veduta, divenne *spiritual bellezza* grande	XXVII, 20–2
dal secolo hai partita *cortesia* e ciò ch'è in donna da pregiar vertute: in gaia *gioventute* distrutta hai l'amorosa *leggiadria*	VII, 13–16

Conversio × *Emphasis*.[1]

già eran quasi che atterzate l'ore del tempo ...	I, 5–6
Amore è qui, che per vostra bieltate lo face, come vol, vista cangiare	IX, 21–2
che 'n voi servir l'ha 'mpronto onne pensero	IX, 27
per la pietà, che 'l vostro gabbo ancide, la qual si crïa ne la vista morta de li occhi, c'hanno di lor morte voglia	XII, 12–14
onde venite che 'l vostro colore par divenuto de pietà simile	XVIII, 3–4
vedeste voi nostra donna gentile bagnar nel viso suo di pianto Amore	XVIII, 5–6
che dà per li occhi una dolcezza al core	XXII, 10
ogne dolcezza, ogne pensero umile nasce nel core ...	XVII, 9–10
che non sospiri in dolcezza d'amore	XXIII, 14

[1] In these examples, the *conversiones* result in phrases that are shorter than their simple equivalents (see above, p. 56). It is rather harder to identify the converted element here because of metaphorical complications.

e' si raccoglie ne li miei sospiri
un sono de pietate,
che va chiamando Morte tuttavia   XXVII, 14–16

These lists have been compiled to demonstrate the relevance of Geoffrey's analysis, and within each of the categories the examples have been arranged to bring out closer similarities between them. In other words chronology has been completely ignored, and the lists give only an average impression of the constructions and of their frequency in these poems. To leave the matter there would be disastrous, for it is only when we consider the distribution of these examples that we shall see the most important general fact about them. This is that there is a marked decrease in their use. In the first four groups of poems[1] in the *Vita Nuova*, the construction is twice as frequent as in the last four groups (respectively 1 in 7 lines and 1 in 14 lines). It is four times more frequent in the first two groups than in the last two.[2] Figures must be treated with some caution here because I have had to exercise my judgement as to what shall or shall not be considered a 'converted' form; and it will be seen that the character of the examples varies considerably from one category to another. Further, we shall have to consider the pattern of distribution still more closely in a moment. Nevertheless, the fall in frequency is striking; and in the later poems, as we shall see, the construction is if anything less common than in the last groups among the *VN* poems.

We have here, then, the first evidence of a *development* in Dante's style. And since we saw that the free use of *conversiones* had been characteristic of the genre to which these poems belong, we may well

---

[1] See introduction p. 47, and pullout chart at the end of the book, facing p. 348.

[2]

Group	No. of lines	Instances of 'Conversiones'		
A	126	20	= approx. 1 in	6·5
B	56	14	1 in	4
C	84	9	1 in	9
D	112	10	1 in	11
E	146	10	1 in	15
F	54	6	1 in	9
G	56	4	1 in	14
H	42	1		
	676	74		

suspect that this decline in their use was not unconnected with a reaction against the style of early 'Italian' love poetry. It would be premature to go more deeply into this matter before we have considered the evidence about other variables. But it may not be untimely to call attention to two other features of this development. First, it is negative rather than positive: it entails a certain limitation of the range of expression; and from the rhetorical point of view, it implies a lowering of the stylistic level. Second, it has not only a stylistic but also a wider linguistic dimension. Part at least of the fascination which *conversiones* held for the earliest 'Italian' poets must have been due to their exotic nature. So it is by no means fanciful to interpret any reaction against the constructions, or even any increasing diffidence in their regard, as evidence of a new purism, of a new trend towards a more homogeneous literary language. The development would in fact be one concrete manifestation of the kind of concern for the actual language of poetry which will later find theoretical expression in the first book of the *De vulgari eloquentia*.[1] To sum up then: *conversiones* appear with such frequency in the earlier poems of the *Vita Nuova*, that it is reasonable to attribute them collectively to the influence of Dante's models, to the prevailing literary fashion; whereas in the later poems in the book, they are so much less frequent that there are grounds for interpreting the decline as part of a reaction against the earlier modes.

This is the picture seen as a whole, and therefore at some distance. A closer inspection, however, will demand some qualifications. In the first place it must be made clear that even in the earliest poems, recourse to *conversiones* is not completely mechanical; or, rather, it is mechanical, but only in certain contexts. Consider for example the following passages drawn from the first and second, then the fourth and fifth poems in the *Vita Nuova*.

(a) Allegro mi sembrava Amor tenendo
   meo core in mano, e ne le braccia avea

---

[1] Cf. Maria Corti on periphrastic forms of the type *son temente*: 'Dopo i poeti di transizione, cioè con lo stilnovismo, *la perifrasi si eclissa* per la nuova tendenza a *un purismo formale*, che in sostanza è un riplasmare sul modello di un ordine classico la sintassi e il lessico' ('Studi', p. 311).

And writing of a similar decline in the use of abstract nouns formed from the past participle (for example *la perduta*) she says of the 'stilnovisti' that 'tesi a rientrare nelle strutture classiche grammaticali, essi liberano la lingua da *incrostazioni impure*' ('Contributi', p. 88).

madonna involta in un drappo dormendo.
Poi la svegliava, e d'esto core ardendo
lei paventosa umilmente pascea:
appresso gir lo ne vedea piangendo.   I, 9–14

(b)   Amor, non già *per* mia *poca bontate*,
         ma *per sua nobiltate*,
         mi *pose* in vita sì dolce e soave,
         ch'io mi sentia dir dietro spesse fiate:
         'Deo, per *qual dignitate*
         così *leggiadro* questi lo *core have?*'
            Or ho *perduta* tutta mia *baldanża*,
         che si *movea d'amoroso tesoro;*
         ond'io pover dimoro,
         in guisa che *di dir* mi *ven dottanża*.   V, 7–16

(c)   Dal secolo hai *partita cortesia*
         e ciò ch'è in donna da pregiar vertute:
         in *gaia gioventute*
         distrutta hai l'*amorosa leggiadria*.   VII, 13–16

(d)   Cavalcando l'altr'ier per un cammino,
         pensoso de l'andar che mi sgradia,
         trovai Amore in mezzo de la via
         in abito leggier di peregrino.   VIII, 1–4

It will be seen that in (a) and (d), which are narrative in character, the
language is simple, whereas it is highly converted in the formal,
oratorical, 'static' poems of lamentation. The contrast is of course in
part natural, one that would arise anywhere and at any time, because it
is inherent in the different themes and aims. But the sharpness of the
distinction between the two modes of expression owes something in
general to the rhetorical concept of 'levels' of style, and a good deal to
the influence of the relevant vernacular genres. In this last respect even
the metrical form is significant. Passages (b) and (c) are taken from
'double sonnets' (with a total of twenty lines), which were clearly felt
to be 'higher' than the ordinary fourteen-line sonnet.

It should also be noted that even among the elevated poems from
Dante's earliest period there are two quite distinct modes. *Conver-*
siones are a relatively unimportant element in the crabbed, congested

and difficult style of the correspondence sonnets, which are addressed
to fellow poets and contain learned discussion about love. But in the
half dozen poems addressed to *madonna*, or containing laments for the
death of a young lady—all poems with an affective aim—*conversiones* are the dominant and distinctive element in their more stately,
more flowing, and more easily intelligible style.[1] As a final example,
take this opening of an isolated *canzone*-stanza:

> Madonna, quel signor che voi portate
> ne gli occhi, tal che vince *ogni possanza,*
> mi *dona sicuranza*
> che voi sarete *amica di pietate;*
>   però che là dov'ei *fa dimoranza,*
> ed ha in *compagnia molta beltate,*
> tragge *tutta bontate*
> a sé, *come principio c'ha possanza.*   LVII, 1–8

Conversely, *conversiones* do not appear with average *in*frequency in
the later *VN* poems. For example, they converge to create an elevated
opening for a *canzone* in which Dante cannot use his favourite vocatives
or exclamations. What in his own prose paraphrase is merely '. . . una
donna giovane e gentile, la quale era lungo lo mio letto', becomes:

> Donna pietosa e di novella etate,
> adorna assai di gentilezze umane,
> ch'era là'v'io chiamava spesso Morte   XX, 1–3

And this kind of convergence is even more apparent when Dante
returns to the genre of the *planctus* in his laments for the death of
Beatrice:

> no la ci *tolse qualità di gelo*
> né di *calore,* come l'altre face,
> ma solo fue sua *gran benignitate;*
>   ché *luce* de la *sua umilitate*
> passò li cieli con *tanta vertute,*
> che fé maravigliar l'etterno Sire,
> sì che *dolce disire*
> lo *giunse* di chiamar *tanta salute*   XXV, 18–25

---

[1] The poems are nos. V–VII, XLVIII–IX and LVII, printed as nos. 8–12 and 22 in Kenelm
Foster and Patrick Boyde, *Dante's Lyric Poetry* (Oxford, 1967), vol. I.

a lei si *volser* tutti i *miei disiri*,
quando la donna mia
fu *giunta* da la *sua crudelitate*;
  perché 'l *piacere* de la *sua bieltate*,
partendo sé da la *nostra veduta*,
divenne spirital bellezza grande,
che per lo cielo *spande*
luce d'amor, che li angeli saluta,
e lo *intelletto loro* alto, sottile
face maravigliar, sì v'è gentile.   XXVII, 17–26

In the earlier passages, the *conversiones* may be considered almost in their totality, as an aspect of a specialized context, and therefore, using Riffaterre's razor, as 'non-style'.[1] Here, shorn of the 'provenzaleggiante' phraseology, and in a context where the construction is no longer mechanical, almost every *conversio* has its contribution to make to a total effect of great beauty and complexity. Dante is now master of the *conversio*; not it of him.

It is not necessary, and indeed it would be scarcely possible, to give a similar survey of *conversiones* in the chosen groups among Dante's later poems.[2] There are few indisputable 'textbook' examples of the constructions, and even if one casts the net widely the numbers are very low. To put it briefly, then, the *conversio* remains a relatively insignificant element in Dante's style in all the later poems.

There are of course a few exceptions. In the allegorical group (group I), the two *canzoni* are virtually innocent of *conversiones*, and the few examples which one does find are individual and would be extremely hard to paraphrase, for example:

Io vi dirò *del cor la novitate*   LXXIX, 10
sed e' non teme *angoscia di sospiri*   ibid., 26
Ché se tu non t'inganni, tu vedrai
di sì *alti miracoli adornezza*   ibid., 49–50

But the *ballata* (*Voi che savete*), which is slightly more archaic in tone, closes with a fine flurry of augmenting *conversiones*:

Ma quanto vuol nasconda e guardi lui,
ch'io non veggia talor *tanta salute*;

---

[1] See introduction, p. 36.   [2] See introduction p. 47 and pullout chart facing p. 348.

però che i *miei disiri avran vertute*
contra 'l *disdegno* che mi dà *tremore*.   LXXX, 25–8

And in its second stanza there is one combination of metaphor with
conversiones of the 'abbreviating' kind which produces an effect that is
quite harsh in the context.

però che intorno a' suoi sempre *si gira*[1]
d'ogni crudelitate una pintura   LXXX, 7–8

There is something of a contrast also between the two doctrinal
canzoni in this respect. In *Le dolci rime* the *conversio* occurs only rarely
until the final stanza, where it plays its part in the description of the
'signs' by which true nobility declares itself—a description which is
in marked contrast to the knotty, technical argumentation of the main
part of the poem. And in that earlier part the *conversiones* had not been
phraseological, but individually expressive. 'Molto ricca' would be no
substitute for 'che lungiamente in gran ricchezza è stata' (LXXXII, 31),
where 'ricchezza' is made to suggest the trappings of wealth. 'Più
ignorante' would be less elegant and therefore in the context less
incisive than 'di più lieve savere' (ibid., 25). 'Fosse sempre esistito'
would have none of the force of 'o che non fosse ad uom cominciamento' (ibid., 71). *Poscia ch'Amor* on the other hand is something of a
throw-back, and among the features which make us feel it to be rather
archaic are precisely the many *conversiones:*

ché *stato* non *avea* tanto gioioso (LXXXIII, 3); che dopo morte *fanno riparo*
ne la mente / a quei cotanti c'*hanno canoscenza* (23–5); *fuggiriano il danno* /
che si *aggiugne* a lo 'nganno (28–9); c'*hanno falso iudicio* in lor *sentenza* (31);
qual non *dirà fallenza* / *divorar cibo* ed a *lussuria intendere?* (32–3); d'*intendimenti* / *correnti* voglion esser iudicati (39–40); ne' *parlamenti* lor *tengono
scede* (50); (vanno a pigliar villan diletto (54)); 'n donne è sì dispento / *leggiadro portamento* (55–6); ché *villania* / *far* mi parria (64–5); (ed è pien di salute

---

[1] *Girarsi* would be a converted preposition in Geoffrey's analysis: cf. '... haec praepositio *circa* notat circuitionem: ponamus ergo verbum hoc *circuit* vel *circinat* pro illa
praepositione. Verbi gratia dicturi sumus ... *iste currit circa domum*, ... dicamus
sic: *cursu circuit vel circinat iste domum*' (*Documentum*, II, 3, 104–5; corresponding to
PN 1,733–4). Compare also 'incerchiare' in xxxv, 8: 'e spesse volte piangon sì,
ch'Amore / li 'ncerchia di corona di martiri', which in the prose paraphrase—a
particularly interesting example of a 'style-less base'—becomes 'e spesso avvenia che
per lo lungo continuare del pianto, *dintorno* loro si facea uno colore purpureo ...'
(*VN*, xxxix, 4).

(71)); sanza *ovrar vertute* / nessun pote *acquistar* verace *loda* (72–3); in gente onesta / di *vita spiritale* / o in abito che di *scienza tiene* (80–2); quante / *sembiante portan* d'omo (rhetorically effective) (103–4); per lo mal c'*hanno in uso* (106); né per *prender* da elle / nel suo effetto *aiuto* (118–19); in ciò *diletto tragge* (120); non s'*induce a ira* (121); per nessuna grandezza / *monta* in *orgoglio* (129–30).

In the remaining poems there are no such exceptions—notwithstanding such a promising-looking opening as *Io sento sì d'Amor la gran possanza* (XCI). They are most numerous in *Doglia mi reca*, but even there one will not find more than 10 in its 155 lines. And largely because of this infrequency the stylistic effect of each example tends to be greater and more varied. Each must be studied in its environment; and to attempt that here would be to exceed my brief.

CHAPTER 2

ASPECTS OF VOCABULARY

———

By a curious chance the earliest surviving classical work to contain
any technical analysis of style and the last theoretical work to be of
direct relevance to this study—respectively Aristotle's *Poetics* and
Dante's *De vulgari eloquentia*—both offer a detailed discussion on the
choice of words,[1] but have little to say about their arrangement. In
this respect, as in so many others, they are not in the least typical of
rhetorical treatises in the intervening centuries. For the typical rhetorician was interested chiefly in the arrangement of words—euphony,
rhythm and the use of figures—not in the words themselves, which
were given proportionally little space and very cursory treatment.[2]
Nor is this in the least surprising if we think back to the ancient theory
of meaning and to the whole rhetorical approach to style discussed
in the introduction. Each word was thought of as the *signum* of a *res*—
which might be an object, being, quality, relationship, action or state.
The meaning of a word was therefore the *res* which it designated and
to which it 'belonged'. Strictly speaking, no *res* should have two *signa*,
and there should therefore be no possibility of choice between words
—only between 'things'. Experience taught otherwise. And to account

---

[1] *Poetics*, chs 21–2; *DVE*, II, vii. The fact that Dante gives an extended account of the
metrical arrangement of words does not invalidate the comparison.

[2] Some of the rhetorical manuals (for example the *ad Herennium*, Isidore, Geoffrey's
Documentum) have no section devoted specifically to the choice of words. Martianus
Capella still follows the classical order (as exemplified in Cicero's *De oratore* III,
Orator, xxxix, 134, and in Quintilian's *Institutio oratoria* VIII, ii, 1–13 and iii, 15–39),
and begins his section on *elocutio* with a study of *singula verba* (*De nuptiis*, v, 509–13).
So in effect does Matthew of Vendôme, whose second book is devoted to *verba polita*
(*Ars versificatoria*, pp. 154–67—the first book having been concerned with matter,
the *interior favus*), and also John of Garland whose *Poetria* deals with vocabulary
immediately after the opening definitions (see pp. 894–6 and 900–2). Horace's *Ars
Poetica* deals with the choice of words in lines 46–72, after reflections on *decorum*.
Geoffrey of Vinsauf's *Poetria Nova* first deals at great length with the ways to begin
a poem, and with the techniques of amplification and abbreviation, but the very short
section on choice of words (lines 739–64) comes at the appropriate place before the
study of tropes and figures.

for the perversities of usage, grammarians taught that where there was some kind of relationship between two *res*, the *signum* of the one might be 'borrowed' or 'transferred' and used 'improperly' of the other. Such an explanation harmonized well with the rhetorical conception of style as a series or a combination of departures from a style-less norm: clearly, the 'proper' use of a word was style-less, whereas the 'improper' use was potentially an element of style. But with that theory of meaning it would be difficult to arrive at a satisfactory treatment of synonymy, which is obviously essential to any discussion bearing on a *choice* of words. And with that approach to style it would have seemed quite futile (even assuming the idea had presented itself) to make any analysis of the different *effects* of a group of words with some common semantic element. At all events, the grammarians and rhetoricians of antiquity confined their attention almost exclusively to an investigation of the 'improper' or 'transferred' uses of words, that is, to a classification of the possible kinds of relationship between two *res*. The result of their labours was the system of tropes—and a very subtle and comprehensive system it was, as we shall see in the next chapter. But its very richness betokens a poverty in other sectors. And of the many aspects of vocabulary which seem of interest in modern stylistics, the ancient theorists deal only with archaisms, neologisms, learned loan-words, and newly derived or invented words.[1] To some extent they considered the phonetic constitution of words; but euphony or cacophony were normally discussed as a feature of arrangement.

The medieval theorists may seem more enterprising, for although they do not devote much space to word selection,[2] they sometimes speak as if they could determine the stylistic level of words, grading them as we might grade marble, sandstone, bricks and mud as building materials. In the best known case—the wheel of Virgil—John of Garland actually tried to assign words to one or other of the three levels of style.[3] It should of course be remembered that this is an ex-

[1] On the use of archaisms (*vocabula prisca, inusitata, ab usu remota, vetera, vetusta*) see Horace, *AP*, 50, 70; *Ep.*, II, ii, 115–18; *Ad Her.*, IV, 15; Capella, V, 509–11; Fortunatianus, III, chs 4–6 (in *Rhetores Latini Minores*, ed. C. Halm (Leipzig, 1863), pp. 123–4). On the creation of new words (*fictio nominis*) of which there is only one example in the chosen poems, 'Contra-li-erranti mia', LXXXII, 141 (cf. *Con.*, IV, xxx, 3), see *Ad Her.*, IV, xxxi, 42; *AP*, 48–59; Capella, V, 510; Fortunatianus, III, ch. 3, p. 122.
[2] Exception made for Matthew of Vendôme.
[3] In accordance with a long-standing tradition, Virgil's three main works are each taken

treme case: other theorists are much more vague than this. But it is nevertheless extremely instructive. It shows how completely medieval thinking about style is dominated by the hierarchical principle embodied in the system of the three styles. It shows, too, how remorselessly a medieval theorist will push an ancient concept to what seems to us absurd consequences.[1] We must be careful to distinguish John of Garland's position from that of such gems of modern pedagogy as 'animals sweat, men perspire, and women glow', or *Menschen essen, Tiere fressen und feine Leute speisen*. He is not saying that in poetry we write 'morn', but in speech we say 'morning', or that 'monarch' and 'sovereign' are loftier synonyms for 'king'. He means that 'king' is a more elevated word than 'knight', and 'knight' than 'shepherd'.

But medieval theorists—and chief among them Dante in the *De vulgari eloquentia*—did not grade words on grounds of meaning alone. It is clear from their examples that other factors, such as length, sound, grammatical status[2] and associations deriving from restricted use in certain registers, all played a part in determining the stylistic level of a word. Thus, assessment of level was necessarily highly subjective. And it is not really feasible to take Dante's own classification of words and use it as a basis for studying the vocabulary of his poems. One would need, rather, to describe that vocabulary first in order to gain a proper understanding of the theory. And so we shall turn first not to the rhetoricians but to the grammarians.

That the grammarians should be relevant to a rhetorically based

---

as examples of one of the three styles. We may tabulate the correspondences as follows:

Eclogues: Humilis	Georgics: Mediocris	Aeneid: Gravis
pastor otiosus	agricola	miles dominans
Tityrus; Meliboeus	Triptolemus; Coelius	Hector; Ajax
ovis	bos	equus
baculus	aratrum	gladius
pascua	ager	urbs; castrum
fagus	pomus	laurus; cedrus

[1] Granted the premiss, the implied argument is by no means absurd; namely, that if the meaning of a *signum* is its *res*, then it must be the dignity of the *res* which determines the dignity of the *signum*.

[2] See chapter 1, p. 58.

study of style need occasion no surprise. We have seen that the main reason for the revival of rhetorical studies in modern times was the realization that authors in the past had been thoroughly imbued with rhetorical concepts, categories and terminology. But there was no instruction in *rhetorica* without prior instruction in *grammatica*, which was truly described as the origin and foundation of all the liberal arts.[1] And in effect *rhetorica* did little more than perpetuate and refine attitudes to language which had already been instilled by the *artes grammaticae*. In short, the two disciplines were intimately related both as to what they taught and in their forbiddingly technical mode of presentation.[2]

The whole of ancient grammatical theory is based on the classification

[1] Cf. Isidore: 'Grammatica est scientia recte loquendi, et origo et fundamentum liberalium litterarum. Haec in disciplinis post litteras communes inventa est, ut iam qui didicerant litteras per eam recte loquendi rationem sciant ... Divisiones autem grammaticae artis a quibusdam triginta dinumerantur, id est, partes orationis octo, vox articulata, littera, syllaba, pedes, accentus, positurae, notae, orthographia, analogia, etymologia, glossae, differentiae, barbarismi, soloecismi, vitia, metaplasmi, schemata, tropi, prosa, metra, fabulae, historiae' (*Et.*, I, v, 1, 4).

There is an excellent introduction to ancient grammatical theory in R. H. Robins, *Ancient and Medieval Grammatical Theory in Europe* (London, 1951). For the interpenetration of grammar and literature, see especially H. I. Marrou, *Histoire de l'éducation dans l'antiquité*, 4th ed. (Paris, 1958), pp. 210–42, 268–82, 364–86, 416–60; and by the same author, *Saint Augustin et la fin de la culture antique*, 4th ed. (Paris, 1958), pp. 3–26, 47–104, 469–540.

[2] The only concession to the student was the occasional use of catechistical form as in Donatus's *Ars minor*, or in the following brief sample of Priscian's exposition of *Aeneid*, x, 1: 'Panditur interea domus omnipotentis Olympi.' '... *Panditur* quae pars orationis est? Verbum. Cuius modi? Indicativi. Cuius formae? Perfectae. Cuius coniugationis? Tertiae. Cuius generis sive significationis? Passivae. Cuius numeri? Singularis. Cuius figurae? Simplicis. Cuius temporis? Praesentis. Cuius personae? Tertiae ...' (The pupil goes on to decline *pando* in all tenses and moods, answers questions on related verbs and derivatives etc.) '*Interea* quae pars orationis est? Adverbium. Quid est adverbium? Pars orationis quae adiecta verbo significationem eius explanat atque implet. Quot accidunt adverbio? Species, significatio, figura. Cuius est speciei? *Inter* quidem ab "in" praepositione videtur esse natum, quomodo a "sub" "subter" et ab "ex" "exter"; *ea* vero primitivum est pronomen ablativi casus singularis vel accusativi pluralis. Cuius est significationis hoc adverbium? Temporis; potest tamen esse et loci. Cuius est figurae? Compositae. Ex quibus? Ex integro et corrupto, si "ea" pluraliter accipimus. "Inter" enim integrum est, quod plerique Latinorum praepositionem accipiunt, Graeci autem adverbium ."ea" vero corruptum etc.' ... Prisciani, *Partitiones duodecim versuum Aeneidos principalium*, in H. Keil (ed.), *Grammatici Latini* (8 vols, Leipzig, 1855–80), vol. III pp. 504–7. The exposition of twelve hexameters occupied 56 generous pages in Keil's edition.

of words into 'parts of speech', traditionally eight in number.[1] Accordingly, 'parsing' was the basic operation in the grammatical analysis of any text. And this it remains even today in any study of the vocabulary of a lengthy text in which it is necessary, for convenience of analysis, to prise words from their contexts, and group like with like. Before we pass on to study any one part of speech in Dante's lyrics however, it will be of interest to present the results of some by-products of the parsing process.

In order to minimize human errors when parsing is done by hand (that is, by copying a text out into the relevant number of columns), it is necessary to keep a numerical cross-check, and ensure that the sum of the columns is indeed equal to the number of words in the passage being parsed. From these figures one can ascertain the proportions in which the various parts of speech appear; and it has long been thought that these proportions—at least in so far as they concern noun, adjective and verb—must either reflect or determine some properties of the style.

Thanks to a study by F. Mariotti published in 1880[2] we shall be able to compare the poems in this respect with the whole of the *Comedy*. And

---

[1] We shall in fact work with *nine* parts, because we shall treat the adjective as a separate part of speech and not, as the ancients did, as a species of noun. The following definitions are from Donatus's *Ars maior* (in Keil (ed.), *Grammatici Latini*, vol. IV):
'*Nomen* est pars orationis cum casu corpus aut rem proprie communiterve significans: proprie, ut *Roma, Tiberis*; communiter ut *urbs, flumen*' (p. 373).
'*Pronomen* est pars orationis, quae pro nomine posita tantundem paene significat, personamque interdum recipit' (p. 379).
'*Verbum* est pars orationis cum tempore et persona sine casu, aut agere aliquid aut pati aut neutrum significans' (p. 381).
'*Adverbium* est pars orationis quae adiecta verbo significationem eius explanat atque inplet, ut *iam* faciam vel *non* faciam' (p. 385).
'*Participium* est pars orationis dicta, quod partem capiat nominis, partem verbi ...' (p. 387).
'*Coniunctio* est pars orationis adnectens ordinansque sententiam' (p. 388).
'*Praepositio* est pars orationis, quae praeposita aliis partibus orationis significationem earum aut mutat aut conplet aut minuit' (p. 389).
'*Interiectio* est pars orationis interiecta aliis partibus orationis ad exprimendos animi adfectus; aut metuentis ut *ei*; aut optantis, ut *o*; aut dolentis, ut *heu*; aut laetantis, ut *evax* ... licet autem pro interiectione etiam alias partes orationis singulas pluresve subponere, ut *nefas, pro nefas*' (pp. 391–2).
[2] F. Mariotti, 'Dante e la statistica delle lingue', *RAL*, CCLXXVII (1879–80), 262–90. The reflections which accompany the figures are almost completely worthless: it is characteristic that the closing pages are devoted to the computation of how long it would take an average speaker to recite the whole of the *Comedy*.

we can say at once that perhaps the most important fact about the proportionate distribution of the parts of speech in Dante is that, notwithstanding the many developments in his style, the proportions remain remarkably constant in his verse of all periods. Here are the percentages for the chosen poems and the three canticles of the *Comedy*:[1]

[1] The actual figures are:

	Subst.	Ep.	Pron.	Verb	Part.	Adv.	Conj.	Prep.	Int.	Totals
VN poems	742	270	702	889	79	258	524	426	11	3,901
Later poems	1,030	380	887	1,123	59	368	847	652	14	5,360
Inf.	6,082	1,866	4,483	6,605	513	3,311	3,508	4,050	26	30,444
Purg.	5,894	2,069	4,309	6,683	554	3,498	3,360	4,260	14	30,641
Par.	6,004	2,280	4,174	6,340	458	3,065	3,476	4,258	5	30,060

The following table shows how the 24 categories used by Mariotti were conflated to produce the 9 used in this book. Decisions which are not self-evident are italicized.

Mariotti	*Boyde*
Articoli; articoli indeterminati; *negazioni*:	*Omitted*
Nomi sostantivi:	Substantives
Nomi aggettivi:	Epithets
Pronomi sostantivi; *pr. aggettivi*: pr. possessivi; pr. personali:	Pronouns
verbi; verbi composti di due parole:	Verbs
Participi, gerundi:	Participles
Avverbi; *avverbi composti di due parole*:	Adverbs
Congiunzioni; congiunzioni 'e'; *pronomi relativi*:	Conjunctions
Segnacasi; segnacasi articolati; preposizioni; preposizioni articolate; *preposizioni composte* *di due parole*:	Prepositions
Interiezioni:	Interjections

'Sunt etiam dictiones, quas incertum est utrum coniunctiones an praepositiones an adverbia nominemus, quae tamen omnes sensu facile dinoscuntur' (Donatus, *Ars maior*, II, ch. 15, in Keil (ed.), *Grammatici Latini*, vol. IV, p. 389). In general I have followed this line, classifying, for example, *perché*, either as conjunction or adverb according to its role in a particular context. Similarly I have allowed context to decide whether a given participle was purely adjectival (Epithet) or retained verbal force (Participle).

Note, however, that the omnipresent *che* has always been counted as a conjunction, irrespective of whether it served as a causal, declarative or relative link. In some ways I now regret this decision; but there are arguments in its favour, and in any case the relative proportions of pronouns and conjunctions will concern us little if at all.

%	Subst.	Ep.	Pron.	Verb	Part.	Adv.	Conj.	Prep.	Int.
VN poems	19·05	7·05	18	22·8	2	6·6	13·4	10·9	0·25
Later poems	19·2	7·7	16·4	20·8	1·1	6·7	15·7	12·2	0·25
Inf.	20	6·1	14·4	21·7	1·7	10·9	11·5	13·3	0·08
Purg.	19·3	6·8	14·06	21·1	1·7	11·4	10·9	13·9	0·04
Par.	20	7·6	13·9	21·1	1·5	10·02	11·6	14·01	0·02

What *significance* do the figures themselves have? Are they distinctive, or would the analysis of other lengthy samples show them to be common to the genre, or to the 'Italian' language of the day, or to Italian of all periods, or even perhaps to the Indo-European languages as a whole? And if they are distinctive, what do they indicate about Dante's style? To these vital questions we can as yet give only a vague and provisional answer. And before doing so it will be necessary to consider a more fundamental and pressing question; namely, how far do these average percentages correspond to the figures for shorter passages? Clearly, not every sentence will conform, nor will every paragraph. But what about the sonnets, or the *canzoni*, or the groups distinguished in the introduction? It is essential to know whether an average figure of, say, 20 per cent is 'typical' or 'representative' of the actual samples. If the majority of the samples lie close to the mean—for example within the range 18–22—the average figure is clearly representative and very probably typical. But if, on the other hand, the majority of the samples have a figure nearer the extremes of 10 and 30 respectively, then these would be the 'typical' figures, and the average would be unrepresentative, and, if unexplained, grossly misleading.

Let us first consider the evidence for the groups.[1] Here and there, an average figure is not 'representative' in the sense we have just suggested for the term. And the divergences are much what one would expect. Adjectives are higher than average (9 per cent) in the poems of lamentation (group F). Verbs are higher (25·5 per cent) in the little 'dramas' of the early Cavalcantian group (group B). Nouns are lower than average (17 per cent) in the poems of the praise-style (group C), where, it may be remembered, *conversiones* were also virtually absent. Conversely, nouns are proportionally more numerous (22·5 per cent) in

[1] Cf. p. 47. The groups are set out in tabular form on a pullout chart facing p. 348.

the *canzoni* of the 'petra'-group (group K), where Dante was seeking to project emotion through the medium of things. But none of these divergences are extreme, and none of them disturb the general balance.[1]

The average figures are still broadly representative of each of the *canzoni* analysed, although, needless to say, the divergences are more frequent in number and greater than at group level. Thus, in the case of nouns, the extremes now range from 14·5 per cent to 25 per cent (in LXXIX and C respectively); for adjectives they range from 5 per cent to 10·5 per cent (LXXXI and XXVII), and for verbs from 18·5 per cent to 25·5 per cent (C and XIV). But with the possible exceptions of *Voi che 'ntendendo* (LXXIX) with low nouns and high verbs, or *Io son venuto* (C) with low verbs and high nouns, there are no striking upsets to the overall pattern.[2]

Obviously, as one reduces the length of sample one will find much less uniformity. There can be startling differences even between poems in one group; and the figures for the double-sonnet *Morte villana* (VII) and the *ballata, Ballata, i' vo'* (IX) are certainly instructive:

[1] Here are the percentages for each group: the figures from which they are calculated will be found at the end of this chapter. Unrepresentative percentages are printed in italics.

Group	Subst.	Ep.	Pron.	Verb	Part.	Adv.	Conj.	Prep.	Int.
A	20·5%	7	17·5	22	2	7	12·5	11	0·5
B	18	5·5	19	25·5	2	6·5	13	10·5	—
C	*17*	7	18	24	*3·5*	7·5	13	10	—
D	20·5	7	17	22	2·5	6	14	11	—
E	18·5	6·5	17·5	24	1·5	6·5	14	11·5	—
F	20·5	*9*	17	20	2	*5·5*	13	12	—
G	20	5·5	*21*	22	1	6·5	12·5	11·5	1
H	17	7·5	18	23	1	6·5	*16*	10·5	0·5
Overall % for *VN* poems	19	7	18	22·8	2	6·6	13·4	10·9	0·25
Group									
I	*16*	6	22	23	—	7·5	14·5	10·5	—
J	18	8	*14·5*	21	1·5	6·5	*17*	13·5	—
K	22·5	6	16	19	0·5	6·5	16·5	13	—
L	20	6·5	16	20	1	10	15	11·5	—
M	20·5	7·5	15	21	1·5	6·5	15	12	0·5
Overall % for later poems	19·2	7·7	16·4	20·8	1·1	6·7	15·7	12·2	0·25

Poem	Sub.	Ep.	Pron.	Verb	Part.	Adv.	Conj.	Prep.	Int.
VII	26·5%	*11*	*12*	22	1	4	9	*13*	1·5
IX	*15·5*		2·5	24·5	26	–	6·5	*16*	9	—
Overall % for *VN* poems	19	7	18	22·8	2	6·6	*13·4*	10·9	0·25

It must however be emphasized that the divergences here are quite exceptional (no other poems disturb the general pattern to this extent); and abnormal distributions are not in the least common even at the level of the minimum sample, that is, the fourteen-line sonnet or the *canzone*-stanza. Of the 25 regular sonnets in the *Vita Nuova*, for example, the average figure is representative of 15; and only of 4 is it

---

[2] Here are the percentages for each *canzone*. The actual figures will again be found at the end of the chapter.

Unrepresentative percentages are printed in italics.

VN POEMS

Canzoni no.	Sub.	Ep.	Pron.	Verb	Part.	Adv.	Conj.	Prep.	Int.
XIV	17·5	6	18·5	25·5	1·5	7	13	11·5	—
XX	18	8	17	23	4	8	13	9	—
XXIV	16·5	7·5	21·5	23	2·5	7·5	*17·5*	4	—
XXV	19·5	7·5	16·5	22	2	6·5	15	11	—
XXVII	20	*10·5*	19·5	*19*	0·5	6	14	10·5	—
Overall % for *VN* poems	19	7	18	22·8	2	6·6	13·4	10·9	0·25

LATER POEMS

Canzoni no.	Sub.	Ep.	Pron.	Verb	Part.	Adv.	Conj.	Prep.	Int.
LXXIX	*14·5*	7·5	23·5	24	1	7	15	8·5	—
LXXXI	17	5	*21·5*	22	—	6	15·5	12	—
LXXXII	17·5	8	16	20	2	6·5	17·5	12	—
LXXXIII	20	9	*13·5*	21	1·5	5·5	15·5	14	—
C	25	7·5	*13·5*	18·5	—	5·5	16	14	—
CIII	19·5	5	18·5	20	1	7	16·5	11	0·5
CIV	21·5	9	*13·5*	20	1	7	15·5	12·5	—
CVI	20	6·5	15	22·5	2	6·5	14	12	1
Overall % for later poems	19·2	7·7	16·4	20·8	1·1	6·7	15·7	12·2	0·25

D

decidedly *un*representative.[1] And it would be fair to say that not less than 60 per cent of all the 'minimum units' conform closely to the relevant average distribution, and that not more than 15 per cent depart from it in any significant way.[2]

This information about the distribution of the parts of speech in Dante's verse will prove of value first and foremost as evidence concerning *context* in the study of the stylistic effects of particular poems or passages.[3] But now we have seen that the proportions remain remarkably constant in all Dante's verse, and that the average distribution is representative of quite short samples, we may return to our earlier question: What do the figures themselves mean? What do they reveal about Dante's personal style? Framed in this way, of course, the questions are unanswerable. And they must be rephrased to read: How far and in what ways do the relative proportions of the parts of speech in Dante differ from those in the work of other authors?[4]

To the best of my knowledge there is no relevant data at present available for other Italian authors. But for English poets it exists in abundance thanks to the labours of Josephine Miles, who has organized the counting of the nouns, adjectives and verbs occurring in the first 1,000 lines of representative works by over 200 poets, the poets being chosen to cover the ground systematically from the Middle Ages to the present day.[5]

Miss Miles argues that the ratio obtaining between the three main parts of speech—expressed in simplified form as the average number of words in each class which would appear in 10 lines of verse—is a significant index to an author's style. It is significant because in each case the ratio implies a particular kind of syntax, or, better, a particular

---

[1] Viz. VI, XVI, XVII, XIX.

[2] A fair picture of typical variations from one unit to another will be gained from a study of the figures given at the end of this chapter showing the actual, unpercentualized distribution of the parts of speech in each stanza of the *canzoni*, *Così nel mio parlar* and *Tre donne*.

[3] Cf. introduction p. 37.

[4] Cf. introduction p. 23.

[5] This work first appeared in book form in *Eras and Modes in English Poetry* (Berkeley and Los Angeles, 1957). This was followed by *Renaissance, Eighteenth-Century, and Modern Language in English Poetry: a tabular view* (Berkeley and Los Angeles, 1960), which gives corrected, additional information, and is far more detailed than the appendices to the first edition of *Eras and Modes*. These tables (with some omissions) are reprinted as the appendices to the second edition of *Eras and Modes* (Berkeley and Los Angeles, 1964).

degree of syntactic organization; and from this in turn we may infer, though with much less certainty, something about the metrical characteristics of the verse, and even something of its stylistic level. Miss Miles herself would distinguish three main modes. At one pole is a substantival or phrasal style revealed in a predominance of adjectives and nouns; at the other is a clausal or predicative style revealed in a predominance of verbs. The former is 'cumulative' the latter 'discursive'. 'The first might say, "Rising and soaring, the golden bird flies into the stormy night of the east"; the second if given the same terms would say, "The golden bird rises and soars; it flies into the night which storms in the east"[1]'. The third mode is classically balanced between the phrasal and clausal types, and is in fact the kind found in the Latin classics and in the work of a Neoclassicist such as Pope.

What can we learn from the material she presents and her interpretation of it? First, we find confirmation that the proportions do vary prodigiously: in Langland she finds 6 adjectives, 21 verbs and 18 nouns in an average 10 lines; in Keats the figures are 12—18—8; in James Thomson 16—18—7. Second, it is clear that the variations are neither casual nor to be ascribed purely to personal taste or idiosyncrasy. Poets of any one age show a broadly similar distribution; and with each new generation (each generation being represented by the mature works of ten poets), there is a general reaction towards either a more phrasal or a more clausal style as the case may be. Third, it appears that, notwithstanding the fluctuations between one poet and another, and between one generation and another, there was a general movement from a predominantly clausal style in medieval authors to a predominantly phrasal style in the later eighteenth century, followed, in the last century and a half, by a reversion towards the earlier mode.

As she herself recognizes, Miss Miles's evidence must be used with circumspection; and a little salt may be required with some of her essays in interpretation. Further, one must not take for granted the relevance of the English evidence for an Italian author. On the other hand, her findings are cumulatively more than enough to substantiate those of her conclusions which I have just summarized; and it would be astonishing if a similar investigation of Italian authors did not produce comparable results. Proceeding with the necessary caution, then, let us compare the figures for Dante with those for the English poets, and see what

[1] *Eras and Modes*, p. 2.

conclusions suggest themselves. Adding the participles not to the verbs, but to the adjectives as Miss Miles (questionably) does, and working now in terms of the number of lines of verse, rather than the total number of words, the figures for the *VN* poems would be 5 adjectives, 11 nouns and 13 verbs in every 10 lines. For the later poems the figures are 5 (4·5)—11—12; for the *Inferno* 5—13—14.[1]

Comparison shows—predictably enough—that this distribution is characteristic of the fourteenth and fifteenth centuries in the low proportion of adjectives. Among all the English poets from the later sixteenth century to the present day only two —Emily Dickinson and A. E. Housman—have less than 6 adjectives in 10 lines: and in both cases the figures are not strictly comparable, as the lines of verse are shorter than in Dante, and the other totals correspondingly lower. The closest general resemblance to Dante's figures are to be found in Gower (4—12—10), Occleve (6—13—14), and the anonymous ballads, dated arbitrarily as 1470 (6—13—11). However, it is reasonable to conclude that even among medieval poets Dante is sparing in his use of adjectives: only Langland shows a significantly lower proportion of adjectives to nouns (6:21). Comparison also reveals something perhaps more interesting. The fact that Dante uses a higher proportion of verbs than nouns distinguishes him from all English poets save one—Thomas Occleve (born *c.* 1368). Typically, in the English poets, nouns exceed verbs by from 50 to 100 per cent. Clearly, these proportions will be reflected in Dante's syntax which will be studied in chapter 4. For the moment we may close this part of our inquiry by noting that Dante's style probably represents the very extreme of what Miss Miles calls the clausal or predicative style.[2]

We have just examined a feature of Dante's style which remained remarkably constant throughout his creative life. Now, by contrast, we shall use similar evidence ('similar' in that the information is expressed in numerical terms and is another by-product of the parsing process) to describe one of the more important *developments* in Dante's style—the increasing richness of his vocabulary in the later poems. 'Richness', in this context, has reference not to the *kind* of words used,

---

1 Miss Miles's figures for the first 1,000 lines of the *Inferno* are 520 adjectives, 1,240 nouns, 1,240 verbs. Mine are calculated from Mariotti's totals, given in the footnote to p. 82.

2 The figures given by Miss Miles for the first 1,000 lines of the *Chanson de Roland* are of interest: 540 adjectives, 1,380 nouns, 1,390 verbs.

but only to the *number*. It has been studied—where concordances exist—by counting the total number of lexical items used by different authors. Mariotti, for example, quotes figures of 15,000 for Shakespeare, 8,000 for Milton, 6,082 for Horace, 5,649 for the Vulgate Bible, 4,972 for Demosthenes, and 3,394 for Sallust. For Dante's *Comedy* he gives the figure of 5,860 lexical items, or 7,475 if personal and proper nouns are also counted (the comparable figure for Ariosto's *Orlando Furioso* being 8,474).[1]

But although such information is not without interest, richness of vocabulary is more economically and accurately studied by comparing the total number of words in a passage of suitable length with the total number of lexical items which actually appear. (The count might of course be limited to nouns, adjectives and adverbs, verbs and participles.) For example, the tables giving the distribution of the parts of speech[2] will show that there are 180 nouns in the allegorical poems (group I). This of course does not mean that there are 180 different nouns in those poems, although this is theoretically possible. In fact there are only 90 and this information is most conveniently expressed by saying there are 90 lexical items (among the nouns) and 90 repetitions. This would seem to indicate a relatively restricted vocabulary. Certainly the richer vocabulary of the two regular *canzoni* in the 'petra'-group declares itself in very different terms. Among the nouns there are 146 lexical items and 66 repetitions. And there are correspondingly fewer repetitions of both adjectives and verbs:

	LXXIX–LXXXI		C AND CIII	
	Items	*Repetitions*	*Items*	*Repetitions*
Adjectives	45	22	46	12
Verbs/participles	107	152	120	70

In this case, it should be noted, the figures may be compared almost without correction, since the passages are roughly equal in length (179 and 155 lines respectively) and in their constitution (although there are three poems in group I against two in group K). But there are many pitfalls for the unwary when comparisons are made between unequal passages. For example, if the sample comprises a number of

---

[1] 'Dante e la statistica delle lingue', pp. 274–77.   [2] See p. 105.

short poems (for example, sonnets) from one genre, the level of repetition is likely to be higher than in one longer poem from the same genre. And the longer the sample, the greater will be the proportion of repetitions. Thus in the 676 lines of the *VN* poems, the figures for the nouns are 229 lexical items and 513 repetitions. But the level of repetition in any one group is on average close to that of the allegorical poems, certainly not twice as high. Nevertheless, the figures for the *VN* poems do indicate clearly that Dante's vocabulary was extremely limited there:

	Items	Repetitions
Nouns	229	513
Adjectives	121	149
Verbs	244	724

And with all possible reservations concerning the length and constitution of the groups, the following figures show unmistakably the increasing richness in the vocabulary of the later poems.

The repetition of lexical items within a poem or group is not of course governed by egalitarian principles. Certain words are repeated

	NOUNS	
Group	Items	Repetitions
I	90	90
J	158	101
K	146	66
L	75	13
M	183	108

	ADJECTIVES	
Group	Items	Repetitions
I	45	22
J	73	45
K	46	12
L	27	3
M	82	25

VERBS

Group	Items	Repetitions
I	107	152
J	142	174
K	120	70
L	66	27
M	166	158

frequently, others not at all.[1] It is plausible, too, that some kind of meaningful relationship will exist between an author's preoccupations, aims and personality, and the words—the 'content'-words—he uses most often. And if it can be shown that some words occur more frequently in one author than in others of his age, or in others writing in his genre, then these distinctive words may offer a key, in Spitzer's sense, to the proper interpretation of his works. Let us, then, take note of the most repeated words in the *VN* poems.

NOUNS

donna	(56)	cielo	(12)	vertute	(9)
amore	(54)	morte	(12)	sospiro	(8)
core	(48)	pensiero	(11)	vita	(8)
occhi	(23)	viso	(11)	salute	(7)
pietà	(22)	madonna	(10)	gente	(7)
anima	(16)	dolore	(10)	pianto	(6)
mente	(13)	cosa	(10)	beltate	(6)
spiriti	(13)	valore	(9)	colore	(6)

ADJECTIVES

gentile	(25)	dolente	(8)	soave	(6)
		novo	(8)	umile	(6)
		amoroso	(6)	dolce	(5)
		bello	(6)	morto	(5)
		degno	(6)	villano	(5)
		pensoso	(6)		

[1] '... the referential vocabulary of adjectives, nouns, and verbs is about half the total in a text ... Of this referential vocabulary, the few most-used words make up about fifty or sixty per cent', Miles, *Eras and Modes*, p. 250.

VERBS

essere	(81)	piangere	(25)	chiamare	(12)
dire	(52)	andare	(21)	intendere	(9)
fare	(52)	volere	(20)	ragionare	(7)
vedere	(49)	potere	(16)	gire	(7)
venire	(28)	parlare	(15)	giungere	(7)
avere	(25)	sentire	(14)	mirare	(7)
		morire	(12)	udire	(7)
				riguardare	(6)

Just how important these words are will become clear when it is realized that they account for *more than two-thirds* of the actual occurrences of nouns, adjectives and verbs in the *VN* poems. They are also of interest, however, in that they offer a fair picture of the vocabulary as a whole. Consider the adjectives, for example: they are typical in that all of them are abstract (that is, non-sensory), and in that most of them can be grouped round two obvious poles: terms of praise for the lady's perfection ('gentile', 'bella', 'umile'), and terms for the lover's suffering ('dolente', 'pensoso'). Notice also the piquant contrast between the simplicity of the verbs and the sophistication of the nouns. The verbs are mostly the basic ones, common in the most prosaic and mundane linguistic situations. Many of the nouns on the other hand, such as 'pietà', 'anima', 'spiriti', 'mente', 'valore', 'vertute', 'salute', belong to more specialized, and, in some cases, exclusively poetic contexts.

It is impossible at this moment to say which if any of these words are distinctively Dantean. A number of them will certainly belong among those most used in Italian poetry of all centuries. For the 200 English poets studied by Miss Miles, the persistent major words include: God, man, love, day, time, life, heart, eye, hand, world; fair, sweet, good, great, high, old; to come, find, give, go, hear, know, make, talk, tell, think.[1] All these are very similar to those in Dante, and very little different from those cited by Miss Miles for classical Latin poets 'the *magnus, bonus, malus, longus, animus, honor, urbs, nox, populus, do, facio, fero, video, volo, opto, timeo* of Horace and Juvenal, and the additionally atmospheric and emotional *altus, summus, laetus, caelum, terra, tellus, unda, sol, ventus, arma, fatum, gens, urbs, nomen* of Ovid

[1] See *Eras and Modes*, pp. 290–1; and for more detail, *Renaissance, Eighteenth century, and Modern Language in English Poetry*, pp. 49–69.

and Virgil, in addition to their more poetically standard *amor*, *deus*, *pater*, *tempus*, *vir*, *homo*'.[1]

The words which Dante uses most frequently of all in the *VN* poems—setting aside such indispensable verbs as 'essere', 'avere', 'fare', 'potere', 'volere' etc.—will almost certainly characterize not Dante but the genre. A glance at the concordance to Cavalcanti's poems in Favati's edition reveals totals such as: 'core' (82), 'amore' (71), 'donna' (52), 'occhi' (37), 'mente' (23), 'gentile' (19), 'novo' (13), 'dolente' (13). It may of course be necessary to take account of relative frequencies even here. Granted that Cavalcanti lays a more constant stress on his sufferings than Dante does, and that it was Dante alone who made the decisive step towards a poetry of disinterested praise, is it perhaps significant that 'core' appears *more* frequently than 'donna' in Cavalcanti, *less* frequently in the *VN* poems? It may be; but it would be rash to build up an interpretation on evidence such as this. On the whole it is more likely that the truly distinctive words, the 'key-words' in a meaningful sense, will be those which appear 4–6 times in a sample as long as the *VN* poems, but less frequently in other poets, provided also that they share a common semantic field. Thus Maria Corti, trusting her literary judgement rather than strict numerical evidence, produces quite distinctive lists of key-words for poets as close to Dante as Guido Cavalcanti and Cino da Pistoia. And although prepared with different criteria, they are worth quoting here for the light they may throw on the most common words in the *VN* poems. For Cavalcanti: 'dolente', 'pauroso', angoscioso', 'tristo', sbigottito', 'dispietato', 'disfatto', 'distrutto', 'dispento', 'morto'.[2] For Cino: 'dolce', 'soave', 'pensoso', 'desioso', 'lontano', 'peregrino', 'smarruto', 'smagato', 'rimembranza', 'vaghezza', 'sovvenire', 'imaginar', 'membrar', 'rimembrar'.[3]

In the later poems there is scarcely any such insistence on a limited number of words. We need make exception only for *Io sento sì* and *Doglia mi reca*, each of which is a thorough exploration of the relationship between a pair of contrasting terms,[4] and of course for the 'petra'-

[1] *Eras and Modes*, p. 39.
[2] M. Corti, 'La fisionomia stilistica di Guido Cavalcanti', *RAL*, ser. VIII, v (1950), 530–52: 531.
[3] 'Il linguaggio poetico di Cino da Pistoia', *CN*, XII (1952), 185–223: 189.
[4] The terms are 'servir'–'merzé' and 'servo'–'signore' respectively. For *Io sento sì*, see Kenelm Foster and Patrick Boyde, *Dante's Lyric Poetry* (Oxford, 1967), vol. II, pp. 200–10; for *Doglia mi reca*, see chapter 9 below.

group: all four poems there are linked by their common stress on the
'stoniness' of the lady; and in two of them—the sestinas—the repetition of key-words is transformed into a structural principle.[1] This
absence of key-words is due in part to the more heterogeneous subject
matter of the poems, but it is also due to the increasing richness of the
vocabulary, which we must now study in more detail. Limiting ourselves to one part of speech, we shall first analyse the nouns in the *VN*
poems, and then trace the lexical innovations in the subsequent groups.

The first significant fact about the nouns in the *VN* poems has
already been noted: they are few in number, and we shall have to classify
a mere 229. The second significant fact is that these nouns are overwhelmingly abstract, or, to use the medieval term, 'incorporeal'.[2]
There are 150 abstract nouns to 79 concrete nouns. And this is no
necessary or constant ratio: in the two 'canzoni petrose' it will be completely reversed—92 concrete nouns to 54 abstract.

It will be convenient to begin this survey with the common, concrete nouns—the *nomina propria* and *nomina appellativa corporalia*.
The common characteristic of those which appear in the *VN* poems
is that they are extremely generic. Although by definition they refer
to beings or things perceived by the senses, they shun particularity.
Consider the proper nouns for example. There are only six, and all
denote 'persons' not places. Two belong to the sphere of religion—
'Dio' (5),[3] 'Maria'. Two do indeed denote living persons, but are
'soprannomi' rather than 'nomi', chosen for their wider, impersonal,
etymological associations[4]—'Primavera', 'Beatrice' (3). The remaining
two are the exceptions that prove the rule; for the same ladies are
named in one place as 'monna Vanna e monna Bice' (XXI, 9). And it
is the shock one feels at such particularity—not to speak of the familiar
forms—which makes one aware just how indefinite the poems usually
are. In this case, too, the familiar names are introduced for deliberate
effect, just before Love *re*-names the ladies 'Primavera' and 'Amore'.

---

[1] See the analyses in Foster–Boyde, *Dante's Lyric Poetry*, vol. II, pp. 265–6, 268–9.

[2] '*Appellativa nomina inde vocantur, quia communia sunt et in multorum significatione
consistunt. Haec in viginti octo species dividuntur, ex quibus *corporalia* dicta, quia vel
videntur vel tanguntur, ut "caelum", "terra"; *incorporalia*, quia carent corpus, unde
nec videri nec tangi possunt, ut "veritas" "justitia" ' (*Et.*, I, vii, 3–4).

[3] Figures in brackets indicate the number of times the word is used in the group: in
this case, groups A–H inclusive.

[4] Cf. *VN*, XXIV.

And the poem is obviously a personal and private one, written in the first instance for Cavalcanti's eyes alone. It belongs less with the other *VN* poems than with some of the lighter pieces among the *Rime del tempo della VN*, where we again meet 'monna Vanna', this time associated with 'monna Lagia' (LII, 9), or where the Garisenda tower is named (LI, 3), or where a date is charmingly fixed as All-Hallows.

> Di donne io vidi una gentile schiera
> questo Ognissanti prossimo passato   LXIX, 1–2

But of course 'Ognissanti' is poetically relevant to the apparition of beautiful ladies in a way that even 'Natale' or 'Pasqua' would not have been. And, in general, even those lighter poems avoid the particular, just as the prose of the *Vita Nuova* does. In that work, ten years are covered by a succession of neutral phrases such as 'un die', 'appresso ciò', 'poscia che ...', 'avvenne poi che ...'; and names are replaced by periphrases, of which the most splendid is 'uno, lo quale, secondo li gradi de l'amistade, è amico a me immediatamente dopo lo primo; e questi fue tanto distretto di sanguinitade con questa gloriosa, che nullo più presso l'era' (*VN*, xxxii, 1). And it is this normal restraint which makes the close of Dante's last *canzone* so moving, when, for the first time in his poems, 'la sopradetta cittade' becomes 'Fiorenza, la mia terra' (CXVI, 77).

Unless they are learned words, like 'Dido', 'Europa', 'Etiopia', 'Ariete' in group K, proper nouns may be said to belong to the lower stylistic levels. Thus, the six sonnets in the *tenzone* with Forese Donati (three by each poet) yield the following: Bicci (4), Forese, conte Guido, Alaghier (3), Salamone (2), Dante, San Simone, Stagno, San Gal, castello Altrafonte, Tana, Francesco, Belluzzo, lo spedale a Pinti, monna Tessa, Gioseppe, Cristo. In the *Comedy*, proper nouns will be nine times more frequent than in the *VN* poems: 21·6 per cent of the total, as opposed to 2·6 per cent.[1] Few of the stylistic differences between the *Comedy* and the early poems can be represented more economically than this, and few are more important.

Among the concrete common nouns, the most important are certainly those denoting certain parts of the body or faculties of the soul: 'core' (48), 'occhi' (23), 'lingua' (3); 'anima' (16), 'mente' (13),

---

[1] 1,615 proper nouns in a total of 7,475 (see p. 89) and 6 in a total of 229.

'spiriti' (13).[1] Their frequency is of course a consequence of the traditional interest shown by courtly poets in the psychology and even the physiology of love. The lover's mental states or processes were at times enacted as dramas in which these nouns were personified, or, to use the term preferred in chapter 1, represented as *agentia*. And in the work of Cavalcanti, and, under his influence, in the young Dante, these dramas of the psyche became a central theme, often to the exclusion of others, and were worked out with a new subtlety and exactitude. The tell-tale word in this respect is certainly *spiriti*—the vital 'spirits', which in medieval science were believed to be the carriers of sensitive life, and which were thought to discharge the functions now ascribed to the central nervous system. In earlier courtly poetry, the *spiriti* appear rarely, if at all: indeed the protagonists are usually limited to the eyes and the heart. In Cavalcanti and the young Dante they are dominant. We shall return to this subject again later; for the moment it will be enough to note that even these words are vague—'core', 'mente', 'anima'—and that all except 'spiriti' had been thoroughly acclimatized in courtly poetry. Exactly the same must be said of the remaining inanimate nouns such as 'cosa' (10), 'cielo' (12), 'nome' (5), 'parola' (4), 'via' (4), 'pietra' (2)[2] and for the animate nouns such as 'donna' (56), 'madonna' (10), 'gente' (17), 'segnore' (5), 'angelo' (4), 'omo' (3).[3]

Among the abstract nouns—already studied from a different point of view in chapter 1—the two most important classes of words are those which describe the lover's 'condizione', and those denoting moral or physical qualities, usually of the lady. In the first category we may range no less than 32, for example: 'amore', (54) 'angoscia' (3), 'disire' (4), 'gioia', 'invidia', 'smarrimento', 'speranza', 'tristizia' (3).[4]

[1] 18 in all: fantasia, ingegno, intelletto (4), intelligenza; braccio, capo, labbia, mano, persona (= 'body') (3), petto, polso, viso (11).

[2] 36 in all: I have introduced some crude categories into the otherwise alphabetical list: aere, inferno, mondo (2), nuvoletta, pioggia, sole, spera, stella (2), terra (2); cammino, città, magione, ostale; abito, chiave (2), corona, drappo, foco, lagrima (2), manna, perla, tesoro, velo; ballata (3), canzone (2); dir, dittare; nota, sono (2), voce (3).

[3] 19 in all: figliuola (2), madre, sorella; donzella (3); amante, beatrice, nemica (2); peregrino (2), messo, servidore, servo, sire (3); augello.

[4] The others are: allegranza, baldanza (2), disdegno, doglia, dolore (10), dottanza, duol (2), ebrietà, ira, letizia, noia (2), orrore, paura (4), pietà (22), spene, superbia, temenza, tremore, vergogna (2); desiderio, disio, voglia (3), volere, voluntate.

In the second, there are 25, for example: 'bieltate' (6), 'cortesia', 'gentilezza' (2), 'salute' (7), 'umiltà' (5).[1] All of them are of course drawn from the common vocabulary of the courtly love lyric. Comparing them with Heinimann's list of similar terms in Marcabru and Bernart de Ventadorn a century earlier, we see that they cover the same ground, and divide it up in much the same way.[2] What developments there are, from the semantic point of view, are probably negative; that is, Dante uses fewer terms, and these are on the whole more homogeneous and more elevated in character. Much the same can be said of Dante's use of two other kinds of abstract noun studied by Heinimann—the substantivized infinitives, and the *deverbale Kurz-formen.* Dante certainly uses both classes, for example: 'l'adoperare', 'l'andare', 'lo perdonare';[3] 'gabbo', 'lamento', 'prego', 'sospiro' (8).[4] But neither class is as common in the *VN* poems as Heinimann shows it to have been in troubadour poetry.[5]

Among the remaining abstract nouns, it is possible and profitable to distinguish three other groups: words relating to the processes of thought or ratiocination (for example 'cagione' (2), 'essenza', 'parvente', 'proprietà',);[6] some very generic words denoting appearance

---

[1] The others are: ardire (2), bellezza, benignitate, bontate, crudelitate, dignitate, dolcezza (4), dolzore, gioventute, gravitate, grazia (3), leggiadria, misura, nobiltate, piacere (= beauty) (2), qualità (3), valore (9), vanità, vertute (9), viltate.

[2] Love, *amor, amansa, amistat, drudaria*; longing, *deʒir, deʒire, deʒiransa, deʒirier, talan, ententa*; desire, *cobeida, cobeʒeʒa, enveia*; pleasure and joy, *plaʒer, plaʒensa, agradatge, alegransa, alegratge, delecha, jauʒimen, esjauʒimen, solatʒ, joi, joia*; hope, *esper, esperans, esperansa*; fear, *doptansa, esglai, esmai, espaven*; oppression and suffering, *afan, aliscara, cura, error, pesansa, sofrensa, maltraih, martire, trebalha*; anger and irritation, *nauʒa, enoi, adiramen, ira, iror*; grief and lamentation, *dol, dolor, badalh, sospir, plor.*

Virtues, *bontat, beutat, pretʒ, valensa, valor; ardimen, proeʒa, vassalatge; cortesia, meʒura*; vices, *malvestat, malvolensa, vilania, vilanatge; avoleʒa, orgolh, sobransa; forfachura, falhimen, falsura, foldat, follatge, follia, folor, nuailla, ufana, ufanaria; glotonia, volpillatge; desonor, frachura, menda.*

S. Heinimann, *Das Abstraktum in der franʒösischen Literatursprache des Mittelalters* (Berne, 1963), pp. 67–8. I follow Heinimann's headings (here translated), ordering and orthography.

[3] The remainder are: il consolare, il durare, il fallare, l'imaginare (3), il lagrimare, il perire, il piangere, il sospirare.

[4] The remainder are: guai (3), loda (2), martiri (2), merzede, offesa, peccato (2), pena (3), pianto (6), preghiero, scusa (2), tormento (2), torto, tremoto.

[5] *Das Abstraktum*, pp. 51–7.

[6] 15 in all: canoscenza, difetto (2), essemplo, mancanza, matera (2), prova, ragione (2), verità, il vero; giudizio, pensiero (11).

(for example 'colore' (6), 'figura' (4), 'sembianti' (2));[1] and words for time and space, again of a very general nature (for example 'etate', 'loco' (3), 'parte' (5)).[2]

All the classes of nouns we have discussed, and indeed most of the nouns themselves, are broadly speaking what one would expect to find in the elevated love lyric of the late thirteenth century. However, lest we accept the 'inevitability' of this kind of vocabulary too readily, let us now examine the nouns in the two 'canzoni petrose' (group K), taking them out of chronological sequence in order to gain the greatest contrast. As we have already noted, the abstract nouns are now outnumbered by almost 2:1 (92:54). Perhaps two of the terms associated with ratiocination, and only a very few of those denoting states or qualities or even appearance have survived.[3] The same nouns for time and place appear,[4] but are joined by more specific words like '*cima', '*termine', '*terza', '*vespro'. Similarly, words like 'guai' and 'martiro' are here outnumbered by more vigorous and somewhat less conventional terms[5]—'*colpo', '*guizzo', '*strida', '*vendetta'. 'Calore' and 'qualità di gelo' of the *VN* poems become 'il *caldo', 'il *freddo', 'la *freddura'.[6]

But it is of course in the number and classes of concrete nouns that the differences are most striking. The proper nouns we have already discussed. Among the 'common animates', we encounter from the *VN* poems, 'donna' (4), 'om', 'augello': but in addition '*pargoletta', '*scherana', 'animale', '*orso'. The parts of the body are well represented, but there is no 'intelletto', or 'anima', and the newcomers are

---

[1] 11 in all: atti (3), forma, imagine, sembianza (3), statura, cospetto, veduta, vista (7).

[2] 11 in all: anno, fine, lato, mezzo, ora, punto (2), stagione (2), tempo.

Other groupings do suggest themselves in the remaining 29, but none are sufficiently large to merit separate treatment: accordanza, atto, compagnia (2), calore, disonore, erranza, fede (3), gelo (2), luce (3), maraviglia (2), miracolo (2), morte (12), natura (2), novella, onore (6), orranza, pace (4), potestate, reame, regno, riposo, rispetto, secolo (4), securtate, segnoria (2), splendore, stato, varietate, vita (8).

[3] Cagione, pensiero; amore (13); dolore, *tema, bellezza, vertù (2); atti, imagine, morte (4), natura (2), onore, pace, vita (3). In this and all the following lists an asterisk indicates that the word has not appeared in any previous group among the poems analysed: in this case groups A–J inclusive.

[4] 13 in all: giorno, loco, ora, parte, punto, stagione, tempo (4), *verno, *volta (2).

[5] 9 in all: *assalto, *guerra, *triegua.

[6] The remaining abstract nouns are: copia, il *dolce, *durezza, *forza, il *fuggire, gelo, *gola, male, merzé, *niego, opra, il parlare, *peso, senso, *verdura.

significant:[1] 'capelli', 'denti', 'sangue', 'trecce', 'vena', 'ventre' (the last two used metaphorically of the earth).

One finds a number of the common concrete nouns from the *VN* poems (for example 'aere' (2), 'cielo' (2), 'terra' (5), 'pietra'),[2] but these are overwhelmed by many others totally alien to the earlier convention: geographical and meteorological terms like '*abisso', '*borro', '*nebbia', '*rena', '*vapore';[3] names of plants and trees, e.g. '*abiete', '*lauro';[4] names of specific stones, '*diaspro', '*marmo'; and above all a group of words with military or generally violent associations like '*ferza', '*saetta', '*scudiscio'.[5]

In other words, Dante deliberately set out to expand his poetic vocabulary in these poems, and in fact, more than half the nouns (89:146) had not been used in all the earlier groups (A–J inclusive). More important still, he expanded his vocabulary to take in not just new words, but new *classes* of words which had been deliberately excluded from the earlier poems. The poems must not be taken as evidence of a general or permanent development; but nevertheless this break with the conventions concerning vocabulary which he observed in the earlier poems is one of the major steps towards the lexical richness and variety of the *Comedy*.

The story for the two intermediate groups is much less dramatic: there are fewer new words, fewer new classes of words, and less extreme ratios between abstract and concrete. In group I only 22 of the 90 nouns had not appeared in the *VN* poems (one would find something like this proportion in any one *VN* poem contrasted with its peers), and the only noticeable change is that the ratio of abstract to concrete now approaches parity (46:44).

The concrete vocabulary is very much of the earlier type, with one

---

[1] The others are: braccio, core (10), mano (2), mente (5), occhi (2), persona, spirito, viso.

[2] 14 in all: mondo, pioggia, sole (3), spera, stella (2), cammino, velo, canzone (2), rima, voce.

[3] 23 in all: (all the following, except 'pianeta', 'raggio', 'fronda', are new to this group, so asterisks have been omitted): acqua, brina, emisperio, falda, mare, neve, ombra, onda, orizzonte, paese, piaggia, pianeta, raggio, rezzo, rivo, suolo, vento, vetro.

[4] 12, including related words: ala, erba, fiore, fioretto, foglia, fronda (2), legno, pino, ramo, scorza (2).

[5] 10 in all: arco, arme, faretra, ragna, scudo, spada, spina. The remainder are: favilla, lima, passo, rota, smalto, squille.

proper noun—'*Paradiso*'—rather generic animate nouns,[1] prominent use of the parts of the body,[2] and similarly generic inanimates.[3] The abstract nouns may be classified under the same categories,[4] and these appear in approximately the same proportions; except perhaps that the 'ratiocinative' nouns are relatively more conspicuous.

With the didactic poems in group J one might reasonably expect some radical changes in vocabulary, since Dante himself proclaims his intention of modifying his style to suit the new themes:

> Le *dolci* rime d'amor ch'i' solia
> cercar ne' miei pensieri,
> convien ch'io lasci; ...
>
> diporrò giù lo mio *soave* stile,
> ch'i' ho tenuto nel trattar d'amore;
> e dirò del valore,
> per lo qual veramente omo è gentile,
> con rima *aspr'* e *sottile*   LXXXII, 1–3, 10–14

However, as the *proemi* of both *canzoni* go on to make clear (LXXXII, 18–20; LXXXIII, 17–19), these poems are not inimical but complementary to love poetry; and the qualities of 'gentilezza' and 'leggiadria' which they seek to define are central to the system of values in courtly poetry. And the promised *asperitas* of style is not that of *Così nel mio parlar voglio esser aspro*; so there is no comparable upheaval. Abstract nouns still outnumber concrete (99:59); 66 nouns are common to this group and earlier ones; and we may recognize the same basic categories in each. But the proportion of nouns in each category has changed

---

[1] *angela, angelo, donna (16), gente; *ancella, *creatore, *creatura, madonna, messo, segnore, sire, sorella.

[2] anima (8), core (7), intelletto (5), mente (2), occhi (9), persona, *piede, spirito (3), spiritello, viso.

[3] aere, cielo (5), mondo, *raggio, sole, stella, *trono, *universo; cosa, *dardo, *fiammella, foco, *pintura; ballata, canzone (2), dire, *parlare (3), *rima; stato, vita (3), voce.

[4] MENTAL STATES: amore (11), angoscia, desiderio, disdegno, disire, paura (2), pietate, tremore.
MENTAL AND PERSONAL QUALITIES: *adornezza, bellezza, bieltate (3), crudelitate, piacere, umiltate, valore (4), virtute (4), *vizio.
'RATIONAL': cagione, difetto, *dimando, essemplo, *essere, pensiero (4), prova, *ragionare, ragione, vero.
TIME AND SPACE: *grandezza, lato, loco, ora (2), parte (2).
MISCELLANEOUS: *aspetto (2), atti (2), fede, figura, loda, maraviglia, merzede, miracolo, natura, *novitate, pace, *riso, salute (3), sospiro (3).

considerably. Naturally enough, the dominant group now are the nouns associated with ratiocination,[1] whilst the nouns denoting states[2] are now greatly outnumbered by those denoting qualities[3] (1:4 instead of 3:2). Among the remaining abstract nouns[4] we find many that are common to the *VN* poems, and many that might well have appeared there, together with a few that would have been out of place, like: '*ischiatta' (2), '*senetta', '*furto', '*scede', '*discorrimento'.

It is among the concrete nouns that differences do begin to make themselves felt—although even here the differences are of degree. Only two are proper nouns, 'Dio' (3) and '*Etica' (the work by Aristotle). Among the animates, the group most often repeated are once again the generic nouns of the *VN* poems: 'donna' (6), 'gente' (2), 'omo' (11). But there are others like '*animale', '*cavaliere' (2), '*dei', '*ladro', '*prenze' which, because of what they signify, or because they are so specific, would have seemed out of place in the earlier poems.[5] The parts of the body and mind are still present,[6] but there is a very significant drop in the number of times they are repeated. Nearly all the concrete nouns that appear for the first time[7] take us outside the narrow

[1] 25 in all: *abito (2), conoscenza, difetto, *effetto (2), essemplo, essere (2), *fallenza, *falso (2), *genere, *intendimento, iudicio, materia (2), *operazione, *opinione, *parere, *parlamento, parlare, *particula, pensiero, *prode, ragione (2), *savere, *scienza, *sentenza, *subietto, vero (3).

[2] 5 in all: amore (7), *diletto (2), *felicità, ira, *orgoglio.

[3] 17 in all: bieltate, bontate, *franchezza, gentilezza (6), *giovinezza (2), grazia (2), *larghezza, *lealtà, leggiadria (3), *lussuria, nobiltate, salute (2), *senno, valore (2), *villania, viltate, virtute (16).

[4] 51 in all; the remainder are:
TIME AND PLACE: *cominciamento, etate (2), fine, grandezza, *levante, mezzo, parte (3), *principio (2), punto (2), tempo (3).
MISCELLANEOUS: *aiuto, atti (3), *biasmo, calore, *cura, *danno, figura (2), *grato, *impero, *inganno, loda (3), luce (2), *male, *messione, *mestiere, morte (2), natura, *nazione, *nero, novella, *opera, peccato, *perso, pianto, *portamenti, *possessione, *reggimenti, *ricchezza (2), *riparo, sembiante (2), *sollazzo, stato, *stile, trattare, *uso, vita (4).

[5] The remaining animates are: amica, *cristiano, *figlio, nemico (2), *nepote, *padre, segnore.

[6] anima (3), *animo, *coraggio, core (2), *corpo, intelletto (4), mente, occhi, persona (4), piede.

[7] See also: *avere (2), *beni, *divizie, *fronda, *frutto, *insegna, *legno, *ornamento, *radice, *rivo, *torre, *vestimento. The remainder are: cammino, cielo (3), cosa, *detto (2), dire (2), *manto, nome, parola (2), *pianeta, raggio, rima (3), *segno, sole (2), stella (3), terra, via.

horizons of the *VN* (for example '*cibo', '*mercato', '*seme', '*vocabulo').

In the five sonnets addressed to Cino, as in the 'canzoni petrose', there is almost a deluge of 'new' words: 39 of the 75 nouns had not appeared in earlier groups. And once again many of the words are new in kind. Thus, the concrete nouns are more specific, and occasionally they denote objects which to a medieval mind would be 'low', or at least inappropriate in an elevated poem; and many of them would be rare in any context, for example: 'fianco', 'foro', 'minera', 'palestra', 'ponte', 'poro', 'prun', 'stecco', 'uncino'.[1] Conversely, abstract terms like 'circulazione', 'consiglio', 'libero arbitrio' would be perfectly at home in a technical philosophical work, but are decidedly less so in a sonnet, especially in the company of concrete nouns such as those we have just considered.[2] In other words, the 'central' courtly vocabulary has been enlarged, and to some extent displaced, by non-courtly items from two very different fields. It must be remembered that these sonnets, like the 'canzoni petrose', have a pronounced experimental character; and most of the more outlandish 'new' words appear in the three 'risposte per le rime' (XCV, CXI, CXIII), where Dante has set himself the task of finding rare words for the rather rare terminations which Cino has in effect imposed on him. But although the lexical richness of these poems must not be thought of as 'normal', or as a consolidated stage in Dante's development, this group does provide a necessary link between the relative poverty of the vocabulary in the lyric poetry as a whole and the prodigious wealth of the *Comedy*.

The most representative documents for a study of Dante's vocabulary in his full maturity as a lyric poet are undoubtedly the two ethical *canzoni*, *Tre donne* and *Doglia mi reca*. Lexically, as in many other ways, they strike a balance between the conservatism of groups A–J and the experimentalism of groups K and L: 'old' and 'new' items are represented in almost equal proportions (94:89), as are abstract and concrete (90:93).

In describing the vocabulary of the later poems, emphasis has naturally been laid upon the innovations; but, since we are equally

---

[1] Other concrete nouns to appear for the first time are: albergo, cerchio, Cino (2), dito, fiume, fronte, lito, messer, nave, nutrice, penna, ploia, sprono, tempesta, volto.

[2] Other abstract nouns to appear for the first time are: †affronto†, caccia, colpa, fatto, partita, pensamento, periglio, riguardo, sapore, sospetto, tacere, umore.

concerned to establish which features of Dante's style remain constant from one group to another, it is only proper to call attention now to the nouns which have 'survived'. The surviving animate nouns, the parts of the body or mind, and the nouns associated with poetry or speech, are those which occurred in all earlier groups, almost without exception,[1] for example 'donna' (10), 'gente' (5), 'omo' (6), 'core' (4), 'mente' (2), 'occhi' (5); 'canzone' (4), 'il parlare' (3). The other 17 concrete nouns are all of the generic kind, and although 11 of them were first used after the *VN* poems, most of them had appeared in at least two groups,[2] for example, 'cielo' (2), 'fronda' (2), 'sole', 'terra'. Among the abstract nouns used before, we note a small select company of states and qualities,[3] for example 'amore' (7), 'doglia' (2), 'vergogna', 'beltà' (7), 'larghezza', 'veritate'; a very small number associated with ratiocination or denoting time and place;[4] and a further 24 miscellaneous items, most of which are to be found in the *VN* poems,[5] for example 'colore', 'lode' (2), 'morte' (4), 'natura', 'pace' (3).

The new elements, which, as we have seen, make up almost exactly half the total vocabulary, contain abstract and concrete in almost exactly equal proportions (42:47), and they consist for the most part of words which do not belong to the well-defined categories used in classifying the nouns in earlier groups. Some of the innovations[6] are

---

[1] ANIMATE (12 in all): Dio; amico (7), ancella, animale, madre, nemico, persona, servo (6), segnore (8).

BODY AND MIND (11 in all): braccio, intelletto, mano (5), petto, sangue, treccia, viso, volto (2).

SPEECH etc. (6 in all): dire, nome, parola (3), voce.

[2] Groups A–H: chiave, cielo (2), foco, mondo (2), sole, terra. Group I: raggi; J: fronda (2), radice; K: ale, arme, fiore, onda, paese; L: cerchio, fiume, penna.

[3] STATES (9 in all): diletto, disdegno, disire, doler (3), ira (2), volere.

QUALITIES (8 in all): bontà, male, misura, vertù (9), viltà.

[4] RATIOCINATIVE (5): cagione, giudizio, matera, prova, ragione.

TIME AND PLACE: parte (3), tempo.

[5] avere, beni (2), colpa (3), danno (2), forza, grado, guerra, lode (2), maraviglia, onore (2), possessione, segno (2), sembianza, signoria, sospiri, vista, vizio; perdonare, tacere.

[6] ABSTRACT. (a) STATES: ardire, onta. (b) QUALITIES (6 in all): amistà, follia, simiglianza. (c) TIME AND PLACE (4): lontananza, mane, sera, numero. (d) VERBAL (6): non cale, donare, negare, tardare, vendere, vincere, (e) MISC. (24): appetito, assembro, briga, comando, commiato, compera, costrutto, destino, difesa, dimanda, dono, essilio, fortuna, lume, merito, perdono, posta, servaggio, sonno, viaggio, vivanda.

CONCRETE. (a) PROPER (4): Bianca, Contessa, Giovanna; Nilo. (b) ANIMATE (11): famiglia, fattore, fera, portato, serva, suora. (c) PARTS OF BODY (5): bocca (always

again bold. On the one hand, we find: 'dismisura', 'drittura', 'tempe-ranza', 'benefizio', 'decreto', 'vassallaggio'; on the other: 'bestia', 'cane', 'veltro'; 'avaro', 'germana'; 'benda', 'casa' (not 'magione' of XVI, 6), 'culla', 'fango', 'orto', 'palude', 'pane', 'pasto', 'strada' (not 'via', 'cammino' as before), 'ossa', 'polpa'. But these uncourtly words do not amount to the overwhelming proportion that we found in groups K and L.

Thus from poems with a traditional, highly specialized abstract vocabulary, through experiments with an almost equally specialized concrete vocabulary, we have come to a vocabulary which draws simultaneously on many fields of human activity, and in which no class may be said to predominate. There are many innovations, but an equal number of conservations, and in fact, whatever aspect one chooses to consider, the key-note now is harmonious variety.[1]

---

paraphrased in A–H), faccia (always 'viso' in A–H), membro. (d) MISC. (27): camera, cintura, colle (2), colonna, corte, dardo, esca, fontana, fonte, gonna, luna, oraggio, panni, pome, porta, rocca, rosa, vinco.

[1] The story of the *epithet* and the *verb* is very much the same in all respects. Just to complete this section, I append a table to demonstrate the level of innovation in each of the three main parts of speech for each of the later groups. The right-hand figure indicates the number of words in each group that have not appeared in all the previous groups taken together. The figures would not of course be significant but for the *constantly* high level of innovation in the later poems. Note, however, that the constant increase in the size of the vocabulary already used makes it progressively more difficult to innovate.

	No. of lexical items	No. not used in all earlier groups
Group I (LXXIX–LXXXI)		
Nouns	90	22
Epithets	45	18
Verbs	107	35
Group J (LXXXII–LXXXIII)		
Nouns	158	92
Epithets	73	52
Verbs	142	55
Group K (C and CIII)		
Nouns	146	89
Epithets	46	25
Verbs	120	51

APPENDIX

DISTRIBUTION OF THE PARTS OF SPEECH

Here are the actual distributions of the parts of speech from which the percentages given in the text were calculated: first, for the thirteen groups, then for the thirteen *canzoni*. These are followed by the actual breakdowns of all the strophes in nos. CIII and CIV.

DISTRIBUTION OF THE PARTS OF SPEECH IN EACH GROUP

Vita Nuova

Group	Total	Sub.	Ep.	Pron.	Verb	Part.	Adv.	Conj.	Prep.	Int.
A	694	143	48	123	153	13	48	88	76	2
B	331	60	18	64	84	6	21	44	34	–
C	635	107	44	114	151	24	48	83	62	2
D	500	101	36	86	111	12	30	69	54	1
E	884	163	59	156	210	13	58	123	101	1
F	296	63	29	50	57	5	16	38	36	2
G	316	63	18	65	67	3	21	40	37	2
H	245	42	18	44	56	3	16	39	26	1
Totals	3901	742	270	702	889	79	258	524	426	11
					Rime					
I	1115	180	67	244	254	5	81	164	118	2
J	1412	259	118	205	293	23	89	237	187	1
K	958	212	58	154	183	7	60	160	122	2
L	443	88	30	71	89	4	43	67	50	1
M	1432	291	107	213	304	20	95	219	175	8
Totals	5360	1030	380	887	1123	59	368	847	652	14

	No. of lexical items	No. not used in all earlier groups
Group L (Cino sonnets)		
Nouns	75	39
Epithets	27	14
Verbs	66	22
Group M (CIV and CVI)		
Nouns	183	89
Epithets	82	31
Verbs	166	54

DISTRIBUTION OF THE PARTS OF SPEECH IN THE CANZONI

Canzoni

No.	Sub.	Ep.	Pron.	Verb	Part.	Adv.	Conj.	Prep.	Int.	Totals
XIV	78	26	83	113	6	30	57	51	1	445
XX	82	36	77	109	18	36	63	44	2	467
XXIV	13	6	17	18	2	6	14	3	—	79
XXV	85	33	73	97	7	28	66	50	—	439
XXVII	27	14	26	25	1	7	18	14	—	132
LXXIX	55	28	90	92	4	27	56	32	1	385
LXXXI	96	30	121	122	1	37	86	66	1	560
LXXXII	134	59	120	161	14	48	134	93	—	763
LXXXIII	125	59	85	132	9	41	103	94	1	649
C	113	33	60	82	1	25	72	64	—	450
CIII	99	25	94	101	6	35	88	58	2	508
CIV	129	55	79	119	6	42	93	72	1	596
CVI	162	52	134	185	14	53	126	103	7	836

DISTRIBUTION OF THE PARTS OF SPEECH IN EACH STROPHE OF CIII AND CIV

CIII

St.	Total	Sub.	Ep.	Pron.	Verb	Part.	Adv.	Conj.	Prep.	Int.
(1)	77	12	7	13	18	0	3	17	7	0
(2)	80	19	2	14	16	0	4	16	8	1
(3)	88	19	0	20	16	2	7	13	11	0
(4)	75	17	5	13	14	2	6	9	9	0
(5)	78	10	6	16	15	0	7	12	11	1
(6)	76	14	4	11	15	2	7	15	8	0

CIV

St.	Total	Sub.	Ep.	Pron.	Verb	Part.	Adv.	Conj.	Prep.	Int.
(1)	99	19	7	11	18	1	12	17	14	0
(2)	100	26	12	11	15	2	6	10	17	1
(3)	96	16	10	16	20	2	7	14	11	0
(4)	92	19	6	11	22	1	8	17	8	0
(5)	104	25	10	13	19	0	5	22	10	0

CHAPTER 3

TROPES

In the first chapter we noted in passing that the example composed by Dante to illustrate the highest level of style was 'studded with tropes'. Since we are now concerned with the figures in this special category, let us take that example as our point of departure and study it in more detail. It runs: *Eiecta maxima parte florum de sinu tuo, Florentia, nequicquam Trinacriam Totila secundus adivit.*

Although it is not a difficult sentence from the syntactic point of view, only a few of those readers who meet it here for the first time will be able to understand it in full. But the first point to notice is that, even when our comprehension is in some way incomplete, we can still proceed to a rhetorical analysis of its style. Contrasting Dante's sentence with various hypothetical 'neutral' or 'style-less' forms, we can see that it is cast in the form of an apostrophe to the inanimate city of Florence. We notice the etymological word-play in 'florum' and 'Florentia'. We see that an ablative absolute construction has been preferred to a finite construction in the opening phrase, and that the grammatical subject of the sentence and the main verb have been held back to the very end. If we analyse the rhythm, we discover that each of the two main phrases terminates with one of the prescribed rhythmical cadences or *cursus* (respectively a *cursus tardus*, 'túŏ Flŏréntĭă,' and a *cursus planus*; 'secúndŭs ădívĭt'). In fact, even in our ignorance of the whole meaning, we could discern almost all the features accessible to the rhetorical analysis of style—all that is, *except the tropes*.

To perceive a trope one must first have *understood* the passage, and understood it well enough to be able either to declare that a word is being used *proprie*, or to supply the 'proper' word for whatever is being signified. The stylistically neutral paraphrase must convey, in this case, the 'plain' or 'naked' or 'literal' meaning: it must be couched in 'verba propria'. To return to Dante's example: before we can understand it we need to know that Charles of Valois, while *en route* to what proved a disastrous expedition to Sicily ('Trinacria'), entered

Florence in November 1301, and that, thanks to his presence, the Black Guelph faction was able to seize control of the city and exile the leaders of the White faction, including, in his absence, Dante Alighieri. We also need to know of a popular tradition that Florence had been destroyed by Totila (a sixth-century Ostrogothic king who was often confused—for example by Villani—with Attila, the Hunnish king of a century earlier). Armed with this information, it is easy to identify the tropes: 'to cast out of the bosom' is to send into exile, whilst the 'flowers' are the leading citizens (sustained metaphor); the 'second Totila' is Charles of Valois (a proper-noun metaphor used hyperbolically); and 'to go in vain' is an ironic understatement, for Villani was to describe the result 'properly' as 'reconne *vergognosa* pace'.[1]

Tropes have this in common with the other figures, then, that they are perceived and defined as departures frhm a style-less norm. But there were excellent reasons, as this analysis will have shown, for the ancient theorists always treating them as a group apart. And, equally, it is not at all hard to see why a Geoffrey of Vinsauf should have transformed this 'separation' into an 'opposition', by introducing a sharp contrast between an *ornata difficultas*, which is produced by tropes, and an *ornata facilitas* produced by a combination of the other figures.[2] Dante's example also makes it abundantly plain why Geoffrey should want to identify his 'difficult ornamentation' with the highest of the traditional three styles.

Let us now consider some of the definitions in our authorities:

Restant enim decem exornationes verborum, quas idcirco non vage dispersimus, sed a superioribus separavimus, quod omnes in uno genere sunt positae. Nam earum omnium hoc proprium est, *ut ab usitata verborum potestate recedatur* atque in aliam rationem cum quadam venustate oratio conferatur.[3]

Tropos Graeco nomine grammatici vocant, qui Latine 'modi locutionum' interpretantur. *Fiunt autem a propria significatione ad non propriam similitudinem.* Quorum omnium nomina difficillimum est adnotare, sed ex omnibus Donatus tredecim usui tradenda conscripsit.[4]

---

1 See A. Marigo's edition of Dante's *DVE*, 3rd ed. (Florence, 1957).
2 *Documentum*, II, iii, 3–4, 48, 103. See ch. 1, p. 58.
3 *Ad Her.*, IV, xxxi, 42.
4 *Et.*, I, xxxvii, 1. The sentence in italics echoes Donatus, *Ars maior*, in H. Keil (ed.), *Grammatici Latini* (8 vols, Leipzig, 1855–80), vol. IV, p. 399. The whole passage is repeated in Matthew of Vendôme, III, 18.

Est igitur tropos sermo *a naturali et principali significatione* translatus ad aliam ornandae orationis gratia vel, ut plerique grammatici finiunt, dictio *ab eo loco*, in quo propria est, translata in eum, in quo propria non est.[1]

It will be seen that a trope may be defined in varying ways, depending on whether one chooses to lay stress on the thing signified, or the sign, and on whether one adopts the viewpoint of the analyst or that of the teacher of expressive style. One can say that a trope occurs when a word is used in a transferred sense; or one can say that the 'proper' term has been displaced by an 'improper' term. Or again, one can say that *res x* is designated by the sign belonging to *res y*—this being possible, and the transference being intelligible, because *res x* and *res y* stand in some kind of real relationship to each other, outside the conventions of language. Each definition is legitimate, but on the whole the third formulation is the most satisfactory. It throws into due relief the interdependence of the system of tropes and the classical analysis of meaning in terms of a *res* and its *signum*; and it permits a succinct and easily remembered classification of the individual tropes, since there are as many tropes as there are kinds of relationships between two 'things' (or as least as many as the ancient theorists were prepared to recognize in this respect).

Before we study the individual tropes in any detail, then, let us try to form a general picture of the tropes as a whole, by looking behind the rhetorical definitions and distinguishing the kind of relationships between two *res* which, in the classical analysis, make it possible for the sign of the one to denote the other.

Where the two *res* are 'sense-objects', the relationship which leads us to associate them in our minds may be one of physical proximity: for example they might be part and whole (in which case the transferred use of their proper terms would be *synecdoche*), or they might be user and thing used, container and thing contained etc. (*metonymia*). Somewhat less concretely, the objects, beings, qualities, states or actions may stand in the relationship of cause and event, or at least of a predictable succession in time (*post hoc* if not *propter hoc*: the resultant trope is still *metonymia*). At a different level of perception, the relationship might be grounded on some similarity, either sensory or conceptual, between the attributes of two *res* which are normally regarded

[1] Quintilian, IX, i, 4, which I quote for its exemplary clarity.

as belonging to distinct categories (and here the resultant trope would of course be *metaphora*). Or, from another point of view again, the relationship might be the negative one of 'contrariety' (yielding the many species of *ironia*, when we say the opposite of what we mean), or at least of an obvious inequality in magnitude or desirability (yielding the trope *hyperbole*).[1]

From the rhetorical point of view, then, proximity, causal dependence, similarity, contrariety and inequality are the most important relationships between things; and synecdoche, metonymy, metaphor, irony and hyperbole are the most important of the tropes. But, although there are no further relationships of this kind to investigate, we have not yet exhausted the list of tropes. To understand the remainder, we must revert to the other formulations suggested above, and lay stress on the element of *transference* or *substitution* involved in all the tropes. In the simplest tropes of all, *antonomasia* and *periphrasis*, a title, epithet, or descriptive phrase is *substituted* for the *res* which it would normally qualify: these are a rich source of cliché, as for example, 'the bard of Avon', 'our feathered friends', 'our cousins across the Atlantic'. In the case of *hyperbaton*, the word is *transferred* from its 'proper place' in the sentence to a position which is 'improper'. With *onomatopoeia* and *catachresis* the criteria differ yet again. The distinctive feature here is that the troped term does not usurp the place of a proper term in the hypothetical style-less base, but fills, as it were, a blank space there: the analyst assumes that the writer was trying to express some *res* which as yet did not possess a *signum proprium*. To fill the 'blank space' the writer had either to coin a new word (*onomatopoeia* was rendered literally into Latin as *fictio nominis*), or to 'misapply' an existing word belonging to another related thing (*catachresis* was translated as *abusio*): in most cases the relationship was that of similarity, and the usage was often described as metaphor *necessitatis* or *inopiae causa*.

Now that we have described the tropes in a general way, we must consider their relevance and utility for the purposes of stylistic analysis today. It will be apparent that the system is not quite so coherent, nor so universally applicable, as one might deduce from the fact that it underwent so few modifications over the centuries. For example,

[1] Logically, one might pair *litotes*, 'understatement', with *hyperbole*: but it is not counted as a trope in the rhetorical manuals.

onomatopoeia and hyperbaton are certainly necessary descriptive terms, but they belong with other distinct variables.[1] Catachresis, on the other hand, is arguably dispensable, since it will rarely be possible to determine whether an apparent metaphor was used *necessitatis causa* or *ornatus causa*.[2] As regards the remaining tropes, we have already said all that is necessary in the introduction. They are tied to a theory of meaning which is too rigid and simplistic to be fully acceptable today. But it is usually possible to grasp the nature and the importance of the linguistic features which the ancient grammarians were trying to describe, even where one would want to modify the theoretical model underlying their description. And we must always remember that tropes were among the stylistic devices which the rhetoricians taught their pupils to exploit. And they put their teaching across with vigour and undeniable efficiency. Here is a key passage from Geoffrey of Vinsauf which illustrates both medieval pedagogical technique and the typical rhetorical conception of metaphor: it is no more than the calculated introduction of *verba translata* to replace proper terms in an otherwise unmodified plain-base or *thema*.

> Verbum, quod ponit ibidem
> Articulus similis proprie, transsume decenter.
> Ut, si forte velis haec dicere: 'Tempora veris
> Exornare solum, primos exsurgere flores,
> Ad placitum fieri tempus, cessare procellas,
> Esse fretum planum, motus sine turbine, valles
> Depressas, montes erectos', discute tecum
> Tale quid in nobis, quod propria verba loquantur.
> Ornatum faciens, 'pingis'; primordia nactus,
> 'Nasceris'; alloquio placidus, 'blandiris'; ab omni
> Re cessans, 'dormis'; immotus, 'stas pede fixo';
> Pressus ad ima, 'jaces'; erectus in aera, 'surgis'.
> Ergo sapit verbum si dicas: 'Tempora veris
> *Pingere* flore solum, *nasci* primordia florum,
> *Blandiri* tempus placidum, *dormire* procellas
> Cessantes, freta *stare* quasi non mota, *jacere*
> Depressas valles, erectos *surgere* montes.'

---

[1] See chapters 2 and 4 respectively.

[2] It is worth noting, however, that in the *Rhetorica ad Herennium* IV, xxxiii, 45, *abusio* is defined in a sense which brings it very close to what Horace called a *callida iunctura* —a bold collocation of familiar words which seems to bring them to life again.

Quando tuum proprium transsumis, plus sapit istud
Quod venit ex proprio.

PN 779–97

In short, the tropes can provide a reasonably satisfactory basis for the
analysis of 'indirectly signified meaning'[1], at least in *certain texts*. They
will obviously be most useful in Latin literary texts which show a
strong rhetorical influence, and least useful in those vernacular texts
which are virtually innocent of that influence. And if we look for tropes
in a text lying somewhere in the middle ground between these extremes, we shall naturally have to proceed with caution and be content
with rather uneven results.

Let us consider two examples. In the elevated opening of Cunizza's
speech in the ninth canto of the *Paradiso*, Dante makes her use Italian
in much the same way that he had used Latin in the sentence we analysed
at the beginning of the chapter. She uses periphrasis and metaphor to
indicate successively the March of Treviso, the hill of Romano, her
brother the murderous Ezzelino, her parents, and her own passionate
disposition. Only one fact is conveyed *proprie*—'Cunizza fui chiamata.'

In quella parte de la terra prava
italica che siede tra Rialto
e le fontane di Brenta e di Piava,
  si leva un colle, e non surge molt'alto,
là onde scese già una facella
che fece a la contrada un grande assalto.
  D'una radice nacqui e io ed ella:
Cunizza fui chiamata, e qui refulgo
perché mi vinse il lume d'esta stella.

Par. IX, 25–33

Now, in the following lines taken from the *congedo* to *Donne ch'avete*,
there is not one trope:

E se non vuoli andar sì come vana,
non restare ove sia gente villana:
ingégnati, se puoi, d'esser palese
solo con donne o con omo cortese,
che ti merranno là per via tostana. XIV, 64–8

[1] I take this useful term from Marie Borroff, *Sir Gawain and the Green Knight. A
Stylistic and Metrical Study* (New Haven and London, 1962).

But this does not mean it was futile even to look for tropes in a passage of this kind. On the contrary, it is only when we have become fully aware of the *absence* of the tropes, together with virtually all other figures, that we can understand and appreciate the directness of these lines. Dante thinks of his poem as a 'daughter' ('io t'ho allevata / per *figliuola* d'Amor giovane e piana,' ibid., 59–60), and he talks to 'her' in language one would use to a child.

When the results are clearly positive or clearly negative, as in the two examples we have just examined, there can be little doubt as to the validity and the utility of tropological analysis. But on occasions the results can be ambiguous or confused, and this all too often the case in the poems of the *Vita Nuova* as a whole. Either the set of keys provided by the rhetoricians are manifestly too crude and clumsy for their delicate mechanisms, or else a key enters a lock with deceptive ease but then fails to turn. It will be relevant to illustrate both kinds of failure, so let us begin with an example of the former.

We may look at the common linguistic phenomenon which the rhetoricians described as *synecdoche* in two ways. In a given sentence, in a given context, we may argue that a particular word has either a *more* comprehensive or a *less* comprehensive meaning than it has in other contexts where we regard it as 'normal' (it is also necessary that there is no element of metonymy or metaphor in this extension or restriction).[1] Or we may choose to say, as the rhetoricians did, that a proper term has been *replaced* by another which should 'properly' designate the genus, of which the thing actually signified is a species (or vice versa), or else the whole, of which the thing signified is a part (or vice versa).[2] As always, such a transference is either a *vitium* or an *ornatus*, depending on the circumstances.

---

[1] As this mode of description implies, there is nothing at all unusual about this process: it happens all the time. Often, extended or restricted meanings become accepted and used by other speakers; and thus they become 'normal' in their contexts. Commonly, indeed, they exist side by side with the primary or original meaning; and, provided that we use them or meet them in the appropriate contexts, we do not usually remember or perceive any relationship with the original meaning. In other cases, they eventually usurp the original meaning which becomes extinct. This explains how the 'ancestors' of *coat* and *place* meant 'petticoat' and a 'public square', whilst the ancestors of *meat, field, deer* and *to starve* meant respectively 'food in general', 'an open tract of country', 'animal', and 'to die'.

[2] '*Intellectio* est cum res tota parva de parte cognoscitur aut de toto pars' (*Ad Her.*, IV, xxxiii, 44).

Now there are a number of usages in the *VN* poems which can be described along these lines. 'Cor gentile' and 'cor villano' are used *pars pro toto* to mean *people* whose nature is noble or base, rather than the organ as such.[1] There is a handful of cases where Dante names a part of the body, or a faculty of the mind, with a term that is either more or less comprehensive; as when he uses 'mente' for what in the prose paraphrase is 'memoria',[2] or when he uses 'labbia' to mean 'bocca',[3] or even 'viso' or 'figura'.[4] To these we may add the instances of 'stagione' used (like Provençal 'sazo') to mean 'tempo',[5] or of 'dire' and 'dettare' used to mean 'sonetto' or 'canzone',[6] or of 'cosa' used to designate a person,[7] as again was not uncommon in Duecento Italian. Dante himself may encourage us in our pedantry when he calls attention to the fact that he has used 'peregrini' in the broader of its two senses.[8] It may also be significant to note that although there is only one example of a singular noun used where the plural is clearly

---

'*Synecdoche* est conceptio, cum a parte totum, vel a toto pars intellegitur. Eo enim et per speciem genus, et per genus species demonstratur; sed species pars est, genus autem totum' (*Et.*, I, xxxvii, 13).

In the Middle Ages the Greek term was corrupted into *Sinodoche* and even *Sidonoche*, but was still used. See also Matthew of Vendôme, III, 33–5; *PN*, 1,022–37; *Documentum*, II, iii, 31–5; *Laborintus*, 419–22. The last is worth quoting for the examples:

'Partem pro toto pono. Placet et vice versa
Totum pro parte ponere saepe mihi.
"In terris *anima* prudens et justa laboret:
Post *carnis* mortem nulla meretur homo".'

Such examples make it clear that the rhetoricians are thinking of *traditional* synecdoches, where the usage has become established in a given context.

[1] See I, 1; XXVI, 2; XIV, 33 (although this last is arguably *proprium*). The use of 'nobile intelletto' to designate the dead Beatrice (XXX, 13) is *proprium*, for she has now become a '*spiral* bellezza' (XXVII, 22).

[2] For example XII, 1 (paraphrase in *VN*, xv, 2); XIII, 1 (*VN*, xvi, 2); XXX, 1 (*VN*, xxxiv, 4); XXI, 12.

[3] XXII, 12.

[4] XXV, 68; XXXII, 5–6: the usage is already in Cavalcanti, *Rime*, XXVI, 7. Cf. also XIII, 14, 'polsi' for 'vene' or 'corpo'; VI, 11, 'imagine' where the prose has 'corpo' (*VN*, viii, 1); and perhaps 'viso' for 'capo' in XVII, 5.   [5] XVI, 8; XXXIII, 2.

[6] I, 2; XVI, 2.   [7] XIV, 43 and 46; XVI, 11; XXV, 28.

[8] 'E dissi "peregrini" secondo la larga significazione del vocabulo; ché peregrini si possono *intendere in due modi*, in uno *largo* e in uno *stretto*: in largo, in quanto è peregrino chiunque è fuori de la sua patria; in modo stretto non s'intende peregrino se non chi va verso la casa di sa' Jacopo o riede. E però è da sapere che in tre modi si chiamano *propriamente* le genti che vanno al servigio de l'Altissimo...' (*VN*, xl, 6, 7).

required,[1] Dante does have a certain preference for the singular construction with 'ogni'. Against 'tutti li miei penser' (x, 1), we may set

del tempo che *onne stella* n'è lucente	I, 6
per che *onne* lor pensero agghiaccia e pere	XIV, 34
e d'*ogni* suo difetto allor sospira	XVII, 6
s'io son d'*ogni* tormento ostale e chiave	V, 6
ogne dolcezza, *ogne* pensero umile	XVII, 9

However, taken together, these examples are hardly very enlightening. They are not striking individually; they do not form part of a pattern of usages in some way peculiar to the courtly lyric;[2] they bear little or no resemblance to the examples in the rhetorical manuals.[3] And if we cannot point to a number of indisputably 'positive' finds in some relevant text, then the fact of finding nothing does not even have the 'negative' value claimed for apparently similar results in other variables. In fact, we have not shown any evidence that this particular stylistic variable exists, as far as these poems are concerned. For where a stylistic choice which is theoretically possible is never made in practice, it has no real existence.

What we have just seen, therefore, is the kind of failure in which we had a key but looked in vain for the corresponding lock. And obviously it was only worth recounting in any detail in so far as it can serve as a warning.

Now let us consider the more instructive kind of failure, in which our key glides effortlessly into an inviting keyhole, but then stubbornly refuses to turn the lock.

There are in the poems of the *Vita Nuova* a certain number of constructions of the type 'my *eyes* see', 'your *ears* hear', 'he has a cruel

---

[1] 'Ab uno plura hoc modo intellegentur: 'Poeno fuit Hispanus auxilio, fuit immanis ille Transalpinus: in Italia quoque nonnemo sensit idem togatus' (*Ad Her.*, IV, xxxiii, 45). (And cf. *Et.*, I, xxxvi, 6.) The example referred to runs:

'Poi mi parve vedere a poco a poco
turbar lo sole e apparir *la stella*,
e pianger elli ed *ella* ...' xx, 49–51

In the prose this is paraphrased: 'e pareami vedere lo sole oscurare, sì che *le stelle* si mostravano di colore ch'*elle* mi faceano giudicare che piangessero...' (*VN*, xxiii, 5).

[2] See chapter 1.

[3] Cf. Isidore's comment on 'Flammas cum regia puppis / extulerat' (*Aen.*, II, 256–7): 'Ubi non solum 'puppis' sed *navis*, et non *navis* sed *qui in ea*, et non *omnes*, sed *unus* flammas extulit' (*Et.*, I, xxxvii, 13).

heart'. And they are perhaps sufficiently frequent for them to merit consideration as potentially significant features of Dante's style in this period. Here are some examples:

Videro li *occhi* miei quanta pietate	XXXI, 1
Li *occhi* dolenti per pietà del core hanno di lagrimar sofferta pena	XXV, 1–2
ch'ogne *lingua* deven tremando muta, e li *occhi* no l'ardiscon di guardare.[1]	XXII, 3–4
e par che de la sua *labbia* si mova un spirito soave pien d'amore	ibid., 12–13
Chi no la piange, quando ne ragiona, *core* ha di pietra sì malvagio e vile	XXV, 32–3

These constructions may certainly be classified as examples of synecdoche, since Dante names only a *part* of the whole human being who was cruel, who heard, or who saw. And it is tempting to gather the examples together under this label, to count them, and then to rest content on the comfortable assumption that one has thus completed an objective and verifiable description of a significant feature, and either helped to show the poems' dependence on the rhetorical tradition, or, at least, to have vindicated the relevance of the rhetorical categories.

But clearly this will not do. It would be necessary to remark that there were almost certainly common locutions, current in Dante's time, which involved the same kind of construction, and which were of no greater stylistic significance than such modern English phrases as 'he could not believe his *ears*', 'he hardened his *heart*', 'his *eye* fell on a misprint', or 'his *mind* went blank'. And modern English experience would suggest that if such constructions acquired a certain relief in formal and rhythmical contexts, then this would have been due to their power to evoke, through association, the language of the Bible or the liturgy.[2] To label these constructions as synecdoche might lead us to

---

[1] Not without suspicion of the *vitium, pleonasmus*. Cf. Matthew of Vendôme: Est enim ... *parysologia* ... plurium dictionum superflua adiectio; *pleonasmus*, unius dictionis, ut apud Virgilium: 'Sic "ore" locuta est' (*Ars versificatoria*, IV, 10).

[2] For example, *Oculi* vestri viderunt omnia quae fecit Dominus (Deut., 4, 3). *Auris* enim verba probat, et *guttur* escas gustu dijudicat (Job, 34, 3). Et *aures* tuae audient verbum post tergum monentis (Isa., 30, 21). ...et *brachia* mea populos judicabunt

overstress one *external* relationship—rhetorical doctrine—at the expense of others which are more relevant, namely, common speech and liturgical language. But to do so might also obscure an internal relationship which is of considerably greater importance. Consider the italicized words and constructions in the following passages:

> Spesse fïate vegnonmi a la *mente*
> le oscure *qualità* ch'*Amor* mi dona,
> e vènmene *pietà*, sì che sovente
> io dico: 'Lasso, avviene elli a persona?'
> ch'*Amor* m'assale subitamente,
> sì che la *vita* quasi m'abbandona:
> campami un *spirto* vivo solamente,
> e *que'* riman perché di voi ragiona.
> . . . .
> e se io levo li *occhi* per guardare,
> nel *cor* mi si comincia uno *tremoto*,
> che fa de' *polsi* l'*anima* partire. XIII, 1–8, 12–14

> così mi sta soave ora nel *core*.
> Però quando mi tolle sì 'l valore,
> che li *spiriti* par che fuggan via,
> allor sente la frale *anima* mia
> tanta dolcezza, che 'l *viso* ne smore,
>   poi prende *Amore* in me tanta vertute,
> che fa li miei *spiriti* gir parlando,
> ed escon for. . . XXIV, 4–11

These constructions are clearly related to those exemplified above. But they could not possibly be described as examples of synecdoche, for there is no question here of any *substitution* of parts for a whole. These passages, and others like them, represent or enact complex mental or psycho-physiological processes in which the various organs *must* be separately named. If a scientist wants to explain in general

---

(Isa., 51, 5). *Os* meum annuntiabit justitiam tuam (Ps. 70, 15 = A.V. 71, 15). . . . loquatur *lingua* mea in faucibus meis (Job, 33, 2).

  Compare *levavi oculos meos, et vidi* (Zach., 1, 18; 2, 1; 5, 1, etc.) with '*Levava* li *occhi miei* bagnati in pianti, / e *vedea*. . .' (XX, 57–8): or 'Li *occhi* dolenti per pietà del *core* / hanno di lagrimar sofferta pena, / sì che per vinti son remasi omai' with *oculi mei languerunt prae inopia* (Ps. 87, 10 = A.V. 88, 9), *turbatus est a furore oculus meus* (Ps. 6, 8 = A.V. 6, 7), *conturbatus est in ira oculus meus, anima mea, et venter meus* (Ps. 30, 10 = A.V. 31, 9).

terms to a young audience how or why we snatch our hand away when we touch a hot saucepan, then it is quite natural for him to say that the *nerve* transmits information to the brain, the *brain* directs the relevant muscles to contract, and the *muscles* pull the hand away. In short, such constructions should not really be studied as products of stylistic *choice*: they are virtually dictated by the context.

It will be seen, also, that constructions with 'viso', 'anima' or 'core', which could in some circumstances be classified as synecdoche, are handled in just the same way as constructions with 'spirito', 'pensiero', 'sospiro', 'intelligenza' or even 'imagine' and 'figura';[1] while these in turn exist on the same plane as constructions involving 'disio', 'pietà', 'paura', which we would have to describe as *conversiones* or metonymies.[2] And we have already noted that these last cannot be isolated from constructions with 'Amore', which are often labelled as personifications. Thus, if one insists on approaching passages such as those just quoted from the stylistic point of view, one must obviously choose *not* synecdoche but a broader concept, such as the *abstractum agens* studied in the first chapter.

In saying that the sophisticated poet, no less than the homely popularizer, is driven almost necessarily to use that kind of construction if he wants to analyse those mental processes, I do not want to suggest that Dante's style is as plain and 'colour-less' as the scientist's would probably remain. It was just such a dramatization of the psyche, in the course of which 'Amore' is represented as moving and speaking and smiling, which led Dante to explain and defend his use of the figure, prosopopoeia ('... parla Amore, sì come se fosse persona umana' *VN*, xxv, 9). And in a few places, Dante's own prose paraphrase discreetly removes a personification and shows the 'verace intendimento'.[3] On one occasion he even provides a completely different *proprium* equivalent for the recurrent 'core' and 'anima':

In questo sonetto fo due parti di me, secondo che li miei pensieri erano

---

[1] For 'spirito' see the passages quoted in the text; for 'pensiero' see xxv, 44; 'sospiro', see xxx, 7–8; 'intelligenza', see xxxvii, 3; 'imagine', see lxvii, 43; 'figura', see lxvii, 81.

[2] See chapter 1, p. 56.

[3] For example 'piansemi Amor nel core, ove dimora' (xx, 31), becomes '... cominciai a piangere fra me stesso di tanta miseria' (*VN*, xxiii, 3). Similarly, 'Allor diceva Amor: "Più nol ti celo"' (xx, 63), becomes 'Allora mi parea che lo cuore, ove era tanto amore, mi dicesse...' (*VN*, xxiii, 8).

divisi. L'una parte *chiamo cuore, cioè l'appetito*; l'altra *chiamo anima, cioè la ragione;* e dico come l'uno dice con l'altro. E che degno sia di *chiamare l'appetito cuore, e la ragione anima,* assai è manifesto a coloro a cui mi piace che ciò sia aperto.

Questo sonetto ha tre parti: ne la prima comincio a dire a questa donna come lo *mio desiderio* si volge tutto verso lei; ne la seconda dico come *l'anima, cioè la ragione,* dice *al cuore, cioè a lo appetito*; ne la terza dico com'e' le risponde.[1]

But this gloss is quite unique; and although the terms of the defence of the 'vesta di figura' in *VN*, xxv rather suggest an opposition between *proprium* and *translatum*, it is not normally possible in these cases to provide *proprium* equivalents. Our only practicable course, then, is to accept the convention, whereby eyes, thoughts, mind and vital spirits may all act as independent agents, as forming part of the *proprium* base. The tropes in such passages will be those which rise above this level, as for example:

> e spesse volte [li occhi] piangon sì, ch'Amore
> li 'ncerchia di corona di martiri   xxxv, 7–8

which in the prose paraphrase becomes: '... spesso avvenia che per lo lungo continuare del pianto, dintorno loro [*sc.* li occhi] si facea uno colore purpureo, lo quale suole apparire per alcuno martirio che altri riceva' (*VN*, xxxix, 4).

Among the other tropes, there are some, like *ironia* or *antiphrasis*,[2] which are totally irrelevant to the study of the *VN* poems. But there are also others which, although unprofitable if pursued without discretion, can nevertheless suggest openings from which one might proceed to the very centre of Dante's poetry. We have not the space to follow up the lines of inquiry in the detail they deserve, but it should be possible, after the lengthy discussion of the problems raised by synecdoche, to convey something of their nature and scope in a few words.

Only three of the *VN* poems contain *aenigmata*;[3] and in all three

---

[1] *VN*, xxxviii, 5 and 7.

[2] Cf. F. Chiappelli, 'Proposta d'interpretazione per la tenzone di Dante con Forese Donati', *GSLI*, cxlii (1965), 321–50.

[3] In rhetorical theory, *aenigma* is treated as a species of *ironia*:
   '*Aenigma* est quaestio obscura quae difficile intellegitur, nisi aperiatur, ut est illud:

cases the *whole* poem offers something of a riddle. They recount a dream (I), or a day-dream (VIII; XXI), in which the actions and words of 'Amore' require some interpretation. To label them as *aenigmata* is, of course, of little or no value. They are to be studied as a genre, not as a trope.[1] But there are many passages in the prose[2] where Dante congratulates himself on having veiled some point in mystery, and it would be very much worthwhile to explore the causes of his esotericism, real or intended, and to define its limits.

If only we could remain sufficiently 'literal minded', we should doubt-

---

"De comedente exivit cibus, et de forte egressa est dulcedo" (Judges, 14, 14), significans ex ore leonis favum extractum' (*Et.*, I, xxxvii, 26).

'*Aenigma* est sententiarum obscuritas quodam verborum involucro occultata, ut apud Virgilium:
"Dic quibus in terris (et eris mihi magnus Apollo)
Tres pateat caeli spatium non amplius ulnas";
vel sic' (the example is from Donatus, *Ars maior*, in Keil (ed.), *Grammatici Latini*, vol. IV, p. 402).
' "Mater me genuit, eadem mox gignitur ex me":
de glacie intelligendum est.' (Matthew of Vendôme, III, 44).

[1] Cf. further, Dante's interpretation of Da Maiano's dream-poem, *Rime*, XXXIX—XL.
[2] The Latin phrase spoken by 'Amore' (*VN*, xii, 4), *Ego tanquam centrum circuli*, etc., is a perfect *aenigma*, as Dante points out: 'mi parea che m'avesse parlato *molto oscuramente*' (ibid., 5). And the prose has many phrases like the following:
'Lo *verace giudicio* del detto sogno non fue veduto allora per alcuno, ma ora è *manifestissimo* a li più semplici' (iii, 15).
'... ne la seconda narro là ove Amore m'avea posto, *con altro intendimento che l'estreme parti del sonetto non mostrano*...' (vii, 7).
'E di ciò toccai alcuna cosa ne l'ultima parte de le parole che io ne dissi, *sì come appare manifestamente a chi lo intende*' (viii, 3).
'Ma tuttavia, di queste parole ch'io t'ho ragionate se alcuna cosa ne dicessi, *dille nel modo che per loro non si discernesse lo simulato amore* che tu hai mostrato a questa e che ti converrà mostrare ad altri' (ix, 6).
'Vero è che tra le parole dove si manifesta la cagione di questo sonetto, si scrivono *dubbiose parole*... E *questo dubbio è* impossibile a solvere a chi non fosse in simile grado fedele d'Amore; e a coloro che vi sono è *manifesto ciò che solverebbe le dubitose parole*: e però *non è bene a me di dichiarare cotale dubitazione*, acciò che lo mio parlare dichiarando sarebbe indarno, o vero di soperchio' (xiv, 14).
'Dico bene che, *a più aprire lo intendimento* di questa canzone, si converrebbe usare di più minute divisioni; ma tuttavia chi non è di tanto ingegno che per queste che sono fatte la possa intendere, a me non dispiace se la mi lascia stare, ché *certo io temo d'avere a troppi comunicato lo suo intendimento* pur per queste divisioni che fatte sono...' (xix, 22).
'...*assai é manifesto* a coloro a cui mi piace che ciò sia *aperto*' (xxxviii, 5).
And cf. iv; v, 3, 4; vii, 2; ix, 13; xii, 7, 17; xxxii, 2; xxxiii, 2.

less detect a strong element of *hyperbole*[1] in *every* account of the lady's beauty or 'virtù', and in *every* description of the lover's joy or suffering. But where hyperbolic claims are constantly and evenly diffused, they become predictable; and we accept them as normal, no matter how wildly exaggerated they may be with respect to our experience of the primary world. Once we have become acclimatized to the rarefied atmosphere, the mountain plateau might just as well be a plain at sea-level. It is therefore appropriate and necessary to confine our attention to the isolated hills and prominences that rise above the level of this plateau.

When taken in this narrow sense, which is clearly how the rhetoricians understood the term, hyperbole is one of the most conspicuous of all stylistic devices. Both in everyday speech and in certain specialized poetic registers, it usually appears in the form of set expressions, or of basic formulae in which some of the elements are variable and permit a certain degree of originality. As it happens, the courtly love-lyric in the period immediately before Dante was particularly rich in such traditional, easily classifiable hyperboles. Baehr goes so far as to describe it as one of the three hallmarks of Guittone's style.[2] Here are some characteristic examples taken from Baehr's lists:

> che certo senza ciò crudele e fella
> morte m'auciderea immantenante
>
> che temo di morir sol d'allegraggio
>
> e sete sì piacente ed amorosa,
> che vi fareste a uno empero amare

---

[1] '*Superlatio* est oratio superans veritatem alicuius augendi minuendive causa' (*Ad. Her.*, IV, xxxiii, 44).

'*Hyperbole* est excelsitas fidem excedens ultra quam credendum est, ut "Sidera verberat unda" (*Aen.*, III, 423) et "Terram inter fluctus aperit" (*Aen.*, I, 107). Hoc enim modo ultra fidem aliquid augetur, nec tamen a tramite significandae veritatis erratur, quamvis verba quae indicantur excedant, ut voluntas loquentis, non fallentis appareat.

Quo tropo non solum augetur aliquid, sed et minuitur: augetur ut "velocior Euro": minuitur, ut "mollior pluma", "durior saxo" ' (*Et.*, I, xxxvii, 21).

Cf. *Laborintus*, 415–19 and *PN*, 1,013–21, concluding:
'Mirifice laudes minuit modus iste vel auget;
Et placet excessus, quem laudat et auris et usus.'

[2] 'Ein drittes Signum des Guittoneschen Stiles tritt uns, wenn wir fortfahren den Text selbst nach seinen hervorstechendsten stilistischen Eigentümlichkeiten zu befragen, deutlich fassbar entgegen: die *Hyperbel.*' R. Baehr, 'Studien zur Rhetorik in den Rime Guittones von Arezzo', *ZRP*, LXXIII (1957), 382.

che natura né far pote né osa
fattura alcuna né maggior né pare
e so che de valor, né de coraggio,
né de piacer, né d'ornata bellezza,
né de far, né de dir cortese e saggio
altra no è de tant'alta grandezza
onni guerra leggera stimo sia
enver di quella, ed onni avversar vano.[1]

This kind of hyperbolic language can certainly be found in the first groups among the *VN* poems, in lines such as these:

e prego sol ch'audir mi sofferiate,
e poi imaginate
s'io son d'ogni tormento ostale e chiave   v, 4–6

che mi comandi per messo ch'eo moia,
e vedrassi ubidir ben servidore.   IX, 33—4

It occurs even in *Donne ch'avete*:

Ancor l'ha Dio per maggior grazia dato
che non pò mal finir chi l'ha parlato   XIV, 41–2

Poi la reguarda, e fra se stesso giura
che Dio ne 'ntenda di far cosa nova   ibid., 45–6

ella è quanto de ben pò far natura;
per essemplo di lei bieltà si prova.   ibid., 49–50

But there is scarcely any trace of this manner in the poems of the new style; and, as in all those cases where Guittone proposes and Dante 'disposes', the absence is a significant one. Of course, the claims that Dante makes for Beatrice far exceed any made for their ladies by earlier courtly poets. But his hyperbole is not accompanied by all the linguistic trappings of the exaggeration. The tone is simple, almost matter of fact, and completely serious:

e par che sia una cosa venuta
da cielo in terra a miracol mostrare   XXII, 7–8

---

[1] Guittone, *Rime*, 72, 13–14; 61, 14; 47, 5–6; 111, 12–13; 70, 3–6; 172, 12–13. The rhetoricians distinguished two main species of hyperbole: those that are *separatim* (*Ad Her.*, IV, xxxiii, 44), or as Dante puts it, 'non avendo rispetto ad altra cosa' (*Con.*, III, vi, 4); and those that are *cum conparatione* (*Ad Her.*, IV, xxxiii, 44), or 'per comparazione a l'altre cose' (*Con.*, III, vi, 1). In Guittone, as these examples suggest, most of the hyperboles are of the type called *cum conparatione a praestantia* ('sweeter than honey'), rather than *cum conparatione a similitudine* ('as white as milk').

> Vede perfettamente onne salute
> chi la mia donna tra le donne vede   XXIII, 1–2

And some of the more interesting hyperboles seem almost *deliberately* muted. Let me give just three examples which can be, and indeed must be, studied in relation to the quasi-scientific pronouncements on love in the little 'trattato',[1] *Amore e 'l cor gentil sono una cosa,* which provides us with our 'plateau', or *proprium* base.

As is well known, this sonnet gives an account of the nature and genesis of love (which in what follows must be understood as 'fin'-amors'), and it establishes three main points. (a) Love is only possible for those whose disposition is noble ('gentile'), and, conversely, the man whose disposition is noble is *always* 'in love', whether actually or potentially. (b) What English idiom describes as 'falling in love' is not a 'birth' but an 'awakening'—not the intrusion or emergence of something new, but the transition from potentiality to actuality. (c) The man must actually *see* a beautiful and virtuous woman before this transition or awakening can occur:

> Bieltate *appare* in saggia donna pui,
> che piace a li *occhi* sì, che dentro al core
> nasce un disio de la cosa piacente   XVI, 9–11

In short, it is *sight* alone that *awakens* love in the *noble* heart.

The very next sonnet in the *Vita Nuova* shows that Dante has presented these facts only in order to use them as a springboard from which he may soar high above them. Beatrice, he says, can awaken love in *everyone* she sees (including the 'villani'); and this means that *everyone* she sees becomes 'gentile':

> Ne li occhi porta la mia donna Amore,
> *per che si fa gentil ciò ch'ella mira*   XVII, 1–2

There is nothing emphatic in the syntax here. But, as the prose gloss makes clear, the implications of these lines are quite staggering. Not only does Beatrice awaken love from potency to act, but

per lei si sveglia questo Amore...non solamente...là ove dorme, ma *là ove non è in potenzia, ella, mirabilemente operando, lo fa venire.* (*VN*, xxi, 1)

---

[1] 'Onde io, pensando che appresso di cotale *trattato* [that is, *Donne ch'avete*] bello era *trattare* alquanto d'Amore, ... propuosi di dire parole ne le quali io *trattassi* d'Amore' *VN*, xx, 2.

This is quite simply a miraculous power because, as Dante will explain in a later poem, 'gentilezza' is the seed of happiness placed *by God* in the well-ordered soul.[1]

Other sonnets repeat these claims for the miraculous *universality* of Beatrice's influence, and further depart from the letter of the truth, as set out in *Amore e 'l cor gentil*, by asserting that Beatrice's 'virtù' is such that it can be transmitted even without the medium of direct vision. In the close of *Vede perfettamente*, Dante declares that anyone who has once seen Beatrice and recalls her to mind, *must* sigh in the sweetness of love:

> Ed è ne li atti suoi tanto gentile,
> che nessun la si può recare a mente,
> che non sospiri in dolcezza d'amore.[2]   XXIII, 12–14

And in *Deh peregrini* it is said that mere words about Beatrice can awaken love, insofar as they will call forth tears for her death, even in those who have never seen her. Here again the astonishing claim is uttered as softly and as unobtrusively as possible. This is an intimate hyperbole; and, as such, it must remain inaccessible to normal rhetorical analysis.

> Ell' ha perduta la sua beatrice;
> e *le parole* ch'om di lei pò dire
> hanno vertù di far piangere altrui.[3]   XXXVI, 12–14

Of the familiar species of metonymy[4] (whereby *ferrum* can mean

---

1 *Le dolci rime*, 119–20.

2 Again, it becomes more explicit in the paraphrase: '. . . ne la terza dico come non solamente ne le donne, *ma in tutte le persone*, e *non solamente ne la sua presenƶia, ma ricordandosi di lei, mirabilmente operava*' (*VN*, xxvi, 15).

3 Compare what Dante says about the sonnet *Tanto gentile*: '. . . propuosi di dicere parole, ne le quali io dessi ad intendere de le sue mirabili ed eccellenti operazioni; acciò che *non pur coloro che la poteano sensibilemente vedere*, ma li altri sappiano di lei quello che le parole ne possono fare intendere' (*VN*, xxvi, 4).

4 *Denominatio* est quae ab rebus *propinquis* et *finitimis* trahit orationem qua possit intellegi res *quae non suo vocabulo sit appellata*' (*Ad Her.*, IV, xxxii, 43).

'*Metonymia*, transnominatio ab alia significatione ad aliam proximitatem translata. Fit autem multis modis' (*Et.*, I xxxvii, 8).

Metonymy becomes extremely important in Geoffrey's theory of the *ornatus difficilis*. Five of its seven sources are species of metonymy; the others being metaphor and synecdoche. See *Documentum*, II, iii, 4–47; *PN*, 960–1,012; and, further, Matthew of Vendôme, III, 30–2; *Laborintus*, 385–410.

'sword', *Bacchus*, 'wine', *fasces* 'the magistracy', etc.) there is hardly a
trace in the *VN* poems. To be complete, one would need to register
only two clear instances of 'container for contained'.[1] The two least
familiar species, however, do offer valuable leads: these are the use of
proprietatem pro subiecto and *consequens pro antecedente*, both of which
have already been discussed in the opening chapter. Dante's frequent
use of the former[2] cannot really be isolated from other constructions
which might be labelled *conversiones*, synecdoches or personifications;
and thus they would only bring us by another gate into the field of
abstracta agentia. But Dante's preference for the effect rather than the
cause[3] does suggest two more general observations.

---

[1] 'Sextus modus construendae difficultatis est ponere *continens pro contento* vel contentum
pro continente. Continens pro contento, quando *locus ponitur pro eo quod est in loco*
... ut ... "murmurat iste locus" id est "isti qui sunt in isto loco murmurant" '
(*Documentum*, II, iii, 36–8).

Lo cielo, che non have altro difetto
che d'aver lei, al suo segnor la chiede   XIV, 19–20
(Madonna è disiata *in sommo cielo*   XIV, 29)
che non piangete quando voi passate
per lo suo mezzo *la città dolente*   XXXVI, 5–6

[2] See chapter 1, p. 68.

[3] 'Septimus modus constituendae difficultatis est *ponere consequens pro antecedente*, quod
quidem fit quando "pallere" ponitur pro "timere", "erubescere" pro "verecundari".
Timor enim est antecedens ad pallorem ... et quando quis verecundatur ex verecundia
erubescit' (*Documentum*, II, iii, 47).

Geoffrey's description and illustration of the third species of the figure *significatio*,
namely *per consequentiam*, is also relevant.

' "Inspectis virgis pueri rubor ora reliquit
Et facies exsanguis erat:" talis color ipsum
Significat timuisse. "Rubor perfuderat ora
Virginis:" haec facies notat hanc puduisse. "Vagando
Crinibus incessit comptis:" modus iste reportat
Luxuriasse. *Datae da signa sequentia formae*;
Praefer res ipsas, sed eas non praefer ut ipsas,
Immo notas rerum solas: pallore timorem,
Comptura Venerem, subitoque rubore pudorem,
Remque notis certis ostende, sequente priorem:
Hic color, hic sexus, haec aetas, ista figura.'   *PN*, 1,549–59

In all the following examples, as Dante explicitly notes about the first of them (cf.
VN, xli, 3), the lover's sighs and tears are the *effects* of his desire and suffering:
Oltre la spera che più larga gira / passa *'l sospiro* ch'esce del mio core, XXXVII, 1–2; e
d'ogni suo difetto allor *sospira*, XVII, 6; / Venite a intender li *sospiri* miei, XXVI, 1;
venite voi da sì lontana gente, / com' a la vista voi ne dimostrate, / che non *piangete* ...
XXXVI, 3–5; Se voi restaste per volerlo audire, / certo *lo cor de' sospiri* mi dice / che
lagrimando n'uscireste pui, ibid., 9–11; venemene un disio tanto soave, / che mi

125

First, that it points ahead to Dante's mature art in the *Comedy*, and to his concentration there on rendering 'il sensato', giving us the 'sembianti' rather than the 'core'; or, better, to his rendering the 'core' (the inner man, or inner meaning) *through* its 'sembianti' (the outward manifestation in gesture or expression).[1] Second, that in the *VN* poems the words which denote the *effects* of suffering—the sighs, tears and trembling—are emotive and affective terms, and it is largely through them that the 'analytical' passages are not just analytical, but also expressive and moving.

It will be recalled that there are very few proper names in the poems of the *Vita Nuova*.[2] Of the three main protagonists, only Love is named frequently and directly: but, then, 'Amore' is not a person, and 'amore' is not a proper noun. Dante is present only as a first person singular pronoun, whilst Beatrice is almost always referred to antonomastically as 'la donna mia' or 'madonna':

Madonna è disiata in sommo cielo	XIV, 29
poi che tu se' ne la *mia donna* stata	XX, 75
Quand'elli è giunto là dove disira,	
vede una *donna*, che riceve onore	XXXVII, 5–6
quando la *donna mia*	
fu giunta da la sua crudelitate	XXVII, 18–19

Since 'donna' or 'madonna' recur on average once in every ten lines in the *VN* poems, antonomasia[3] has some claim to the status or title

---

tramuta lo color nel viso, XXV, 47–8; *Color* d'amore e di pietà sembianti, XXXII, 1.
This species of metonymy has its moment of glory in nos. XVIII and XIX which are hardly more than *expolitiones* or *interpretationes* of the underlying idea: see Kenelm Foster and Patrick Boyde, *Dante's Lyric Poetry* (Oxford, 1967), vol. II, p. 109.

[1] The terms used here are derived from two key passages in the *Comedy*: *Par.*, IV, 40–8; *Purg.*, XXVIII, 44–5.

[2] See chapter 2, p. 94.

[3] 'Antonomasia est pro nomine, id est vice nominis posita, ut "Maia genitus" pro Mercurio.
Inter antonomasiam autem et epitheton hoc differt, quod *antonomasia pro vice nominis ponitur*, epitheton autem numquam est sine nomine' (*Et.*, I, xxxvii, 11–12).
In *Ad Her.*, IV, xxxi, 42 it is called *pronominatio*.
Both traditions agree that the epithets may be *ab animo*, *a corpore* or *extrinsecus*; and Bede, in his *De schematibus et tropis* (ed. C. Halm, in *Rhetores Latini Minores* (Leipzig, 1863), p. 613), subdivides the third category into *a genere*, *a loco*, *ab actu*, and *ab eventu*.
Geoffrey of Vinsauf understands the term *pronominatio* to mean metaphor by use of proper nouns ('Tullius', 'Paris', etc.): see *Documentum*, II, iii, 5; *PN*, 923–35.

of the 'dominant' trope. But having said this, it must be noted that this received and ubiquitous usage is far removed from the kind of examples given in the rhetorical manuals. And the half dozen remaining examples of the trope in the *VN* poems are hardly less modest or unpretentious:

fu posta da l'*altissimo signore*	XXX, p.c. 3
che fé maravigliar l'*etterno Sire*	XXV, 23
dicea, guardando verso l'*alto regno*	XX, 82
Ita n'è Beatrice in l'*alto cielo* (the Empyrean)	XXV, 15
sì come *il saggio* in suo dittare pone (Guinizzelli)	XVI, 21

People may also be designated by a short periphrasis[2] introduced by a pronoun such as 'quello' or 'colui':

O voi che per la via d'Amor passate	V, 1
chi d'amor per innanzi si notrica	VII, 12
però che *quella* che ti dee audire (Beatrice)	IX, 11
Madonna, *quelli* che mi manda a vui (Dante)	ibid., 18
E dì a *colui* ch'è d'ogni pietà chiave (Amore)	ibid., 35
quando 'l pensero ne la mente grave mi reca *quella* che m'ha 'l cor diviso	XXV, 44–5
quella donna gentil cui piange Amore	XXX, 2

Places are also indicated by a periphrasis, usually with the favourite 'ove', or 'là ove':

e disse: 'Io vegno di lontana parte, *ov'*era lo tuo cor per mio volere'	VIII, 10–11
Quand'elli è giunto *là dove* disira	XXXVII, 5
nel ciel de l'umiltate, *ov'*è Maria	XXX, p.c. 4
Ita n'è Beatrice in l'alto cielo, nel reame *ove* li angeli hanno pace	XXV, 15–16
ch'era *là 'v'* io chiamava spesso Morte (= 'lungo lo mio letto' *VN*, xxiii, 11)	XX, 3

---

[1] Cf. further, XI, 14; XXVI, 3; XXXIV, 13; XXXV, 12.

[2] 'Circumitio est oratio rem simplicem adsumpta circumscribens elocutione' (*Ad Her.*, IV, xxxii, 43). The definition from Isidore was quoted in ch. 1. See also Matthew of Vendôme, IV, 21. In the *Poetria Nova*, 225–40, and its descendants, periphrasis becomes one of the means of *amplificatio* (for example, *Laborintus*, 305–10).

guardando in quella parte *onde* venia	XXI, 8
venire inver lo loco *là 'v'* io era	ibid., 10
che *là 've* giugni tu diche pregando	XIV, 61
Oltre la spera che più larga gira	XXXVII, 1

And in both cases we have something very unlike the periphrasis of rhetoric, and very characteristic of the Romance vernaculars in the early centuries. The only group of periphrases to show any similarity with the rhetorical examples are those which render the concept, 'morire'. Geoffrey's *Documentum*, in fact, exemplifies the figure *circumitio* with eight periphrases of *mortuus est.*[1] But here again a closer examination will only heighten our sense of the differences. Geoffrey's examples are the tired euphemisms we use to skirt round an unpleasant reality. The lyricism, restraint, and beauty of Dante's lines are a poetic demonstration that death has indeed become a 'cosa gentile' now that 'it has been in his lady' (xx, 74–5). They are a *celebration* of death, a death that is a *dies natalis*:[2]

... che si n'è gita al secol degno de la sua vertute	XXVI, 10–11
oggi fa l'anno, che nel ciel salisti	XXX, 14
Ita n'è Beatrice in l'alto cielo	*xxv*, 15
la gentil donna che per suo valore fu posta da l'altissimo signore nel ciel de l'umiltate, ov'è Maria	XXX, p.c. 2–4
...poscia che la mia donna andò nel secol novo	XXV, 60–1
Partissi de la sua bella persona piena di grazia l'anima gentile, ed èssi gloriosa in loco degno	XXV, 29–31
divenne spirital bellezza grande[3]	XXVII, 22

---

1 'Naturali sorte assumptus est', 'Fati munus implevit', 'Diem clausit extremum', 'Consummavit cursum vitae', 'Debitum naturale persolvit', 'Viam universae carnis ingressus est', 'Sublatus est e medio', 'Concessit in fata' (II, ii, 15).

Baehr, 'Studien zur Rhetorik' (1957), p. 224, notes that in Guittone, also, 'morire' is frequently paraphrased; and when it is used, it is normally as a hyperbole for 'soffrire.'

2 Cf. V. Branca, 'Poetica del rinnovamento e tradizione agiografica nella *Vita Nuova*', *Studi in onore di Italo Siciliano* (Florence, 1966), vol. 1, pp. 123–48.

3 Other periphrases for 'morire' will be found in: VI, 5–6; XIII, 14; XXVII, 18–19; XXV, 12–13, 18–19, 42. Cf. also the following periphrases for 'piangere': mostrando amaro duol

The most striking use of these two tropes, by virtue of their density, comes in the words spoken by God in the second stanza of *Donne ch'avete*. What He is saying in bald, proper terms might be reduced to this: 'Angels and souls of the blessed, accept my will that Beatrice should remain somewhat longer in Florence, where Dante is; Dante, who knows he must one day lose her, and who will say in Hell, "Lost souls, I have seen Beatrice".' With the exception of 'inferno', every single name is softened and veiled in mystery by simple periphrases and antonomasiae.

> *Diletti miei*, or sofferite in pace
> che *vostra spene* sia quanto me piace
> *là've alcun* che perder lei s'attende,
> e che dirà ne lo inferno: '*O mal nati*,
> io vidi *la speranza de' beati*'.
>
> XIV, 24–8

And in this context a phrase of St Augustine's comes to mind, where he speaks of the eloquence of the prophets 'ubi per tropologiam multa obteguntur'.[1]

Antonomasia and periphrasis are tropes, but, as we have seen, they are very simple tropes. And so perhaps we may allow them to symbolize that pleasing blend of openness and reserve, of simplicity and elusiveness which is so characteristic of the *VN* poems, and which in fact these two tropes do much to create.

By almost universal consent, the most arresting, versatile, creative, and therefore the most important of the tropes is metaphor.[2] And as the foregoing remarks will have suggested, metaphor[3] has only a very

---

per li occhi fore, VI, 4; veggendo li occhi miei pien di pietate, XX, 4; Ell'ha nel viso la pietà sì scorta, XIX, 12; di dimostrar con li occhi mia viltate, XXXI, 8; Amor sente a Pietà donne chiamare, VI, 3.

[1] *De doctrina christiana*, IV, vii, 48, in W. M. Green (ed.), *Corpus scriptorum ecclesiasticorum latinorum*, vol. LXXX (Vienna, 1963).

[2] Modern theorists find themselves in agreement with Aristotle (*Poetics*, ch. 22), and Matthew of Vendôme (III, 24).

[3] 'Translatio est cum verbum in quandam rem transferetur ex alia re, quod propter similitudinem recte videbitur posse transferri' (*Ad Her.*, IV, xxxiv, 45).

'*Metaphora* est verbi alicuius usurpata translatio, sicut cum dicimus "fluctuare segetes" "gemmare vites", dum in his rebus fluctus et gemmas non invenimus, in quibus haec verba aliunde transferuntur' (*Et.*, I, xxxvii, 2).

Types of metaphor were usually distinguished by their 'source', in the sense of the

limited role to play in the poems of the *Vita Nuova*. Dante *became* a metaphorical poet. He did not begin as one. Virtually all the metaphors used in these poems are traditional in character. And if we adopt some relevant categories current in the Middle Ages, nearly all of them may be accommodated under just three heads. Thus:

AB HOMINE AD INANIMATUM[1]

NOUNS

di dolor *madre* antica ('Morte')	VII, 2
...perch' io t'ho *allevata* per *figliuola* d'Amor giovane e piana ('canzone')	XIV, 59–60
e rituova le donne e le donzelle a cui le tue *sorelle*[2]	XXV, 72–3

---

relationship obtaining between the *res* which is meant and the *res* which provides the *signum*. Thus, the ancient classification was based on the four permutations possible with 'animate' and 'inanimate' (that is, 'from animate to animate', 'from animate to inanimate', etc.) (*Et.*, I, xxxvii, 3–4; Matthew of Vendôme, III, 19–24).

Geoffrey prefers to simplify this into 'from man to thing', and 'from thing to man' (*PN*, 765–829; *Documentum*, II, iii, 12–16). He also distinguishes transference from one species of human activity to another (*Documentum*, II, iii, 21–2). John of Garland makes a similar 'internal' division—transference from *anima* to *corpus* (p. 896); and later he revives what had been Aristotle's classification in the *Poetics*: transference from genus to species, and species to genus (p. 904). Capella (V, 512) recognized transferences from senses to abstractions (*ab oculis, a gustu*).

Geoffrey also made the first attempt at a *grammatical* classification of metaphor. He carefully distinguishes between nouns, verbs and epithets, and tries to establish whether a metaphorical sense is determined by the verb's subject or its object, or by the noun itself or its dependent. (See Christine Brooke-Rose, *A Grammar of Metaphor* (London, 1958), who builds on Geoffrey's humble beginnings.)

In the *Ad. Her.* there is a different classification, based on *purpose* or *effect*: 'rei ante oculos ponendae causa ... brevitatis ... obscenitatis vitandae ... augendi ... minuendi ... ornandi causa'.

Classification by *source* in the narrower, modern sense (for example from the field of law, the natural sciences, the sea, etc.) was virtually unknown. The nearest approach is in Bede's fascinating *De schematibus et tropis* (ed. Halm in *Rhetores Latini Minores*), where we read: 'Hic tropus et ad Deum fit multifarie: a volucribus ... a feris ... a membris humanis ... ab homine interiore... a motibus mentis humanae ... a rebus insensibilibus' (p. 612).

[1] Si de quo loqueris sit *non homo*, lora retorque/mentis ad id quod homo' (*PN*, 778–9).
[2] The same usage in LXXXI, 74 is glossed: 'Per similitudine dico "sorella"; ché sì come sorella è detta quella femmina che da uno medesimo generante è generata, così puote l'uomo dire "sorella" de l'opera che da uno medesimo operante è operata; ché la nostra operazione in alcuno modo è generazione' (*Con.*, III, ix, 4).

e tu, che se' *figliuola* di tristizia .... ibid., 75
e per la *ebreità* del gran *tremore*
le pietre par che gridin: 'Moia, moia' .... XII, 7–8

VERBS

Ciò che m'incontra, ne la mente *more* .... XII, 1
la qual si *cria* ne la vista *morta*
di li occhi, c'hanno di lor morte voglia .... ibid., 13–14
     ...che dentro al core
nasce un disio de la cosa piacente .... XVI, 10–11
     ...sospiri,
che *nascon* de' penser che son nel core .... XXXV, 1–2
Amor per sire e 'l cor per sua magione,
dentro la qual *dormendo* si *riposa* .... XVI, 6–7
che fa *svegliar* lo spirito d'Amore .... ibid., 13
Amor...
s'era *svegliato* nel destrutto core .... XXX, 6
benignamente d'umiltà *vestuta* .... XXII, 6
anzi le face andar seco *vestute*
di gentilezza, d'amore e di fede .... XXIII, 7–8
e d'onne consolar l'anima *spoglia* .... XXV, 40
turbar lo sole e apparir la stella,
e *pianger* elli ed ella .... XX, 50–1

AB INANIMATO AD HOMINEM[1]

NOUN

che si movea d'amoroso *tesoro* .... V, 14
s'io son d'ogni tormento *ostale* e *chiave* .... ibid., 6
E dì a colui ch'è d'ogni pietà *chiave* .... IX, 35
core ha di *pietra* sì malvagio e vile .... XXV, 33

(VERB)

(lei paventosa umìlmente *pascea*) .... (I, 13)

---

[1] Si sit homo de quo fit sermo, transferor ad rem / expressae similem...' (*PN*, 766–7). Note that these are confined to the early group, and were already clichés in Provençal.

VERBS OF VIOLENT ACTION USED OF PSYCHOLOGICAL PROCESSES[1]

che *fere* tra' miei spiriti paurosi, e quale *ancide*, e qual *pinge* di fore	XI, 9–10
per la pietà, che 'l vostro gabbo *ancide*, la qual si cria ne la vista *morta* de li occhi, c'hanno di lor morte voglia	XII, 12–14
ch'Amor m'*assale* subitanamente	XIII, 5
De li occhi suoi, come ch'ella li mova, escono spirti d'amore *inflammati*, che *feron* li occhi...	XIV, 51–3
Lasso, per *forza* di molti sospiri, ... li occhi son *vinti*	XXXV, 1 & 3 (cf. XXV, 3)
ch'io temo forte non lo cor *si schianti*	XXXII, 8
Amor... s'era svegliato nel *destrutto* core	XXX, 5–6
Eo non posso tener li occhi *distrutti*	XXXII, 9
Era la voce mia sì dolorosa e *rotta* sì da l'angoscia del pianto	XX, 15–16
Color d'amore e di pietà sembianti non *preser* mai così mirabilmente viso di donna...	XXXII, 1–3
mi reca quella che m'ha 'l cor *diviso*	XXV, 45
Pianger di doglia e sospirar d'angoscia mi *strugge* 'l core ovunque sol mi trovo	ibid., 57–8
gitta nei cor villani Amore un *gelo*, per che onne lor pensero *agghiaccia* e *pere*	XIV, 33–4
che de la voglia si *consuman* tutti	XXXII, 13
and cf. nel cor mi si comincia uno *tremoto*	XIII, 13

---

[1] One might take these with Geoffrey's class:

'Unde sciendum est, quod verba, quae dicuntur de homine *proprie*, eadem dicta de homine ponuntur *translative* et hoc ratione obliqui sequentis. Possumus verbum quod dicitur de homine *proprie in uno genere rei*, ut "polire" in marmore, "pectere", vel "comere" in capillis, dicere de homine *in alio genere rei*, et ita ponere illud *translative*, non ratione hominis, sed ratione illius generis rei, ut "polire", "pectere", "comere" in *verbo*' (*Documentum*, II, iii, 22).

There are a number of quasi-metaphorical expressions which have more nerve than the majority of those just listed. But such energy as they possess derives rather from syntactic compression than from any illuminating 'juxtaposition' or 'superimposition' of things, concepts, or areas of experience that are normally distinct:[1]

E fatti son che *paion due disiri*	
di lagrimare e di mostrar dolore	XXXV, 5–6
pensatel voi, da che *non mutò 'l core*	IX, 24
ond'io *mi cangio in* figura d'altrui	XI, 12
Color di perle ha quasi...	XIV, 47
Color d'amore e di pietà sembianti	XXXII, 1
Lo viso mostra *lo color del core,*	
che, *tramortendo, ovunque pò s'appoia*	XII, 5–6
Vedeste voi nostra donna gentile	
bagnar nel viso suo di pianto Amore?	XVIII, 5–6
voi le vedete *Amor pinto nel viso*	XIV, 55

There are a few notable exceptions: the dream-ladies' laments, which shoot *arrows* causing the *fire* of grief ('che di tristizia saettavan foco', XX, 48); or again the beautiful close to the sonnet *Lasso, per forza di molti sospiri,* where the book image appearing unobtrusively in line 13 is sustained gently but with infinite suggestiveness in the last line:

però ch'elli hanno in lor li dolorosi	
quel dolce nome di madonna *scritto,*	
e de la morte sua *molte parole.*	XXXV, 12–14

And, finally, there are the metaphors which express Beatrice's 'virtù' in terms of *light,* and which possess an importance out of all proportion to their number or intensity of expression. Without them the figure of

---

Or, better still, with John of Garland:
  '*De arte transumendi verba.* Item quedam verba pertinent ad *animam,* ut "discerno", "doceo"; quedam ad *corpus,* ut "seco", "cano"; quedam ad utrumque, ut "langueo", "doleo". Congrua fiet transumptio verborum duram excludens transumptionem si *verbum quod pertinet ad corpus transferatur ad animum et e contrario,* ut: "pungere mentem contricione"; "lavare sordes anime"; "elementa docent, prata rident'" (p. 896).

[1] What I mean by compression is best explained by comparing the first example with its prose paraphrase: 'Per questo raccendimento de' sospiri si raccese lo sollenato lagrimare in guisa che li miei occhi pareano *due cose che disiderassero pur di piangere*' (*VN,* xxxix, 4).

Beatrice simply would not exist as we know it. For it is of her essence that she is not just 'goodness', but an *active, more-than-human* goodness. And it is light, and light alone, that can convey the one-ness, or the simultaneity of such concepts as goodness, beauty, generosity, truth and divinity, or that can suggest their overwhelming impact on the beholder, and the joy of that impact:[1]

> Sire, nel mondo si vede
> maraviglia ne l'atto che procede
> d'un'anima che 'nfin qua su *risplende*.　　　　xiv, 16–18
>
> ché *luce* de la sua umilitate
> passò li cieli con tanta vertute,
> che fé maravigliar l'etterno Sire　　　　xxv, 21–3
>
> divenne spirital bellezza grande,
> che per lo cielo spande
> *luce* d'amor, che li angeli saluta　　　　xxvii, 22–4
>
> vede una donna, che riceve onore,
> e *luce* sì, che per lo suo *splendore*
> lo peregrino spirito la mira.　　　　xxxvii, 6–8

The three poems of group I (*Voi che 'ntendendo, Voi che savete, Amor che ne la mente*) show very little change or development in their use of tropes with respect to the later poems of the *Vita Nuova*; or, to state the matter a little more precisely, a study of these poems taking the ancient tropes as a starting point would have to proceed along similar lines, and would reach much the same conclusions. There is, however, one apparent exception. These poems were written and interpreted by Dante as *allegories*. His new love is a love of philosophy. Using the conventions of the love poetry written for Beatrice, he is expressing allegorically his early difficulties in the study of philosophy (lxxix, lxxx),[2] and his triumph over them (lxxxi).

---

1 Any proper discussion of Dante's light imagery would start from the *Paradiso*, not the *Vita Nuova*. Here it must suffice to note that there was a rich tradition of light imagery in medieval Christian culture, and that Dante may well have been influenced in particular by its use in Guinizzelli's *Al cor gentile*. We shall return to Beatrice's 'mirabili operazioni' in chapter 4.

2 The difficulties were partly intrinsic—that is, he found certain concepts hard to grasp (lxxx)—and partly purely personal (lxxix): Dante had just interpreted the whole of his early development (in the *prose* of the *Vita Nuova*) as his gradual discovery of the full meaning of Beatrice for him. His new studies seemed to mark a radical *break* with his past, and therefore to be in *conflict* with his earlier culture, personality and ideals.

Now, allegory was a trope.[1] But it would clearly be absurd to approach this kind of allegory from a narrowly rhetorical point of view; and we must therefore take as our plain-base the 'sentenzia litterale' as Dante expounds it (for nos. LXXIX and LXXXI) in the first parts of his commentaries in the *Convivio*[2]. We shall set the allegory on one side; just as we shall continue to set on one side the general, diffuse hyperbole in the *canzone* of praise (LXXXI), and the 'synecdochic' dramatization of the psyche in the poems of conflict (LXXIX, LXXX).[3]

Metonymy is still virtually restricted to the categories of 'effect for cause' or *consequens pro antecedente*.[4] Once again, the dominant tropes

---

[1] 'Allegoria est alieniloquium. Aliud enim sonat, et aliud intellegitur, ut "Tres litore cervos / conspicit errantes" (*Aen.*, I, 184–5). Ubi tres duces belli Punici, vel tria bella Punica significantur. Et in Bucolicis "Aurea mala decem misi" (III, 71), id est ad Augustum decem eglogas pastorum' (*Et.*, I, xxxvii, 22). And cf. Donatus, *Ars maior*, in Keil (ed.), *Grammatici Latini*, vol. IV p. 401; Matthew of Vendôme, III, 43.

'Permutatio est oratio aliud verbis aliud sententia demonstrans. . . . Per similitudinem sumitur *cum translationes plures frequenter ponuntur a simili oratione ductae*, sic: "Nam cum canes funguntur officiis luporum, cuinam praesidio pecuaria credemus" ' (*Ad Her.*, IV, xxxiv, 46). Cf. *PN*, 936–44; *Laborintus*, 381–4.

In Bede's *De schematibus et tropis* (in Halm (ed.), *Rhetores Latini Minores*, p. 617) the definition of *allegoria* takes in all the senses elaborated in scriptural exegesis, and the whole section is remarkably close to *Con.* II, i.

[2] It is worth adding that, unlike the *Vita Nuova*, where much of the prose is poetic in the fullest sense of the word, the prose of the *Convivio* is prosaic and truly 'subietto'. Thus a phrase like:

> un soave penser, che se ne già
> molte fïate a' pie' del nostro Sire   LXXIX, 15–16

will be glossed: 'cio è a dire, che *io pensando contemplava* lo regno de' beati . . . (II, vii, 5).

[3] Note the very different definitions of 'core' and 'anima' from those given for the *Gentil pensero* sonnet in *VN*, xxxviii.

'E da sapere è che in tutta questa canzone...lo "core" si prende per *lo secreto dentro*, e non *per altra spezial parte de l'anima e del corpo*' (II, vi, 2). ' "L'anima" s'intende...per lo *generale pensiero col consentimento*' (II, vii, 8; but in III, iii, 14: 'la mia "anima", cioè lo mio affetto'). Cf. further '... non dico che vegna questo "spirito", cioè questo pensiero...' (II, vi, 9).

[4] Sometimes Dante gives *both* cause *and* effect, for example:

> L'anima *piange* (*sì ancor len dole*)   LXXIX, 30
> che *fa chinare gli occhi* (*di paura*)   LXXX, 6

and in the *VN* poems:

> *Pianger* (di doglia) e *sospirar* (d'angoscia)   XXV, 57

Other simple examples are:
come l'anima trista *piange* in lui, LXXIX, 11; ch' a l'anima gentil *fa dir*: '*Merzede*', LXXX, 10; *trae li sospiri* altrui fora del core, ibid., 12; contra 'l disdegno che *mi dà tremore*, ibid., 28; che 'l cor ne *trema* che di fuori appare, LXXIX, 22; che prendon aire e *diventan sospiri*, LXXXI, 36.

are antonomasia and periphrasis; and again it must be stressed that the examples are in no way Latinate or rhetorical. Under antonomasia we can take the constant 'donna' (LXXIX, 16, 17, 23, 25, 34 etc.), adjectival usages like:

> *questo piatoso* che m'ha consolata.
> De li occhi miei dice *questa affannata*   LXXIX, 32–3

and the simple:

> molte fiate a' piè del *nostro Sire*   LXXIX, 16
> che vien pe' raggi de la *vostra stella*   ibid., 13

While under periphrasis we may distinguish some for God:

> Quei che lel dà   LXXXI, 27
> Chi mosse l'universo   ibid., 72

others for 'li fedeli d'Amore',

> e quella gente che qui s'innamora   ibid., 24
> Voi che savete ragionar d'Amore   LXXX, 1

others for Venus,

> il terzo ciel   LXXIX, 1
> El ciel che segue lo vostro valore   ibid., 4

For other persons or spirits there are,

> *Voi che* 'ntendendo il terzo ciel *movete*   ibid., 1
> *la donna*, di cui dire Amor mi face   LXXXI, 22
> ch'io ci porto entro *quel segnor gentile*
> che m'ha fatto sentir de li suoi dardi   LXXX, 15–16
> *d'un'angela* che 'n cielo è coronata   LXXIX, 29
> *questa* che sente Amor ne gli occhi sui   LXXX, 24
> Or apparisce *chi* lo fa fuggire   LXXIX, 20
> Trova contraro *tal che* lo distrugge   ibid., 27

The only other metonymic usages worthy of note are 'dico ne li occhi e nel suo dolce *riso*' ("bocca") (LXXXI, 57), and, 'udite la ballata mia *pietosa*' (LXXX, 2), which may perhaps be understood as 'per efficientem, id quod efficitur, sicut . . . "timor pallidus", eo quod pallidos homines reddat' (*Et.*, I, xxxvii, 10).

> de' star *colui che* le mie pari ancide   ibid., 37
>
> che non mirasser *tal, ch'*io ne son morta.   ibid., 39

And there are a number of simple periphrases for 'condizione':

> mi tragge ne lo *stato ov'io mi trovo*   ibid., 6
>
> Onde 'l parlar de *la vita ch'io provo*   ibid., 7
>
> ha transmutata in tanto *la tua vita*   ibid., 44

Finally, note that for *body:*

> lo manifesta in *quel ch'ella conduce*   LXXXI, 32

Metaphor again plays a very subordinate role, although it does become a little more important in the last of the three poems, *Amor che ne la mente.* In *Voi che 'ntendendo* and *Voi che savete* it is limited to a few hyperbolic verbs of action:

> Or apparisce chi lo fa *fuggire*
>
> e *segnoreggia* me di tal virtute   LXXIX, 20–1
>
> Trova contraro tal che lo *distrugge*   ibid., 27
>
> de' star colui che le mie pari *ancide*   ibid., 37
>
> che non mirasser tal, ch'io ne son *morta*   ibid., 39
>
> la qual m'ha *tolto* il cor per suo valore   LXXX, 4

and a pair of extremely effective compressions:

> ... tu vedrai
>
> *di sì alti miracoli adornezza*   LXXIX, 49–50
>
> però che intorno a' suoi [*sc.* occhi] sempre *si gira*
>
> *d'ogni crudelitate una pintura*   LXXX, 7–8

In *Amor che ne la mente* we meet the more striking:

> che lo 'ntelletto sovr'esse *disvia*   LXXXI, 4

and:

> che li occhi di color dov'ella *luce*
>
> ne mandan *messi* al cor pien di desiri,
>
> che *prendon aire* e diventan sospiri.   LXXXI, 34–6

There are also two passages in which the metaphor arises from an interchange between the senses:

> Li *atti* soavi ch'ella mostra altrui
>
> vanno *chiamando* Amor *ciascuno a prova*
>
> in quella *voce* che lo fa sentire.   ibid., 45–7

> ma li nostri *occhi* per cagioni assai
> *chiaman* la stella talor tenebrosa.   ibid., 79–80

And a fine climax to the poem is reached with a whole series of metaphors:

> Sua bieltà *piove fiammelle di foco*,
> *animate* d'un spirito gentile
> ch'è *creatore* d'ogni pensier bono;
> e *rompon* come trono
> l'innati vizii che fanno altrui vile.   ibid., 63–7

But one still cannot regard metaphor as an important constituent of Dante's style in this group.

We have seen that hyperbole, synecdoche and allegory could be described as important tropes in Dante's early poetry if these terms are understood in a very general way—as figures of 'thought', rather than figures of 'speech'. But in the doctrinal poems of group J, there is clearly no place for the first two, and Dante deliberately renounced the use of allegory:

> E però che in questa canzone s'intese a rimedio così necessario, non era buono sotto alcuna figura parlare ... Non sarà dunque mestiere ne la esposizione di costei alcuna allegoria aprire, ma solamente la sentenza secondo la lettera ragionare.   *Con.*, IV, i, 10–11

In the absence of these 'figure of thought' tropes, the language becomes almost as *proprium* as it is possible for any work in metre and rhyme to be. Metonymy and synecdoche are almost unknown.[1] Antonomasia has become much less important in the absence of *madonna*,[2] although periphrases of the same simple types are still quite common, being rather more frequent in *Poscia ch' Amor*.

---

[1] Save for *rima*, used in LXXXII, 1, 14, and LXXXIII, 68, as in earlier poems, '*largamente* ... quando ... s'intende per *tutto quel parlare* che 'n numeri e tempo regolato in rimate consonanze cade...' (*Con.*, IV, ii, 12); *tempi* = 'età' in LXXXII, 139; *meo core* = 'me' in LXXXIII, 5; *cor gentile*, ibid., 107; *peccato* = 'vizio', 'cattiva abitudine', ibid. 8.

[2] 'Donna' in LXXXII, 6, 19, 143; 'amica vostra', ibid., 146; 'di cotal valente', ibid., 36; 'merzé d'una gentile', LXXXIII, 62; 'la disviata', ibid., 77; 'gran pianeto', ibid., 96; and 'prenze delle stelle', ibid., 114. 'Leggiadria' is not used in the last two stanzas of LXXXIII, even though it is frequently the subject of the verb.

...chiamo *quel signore*
ch'a la mia donna ne li occhi dimora · LXXXII, 18–19

e *altri* fu di più lieve savere · ibid., 25

Ma vilissimo sembra, a *chi* 'l ver guata · ibid., 38

quei c'han tal grazia fuor di tutti rei · ibid., 115

è ne la *prima etate* · ibid., 126

poi ne *la quarta parte* de la vita · ibid., 136

contemplando *la fine che l'aspetta* · ibid., 138

tu sarai / *in parte dove* sia la donna nostra · ibid., 142–3

Tale imperò... · ibid., 21

...*chi* tenne impero · ibid., 45

valore, / *per lo qual* veramente omo è gentile[1] · ibid., 12–13
credon potere
capere là *dove li boni stanno,*
che dopo morte *fanno*
riparo ne la mente
a *quei cotanti c'hanno canoscenza* · LXXXIII, 21–5

...*la gente*
c'hanno falso iudicio in lor sentenza · ibid., 30–1

...*una gentile*
che la mostrava in tutti gli atti sui · ibid., 62–3

negata là 'v'è *più vertù richesta,*
cioè in *gente onesta*
di *vita spiritale*
o in *abito che di scienza tiene*[2] · ibid., 79–82

Eo giuro *per colui*
ch'Amor si chiama ed è pien di salute · ibid., 70–1

che dal levante
avante in fino a tanto che s'asconde · ibid., 97–8

non moveriano il piede / per donneare... · ibid., 51–2

...vanno a pigliar villan diletto · ibid., 54

---

[1] Note how much more pointed this is than 'gentilezza', when Dante is going to begin by refuting false opinions. And he himself explains why he did not use 'emperor': '... non dicendo "imperadore", ma, "quelli che tenne imperio", a mostrare ... questa cosa determinare essere fuori d'imperiale officio' (*Con.*, IV, x, 5).

[2] This is the most complex yet encountered.

Metaphors on the other hand are slightly more frequent, and a little more varied. There are quite a number which we might classify as *a corpore ad animum.*

Le dolci rime d'amor ch' i' solia	
cercar ne' miei pensieri,	
convien ch'io *lasci*; non perch' io non speri,	
ad esse *ritornare*,	
ma perché li atti...	
... m'han *chiusa la via*	
de l'usato parlare.	LXXXII, 1–8
diporrò giù lo mio soave stile	ibid., 10
Di retro da costui *van* tutti quelli	ibid., 29
cui è *scorto* 'l *cammino* e poscia l'*erra*,	
e tocca a tal, ch'*è morto* e *va* per terra![1]	ibid., 39–40
e da lor *mi rimovo*	ibid., 77
onde l'*animo* ch'è *dritto* e verace	
per lor *discorrimento* non si *sface*	ibid., 59–60
Per che a 'ntelletti sani[2]	ibid., 74
che lo 'ntelletto cieco non la vede	LXXXIII, 44
onde lor ragion par che sé offenda	LXXXII, 65
conven che di sé vesta	
l'un bene e l'altro male	LXXXIII, 86–7
... e fuggiriano il danno,	
che si aggiugne a lo 'nganno	ibid., 28–9
che leggiadria / disvia cotanto...	ibid., 59–60
sarà vertù o con vertù s'annoda	ibid., 76

Then there is a small group in which there is a transference from 'man' to 'abstractions'.

L'*anima* cui *adorna* esta bontate...
e sua persona *adorna* di bieltate...
ché dal principio ch'al corpo *si sposa*...
a Dio si *rimarita*...

---

[1] Dante defends the paradox: 'Onde è da sapere che *veramente* morto lo malvagio uomo dire si puote...' (*Con.*, IV, vii, 10).

[2] 'E dico "sani" non sanza cagione. Onde è da sapere che lo nostro intelletto si può dir sano e infermo...' (*Con.*, IV, xv, 11).

... in lealtà far *si diletta*...
e 'n se medesma *gode* / d'udire...
e *benedice* li tempi passati   LXXXII, 121–41
                  (with some lines transposed)

[il sole] mai non *sen dole*   LXXXIII, 116

ma l'uno e l'altro in ciò *diletto tragge*   ibid., 120

lo qual [*sc.* abito] *dimora* in mezzo solamente   LXXXII, 87

... u' la vertù *dimora*   LXXXIII, 16

And there is a further small group (all common), 'from things to man':

vien da una *radice*   LXXXII, 82

... *seme* di felicità   ibid., 119

... e non responde
il lor *frutto* a le *fronde*   LXXXIII, 104–5

che paiono *animai* sanza intelletto.   ibid., 57

But metaphor is still not an important element in Dante's style at this stage. Here, as in the previous poems, all the metaphors are conventional and conceptual: none make any appeal to the senses. More important still, it is comparatively rare to find three words used metaphorically in any given context—let alone three metaphors drawn from a common source. The sequence of ideas, and the course of the argument are still determined by logic.[1]

The two regular *canzoni* (*Io son venuto* and *Così nel mio parlar*) written for the 'donna petra' offer a dramatic contrast. It is scarcely too much to say that their language is deliberately and predominantly tropological. And this is the consequence or cause of two facts which we have already noted: the abstract *content* of the poems is by no means unlike that of many other courtly lyrics, which describe the torments of unrequited love; but the *vocabulary* is radically different. And since the new words, which are here used to express the substantially similar feelings and ideas, are also concrete and particular, they must neces-

---

[1] Among the exceptions, note no. XI where the assault and occupation by Love is sustained—although Dante never seeks to bring out the military idea; no. XII (*perir, moia moia, ancide, morta, morte*); no. XXXV (*scritto*—molte *parole*); the opening of LXXXII, with its verbs of movement; lines 52–60 of that poem, in which the 'animo dritto' of line 59 seems to pick up the '*diritta* torre' of line 54, and where there is a lesser parallel between 'corre' (55) and 'discorrimento' (60).

sarily be used in extended senses: that is, they must be used tropologically.

The two *can̄oni* are, however, very different one from another. In *Io son venuto*, periphrasis becomes what we have called a 'figure of thought' trope. For what the poem does is to express no less than five times the proposition that 'my love is so great that I burn with love even in the coldest, most unpropitious season'. But since the periphrases are also descriptions, we shall examine them in proper detail in chapter 8, and treat them in the meantime as part of the plain-base, or 'sentenza litterale'.

Periphrasis of the elementary kind found in earlier poems is important also; but if we examine those in the first stanza, we shall find that they differ from those in earlier poems in at least three important respects. First, they do not blur or conceal, but declare and make precise. Second, the objects or phenomena which they convey through description are of a totally different kind—successively, conjunction ('al punto de la rota che' ...), sunset ('quando il sol si corca'), the constellation of Gemini ('il geminato cielo'), Venus ('la stella d'amor'), Saturn ('quel pianeta che conforta il gelo'), part of the ecliptic ('lo grand'arco'), planet ('ciascun di sette'). Thirdly, they derive vigour and force from a series of isolated verb-metaphors, most of which are quite without precedent in Dante's earlier poems: the verbs are 'coricarsi', 'partorire', 'inforcare', 'farsi velo', 'confortare', 'disgombrare'. Together, periphrases and metaphors generate something quite new:

> Io son venuto al punto de la rota
> che l'orizzonte, quando il sol si corca,
> ci partorisce il geminato cielo,
>   e la stella d'amor ci sta remota
> per lo raggio lucente che la 'nforca
> sì di traverso, che le si fa velo;
>   e quel pianeta che conforta il gelo
> si mostra tutto a noi per lo grand'arco
> nel qual ciascun di sette fa poca ombra:
> e però non disgombra
> un sol penser d'amore, ond'io son carco,
> la mente mia, ch'è più dura che petra
> in tener forte imagine di petra.   c, 1–13

The opening of the second stanza is perhaps more remarkable for its *proprietas* (with the exception of the 'vento *peregrino*', and 'chiude e *salda*'); and this renders all the more striking the metaphor *ab homine* in line 22, which in effect re-expresses the sense of the two preceding lines:

> e poi si solve, e cade in bianca falda
> di fredda neve ed in noiosa pioggia,
> onde l'aere *s'attrista tutto e piagne*.   c, 20–2

The following stanza again makes frequent use of elementary periphrasis.[1] The fifth stanza, like the second, begins with devastating propriety; but then it sustains, if unobtrusively, a number of metaphors drawn from warfare.[2] In general, one could say that the most important 'figure-of-*speech*' tropes in *Io son venuto* are synecdoche,[3] periphrasis,[4] and not infrequent but isolated metaphor.[5]

In *Così nel mio parlar*, metaphor is at once more important and more sustained. What is most striking about the poem, in this context, is that it develops and particularizes the ancient image of love as a violent *contest* between man and woman, without any diminution in its power following a decline into wit or self-conscious artifice. This imagery falls into three distinct sections. In the first, the man and the woman both attack and defend, but the woman's onslaught is overwhelming. In the second, Love stands like a victorious gladiator over his prostrate victim, threatening to dispatch him at any moment. In the third, the poet dwells on the 'counterattack' which he is planning in the unrestricted freedom of his overheated imagination.

---

[1] ogne *augel che 'l caldo segue*, 27; del *paese* d'Europa, che *non perde/le sette stelle gelide* unquemai, 28, 29; *posto* a le lor voci *triegue*, 30; infino al *tempo verde*, 31; donna... c'ha picciol tempo, 39; *per cagion di guai*, 32; tutti li *animali che son gai*, 33.

[2] del verno il grande *assalto*, 58; la freddura che *di fuor la serra*, 61; e io de la mia *guerra* / non son però *tornato un passo a retro*, 62–3.

[3] la mente mia, 12; tollerar la *brina*, 48; *al bel giorno*, 56; per questi *geli*, 69; fia per *core un marmo*, 72.

[4] Apart from those already quoted: Passato hanno lor termine le fronde, 40; la vertù d'Ariete, 41; alcun che sua verdura serba, 45; ch'io sarò in vita, 52; l'altro / dolce tempo novello, 66–7; un uom di marmo, 71.

[5] Apart from those already noted: Amor, che sue *ragne* / *ritira* in alto, 23–4; *Fuggito* è ogne augel, 27; son d'amor *disciolti*, 34; 'l freddo lor spirito *ammorta*, 35; li dolzi pensier non mi son *tolti*, 37; ramo... a noi s'*asconde*, 43; *spina* / però Amor di cor non la mi *tragge*, 49–50; cammino... ora è *fatto* rivo, 56–7; l'acqua *morta* si converte in *vetro*, 60; *piove* / amore in terra; 67–8.

To appreciate the novelty of the first section, we should first re-read the following lines from Dante's early sonnet *Con l'altre donne:*

> ché Amor, quando sì presso a voi mi trova,
> prende baldanza e tanta securtate,
> che fere tra' miei spiriti paurosi,
> e quale ancide, e qual pinge di fore,
> sì che solo remane a veder vui   XI, 7–11

By contrast, the 'two-sided' battle in the first stanza of *Così nel mio parlar* is more explicit and more fully elaborated. Note in particular the concern for symmetry. Both parties are shown as attacking with arrows ('*saetta*' ... '*colpi mortali*, che, com'avesser *ali*'); and each defends itself with armour and by taking evasive action, the woman successfully ('*veste* sua persona d'un *diaspro*' ... '*ella s'arretra*'), the man unsuccessfully ('si *chiuda*' ... '*spezzan ciascun'arme*' ... '*non trovo scudo*' ... 'si *dilunghi*' ... '*né loco che m'asconda*'):

> e *veste* sua persona d'un *diaspro*
> tal, che per lui, o perch'ella s'*arretra*,
> non esce di *faretra*
> *saetta* che già mai la *colga ignuda*:
> ed ella *ancide*, e non val ch'om *si chiuda*
> né si *dilunghi* da' *colpi mortali*,
> che, com'avesser ali,
> *giungono* altrui e spezzan ciascun'*arme*;
> sì ch'io non so da lei né posso atarme.
>   Non trovo *scudo* ch'ella non mi *spezzi*
> né *loco* che dal suo viso m'*asconda*   CIII, 5–15

Here the metaphors are kept up without break for eleven lines. In the second section, the image of love as gladiatorial victor is sustained, with intervals, over fully twenty lines; and the scene is much more clearly visualized and pictorial.

> E' m'ha percosso in terra, e stammi sopra
> con quella spada ond'elli ancise Dido,
> Amore, a cui io grido
> merzé chiamando, e umilmente il priego;
> ed el d'ogni merzé par messo al niego.
>   Egli alza ad ora ad or la mano, e sfida
> la debole mia vita, esto perverso,

> che disteso a riverso
> mi tiene in terra d'ogni guizzo stanco: CIII, 35–43

> Elli mi fiede sotto il braccio manco
> sì forte, che 'l dolor nel cor rimbalza ibid., 48–9

The third section offers a fantasy of erotic violence which has all the more impact because it no longer draws its images from ritualized or formalized modes of combat. Dante sees himself as a 'cave-man' dragging his tormentor off by her hair, playing with her as roughly as a sportive bear, and then (we presume) having his will of her:

> S'io avessi le belle trecce prese,
> che fatte son per me scudiscio e ferza...

> e non sarei pietoso né cortese,
> anzi farei com'orso quando scherza...

> e poi le renderei con amor pace. CIII, 66–7,
> 70–1, 78

Nor have we by any means exhausted the imagery of *Così nel mio parlar*. And a further comparison with the *VN* poems will demonstrate the new urgency of Dante's metaphorical language in the lines which represent the effects of Love on his mind and body. The earlier poems were rarely more forceful or precise than in the following lines:

> Però quando [Amore] mi tolle sì 'l valore,
> che li *spiriti* par che fuggan via,
> allor sente la frale *anima* mia
> tanta dolcezza, che 'l *viso* ne smore XXIV

Against these, set the following:

> Ché più mi *triema* il *cor* qualora io penso
> di lei in parte ov'altri *li occhi* induca,
> per tema non *traluca*
> lo mio *penser* di fuor sì che si scopra,
> ch'io non fo de la morte, che ogni *senso*
> co li *denti* d'Amor già mi *manduca*;
> ciò è che 'l *pensier bruca*
> la lor vertù, sì che n'allenta l'opra. CIII, 27–34

With the exception of the rhyme-sounds -*uca* and -*opra*, of the elegant '*indurre* li occhi', and the metaphor in 'tralucere', the opening four lines might conceivably have appeared in the *VN* poems—at least as far as their vocabulary is concerned. But the 'denti—manducare —brucare' sequence would have been quite unthinkable! And in the continuation, ten lines below, it is once again the combination of more 'corporeal' parts of the body ('sangue', 'vene', 'braccio') with verb-metaphors ('*surgon*... strida'!, ' 'l sangue *fuggendo corre* ...', ' 'l dolor... *rimbalza*') which transform the whole passage to such an extent, that we scarcely recognize it as something continuous with the earlier poetry:

> allor mi *surgon* ne la mente *strida*;
> e 'l *sangue*, ch'è per le vene disperso,
> *fuggendo corre* verso
> lo cor, che 'l chiama; ond'io rimango bianco.
> Elli mi fiede sotto il *braccio* manco
> sì forte, che 'l dolor nel *cor rimbalza*   CIII, 44–9

The following brief *allegoria* is also worth noting, partly as further evidence of Dante's new power to sustain a metaphor, and partly for its interesting mixture of 'proper' and 'improper' elements:

> Ahi angosciosa e dispietata *lima*
> che sordamente la mia vita *scemi*,
> perché non ti ritemi
> sì di *rodermi* il core *a scorza a scorza*,
> com'io di dire altrui chi ti dà forza?   CIII, 22–6

Note also how a simile suggests a metaphor in the following:

> Cotanto del mio mal par che si prezzi
> quanto legno di mar che non lieva onda;
> e 'l *peso* che m'*affonda*...[1]   ibid., 18–20

Other vivifying metaphors include:

[1] This kind of 'spontaneous birth' is not, however, characteristic of the 'petrose'-group. Although the metaphors are now sustained, they are still clearly ornaments on a logical base. The only real exception is in the opening of the sestina (CI), where, as Contini notes, each of the italicized words seems to suggest its successors:
> 'Al poco giorno e al gran cerchio d'ombra
> son giunto, lasso, ed al *bianchir* de' colli,
> quando si perde lo *color* ne l'*erba*:
> e 'l mio disio però non *cangia* 'l *verde*,
> sì è *barbato* ne la *dura petra*
> che parla e sente come fosse donna.'

Morte m'avrà *chiuso*	51
Così vedess'io lui *fender* per mezzo	
lo core a la crudele che 'l mio *squatra*!	53–4
Omè perché non *latra* / per me...[1]	59–60
...le belle trecce...	
che fatte son per me *scudiscio* e *ferẓa*	66–7
e *dàlle* per lo cor d'una *saetta*	82

As one would expect, periphrasis has become less important,[2] whilst the antonomasiae have acquired real bite.[3] So too have the metonymies, which are no longer limited to the *consequens pro antecedente* species.[4]

The *canẓone*, *Tre donne*, is the only poem among those chosen which bears any resemblance to the most familiar kind of allegorical composition, in which various virtues and vices are represented by female figures. But, as so often in Dante, one notes a general resemblance to a traditional feature only in order to call attention to his individual handling of the convention. So, in this case, we soon discover that the three ladies whom he introduces represent not three different virtues, but three different aspects of the one virtue, *justice*. It is the reader's task to ascertain their precise identities, which he must infer from the allegorical description of their relationship to each other. And this must surely be the most elaborate and the most intrinsically difficult of all the concepts to be 'signified indirectly' in Dante's lyric poetry.[5]

The meaning conveyed allegorically by the action of the poem as a whole is, however, perfectly clear, even if it is extremely difficult to

---

[1] *Latrare* ('adlatrari') is given in an example of metaphor as early as Quintilian (VIII vi, 9).

[2] Periphrasis: *la mia vita* scemi, 23; sfida / la debole *mia vita*, 40–1; *chi* ti dà forza, 26; *in parte ov'* altri li occhi induca ,28; sotto il braccio manco, 48; a *quella* donna / che m'ha ferito il core, 79–80; *quello* ond' io ho più gola, 81.

[3] Antonomasia: a la crudele, 54; questa scherana micidiale e latra, 58; nel caldo borro, 60:

[4] Metonymy: ond'io rimango bianco, 47; legno (= 'ship'), 19; con esse passerei *vespero* e *squille*, 69; tanto dà nel *sol* quanto nel *reẓẓo*, 57; quello ond' io ho più *gola*, 81. In terms of the allegory, the three ladies are mother, daughter and granddaughter. Each successive birth was, however, a *virgin* birth. In other words, the essence of the relationship is that the second derives from the first, and the third from the second, without the intervention or admixture of any other principle. And this being so, the most convincing interpretation is that given by Dante's son, Pietro, in the course of a note to *Inf.* VI, 73 where he identifies the ladies as *jus divinum ac naturale, jus gentium sive humanum, lex.* See Foster-Boyde, *Dante's Lyric Poetry*, vol. II, p. 287.

formulate without recourse to Dante's own imagery. The first and simplest proposition is that Dante has been *unjustly* exiled from Florence, and that he prefers to remain in exile, rather than be party to any *unjust* settlement. But there is also a wider and more important claim; namely, that his exile was not an isolated act of injustice, but just one example of an injustice that is universal.

Now, what Dante actually says is that justice, personified as the three ladies, has been driven out and *exiled* from human society. What he has done, therefore, is to take terms that can be used *properly* of his own case, and apply them *in a transferred sense* to the general situation. Or, to put it another way, the terminology of the two propositions is identical; but in the first case it is used 'properly', in the second, 'tropologically'.

The same transference will be found in the poem's conclusion, where Dante affirms his conviction that, in the fullness of time, justice will be restored, and consoles himself meantime with the thought that his cause is just. What he actually says is that the ladies will return from 'exile', and that in the company of such noble 'refugees', he considers his own exile not a disgrace but an honour. All this is said in precisely the same kind of terms with which he expresses—'properly' this time—the hope that he will one day be allowed to return to his beloved Florence. The interpenetration of proper and tropological language is unique here, because it is grounded in unique circumstances; and I think it does much to explain the poem's lasting fascination. The allegorical passages have the urgency and immediacy of lived experience; the 'proper' passages take on a splendour and nobility from a context in which Dante's exile is itself the type or figure of the exile of justice.

We must now set the general allegory of *Tre donne* on one side, and pass on to examine the figure-of-speech tropes as they appear word by word and phrase by phrase. To do justice to the facts at this humbler level we must divide the poem into two distinct parts, lines 1–72, and lines 73–107. The first four stanzas (lines 1–72) are given over mostly to the general allegory, and they make a rather conventional and sparing use of tropes. The only phrases that stand out in any way are the metaphors in:

> il nudo braccio, *di dolor colonna*,
> sente l'*oraggio* che cade dal volto   CIV, 22–3

and in:

> Oh di pochi *vivanda*   ibid., 31

and also the periphrasis for the torrid zone (and, more narrowly, for the Earthly Paradise):

> quivi dove 'l gran lume
> toglie a la terra del vinco la fronda:[1]   ibid., 47–8

But the fifth stanza is more densely tropological than any passage we have yet encountered. Heightening the *sententiae*, antitheses and personification, we find the following tropes:

	ché, se giudizio o forza di destino
metonymy	vuol pur che il *mondo* versi
metaphors (flower and colour)	i *bianchi fiori* in *persi*,
catachresis	*cader* co' buoni è pur di lode degno.
periphrasis	E se non che *de gli occhi miei 'l bel segno*
(inc. metaphor and synecdoche)	
metaphor (just): synecdoche	per lontananza m'è *tolto* dal *viso*,
metaphor	che m'have in *foco miso*,
metaphor	*lieve* mi conterei ciò che m'è *grave*.
metaphor	Ma questo *foco* m'have
metaphor, synecdoche	già *consumato* sì l'*ossa* e la *polpa*
synecdoche:	che Morte *al petto* m'ha *posto la chiave*.
periphrasis (inc. metaphor)	
	Onde, s'io ebbi colpa,
metonymy	più *lune* ha volto *il sol* poi che fu *spenta*,
(periphrasis); metaphor	
metaphor	se colpa *muore* perché l'uom si penta.

>   CIV, 77–90

---

[1] Other tropes in the first four stanzas are:

Metaphor: più nel dolor s'*accese*, 43; di fonte *nasce* il Nilo, 46; l'uno e l'altro *dardo*, 59; l'armi, 61...per *non usar*...son *turbate*, 62; questo *dardo* farà star *lucente*, 72; se noi siamo or *punti*, 70.

Periphrasis: 'l possente segnore, / dico quel ch'è nel core, 6–7; in parte che il tacere è bello, 28; son suora a la tua madre, 35; sovra la vergin onda, 49; Drizzate i colli, 60; sono a' raggi di cotal ciel giunti, 68; noi, che semo de l'etterna rocca, 69.

Antonomasia: lo mio segnore, 39; gran lume, 47; le germane, 58; l'etterna rocca, 69; alti dispersi, 75.

Metonymy: (limited to 'effects for cause') voce con *sospiri* mista, 32; sì di *pianger* pronta, 41; fenno i *sospiri* Amore un poco tardo; / e poi con gli *occhi molli*, 55–6; *piangano* gli *occhi* e dolgasi la *bocca*, 66.

F   149

The poem has two 'tornate' or 'congedi', and both of them make use of extended metaphor. The most striking and the most original is certainly the second, in which Dante sends his poem to find and conciliate his enemies and pursuers, the Black, and now also the White Guelph factions, who are imaged as falcons and greyhounds:

> Canzone, *uccella* con le *bianche penne*;
> canzone, *caccia* con li *neri veltri*,
> che fuggir mi convenne ...   ibid., 101–3

But the first 'tornata', although apparently more conventional, is of considerable interest, because there are several indications that Dante is here composing 'poetically'. First, we note that the image of a 'bella donna' (the allegorical or inner meaning) and her 'panni' (the literal or outer meaning) was probably suggested by the description of 'Drittura' in the second stanza:

> discinta e scalza, e sol di sé par donna.
> Come Amor prima per la rotta gonna
> la vide in parte che il tacere è bello ...   ibid., 26–8

But, as we have seen, the allegorical meaning of those lines was quite different. Second, the image of beauty adorned, and beauty *un*adorned, is an ambivalent one in Dante. It can express or symbolize different oppositions, and convey differing emotional emphases. For example, in the course of his defence of 'Italian' prose in the first book of the *Convivio*, Dante uses the image with much the same emotional charge as here. The 'natural' beauty of a language consists in its 'bontate', in its power to give adequate and fitting expression to lofty concepts; and this 'bontate' is best judged in prose, when it is 'da tutto accidentale adornamento discompagnata' (*Con.*, I, x, 13). The beauty of verse— 'cioè la rima e lo ritimo e lo numero regolato' (ibid., 12)—is precisely the kind of 'accidentale adornamento' which often wins more admiration than the actual beauty of the person so adorned.[1] In the second book of the *Convivio*, however, when making a similar distinction between the 'bontade' and the 'bellezza' of *Voi che 'ntendendo*, the emphasis falls on the poem's beauty as something positive. It is unfortunate that some people will be unable to understand the poem;

---

[1] '... sì come non si può bene manifestare la bellezza d'una donna, quando li adornamenti de l'azzimare e de le vestimenta la fanno più ammirare che essa medesima' (*Con.*, I, x, 12).

but let them nevertheless take delight in its beauty. 'Ponete mente almen com'io son bella!'[1] Further, it is most unusual for Dante to speak slightingly of 'rima', 'ritimo' and 'numero regolato', since it is the verbal harmony of poetry which he regards as its chief and distinctive feature.[2] And, in any case, he must have been extremely and justifiably proud of the 'panni' of this particular poem. We must therefore be careful not to commit ourselves to any narrow or one-sided paraphrase of this 'tornata':

> Canzone, a' panni tuoi non ponga uom mano,
> per veder quel che bella donna chiude:
> bastin le parti nude;
> lo dolce pome a tutta gente niega,
> per cui ciascun man piega.
> Ma s'elli avvien che tu alcun mai truovi
> amico di virtù, ed e' ti priega,
> fàtti di color novi,
> poi li ti mostra; e 'l fior, ch'è bel di fori,
> fa' disïar ne li amorosi cori.   CIV, 91–100

Note, further, how, within the 'tornata' itself, the '*fior* ch'è bel di fori' of line 99 seems to have been suggested by 'lo dolce *pome*' of line 95. On a first reading, we probably understood 'pome' as a familiar, metaphorical euphemism for the 'parte che il tacere è bello' (line 28). But the two terms together adumbrate a second image-cluster— 'blossom and fruit'—which is very much relevant to the first. And, finally, note now the line 'fàtti di color novi' is appropriate to both images—spring *blossom*, or festive *clothes*.

In the remaining poems—*Doglia mi reca* and the sonnets addressed to Cino—we find certain passages which, if they had not existed, would have to have been 'invented', so well do they supply a link between the use of metaphor in the *Inferno* and that in the 'canzoni petrose'.

In the *canzone* one feels for the first time that extensive sections were actually *conceived* in figurative language, and that the argument was influenced or even shaped by association and metaphor—that is at a poetic and not a logical level. This is a development of the utmost importance. It means that a metaphor cannot be studied within the confines of a single clause or sentence, nor within the bounds of a

---

[1] LXXIX, 61; *Con.*, II, xi, 8–10.   [2] See below, chapter 5.

'tornata'. It means that extended metaphor is no longer convertible element by element into a neat and consistent paraphrase. It means that metaphor can no longer be analysed as an 'improper' term used to replace—*ornatus causa*—the obvious and pre-existent 'proper' term. It means that *metaphor is no longer a trope*. The metaphorical element in the *canzone* therefore requires a very different kind of analysis, and this will be attempted in a more appropriate place in the final chapter.

In the sonnets addressed to Cino the development is of a very different kind. The metaphors here may still be analysed as tropes, but they are individually more ambitious than any we have yet examined, and they present real obstacles to the understanding. The difficulties are of three sorts: the words are unfamiliar in themselves; the metaphors are drawn from fields which are relatively unfamiliar; and the point of contact between the proper and the metaphorical term is not always self evident. For the first time, we see why Geoffrey should describe the product of metaphor and metonymy as an 'ornata *difficultas*'. And perhaps the best way to approach them is via a passage in the *Poetria Nova*, where Geoffrey warns against the danger of obscurity or unintelligibility following the abuse of these tropes:

> Si niti gravitate velis, his utere velis.
> Hunc portum teneas, hic fixa sit anchora mentis.
> Sic tamen esto gravis ne res sub nube tegatur,
> Sed faciant voces ad quod de jure tenentur.
> Quae clausum reserent animum sunt verba reperta,
> Ut quaedam claves animi: qui vult aperire
> Rem clausam, nolit verbis inducere nubem;
> Si tamen induxit, facta est injuria verbis:
> Fecit enim de clave seram. Sis claviger ergo,
> Rem citius verbis aperi. Si namque per aures
> Intrat in aspectus animi sine luce loquela,
> In fluvio fundat, in sicco plantat, in aura
> Verberat, in sterili sulcum deducit arena.
> *Si qua feras igitur peregrina vel abdita verba,*
> *Quid possis ex hoc ostendis* jusque loquendi
> Non attendis.   *PN*, 1,061–76

The last lines of this passage provide the key: Dante is quite definitely setting out to show 'what he can do'; and the prime source of the difficulty lies in the *peregrina verba*. The tropes in question come only in the three sonnets which are replies *per le rime* to inquiries by Cino, and they are the direct result of Dante's exceptionally whole-hearted acceptance of the challenge offered by this convention. Circumscribed not only by the normal difficulties of the sonnet-form, but also by the need to use the same rhyme-sounds employed by Cino, Dante imposes on himself the additional restriction of using only *rare* words with these sounds. Thus, the rare rhymes ('rimas caras') imply the use of *peregrina verba*, which must almost inevitably be used in transferred senses. And the other sources of difficulty follow with equal inevitability from the first.

Let us exemplify first the rarity of the rhyme words. In *I'ho veduto* (XCV, 1–8) we meet:[1] radice, *elice, *contradice, *notrice; *gagliardo, *lombardo, *riguardo, *bugiardo. In *Io sono stato* (CXI): insieme, geme, *sprieme, *sceme; *nona, *sprona, sona, tona; *palestra, *balestra, *addestra; *franco, *fianco, stanco. In *Degno fa voi* (CXIII): tesoro, *foro, *poro, *discoloro; *latina, *disvicina, *medicina, s'affina; fronte, conte, *ponte; poia, *croia, *ploia. More than two-thirds of these had not been used at all (let alone in rhyme) in earlier groups, and nearly half seem truly rare in the sense that one would not find words of that type in the earlier poems.

As regards the unfamiliar *sources*, we find images drawn from classical mythology (XCV, 3–4), from astronomy (CXI, 2), from meteorology (CXI, 6–8), from botany (XCV, 1–8), from medicine (CXIII, 5–8, 9–11), and from 'sports', including archery (CXIII, 4–5), the hunt (XCV, 14) and equestrianism (CXI, 3–4, 9–14), as well as others of the familiar *ab homine* type.

And finally, as regards the difficulty of comprehension, there are no passages elsewhere in Dante's poems that are so difficult on tropological grounds as the opening of XCV, the close of CXI, or the second quatrain of CXIII, which will serve as our final example.[2]

> Io che trafitto sono in ogni poro
> del prun che con sospir si medicina,
> pur trovo la minera in cui s'affina
> quella virtù per cui mi discoloro.   CXIII, 5–8

---

[1] Those not used in earlier groups are marked with an asterisk.

[2] Here, for the sake of completeness, is a list of the tropes in all five sonnets:
Metaphor: XCV: per omor tanto *gagliardo*, 2; sarìa *bugiardo* / sapor non fatto da *vera notrice*, 7–8; ... a dentro è *gita*... è stata la *partita*, 10–11; la tua *caccia* non *seguer*

de', 14; XCVI: 'l ben non trova chi *albergo* li *doni*, 8; 'l ben è si poco *ricolto*, 14; CXI: come [Amore] *affrena* e come *sprona*, / e come *sotto* lui..., 3–4; le *guerre* de' vapori *sceme*, 8; nel *cerchio* de la sua *palestra* / libero arbitrio già mai non fu *franco*, / ... invan vi si balestra / ... con nuovi *spron punger* lo fianco, / ...piacer che ora n'*addestra*, / *seguitar* si convien, se l'altro è *stanco*, 9–14. CXIII: *stecco* d'Amor mai non *fé foro* 4; io che *trafitto* sono in ogni *poro*, 5; del prun che con sospir si *medicina* / pur trovo la *minera*, 6–7; de gli occhi *ploia*, 12; non mi *porreste di sospetto in ponte*, 14; CXIV: esser *partito* / da queste nostre rime, ... 1–2; ...altro cammino / a la mia *nave* più lungi dal *lito*, 3–4; che *pigliar* vi lasciate a ogni *uncino*, 6; ... e sé *lega* e *dissolve*, 10; Amor leggermente il *saetti*, 11.

Catachresis: XCVI: li nostri *diri*, 13; CXI: chi ragione o virtù contra gli *sprieme*, 5; le guerre ... *sceme*, 8; 'l piacer (= 'bella persona',) 13; CXIII: la voce sì dolce e *latina*, 2.

Metonymy: XCVI: che per lui *sospiri*, 10; CXIII: con *sospir* si medicina, 6; per cui mi *discoloro*, 8; CXI: e come sotto lui si *ride* e *geme*, 4; CXIII: la *voce* vostra (poetry), 2; *stecco* d'Amor (= 'dardo'), 4.

Synecdoche: XCV: legno (= tree), 2; CXIII: volgibile *cor* ven disvicina, 3; CXIV: leggier *cor* così vi volve, 12; CXIII: se l'orba fronte (= 'occhi ciechi',) 9; CXIV: da queste nostre *rime*, 2; a questa penna lo stancato *dito*, 8.

Periphrasis: XCV: che que' che vide (Sun) nel fiume lombardo (Po) / cader suo figlio (Phaethon), 3–4; XCVI: del signor a cui siete voi ed io, 2; donna non ci ha ch'Amor le venga al volto, 9; CXI: Io sono stato con Amore insieme, 1; da la circulazion del sol mia nona, 2; colà dove si tona, 7; CXIII: del prun che con sospir si medicina, 6; quella virtù per cui mi discoloro, 8; CXIV: piacemi di prestare un pocolino / a questa penna lo stancato dito, 7–8.

CHAPTER 4

ASPECTS OF SENTENCE
STRUCTURE

The periodic sentence is often described as one of the most important, most characteristic, and most enduring collective achievements of Greek and Latin culture.[1] So it is perhaps curious that the ancient theorists offer so little analysis of its structure. But, in fact, the grammarians treated questions of syntax only indirectly in their accounts of the parts of speech or of conjugation and declension; whilst the rhetoricians, true to the nature of their discipline, concerned themselves exclusively with those aspects of syntax which might constitute 'expressive departures' from the 'norm'. Such departures were of two main kinds: on the one hand, the attainment of balance and rhythm; and, on the other, all such potential faults as the grammatical solecism, dislocation of word order, asyndeton and polysyndeton, or the various species of ellipse and pleonasm. The only *structural* terms to be at all widely used were *comma* (*articulus, incisum, caesum*), *colon* (*membrum*) and *periodos* (*continuatio, circuitus*).[2] But although these were defined partly in terms of their meaning, they were felt predominantly as units of *rhythm*. And, in any case, the scheme they offer is hardly a subtle or a comprehensive one. In short, where a rhetorical manual, be it classical or medieval, deals at any length with the structure of the period, most of its space will be devoted to questions of prosody.[3] It will seek to determine which rhythms are to be avoided at all times, which are to be preferred in the opening of a sentence, and which form the most satisfactory cadences—this last being the most fruitful subject of all.

[1] See the works by Norden, Auerbach and Wilkinson cited in the bibliography, and especially the studies by F. Di Capua.
[2] Sometimes *commata* and *cola* are seen as the constituent parts of a *periodos*; at other times the 'legato' sweep of the period is contrasted with the 'staccato' jabs of *commata* or *cola*.
[3] For example, *Orator*, 163–236; Quintilian, IX, iv, 45–147; Capella, V, 517–22; Guido Faba, *Summa dictaminis*, ed. A. Gaudenzi, *Il Propugnatore*, n.s. III (1890), 336–8, 345–8.

Thus the categories and terminology used in this chapter are *not* for the most part founded on rhetorical authorities. But they are nevertheless 'traditional', in the double sense that they are not here distinguished for the first time, and they all derive ultimately from analysis of the literary monuments of the classical languages, made before the development of twentieth-century linguistic science. It is worth adding that the variables to be studied represent only a small fraction of those which have been or could be distinguished. Selection has been largely empirical, but each of the chosen variables will be found to satisfy three demands. It has proved its relevance in existing studies[1] of the syntax of Dante and his contemporaries; it determines some of the general characteristics of a personal style, in the sense given to this notion in the introduction; and the alternatives which it comprises are sufficiently clear-cut to make possible a numerical expression of the findings.

Our first aim will be to reach some assessment of the complexity of Dante's syntax. We shall begin, therefore, by studying the sentence structure in the chosen poems from a purely logical point of view, taking the clause[2] as the minimum unit. We shall establish the pro-

---

[1] G. S. Lisio, *L'arte del periodo nelle opere volgari di Dante Alighieri e del secolo XIII* (Bologna, 1902). B. Terracini, *Stile e lingua della 'Vita Nuova'* (Turin, 1951) (Corso di storia della lingua italiana: cyclostyled). Material from this work appears as: 'Analisi dello stile legato della *Vita Nuova*' and 'Analisi dei toni narrativi della *Vita Nuova* e loro interpretazione', in *Pagine e appunti di linguistica storica* (Florence, 1957), pp. 247–72. But my references are to the original work. C. Segre, 'La sintassi del periodo nei primi prosatori italiani', *RAL*, ser. VIII, IV (1952), 41–193; reprinted in his *Lingua, stile e società* (Milan, 1963), pp. 81–270. My references are to the original article. M. Corti, 'Studi sulla sintassi della lingua poetica avanti lo stilnovo', *AMAT*, XVIII, n.s. IV (1953), and the relevant pages of her studies of Guido and Cino. A. Schiaffini, *Tradizione e poesia*, 2nd ed. (Rome, 1943). L. Malagoli, *Motivi e forme dello stile del Duecento* (Pisa, 1960) (esp. ch. 1 'Paratassi e sensibilità stilistica medievale' and ch. 3 'Ritmo chiuso e aperto', which, in spite of its title, is *not* concerned with rhythm); *Linguaggio e poesia nella D.C.* (Genova, 1949); *Stile e linguaggio nei poeti del '200*, Anno Acc. 1953–4 (Pisa, 1954) (cyclostyled: texts pp. 1–135, discussion pp. 136–313): esp. pp. 265–70. G. Bertoni, 'La prosa della *V.N.* di Dante' (first pub. 1914, now in *Lingua e Cultura* (Florence, 1939), pp. 165–222. A very uneven study). M. Fubini, *Metrica e Poesia*. Vol. I: *Dal Duecento al Petrarca* (Milan, 1962), chs 1–4. E. Auerbach, *Dante als Dichter der irdischen Welt* (Berlin, 1929), translated by R. Manheim as *Dante, Poet of the Secular World*, (Chicago, 1961), ch. 2, 'Dante's Early Poetry' (esp. pp. 29–59 of the English edition).

[2] A *clause* will here be defined, traditionally, as a structure possessing a subject and a predicate. It may be assumed, except where specific exception is made, that a clause contains one verb (and not more than one) in a finite form. 'Non-finite clauses'—that is,

portions of simple and complex sentences,[1] and study the organization of the latter in terms of the number and type of dependent clauses they contain, and also of the role of *sub*-subordination[2] and coordination within the sentence. This section will be completed by a survey of the coordination of sentences and the use of non-finite clauses. Then we shall consider the relationship between syntax and metre; and finally we shall turn to the potentially more expressive aspects of syntax, and consider the order of clauses within the sentence and the order of words within the clause.[3]

A simple but remarkably sensitive index to the complexity of syntactic structures can be obtained by establishing the relative proportions of simple and complex sentences, and by calculating the percentage of complex sentences with three or more dependent clauses. A study of these figures for the various groups within Dante's poems reveals a pattern which will be confirmed and further illuminated as we study each of the other main variables.

In the *VN* poems, simple sentences amount to just over 34 per cent of the total. In the selected later poems, the proportion falls slightly but perceptibly to 30 per cent.[4] This fall in the number of simple sentences, indicating of course a modest increase in complexity, is both confirmed and slightly magnified if we add to the simple sentences those 'complex' sentences with only *one* dependent clause. Together, these sentences with not more than two clauses account for 66 per cent of the total in the *VN* poems but only 57 per cent in the later poems.[5] The same slight difference appears in our other main

---

phrases containing a gerund or participle—are treated as part of their governing finite clause for the main part of the analysis.

[1] A *sentence* is a *free* structure possessing at least one subject and predicate. It may consist of one clause only: in that case it is called a *simple sentence*. It may consist of a 'main' clause accompanied by one or more clauses which are 'dependent' on the main clause (*a complex sentence*). In this chapter, it will be assumed, by definition, that a sentence cannot have more than one main clause. Where the need arises, I shall use the term '*period*' to cover two or more sentences closely linked by coordinating conjunctions.

[2] By *sub*-subordination I mean the subordination of one dependent clause to another dependent clause.

[3] Some readers may wish to pass over the first two-thirds of this chapter and turn straight to p. 187.

[4] In the *VN* poems, 106 simple sentences in a total of 308; in the later poems, 110 in 363.

[5] *VN* poems: 205 in 308; later poems: 206 in 363.

index. In the *VN* poems, only 25 per cent of *complex* sentences have three or more dependent clauses; in the later poems, these amount to nearly 38 per cent.[1]

These key-figures suggest that, on the whole, Dante's syntax is relatively simple, but that there is a general trend to a greater degree of complexity. However, a study of the same figures at group level reveals a different and more interesting story. Represented as a graph, the curve of development might look something like this:

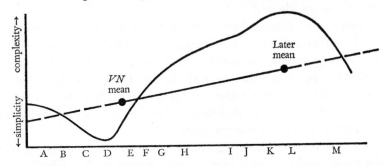

In other words, from a degree of complexity in group A which is close to that of the mean figure for the *VN* poems as a whole, there is a progressive simplification in groups B, C and D. From group E onwards, the syntax is markedly more complex than the relevant average figure, reaching its highest point in group L. In the final group there is a return to the mean level of the later poems. The gap that separates group D and group L is enormous.

Let us consider some of the figures. In group D, the proportion of simple sentences rises from 1 in 3 to 1 in 2 of the total. But in groups F–H that proportion falls to 1 in 4.5; and this low level is maintained, with the exception of group J, until group M, when it falls back to the mean level of slightly less than 1 in 3.[2]

---

[1] *VN* poems: 50 in 202 *complex* sentences; later poems: 95 in 253 *complex* sentences.
[2] Here are the totals for each group:

Groups	Simple	Total		
A	16	51	approx.	1 in 3
B	9	28		1 in 3
C	13	39		1 in 3
D	31	67		1 in 2
E	25	68		1 in 2·5
F	4	18		1 in 4·5

Applying our variant of this first test (that is, adding together the simple sentences and complex sentences with only one dependent clause), we can see the process of simplification beginning even in groups B and C.[1] Sentences with one or two clauses—*including* the main clause—mount from 3 in 5 of the total in group A, to 3 in 4 and 2 in 3 respectively: in group D they reach 5 in 6.

The evidence from the second index is perhaps more equivocal.

G	7	23	1 in 3·5
H	1	14	
VN poems	106	308	
Groups			
I	17	77	1 in 4·5
J	33	91	1 in 3
K	15	57	1 in 4
L	4	24	1 in 6
M	41	114	1 in 2·75
Later poems	110	363	

1

Groups	Sentences with one or two clauses	*Total*	
A	32	51	approx. 3 in 5
B	20	28	3 in 4
C	25	39	2 in 3
D	56	67	5 in 6
E	42	68	2 in 3
F	10	18	1 in 2
G	14	23	2 in 3
H	6	14	1 in 2
VN poems	205 (66%)	308	
Groups			
I	40	77	1 in 2
J	49	91	1 in 2
K	27	57	1 in 2
L	12	24	1 in 2
M	78	114	less than 3 in 4
Later poems	206 (57%)	363	

Although in group D, only one sentence in 67 has three or more dependent clauses, whereas in group I there are 27 in 77, the figures on the whole are closer to the mean.[1] And, as we shall see in due course, the *canzone*, *Donna pietosa*, in group D, makes extensive use of non-finite clauses.

Let us now leave on one side the question of variations and development, and proceed to a more detailed analysis of the structure of Dante's complex sentences, with the particular aim of defining more closely the degree of their complexity. This will obviously be difficult in the absence of comparable figures for other authors. But the variations between one group and another do provide some indication of the possible extremes; and it is obvious that, taken as a whole, the syntax of these poems is neither very simple nor very complex. Certainly, any attempt to place it decisively nearer one pole than the other will call forth an immediate qualification or counter-claim. For example, one might infer the essential simplicity of Dante's syntax from the fact that 75 per cent of all *complex* sentences in the *VN* poems, and 62 per cent of all those in the later poems, have not more than two dependent clauses, that is, three clauses in all.[2] But against this, one

1

	Sentences with more than 3 clauses	Total sentences	No. of clauses in sentences with more than 3 clauses	Total clauses
VN poems	50 (16%)	308	258 (34%)	720
Later poems	95 (27)	363	484 (49)	982
Key-groups				
C	7 (18)	39	31 (35)	89
D	1 (2)	67	7 (5)	128
E	14 (20)	68	78 (48)	165
I	27 (35)	77	128 (58)	221
K	13 (23)	57	77 (46)	167
M	17 (15)	114	87 (32)	268

2

	Complex sentences with 1 and 2 dependents	Total complex sentences
VN poems	152	202
Later poems	158	253

must note that a third of all the *clauses* in the *VN* poems, and half the *clauses* in the later poems, occur in sentences with at least three dependents, that is, at least four clauses in all.[1] Moreover Dante does construct a significant number of sentences with *four* or more dependents, that is, with five or more clauses in all. There are 76 such sentences, constituting 11 per cent of the total.[2]

Complexity cannot, of course, be measured simply in terms of the number of dependent clauses. We need some indication of the 'tightness' or 'coherency' of the structures. For this purpose, we must distinguish those sentences, in which all clauses are dependent on the main clause, from those which contain *sub*-subordinated clauses; and within this latter group we must take into account the number of cases of sub-subordination. Here are examples with one, two and three cases respectively, the *sub*-subordinated clauses being placed in parentheses:

> Ora, s'i' voglio sfogar lo dolore,
> (che a poco a poco a la morte mi mena,)
> convenemi parlar traendo guai. XXV, 4–6

> E perché me ricorda (ch'io parlai
> de la mia donna, [mentre che vivia,]
> donne gentili, volentier con vui),
> non vòi parlare altrui,
> se non a cor gentil che in donna sia; XXV, 7–11

> E quando trova alcun (che degno sia
> di veder lei), quei prova sua vertute,
> ché li avvien, ciò (che li dona), in salute,
> e sì l'umilia, (ch'ogni offesa oblia).[3] XIV, 37–40

[1] See note to p. 160.

[2]

	No. of dependent clauses per sentence							Total
	3	4	5	6	7	8	9	
VN poems	21	16	4	5	3	–	1	50
Later poems	48	22	10	4	7	2	2	95
Total	69	38	14	9	10	2	3	145

[3] If two clauses are sub-subordinated to the *same* dependent clause this does *not* constitute two cases of sub-subordination, e.g. in the last line of this example (beginning in mid-sentence):

> ché 'n sue bellezze son cose vedute

Sub-subordination is extremely common in Dante's poems. Of the complex sentences with the necessary two or more dependent clauses, 70 per cent contain sub-subordinated clauses.[1] In the majority of these sentences (60 per cent), there is only one instance of sub-subordination, and sentences of this type are perhaps hardly distinct from those with none. But 40 per cent do have more than one case, and, as we have seen, a great many clauses appear in sentences of this type.[2] They are certainly typical of Dante's syntax.

> che li occhi di color (dov'ella luce)
> ne mandan messi al cor pien di desiri,
> (che *prendon* aire e *diventan* sospiri).   LXXXI, 33–6

And in the following example, both the 'quando' clause and the 'sì' clause modify the consecutive clause 'che ... io no lo intendo', and thus the sentence is taken to have only two, not three, cases of sub-subordination:

> Vedela tal, che (quando 'l mi ridice),
> io no lo intendo, (sì parla sottile
> al cor dolente), [che lo fa parlare].   XXXVII, 9–11

[1] In the *VN* poems, there are 30 *without*, 73 *with*; in the later poems, 47 *without*, 110 *with*.
[2] The percentage is constant in both the *VN* poems and the later poems: 29 in 73 and 44 in 110. Here is the full break-down:

Sentences with one case of sub-subordination

	with	2	3	4	5		dependents	*Grand totals*
VN poems		27	13	3	1			44
Later poems		29	29	6	2			66
Total		56	42	9	3			110

Sentences with two cases . . .

	with	3	4	5	6	7	8	dependents	
VN poems		6	10	2	2	1	–		21
Later poems		6	12	6	1	2	1		28
Total		12	22	8	3	3	1		49

Sentences with three cases . . .

	with	4	5	6	7		dependents	
VN poems		1	1	3	1			6
Later poems		3	2	1	3			9
Total		4	3	4	4			15

Sentences with four cases . . .

	with	6	7	8	9		dependents	
VN poems		–	1	–	1			2
Later poems		2	2	1	1			6
Total		2	3	1	2			8

There is one sentence with five cases of sub-subordination and nine dependents (CIII, 27–34 quoted below).

Experience suggests that two or more cases of sub-subordination have a pronounced effect on the character of the syntax, but it is impossible to generalize as to the nature of the effect. They may point to an assured mastery of the periodic sentence; they may equally be evidence of 'incompetence', clause after clause being thrust into a dependent role which its meaning will not bear. A great deal depends on the ratio between the number of dependents and the number of cases of sub-subordination, and even more, perhaps, on clause order: the sentence will seem more tightly constructed if the main clause is delayed, than if it stands at the head of the sentence. Here are some examples to illustrate this variety. The first pair are drawn from the same *canzone*, *Quantunque volte*. Analysed in the light of the simple variables we have so far discussed, they are not unalike. In the first sentence, there are four dependent clauses, of which two are sub-subordinated (here placed in parentheses); in the second, there are five dependents and three cases of sub-subordination (here indicated by dashes). But in the first sentence the main verb (*assembra*) is delayed; in the second it occurs at the very beginning (*si volser*). As a result the movement of each sentence is totally different:

> Quantunque volte, lasso, mi rimembra
> (ch'io non debbo già mai
> veder la donna) (ond' io vo sì dolente),
> tanto dolore intorno 'l cor m'*assembra*
> la dolorosa mente,
> ch'io dico ... XXVII, 1–6

> a lei si *volser* tutti i miei disiri,
> quando la donna mia
> fu giunta da la sua crudelitate;
> perché 'l piacere de la sua bieltate,
> partendo sé da la nostra veduta,
> divenne spirital bellezza grande,
> —che per lo cielo spande
> luce d'amor,—che li angeli saluta,
> e lo intelletto loro alto, sottile
> face maravigliar—sì v'è gentile. ibid., 17–26

The next two sentences have the greatest number of clauses in all those analysed. It will be seen that the first, taken from an early sonnet, is the 'looser' or more 'open-ended', in that once sub-subordination has begun, no further clauses are dependent on the main clause. The sentence is given a little bonding and some articulation by the use of coordination (*e ... e ... ma*), but the impression one receives of a forward sprawl is intensified by the fact that all the later clauses are consecutives:

> Se lo saveste, non *poria* Pietate
> tener più contra me l'usata prova,
> ché Amor, (quando sì presso a voi mi trova),
> prende baldanza e tanta securtate,
> —che fere tra' miei spiriti paurosi,
> *e* quale ancide, *e* qual pinge di fore,
> —sì che solo remane a veder vui:
> —ond' io mi cangio in figura d'altrui,
> *ma* non sì ch'io non senta bene allore
> li guai de li scacciati tormentosi.[1]   XI, 5–14

But there is nothing paratactic about the next example taken from the last 'canzone petrosa', although it has not four but five cases of sub-subordination among its nine dependents. This is because all but one of the sub-subordinated clauses are dependent on clauses immediately dependent on the main clause, and because two of them are placed between the main verb (*triema*) and the comparative (*più ... ch'io non fo*) which completes its sense:

> Ché più mi triema il cor qualora io penso
> di lei in parte (ov' altri li occhi induca),
> per tema non traluca
> lo mio penser di fuor (sì che si scopra),

---

[1] The last three lines could be taken as a distinct sentence; and reviewing the passage now, some years after making the original analyses, I would be inclined to treat the initial *onde* as an adverb rather than a subordinating conjunction (see note to p. 181 below). But to correct the analysis now would involve the risk of producing a series of errors in the various tables; and in any case Dante was concerned to stress the consequence.

Malagoli in his *Stile e linguaggio nei poeti del '200*, pp. 265–70, prints a number of examples as typical of the Tuscan school (Meo Abbracciavacca, Lemmo Orlandi, Bonagiunta, Panuccio del Bagno), which have just this kind of 'loose complexity'. He describes them in these terms:

'È una sintassi semplice e frontale che procede per aggiunte, anche se il ragionamento tende a intaccarla; ma non vi riesce, e l'involuzione del periodo conserva dentro di sé questo accento di distacco e questa tendenza alla proposizione frontale' (pp. 265–6).

ch'io non fo de la morte—che ogni senso
co li denti d'Amor già mi manduca;
—cio è che 'l pensier bruca
la lor vertù,—sì che n'allenta l'opra.   CIII, 27–34

Another aspect of the general increase in complexity in the later
poems may be seen in the slight rise in the frequency of coordination
within the complex sentence. In the *VN* poems, such internal coordination occurs in 1 in every 20 sentences: in the later poems in 1 in
9.[1] If one relates the number of instances to the number of sentences
in which such coordination is possible,[2] the ratios become 1 in 4·5, and
1 in 2·75 respectively. The pattern of distribution at group level is
however slightly different, for the usage is evenly diffused in the *VN*
poems and is absent in LXXXIII. But there is still a marked increase in
LXXXI and LXXXII, continuing and reaching a peak in the 'canzoni
petrose', and becoming less frequent in the final group.[3]

It will be noted that I have made no attempt to establish typical
distributions at the level of the strophe. Even with regard to these
simple variables, the variety is too great.[4] There are, however, a few

---

[1] 15 in 308 in the *VN* poems; 42 in 363 in the later poems.

[2] That is, discounting simple sentences; complex sentences with one dependent;
complex sentences with two dependents of which one is sub-subordinated, or with
three dependents of which two are sub-subordinated.

[3]

COORDINATION OF SUBORDINATES

Groups	No. of instances	No. of sentences in which possible	
VN poems	15	67	approx. 1 in 4·5
I	5	34	1 in 5
J	10	26	1 in 2·5
(no. LXXXII)	(10)	(18)	(1 in 2)
K	13	25	1 in 2
L	6	11	1 in 2
(nos CXI,			
CXIII, CXIV)	(6)	(6)	(1 in 1)
M	8	24	1 in 3

[4] This variety can be gauged by comparing the number of sentences with the number of
clauses in a sequence of equal strophes (this ratio being another useful rough guide to
the degree of complexity). Here are the ratios for the first regular sonnets in the *Vita
Nuova*, and for the stanzas of *Tre donne*:

'coincidences' to which it will be worth calling attention. Many critics have noticed that the opening stanzas of the *canʒoni* are the occasions for a display of syntactic virtuosity, and this implies the use of a few complex sentences rather than numerous simple ones (the dominant syntactic variables will be those we have yet to consider: clause length, and in particular, clause and word order). By contrast, the *congedi* usually have a very simple structure. Here are fairly extreme examples of each, with the main verbs again printed in italics and the cases of sub-subordination shown by parentheses and dashes:

> Poscia ch'Amor del tutto m'*ha lasciato*,
> non per mio grato,
> (ché stato non avea tanto gioioso),
> (ma però che pietoso
> fu tanto del meo core,
> —che non sofferse d'ascoltar suo pianto);
> i' *canterò* così disamorato
> contra 'l peccato
> ch'è nato in noi, di chiamare a ritroso
> tal (ch'è vile e noioso)
> con nome di valore,
> cioè di leggiadria—ch'è bella tanto
> —che fa degno di manto
> imperial colui—dov'ella regna.   LXXXIII, 1–13

> Canzone, *uccella* con le bianche penne;

Poem no.		No. of sentences	No. of clauses
I		7	12
V		3	12
VIII		9	14
X		8	17
XI		3	15
XII		8	21
XIII		9	16 etc.
CIV	st. 1	7	18
	st. 2	10	15
	st. 3	8	18
	st. 4	8	20
	st. 5	4	16
Congedi 1 and 2		11	21

canzone, *caccia* con li neri veltri,
che fuggir mi convenne,
ma far mi *poterian* di pace dono.
Però nol *fan* che non san—quel che sono:
camera di perdon savio uom non *serra*,
ché 'l perdonare è bel vincer di guerra.[1]   CIV, 101–7

Both the pre-exilic doctrinal *canzoni* (in which one finds the 'average' proportion of complex sentences) become markedly simpler in their final stanzas, after the close reasoning has been concluded, and the virtues are depicted as they truly are. But there is a contrary movement in *Tre donne*, where the opening stanzas are comparatively simple, but the all-important fifth stanza (quoted for its tropes in ch. 3) assumes *constructiones* worthy of the high style.

Another not infrequent pattern is for the syntax of the *frons* and that of the *sirima* to be contrasted within one strophe: usually the movement is from complex to simple, more rarely vice-versa.[2]

We now turn to examine the *kinds* of subordination most used by Dante. In the *VN* poems, the dominant species are the relative (20 per cent of all clauses including main clauses) and the consecutive (12·5 per cent). These are followed at some remove by the declarative or noun clause (8 per cent), the causal (6 per cent) and the temporal 4·5 per cent. In the later poems, the same species predominate, but with significant differences in their relative proportions. The proportion of main clauses has fallen from 43 per cent to 37 per cent, this being another aspect of the slightly more complex syntax in the later poems. The percentage of relative clauses rises by fully 10 per cent to 30 per

---

[1] Lisio (*L'arte del periodo*, p. 109) notes that in *canzoni* where *frons* and *sirima* are metrically very distinct, '... anche il periodare, di solito, differisce così, che nella prima parte (specie nella prima stanza della canzone) si apra a respiri ampi e costrutti ben legati, nella seconda par che si restringa, si spezzi e preferisca i costrutti più brevi e coordinati'. This type he found in XX, LXXIX and C but not in LXXXII and LXXXIII.

Maria Corti ('Il linguaggio poetico di Cino da Pistoia,' *CN*, XII (1952), 197–9) finds a similar process in Cino, and she prints and analyses nos XLVI, 1ff.; XC, 49ff.; and LXI, 1 (ed. Zaccagnini). Of the last she says: 'Si osservi l'andamento sintattico delle prime due quartine ... cioè la *struttura prolettica del periodo* [che] serve a scandire l'atmosfera di pensosità in cui si dispiega la narrazione ... una volta creato il tono, il poeta passa a *un andamento narrativo a base di coordinate e polisindeti: duplice tecnica* che si ritrova *molte volte applicata*'. (On pp. 211–13, she makes similar comments on nos. CXI, 19 ff.; XLII, 1 ff.; CXVIII, 1 ff.).

[2] Examples of change from complex to simple: I; VII; XIV, st. 3; XX, st. 1, 3, 4; XXV, st. 4; XXXII; XXXIII; XXXVI. Examples of change from simple to complex: V; XII; CXIV.

cent, whilst the percentage of causal clauses rises by 3 per cent to become nearly twice as frequent, instead of half as frequent, as the consecutives which fall to 5·5 per cent.[1]

The distribution of these clauses at group level is on the whole reasonably close to that of the relevant average distribution.[2] But at the level of the strophe, the variations are so great that it is quite impossible to print a 'representative' passage. Before we attempt any comment on the significance of these figures, however, it will be useful to establish the typical flavour of the relative, consecutive and causal clauses. Here, then, are three short passages in which each is dominant in turn:

> Quivi dov'ella parla, si dichina
> un spirito da ciel, *che* reca fede

[1] Here are the distributions:

| | VN poems | | Later poems | |
Clause type	Total	Percentage	Percentage	Total
MAIN	308	43	37	363
NOUN	56	8	8	81
RELATIVE	143	20	30	299
ADVERBIAL				
Consecutive	90	12·5	5·5	52
Causal	45	6	8·5	84
Final	3	—	—	5
Hypothetic	23	3	4·5	43
Concessive	—	—	—	2
Modal	9	1·5	1·5	13
Local	3	—	—	—
Temporal	36	4·5	2·5	25
Parenthetical	4	—	1·5	15
Totals	720			982

[2] Among the exceptions, we may note that in group A the causal clauses just outnumber the consecutives, and the temporals are nearly as frequent (10, 9, 7 respectively). Groups B and C have an exceptionally high proportion of consecutives (17 per cent and 22 per cent respectively). There is a general increase in the proportion of relative clauses throughout the *VN* poems, accompanied by a decline in the noun clauses, the actual totals in each group being: A 22, 16; B 9, 6; C 16, 4; D 19, 6; E 33, 14; F 17, 2; G 13, 5; H 14, 3. The change in ratio between causal and consecutive is, not unnaturally, sharpest in group J (30, 9), but is marked in group M (21, 9). In the allegorical and correspondence groups (I+L), the causals are only slightly more frequent, and in group K the ratio is again reversed (11, 15).

come l'alto valor *ch*'ella possiede
è oltre quel *che* si conviene a nui.
Li atti soavi *ch*'ella mostra altrui
vanno chiamando Amor ciascuno a prova
in quella voce *che* lo fa sentire.   LXXXI, 41–7

e spesse fiate pensando a la morte,
venemene un disio *tanto* soave,
che mi tramuta lo color nel viso.
E quando 'l maginar mi ven ben fiso,
giugnemi *tanta* pena d'ogne parte,
ch'io mi riscuoto per dolor ch'i' sento;
e *sì* fatto divento,
che da le genti vergogna mi parte.   XXV, 46–53

Similemente fu chi tenne impero
in diffinire errato,
ché prima puose 'l falso e, d'altro lato,
con difetto procede:
ché le divizie, sì come si crede,
non posson gentilezza dar né torre,
però che vili son da lor natura:
poi chi pinge figura,
se non può esser lei, non la può porre,
né la diritta torre
fa piegar rivo che da lungi corre.   LXXXII, 45–55

At first sight the figures showing the distribution of subordinate clauses in Dante's poems do no more than confirm that he was a man of his time: many critics have noted the predominance of relative and consecutive clauses in thirteenth-century Italian and in Old French, both in prose and in verse.[2] It would therefore seem permissible to use

---

[1] I repeat that this, like the others, is an extreme example. It bears out a comment made by Corti in her article on Cino: 'Sono tipiche della struttura poetica stilnovistica *queste relative ritmiche che occupano la seconda metà del verso*' ('Il linguaggio poetico di Cino da Pistoia', p. 197).

[2] '... il sonetto ... porta con sé, secondo che ho osservato in tutta la lirica del Duecento, il predominio delle forme più semplici, delle coordinate ... ipotetiche, causali, temporali, *e più frequenti che mai, relative e consecutive*,' Lisio, *L'arte del periodo*, p. 107. And of Dante's mature style Lisio wrote: 'Quanto al resto, i modi prevalenti sono i relativi, i consecutivi, i coordinati, e quelli di discorso diretto; vengono appresso, ma a distanza, i causali, poi quelli gerundivi, in fine gli ipotetici, i comparativi, gli ottativi',

the figures as further evidence of the 'incapacità costruttiva' of the nascent vernaculars, which is how Terracini and Segre tend to explain the frequency of these constructions, or alternatively, to use them to support a Spitzerian interpretation of a medieval view of the world along the lines of those given by Malagoli, Miss Hatcher[1] and others. But in either case it would not seem possible to draw any conclusions about Dante himself. Nevertheless, I believe a *prima facie* case can still pe made for regarding the free use of the consecutive clause in the *VN* boems as both distinctive and meaningful.[2] Some of the evidence in support of this claim is 'internal'. Thus, the fact that the consecutive clauses are very much less frequent in the later poems as a whole, than in the *VN* poems as a whole, shows that the level of 12 per cent is by no means 'necessary' in a reasonably extensive sample of thirteenth-century verse. And this is further confirmed by the distribution of the clause within the *VN* poems. Of the 48 strophes, only 26 have two or more consecutive clauses, and most of these have a common *materia*. They represent the condition of being in love, as it is experienced by the 'omo gentile'. This condition is experienced at times as bliss, and at times as suffering; and the suffering is essentially the same in its nature and manifestations, both when the lady denies the lover her greeting,

---

ibid. p. 186. '*I costrutti consecutivi e relativi si possono dire elementi essenziali*, che costituiscono come la più *comune saldatura logica* naturale al pensiero e al periodo dantesco' (ibid., pp. 186–7).

For the consecutive clause see further Terracini, *Stile e lingua*, who comments on their role in the *Cronachetta Fiorentina* ('la consecutiva ... una delle forme più care a questa lingua', p. 18), in the *Novellino* (p. 30), in Brunetto Latini ('proposizioni ricche di contrapposizioni causali e consecutive nei tipi più consueti di questa prosa', p. 69), in the prose of the *Vita Nuova* (pp. 92, 120) and in Dante's lyrics (pp. 95–6). See also Corti's article on Cavalcanti, 'La fisionomia stilistica di G. Cavalcanti, *RAL*, ser. VIII, v (1950), 543–5; and Malagoli, *Motivi e forme*, p. 71. For the relative clause see also Terracini, *Stile e lingua*, p. 90 where, in discussing the prose of the *VN*, he speaks of 'l'agganciarsi l'una all'altra senza una precisa ragione subordinante di proposizioni relative'; also p. 94. See further Corti's article on Cino da Pistoia, 'Il linguaggio poetico', pp. 197–8, and Segre, 'La sintassi del periodo nei primi prosatori italiani', p. 140.

On the consecutive clause in Old French, see P. M. Schon, *Studien zum Stil der frühen französischen Prosa, Analecta Romanica*, vol. VIII (Frankfurt am Main 1960), pp. 153–7.

1 Anna G. Hatcher, 'Consecutive clauses in Old French. A contribution to medieval syntax and psychology', in *Revue des études indoeuropéennes*, II (1939), 30–66.

2 There are 90 in all. The introductory conjunctions are *onde* (5), *per che* (5), *sì che* (27), *s'*+adjective or adverb+*che* (31), *tal che* (3), *tanto*+noun, adjective or verb+*che* (19).

and when she herself is denied to the lover by death. Only two strophes represent the condition, so defined, without using at least two consecutive clauses, and only four strophes have two consecutives, but do *not* describe one or other 'aspect' of the lover's condition.[1]

The 'external' evidence has still to be assembled, but I have been able to confirm two impressions: first, that the constructions are much less common in a comparable sample of poems by Guinizzelli and Petrarch;[2] and second, that they occur frequently, although not so frequently, in the poems of the other 'stilnovisti',[3] where they are used in much the same contexts. The two passages quoted above, in which consecutive constructions were dominant (XI, XXV), both represented love as *suffering*. As an example of love as *bliss*, let us now quote not from Dante's *Tanto gentile*, but from Cino's *Una gentil piacevol giovanella*:

Una gentil piacevol giovanella

[1] The following are the 22 strophes that satisfy my conditions. Love as bliss: XIV, st. 3; XVI; XVII; XXII; XXIII; XXIV. Love as suffering, (a) 'in vita': V; X; XI; XIII; XX, st. 2, 3, 6; XXXII; XXXIII; XXXIV; (b) 'in morte' XXV, st. 2, 3, 4, 5; XXVII, st. 1; XXXV.

The exceptions are XIV, st. 1, XVIII, XIX and XXXVII, which have two or more consecutive clauses, but do not represent the lover's condition; and XII and XIII which represent the condition, without having at least two consecutives.

[2] Guinizzelli, *Opere* (ed. Di Benedetto)   632 lines   23 consecutive clauses
Petrarch, I–XXVII   711 lines   38 consecutive clauses
Dante, *VN* poems   676 lines   90 consecutive clauses

[3] Using the text established by L. Di Benedetto (*Rimatori del Dolce Stil Novo* (Bari, 1939)), the figures were:

Lapo Gianni, *Opere*	683 lines	41 consecutive clauses
Dino Frescobaldi, *Opere*	572 lines	48 consecutive clauses
Cino da Pistoia, I–XLIV	708 lines	66 consecutive clauses
Guido Cavalcanti, I–XXXIV	702 lines	77 consecutive clauses
Dante, *VN* poems	676 lines	90 consecutive clauses

It will be seen that, after Dante, it is Cavalcanti who uses them most frequently—that is, in all probability, the man from whom Dante took both the conception of love and the representational device. Corti when speaking of the use of *direct speech* in Cavalcanti (frequent as in Dante), notes: 'Il discorso diretto di Guido è sempre preceduto da un *periodare fatto di una o più proposizioni consecutive* che vogliono raggiungere il massimo della tensione stilistica, a cui segue il tono completamente diverso, grave, sentenzioso o meditativo di Amore: si può parlare perciò anche qui di un vero schema costante stilistico di Guido' ('La fisionomia stilistica', p. 543, apropos of XXVIII; similarly p. 544 apropos of XIII and XXVII).

Such periods in Dante are quite common, although there are many consecutives which do not terminate in direct speech.

adorna ven d'angelica vertute,
in compagnia di *sì dolce salute*
che qual la sente poi d'amor favella.

Ella m'aparve agli occhi *tanto bella,*
che per entr' un penser al cor venute
son parolette, *che* dal cor vedut'è
abbia 'n vertù d'esta gioia novella;

la quale ha *presa sì* la mente nostra
e l'ha coverta di *sì dolce amore,*
*ch'*ella non può pensar se non di lei[1]   III, 1–11

Such then is the preliminary evidence that the use of consecutive
clauses in certain *VN* poems is both frequent and *distinctively* frequent.
It is not easy to pin down the full *significance* of the findings, but I
suggest that they will have some bearing on two important points—
on the relationship of the 'stil novo' to earlier courtly love poetry, and
on the homogeneity of the 'stil novo' itself. As to the first point, the
findings would serve to confirm that one of the most distinctive
features of the 'stil novo' is its emphasis on *action*—on the *representation* of the condition of being in love as a sequence of effects, all of
which can be traced back to their efficient cause, the 'more than human'
beauty of the lady. In Dante's poems at least, 'madonna' is transformed
from a term of desire into an active principle, a 'beatrice'. And the most
important linguistic resources by which he conveys to us her 'mirabili
operazioni' are light imagery on the one hand, and consecutive constructions on the other.

As to the homogeneity of the 'stil novo', I would stress once again
that consecutive constructions are equally prominent, whether love is
bringing suffering or joy. And this is an important point, because it
suggests that it is the *technique* of representation (together with the
linguistic and stylistic purification described in other chapters) which
constitutes the 'school'; whereas the implication of the prose of the *Vita
Nuova* (especially chapter xviii) is that the dividing line between the
old poetry and the new is to be located between the conception of love
as self-centred suffering, and the conception of love as disinterested,
joyful and issuing in spontaneous praise. There is of course no necessary contradiction: but we must be careful to distinguish what is

[1] Text from *Poeti del Duecento*, ed. G. Contini (Milan–Naples, 1960), vol. II, p. 643.

significant for Dante, and for his poetic career as a whole, from what is significant for the development of courtly love poetry in the 1280s. Let me clinch this point and close the matter for the present by quoting two passages from Cavalcanti[1] in which the consecutive constructions are equally prominent, the first from a poem of lament, the second from a poem of praise:

> Ch'una paura di novi tormenti
> m'aparve allor, *sì crudel e aguta*,
> *che* l'anima chiamò: "Donna, or ci aiuta,
> *che* gli occhi ed i' non rimagnàn dolenti!
>
> Tu gli ha' lasciati *sì, che* venne Amore
> a pianger sovra lor pietosamente,
> *tanto che* s'ode una profonda voce
> la quale dice ..."   XIII, 5–12

> Posso degli occhi miei novella dire,
> la qual è *tale* che piace *sì* al core
> *che* di dolcezza ne sospir' Amore.
>
> Questo novo plager che 'l meo cor sente
> fu tratto sol d'una donna veduta,
> la qual è *sì gentil e avenente*
> *e tanto adorna, che* 'l cor la saluta.   XXIV, 1–7

Very little need be said concerning Dante's use of the past participle. It is by no means common[2] and in the great majority of cases its function is not equivalent to that of a finite verb, since it is used adjectivally or adverbially, for example:

A ciascun' alma *presa* ...	I, I
li quai *disconsolati* vanno via	XXVI, 3
Levava li occhi miei *bagnati* in pianti	XX, 57

The only cases to be of any interest syntactically are the imprecations and the construction with *ecco* in *Doglia mi reca*, an ablative absolute in *Donna pietosa*, and a Latin accusative and infinitive construction[3] in

---

[1] Texts from *Poeti del Duecento*, ed. Contini, vol. II, pp. 505, 519.

[2] There are 27 in the *VN* poems, 41 in the later poems. Note that a number of words which are past participles in form have been classed as adjectives, and are not included in these totals.

[3] See Segre, 'La sintassi del periodo nei primi prosatori italiani', pp. 68–71 and 177 for the frequent use of this construction in the prose of the *Convivio*.

the sonnet, *Io sono stato:*

Maladetta tua culla	cvi, 78
Maladetto lo tuo perduto pane	cvi, 80
Ecco *giunta* colei che ne pareggia	cvi, 74
Poi mi partia, *consumato ogne duolo*	xx, 80
credendo *far* colà dove si tona	
esser le guerre de' vapori *sceme.*	cxi, 7–8

The story of the gerund is much more interesting. In the *VN* poems it occurs rather frequently, on average once in every 13 lines. But it suffers a sharp decline in the later poems, where it occurs only once in every 50 lines. Now this decline is fairly obviously another aspect of that general trend towards more complex syntactic structures which we have already noted; and indeed the pattern of distribution for gerunds in the groups is remarkably like that for simple sentences and sentences containing only one dependent clause. Thus, the level in group A is identical with that in the *VN* poems as a whole: it increases slightly in groups B and C, reaches a peak in group D (with one gerund every 8 lines), and then falls sharply away.[1] There is probably more to it

[1]   USES OF THE GERUND

Groups	Instances	Total lines	
A	10	126	approx. 1 in 13
B	5	56	1 in 10
C	8	84	1 in 10
D	14	112	1 in 8
E	9	146	1 in 16
F	3	54	1 in 18
G	3	56	1 in 18
H	2	42	1 in 21
VN poems	54	676	1 in 13
Groups			
I	2	179	1 in 90
J	6	279	1 in 48
K	3	155	1 in 50
L	1	70	1 in 70
M	6	265	1 in 44
Later poems	18	948	1 in 52

These figures show that one must qualify Segre's assertion that the *Convivio* avoids,

than this, however, for the level in the later poems is very much lower than in the poems of the *Vita Nuova*, and it does not rise appreciably even in the last group, where other variables revealed a certain simplification of syntax. To see what lies behind the development we must glance very briefly at the history of the gerund. This is how Segre summarizes the conclusions reached in numerous studies of the gerund in earlier texts:[1]

Nelle lingue romanze l'uso del gerundio è, nel periodo delle origini, molto frequente e alquanto confusionario, avendo esso assunto contemporaneamente le funzioni, oltre che del gerundio ablativo e del participio presente, di gerundivo e di infinito. Esso è prediletto, tra i nostri antichi scrittori, dai poeti lombardi e veneti, da Jacopone e dal nostro Guittone. Diversa la fortuna che avrà esso nel Trecento, perché allora le sue accezioni si polarizzeranno intorno al valore fondamentale del gerundio ablativo.[2]

Now, one cannot speak of any 'abuse' of the gerund even in the *VN* poems. There are no comparable figures for other authors, but one could hardly describe an average of one gerund in thirteen lines as exceptionally frequent.[3] And, perhaps more important, Dante almost always uses the gerund in the unambiguous acceptations which were to prevail in literary Italian.

It is not used with a preposition,[4] nor where one would expect an infinitive.[5] Its use in place of the present participle is confined to the

---

for the first time, 'il libero uso di gerundi, anch'esso comune alle *Rime* e alla *Vita Nuova*' (ibid., p. 165).

For a bibliography of the grammatical studies by Diez, Meyer-Lübke, Škerlij, Pezzuto, Lyer and others, see the articles by Segre and Corti. The fullest treatment in the relevant articles is that by Corti ('Studi', pp. 342 ff.). Malagoli has some of his most subtle observations on the poetic use of the gerund in Dante: *Linguaggio e poesia nella D.C.*, pp. 29–37. The relevant pages in Segre, 'La sintassi', are 72–80.

[2] Segre ibid., pp. 72–3. It is very common in Duecento prose: see Terracini, *Stile e lingua*, p. 20 (*Cronachetta* . . . 'consueto procedere di gerundi circostanziali prolettici'); p. 42 (*Tristano* . . . 'monotone e caratteristiche prolessi di gerundi' . . .); pp. 95, 114–16 (for use in VN prose).

[3] Contrast Segre on the gerund in Guittone's prose: '. . . l'*abuso* dei gerundi . . . ci indica . . . lo scarso interesse di Guittone per la precisione nell'indicazione dei rapporti, ed insieme i suoi legami con la tradizione dettatoria, che consigliava appunto l'uso dei gerundi per evitare . . . una coordinazione. . . . *Non c'è* pagina di *Guittone che non sia costellata di gerundi*' ('La sintassi', p. 62).

[4] Cf. Corti, 'Studi', pp. 349, 353.

[5] Cf. ibid., p. 342, p. 355 ff.; Segre, 'La sintassi', pp. 76–8.

first sonnet.[1] The periphrastic form with 'andare'+gerund is not common.[2] In all except a very few cases, the subject of the gerund is that of the verb in the governing clause, and even in these exceptional cases the gerund is firmly anchored to some part of the clause.[3] Pregnant uses,[4] such as the following, are uncommon:

sarebbe innanzi lei *piangendo* morta	XIX, 14
ch'ogne lingua deven *tremando* muta	XXII, 3
farei *parlando* innamorar la gente	XIV, 8

The last variable to be studied in this first section is *coordination*. The general picture will by now be familiar, although there are some interesting deviations. In the *VN* poems, there is approximately one instance of the conjunction *e* used *to link sentences*[5] in every 3 sentences. In the later poems, the ratio changes to 1:4·2.[6] At group level, there is

---

1 'madonna involta in un drappo *dormendo*. / Poi la svegliava, e d'esto core *ardendo*' I, 11–12. Cf. Corti, 'Studi', p. 343.

2 The following examples have *not* been included in the totals on the previous page.

che fa li miei spiriti *gir parlando*	XXIV, 10
li spirti miei, che ciascun *giva errando*	XX, 38
venian dicendo: Oi nobile intelletto	XXX, 13
che *va dicendo* a l'anima: Sospira	XXII, 14
che *va chiamando* Morte tuttavia	XXVII, 16

Cf. Corti, 'Studi', pp. 346–7: 'Per il momento mi limito a osservare che i poeti *prestil-novisti*, di qualunque corrente e di qualunque livello linguistico usano con tale frequenza le due perifrasi e soprattutto *andare+gerundio*, e con tale promiscuità nei riguardi dei verbi semplici, che in un buon numero di casi si può giungere all'affermazione di un completo logorìo della perifrasi, di una sua riduzione a sintagma fisso ...' Cf. also 'Il linguaggio poetico', pp. 193–5.

3 E poco *stando* meco il *mio* segnore, / *guardando* in quella parte onde venia, / *io* vidi ... XXI, 7–9; e poscia *imaginando*, / di caunoscenza e di verità fora, / visi di donne *m*'apparver ... XX, 39–41; altro *sperando* m'apporta dolzore, X, 5.

4 Cf. Corti, 'Studi', pp. 351–2. 'Questa enorme disponibilità sintattica del gerundio produce naturalmente tutta una messe di gerundi *assoluti* nei quali hanno pieno sfogo le tendenze anacolutiche della sintassi medievale e il gusto delle costruzioni equivoche, condito qua e là di incapacità costruttiva dei rapporti di subordinazione.'

5 Using 'sentence' in the sense which it has throughout this chapter, and in which it can be opposed to 'period'. See note to p. 157.

6 This seems the most convenient and economical measurement. Note, however, that it is not possible to determine from these figures what proportion of sentences are actually coordinated. For example in a grouping like 1 +1, 1 +1, 1 +1, 1 +1, eight sentences would all be coordinated even though there were only four conjunctions. But if the grouping were 1 +1 +1 +1 +1, 1, 1, 1, there might still be three totally uncoordinated sentences with the same number of conjunctions.

a slight increase in the use of coordination in groups B and C (1:2·5), but group D shows the average ratio, and there is no really clear-cut differentiation between groups B–D on the one hand and F–K on the other. The 'surprise' comes in the final group where one might have expected, if anything, a slight increase in coordination. In fact the level is as low as 1:7—almost as low as it had been in group L.[1] In the *canzone*, *Doglia mi reca*, in which there are 66 sentences and 158 lines, *e* appears as a coordinating conjunction only 7 times, a fact which we shall consider in its context in the last chapter.

It is fairly common for a *pes* or *volta* to be formed of one period, comprising two coordinated sentences, for example:

> Gentil pensero che parla di vui
> sen vene a dimorar meco sovente,
> *e* ragiona d'amor sì dolcemente,
> che face consentir lo core in lui.   XXXIV, 1–4

> La vostra vanità mi fa pensare,
> *e* spaventami sì, ch'io temo forte
> del viso d'una donna che vi mira.   XXXIII, 9–11

[1] The group distribution is as follows:

Groups	Cases of coordination	No. of sentences	
A	17	51	approx. 1 in 3
B	12	28	1 in 2·5
C	15	39	1 in 2·5
D	22	67	1 in 3
E	24	68	1 in 3
F	3	18	1 in 6
G	6	23	1 in 4
H	4	14	1 in 3·5
VN poems	103	308	1 in 3
I	17	77	1 in 4·5
J	29	91	1 in 3
K	21	57	1 in 3
L	3	24	1 in 8
M	17	114	1 in 7
Later poems	87	363	1 in 4·2

It must be emphasized, however, that the perfect symmetry and balance of the first example is extremely rare; and this, in turn, probably explains why there are no significant patterns in the use of coordination at strophe level. One can safely say that coordination is usually limited to pairs of sentences, or that a sequence of short sentences juxtaposed without a link of any kind is most *unusual*. But there is no *typical* strophe; and there are also some important exceptions to these general rules. For example, there are sonnets like *Io mi senti' svegliar* (XXI) and *Un dì si venne a me Malinconia* (LXXII), in which every sentence that can be is coordinated. This means (granted the high coincidence of line and clause) that in the latter poem 9 lines out of 13 begin with *e*. Here is a sample:

> *E* io le dissi: 'Partiti, va' via';
> *ed* ella mi rispose come un greco:
> *e* ragionando a grande agio meco,
> guardai *e* vidi Amore, che venia
>
> vestito di novo d'un drappo nero,
> *e* nel suo capo portava un cappello;
> *e* certo lacrimava pur di vero.   LXXII, 5–11

Two points must be made about these sonnets. In the first place, they are in every way offhand and familiar, and Dante is clearly using the syntax of colloquial speech for particular effect. And secondly, such elementary parataxis would be normal, or at least not abnormal, in many medieval texts, both Latin and vernacular, both informal and formal.[1] It is only within the context of Dante's 'personal style', that one might remark on the high number of lines beginning with *e* in such *canzoni* as *Donna pietosa* and *Li occhi dolenti*,[2] where the frequent coordinations, together with the free use of consecutive clauses and of direct speech, remind us that much of the individuality and the fascination of the 'sweet new style' lies in its synthesis of esoteric and popular elements.

There is one passage in *Donna pietosa* where the *e*'s are so insistent

---

[1] See for example Lisio, *L'arte del periodo* pp. 174–88; Terracini, *Stile e lingua*, pp. 30, 70; Segre, 'La sintassi', pp. 65, 116, 138; Malagoli, *Motivi e forme*, ch. 1.

[2] XX, lines 5, 7, 10, 12, 16, 18, 25, 27, 30, 36, 38, 45, 51, 53, 54, 58, 60, 62, 67, 69, 76, 81; XXV, lines 7, 12, 14, 17, 26, 31, 37, 40, 46, 49, 52, 56, 60, 63, 70, 72, 75.

that one might be tempted to recognize a conscious use of the figure polysyndeton:[1]

> *ed* esser mi parea non so in qual loco,
> *e* veder donne andar per via disciolte,
> qual lagrimando, *e* qual traendo guai ...
> Poi mi parve vedere a poco a poco
> turbar lo sole *e* apparir la stella,
> *e* pianger elli *ed* ella;
> cader li augelli volando per l'are,
> *e* la terra tremare;
> *ed* omo apparve ...   xx, 45–7, 49–54

But if it is felt necessary to invoke any influence to account for this passage, it is best sought not in the rhetorical manuals but in the Vulgate, for example:

Et vidi, cum aperuisset sigillum sextum, *et* ecce terrae motus magnus factus est, *et* sol factus est niger tanquam saccus cilicinus, *et* luna tota facta est sicut sanguis; *et* stellae de caelo ceciderunt super terram ... *et* caelum recessit sicut liber involutus, *et* omnis mons, *et* insulae de locis suis motae sunt.

Apoc. 6, 12–14

Videbam, *et* ecce arbor in medio terrae, *et* altitudo eius nimia. Magna arbor, *et* fortis, *et* proceritas eius contingens caelum; ... folia eius pulcherrima, *et* fructus eius nimius, *et* esca universorum in ea ... Videbam in visione capitis mei super stratum meum; *et* ecce vigil, *et* sanctus de caelo descendit. Clamavit fortiter, *et* sic ait: Succidite arborem, *et* praecidite ramos eius; excutite folia eius, *et* dispergite fructus eius; fugiant bestiae, quae subter eam sunt, *et* volucres de ramis eius.

Dan. 4, 7–11

It would be less misleading, but still rash, to see the contrary figure, asyndeton,[2] in these lines:

---

[1] '*Polysyntheton* est dictio multis concatenata coniunctionibus, ut "Tectumque, laremque, / armaque, Amicleumque canem"' (*Georgics*, III, 344–5), (*Et.*, I, xxxvi, 19).

'*Polissinteton* est cum multis coniunctionibus clausularum copulativa connexio, ut apud Virgilium: "Acamasque, Thoasque, / Pelidesque Neoptolemus" etc. (*Aen.* II, 262–3)' (Matthew of Vendôme, III, 14).

[2] '*Dissolutum* est quod, coniunctionibus verborum e medio sublatis, separatis partibus effertur hoc modo: "Gere morem parenti, pare cognatis, obsequere amicis, obtempera legibus". Item: "Descende in integram defensionem, noli quicquam recusare, da servos in quaestionem, stude verum invenire"' (*Ad Her.*, IV, xxx, 41).

'*Dialyton* vel *asyntheton* est figura quae e contrario [sc. polysyntheton] sine coniunctionibus solute ac simpliciter effertur, ut "Venimus, vidimus, placuit"' (*Et.*, I, xxxvi, 20).

Dice di lei Amor: 'Cosa mortale
come esser pò sì adorna e sì pura?'
Poi la reguarda, *e* fra se stesso giura
che Dio ne 'ntenda di far cosa nova.

Color di perle ha quasi, in forma quale
convene a donna aver, non for misura:
ella è quanto de ben pò far natura;
per essemplo di lei bieltà si prova.
De li occhi suoi ...   XIV, 43–51

The usage is certainly deliberate here, and it is particularly striking
in the context of *Donne ch'avete*. The juxtaposed imprecations in
Doglia mi reca, on the other hand, do not stand out in quite the same
way. The only comparable passage occurs in the corresponding section
of *Amor che ne la mente*:

Però qual donna sente sua bieltate
biasmar per non parer queta e umile,
miri costei ch'è essemplo d'umiltate!
Questa è colei ch'umilia ogni perverso:
costei pensò chi mosse l'universo.   LXXXI, 68–72

And the device is too obviously tied to this one sort of context to be
classed as a figure.

We shall consider Dante's use of antithesis and direct speech in later
chapters, so we may bring this section to a close with a brief glance at
his use of initial adverbs. The use of initial adverbs to bring a sentence
into a temporal or causal relationship with its predecessor is very
characteristic of the Romance vernaculars. Typically, they are used
most freely when the syntactic resources are most meagre.[1] In Italian,
the most favoured adverbs were such as the following: 'appresso',
'allora', 'poscia', 'poi'; 'così'; 'dunque', 'però' (= 'perciò'). And to
them we must add words like 'onde', 'per che', 'sì che', 'ché' and 'dico',
which at times may introduce a true subordination, but at other times

---

It is also known as *disiunctum* and *dissolutio*. See further Capella, V, 536; Matthew of
Vendôme, III, 15; *PN*, 1,201–12; *Laborintus*, 515–17.
[1] See Schon, *Studien zum Stil der frühen französischen Prosa* pp. 149–51. The adverbs
most common in the Old French chronicles are (*a*)*lors*, (*a*)*dont*, *aprés*, *puis entre-
mentiers*.

function exactly like an adverb.[1] In the chosen poems there are 63 such initial adverbs.[2] They are distributed fairly evenly, although, as one would expect, they occur more frequently in poems which are predominantly narrative or ratiocinative than in those which are more neutral in character.[3] They are perhaps sufficiently numerous, in certain passages at least, to remind us that Dante was a medieval writer, in a way that Petrarch is not. But even in the absence of comparable figures for other authors, it seems clear that Dante relied on them far less than the majority of his predecessors.

We now pass on to the second main object of study: the relationship between Dante's syntax and his metric. We shall be under no obligation here to prove that the metrical and syntactic units which he used were originally identical—although no one would now seriously call this into question. It is quite sufficient to note that there is a *natural parallelism* between the clause and the line, or between the period and the strophe or independent part of a strophe; and that it is possible to 'respect' this parallelism or to disregard it in varying degrees. What we must establish for any text is the degree to which the syntactic and metrical units coincide, and the nature and degree of the 'dissidences'.

The relationship between syntax and metre in *all* Dante's verse has already been studied by Lisio (*L'arte del periodo*, pp. 87–120); and his findings were expressed in numerical form. In what follows, I shall

---

[1] Cf. Segre on Brunetto Latini: 'parimente l'*onde*, tanto comunemente introdotto tra una causa e la sua conseguenza per la possibilità che offriva di *evitare costruzioni subordinate più difficili a maneggiare*... entra non solo all'inizio della minore d'un sillogismo, secondo un uso di cui c'è traccia anche in Dante, ma anche, con funzione poco dissimile da quella dell'*et*, a segnare il passaggio tra due parti d'una trattazione' ('La sintassi', p. 140).

I have taken 'onde' as a subordinating conjunction in the following cases: V, 15; VII, 5; XI, 12; XVII, 11; LXXXI, 53; LXXXII, 59; C, 22, 56; CIII, 47.

On 'dico' see Foster-Boyde, *Dante's Lyric Poetry*, vol. II, Index, *s.v.*

[2] *appresso* I, 14; *già* I, 5; LXXXIII, 121; *or(a)* V, 13; XIV, 30, 59; XXV, 4; XXXIII, 5; LXXIX, 20; CIV, 15; *allor(a)* VIII, 13; XX, 13, 63; XXXI, 5; CIII, 50; *poscia* XIII, 9; XXV, 54; *poi* I, 12; XIV, 45; XX, 43, 49, 80; LXXXII, 136; CIII, 55; CIV, 45, 99; CVI, 158; *però* XXIV, 5; LXXIX, 9; LXXXI, 14, 54, 68; LXXXII, 112; XCV, 13; CXI, 9; CXIV, 12; CIV, 65; CVI, 3; *così* X, 11; XXXIII, 14; LXXXI, 81, 87; CVI, 126; *dunque* IX, 23; LXXXII, 109; LXXXIII, 74, 83; *sì che* V, 17; *per che* LXXXII, 74; LXXXIII, 17, 67; *ancor(a)* XIV, 41; LXXXII, 69; CIII, 74; *onde* X, 9; XXVII, 10; LXXIX, 7, 56; LXXXII, 65, 96; CIV, 88; *ché* LXXIX, 49; CIII, 27.

[3] There are 25 in the *VN* poems, 38 in the later poems. There is marked increase in the use of *però* in the later poems.

---

be concerned more to fill out his picture than to offer any substantial revision. But this being said, I must also call attention to an important difference in method. We are obviously in agreement on basic principles. Identity or coincidence of the two orders is assumed to be the norm; and deviations or dissidences are of two kinds only: either the syntactic unit may overrun the metrical unit, or it may be terminated, and a new unit begun, within the metrical unit. But Lisio is rather vague as to what constitutes a syntactic unit, and in practice his criterion is 'prosodic' rather than 'logical'. In other words, he seems to adopt the common-sense view that the end of a syntactic unit is indicated by the perceptible break in delivery, which a speaker would make when giving a meaningful reading of the poem. 'Perché l'armonia d'un verso vada sperduta o soltanto dileguata', he writes, 'conviene sia rotto fortemente a mezzo, o vero che la sua fine si attacchi così stretta al principio seguente, da non permettere con la pausa ritmica la più lieve pausa del senso.'[1]

The advantages of this approach are its simplicity and its concentration on a stylistic device of undoubted importance. But it also has disadvantages. It must be subjective because agreement on the 'value' of 'sense-pauses' is extremely hard to reach; and it does not permit sufficient discrimination.[2] I have therefore chosen the *clause*, not the phrase or the period, as the syntactic unit which is presumed to coincide with the line. Of course, the clause-boundary will often coincide with a sense-pause, but the two may also be distinct. There may well be sense-pause at the end of a line, even though the clause is incomplete; and, at the other extreme, one would hardly recognize a sense-pause, strong enough to constitute an exception, at the clause-boundary within a line like this:

allor ti priego / che ti riconforte   LXXIX, 59

Four figures are necessary to provide an adequate picture of the relationship between syntax and metre: the number of lines in the passage; the number of perfect coincidences between clause and line;[3]

---

[1] *L'arte del periodo*, p. 92.

[2] It is worth adding that in his published figures Lisio does not distinguish between the two kinds of dissidence. On the other hand, since there are so few 'internal pauses' in Dante's verse, almost all the exceptions are cases of *enjambement*, and his figures may be understood and used accordingly.

[3] I have found it empirically desirable to make one exception. Where one clause occupies two lines exactly, I have taken it as equivalent to two cases of coincidence, rather than

the number of open-ended or 'unstopped' lines; the number of 'mid-stopped' lines. Their usefulness may be gauged by an analysis of the sonnets *Vede perfettamente* (XXIII) and *Ciò che m'incontra* (XII). By Lisio's test, both sonnets show a perfect coincidence of metre and syntax (although he was prepared to admit an internal pause in the last line of the latter, p. 93). But this is what the sonnets look like when printed out clause by clause.

XXIII

Vede perfettamente onne salute
chi la mia donna tra le donne vede
quelle che vanno con lei
son tenute di bella grazia a Dio render merzede.
E sua bieltate è di tanta vertute
che nulla invidia a l'altre ne procede
anzi le face andar seco vestute
di gentilezza, d'amore e di fede.

La vista sua fa onne cosa umile
e non fa sola sé parer piacente
ma ciascuna per lei riceve onore.
Ed è ne li atti suoi tanto gentile
che nessun la si può recare a mente
che non sospiri in dolcezza d'amore.

XII

Ciò che m'incontra
ne la mente more
quand'i' vegno a veder voi bella gioia
e quand'io vi son presso
i' sento Amore
che dice
Fuggi

---

two cases of dissidence. In such a case I have not counted the first line as 'unstopped', even where there is *enjambement*!

e.g. Allor lassai la nova fantasia,
    chiamando il nome della donna mia.   XX, 13–14

    Ahi angosciosa e dispietata lima
    che sordamente la mia vita scemi   CIII, 22–3

    Ubidente, soave e vergognosa
    è ne la prima etate   LXXXII, 125–6

se 'l perir t'è noia.
Lo viso mostra lo color del core
che tramortendo s'appoia
ovunque pò
e par
che per la ebrietà del gran tremore le pietre gridin
Moia moia.

Peccato face
chi allora mi vide
se l'alma sbigottita non conforta sol dimostrando
che di me li doglia per la pietà
che 'l vostro gabbo ancide
la qual si cria ne la vista morta de li occhi
c'hanno di lor morte voglia.

My case is that the differences between these sonnets are worth registering, and that the indices do this quite adequately:

	Clause–Line coincidences	Unstopped lines	Midstopped lines
XXIII	12	1	1
XII	2	3	9

Analysis of the relationships between clause and line reveals much the same pattern of distribution as we have seen in earlier syntactic variables, and generally confirm Lisio's findings. Thus, the proportion of coincidences is as high as 51 per cent in the *VN* poems, but falls to 39 per cent in the later poems. The proportion of unstopped lines (not to be confused with *enjambements*) rises from 11 per cent to 22 per cent, whilst the less significant proportion of midstopped lines rises only slightly from 33 per cent to 39 per cent.[1]

1

Lines	Coincidences		Unstopped lines		Midstopped lines	
	Total	%	Total	%	Total	%
676	349	51·5	86	11	225	33
948	371	39	212	22	373	39

Coincidence and dissidence of clause and line

At group level,[1] we may note yet one more aspect of the simplification of the syntactic structures in group D, where the proportion of coincidences is as high as 63 per cent: a figure which is once again thrown into relief by the below average figure of 37 per cent in groups F–H. In the allegorical poems, the proportion of coincidences is close to that of the last groups in the *VN* poems, but the proportion of 'unstopped' lines is as low as 16 per cent. The extremes of dissidence are to be found in the didactic *canzoni* and in the 'canzoni petrose', the former having more unstopped lines (30 per cent), the latter more midstopped lines (47 per cent). But the last group restores the balance, and in *Tre donne*

[1] Lisio recognized a dozen or so exceptions in the *VN* sonnets (he is purposely a little vague) and five in the *VN canzoni*. Taking all the poems as a whole he suggests (*L'arte del periodo*, p. 96) that approximately one verse in 16 does not 'concord with the grammatical pause'. In the *Comedy* as a whole he found that the proportion of exceptions reaches approximately 1 in 8 lines; in the *Inferno* 1 in 15, in the other two *cantiche*, approximately 1 in 5.

Groups	No. of lines	Coincidences		Unstopped lines		Midstopped lines	
		Total	%	Total	%	Total	%
A	126	74	58	5	4	30	24
B	56	26	46	8	14	22	39
C	84	44	53	10	12	27	33
D	112	71	63	9	8	33	30
E	146	77	54	22	15	54	37
F	54	20	37	13	24	20	37
G	56	26	46	10	18	16	29
H	42	11	26	9	21	23	55
VN poems	676	349		86		225	
Groups							
I	179	61	34	28	16	89	50
J	279	108	38	84	30	91	32
K	155	49	32	40	26	73	47
L	70	33	46	10	14	31	44
M	265	120	45	50	19	89	33
Later poems	948	371		212		373	

It should be noted that the number of unstopped and midstopped lines together with the clause–line coincidences need not be identical with the number of lines in the passage.

the proportion of coincidences rises to 53 per cent, whilst unstopped lines fall to 16 per cent.[1]

Turning now to the crucial lines which occur before a *metrical boundary*—that is before a boundary between the constituent parts of a strophe—we find that only 3 out of 231 are not 'clause-stopped',[2] and that in over 80 per cent of cases, the metrical boundary coincides with a boundary between *sentences*. It is worth adding, too, that where a sentence does extend over the metrical boundary, the new subordinate clause will be only loosely attached to the earlier part of the sentence. Typically, it will be a consecutive clause, or a causal clause introduced by 'ché'. There is little variation or development within the poems in this respect.[3]

[1] Lisio's figures point the same way. He finds 'scarcely' one exception in each of nos LXXIX, LXXXI, and XC, but 25 in nos C and CIII, and 45 in the four 'later philosophical poems'. *Tre donne* has 'scarcely' two exceptions (*L'arte del periodo*, p. 94). There is therefore a clear correlation between the proportion of lines which are not 'clause-stopped' and the proportion of *enjambements*.

[2] In nos XX, 45–6; XXXII, 4–5; CIV, 22–3. Each is heavily 'phrase-stopped'.

[3] INFRINGEMENT OF METRICAL BOUNDARIES

Groups	pes-pes	volta-volta	frons-sirima	No. of boundaries
A	1	1	—	19
B	1	1	1	12
C	2	—	1	17
D	2	—	—	18
E	2	×	2	20
F	2	1	2	10
G	1	—	—	12
H	1	—	—	9
VN poems	12	3	6	117
Groups				
I	4	×	1	25
J	3	×	4	28
K	3	×	1	22
L	1	—	—	15
M	2	×	—	24
Later poems	13	—	6	114

Infringement of boundary between *pedes*: VI, X; XIV, st. 3, 5; XVII; XX, st. 1, 3, 4; XXI; XXVI; XXXII; XXXVI; LXXIX, st. 2; LXXX, st. 1, 2, 3; LXXXII, st. 1; LXXXIII, st. 1, 4; XCV; C, st. 5; CIII, st. 1, 3; CIV, st. 2, 5.

One last aspect of the determining influence of the metrical forms on Dante's syntax is worth brief consideration, for it alone would suffice to distinguish his prose from his verse. In the prose works one can find clauses as long as the following on almost any page:

Contra questo avversario de la ragione si levoe un die, quasi ne l'ora de la nona, una forte imaginazione in me ...   *VN*, xxxix, 1

La prima similitudine si è la revoluzione de l'uno e de l'altro intorno a uno suo immobile.   *Con.*, II, xiii, 3

But in all the poems analysed, only 37 clauses exceed 22 syllables in length, and the great majority have 11 syllables or less.

We must now consider what I earlier called the potentially more expressive aspects of Dante's syntax, namely the order in which clauses appear within the sentence, and the order in which words appear within the clause.[1] The description will take the form used in other chapters. It will be assumed that certain sequences constitute a norm: and these will be defined in terms of logical relationships, not in terms of 'naturalness' or frequency of use. We shall then find out how often Dante departs from the norms, and establish the kind, number and distribution of those deviations. Taken all together, these findings will provide the evidence concerning the *true* norm, which, in turn, will enable us to identify with some confidence those sequences that are of 'low predictability' in their context, and may therefore have some expressive force.[2] The findings will also document yet another aspect of the complexity or simplicity of Dante's style.

With regard to clause-order, we may define the norm as follows: all

---

Infringement of boundary between *voltae* (where they exist): v; xI; xxvI. Infringement of boundary between *frons* and *sirima*: xI; xIV, st 2; xxI; xxv, st. 2; xxvII, st. 1, 2; LxxIx, *congedo*; LxxxII, st. 3; LxxxIII, st. 1, 6, 7; cIII, st. 5.

Lisio, *L'arte del periodo*, ch. 2, found by his test that 'metro' and 'periodo' did not coincide 6 times in 165 in the sonnets (p. 107), and 25 times in 207 in the *canzoni* (p. 110, where he seems to recognize *voltae* in LxxxIII, cIV and cvI). In the *Comedy*, he found that the trend towards dissidence is reversed: he found 101 exceptions in the *Inferno*, but a mere 44 in the *Paradiso* (p. 114n).

[1] For the sake of clarity, I shall maintain a sharper distinction between these two categories than is customary, even though certain dislocations of word-order clearly depend on dislocations of clause-order.

[2] See introduction, p. 35.

dependent clauses *follow* their governing clause, whether in subordination or sub-subordination. And it will be assumed that deviations from the norm may be of two kinds only: *inversion* or *interpolation*. It would obviously be possible to make finer subdivisions under each head, but, as the examples will show, it is the number of deviations within a sentence, rather than their kind, which is stylistically significant.

Inversion (or prolepsis) occurs when a clause precedes its governor. In Dante's poems, up to four clauses may be inverted, for example:

ONE CLAUSE

> ... Sì come saper dei, /
> di fonte *nasce* il Nilo picciol fiume   CIV, 45–6

> S'i' vi vedesse uscir de gli occhi ploia
> per prova fare a le parole conte, /
> non mi *porreste* di sospetto in ponte.   CXIII, 12–14

TWO CLAUSES

> e quando tu sarai
> in parte / dove sia la donna nostra, /
> non le *tenere* il tuo mestier coverto: LXXXII, 142–4

> e qual che sia 'l piacer / ch'ora n'addestra, /
> seguitar si *convien* ...   CXI, 13–14

THREE CLAUSES

> Perch'io non trovo / chi meco ragioni
> del signor / a cui siete voi ed io, /
> *conviemmi* sodisfare ...   XCVI, 1–3

> ... se per ventura elli addivene /
> che tu dinanzi da persone vadi /
> che non ti paian d'essa bene accorte, /
> allor ti *priego* ...   LXXIX, 56–9

FOUR CLAUSES

> Chi s'innamora (sì come voi fate),

or qua or là, / e sé lega / e dissolve, /
mostra ...   CXIV, 9–11

Poscia ch'Amor del tutto m'ha lasciato,
non per mio grato, /
ché stato non avea tanto gioioso, /
ma però che pietoso
fu tanto del meo core, /
che non sofferse d'ascoltar suo pianto; /
i' *canterò* ...   LXXXIII, 1–7

Interpolation occurs when a dependent clause is 'inserted' into the body of the governing clause, which thus both precedes and follows its dependents. Up to three clauses may be incapsulated in this way in the chosen poems, for example:

ONE CLAUSE

e però non *disgombra*
un sol penser d'amore (ond'io son carco),
la mente mia ...   C, 10–12

Fassi dinanzi da l'avaro volto
vertù, (che i suoi nimici a pace invita),
con matera pulita,
per allettarlo a sé ...   CVI, 106–9

TWO CLAUSES

e Amor, (che sue ragne
ritira in alto pel vento / che poggia),
non m'*abbandona* ...   C, 23–5

E questa, (ch'era sì di pianger pronta, /
tosto che lui intese),
più nel dolor s'*accese*   CIV, 41–2

THREE CLAUSES

Ancor ne li occhi, (ond'escon le faville /
che m'infiammano il cor, / ch'io porto anciso),
guarderei presso e fiso   CIII, 74–6

Ma (s'elli avvien / che tu alcun mai truovi
amico di virtù, / ed e' ti priega),
fatti di color novi   CIV, 96–8

As the last of these examples shows, the borderline between inversion
and interpolation is sometimes hard to define.[1] But it is in any case
reasonable to consider both classes together when measuring the
extent to which an author departs from the logical norm.

We may begin by confirming Terracini's observation[2] that prolepsis
is anything but unknown in these poems. There are 50 cases of pure
inversion of clauses in the *VN* poems, and 59 cases of interpolation.
This means that 54 per cent of the complex sentences show one or
other kind of deviation in clause order. In the later poems, this proportion rises to 59 per cent, and the interpolations outnumber the
inversions by more than two to one (106:45).[3]

As always, it is hard to assess the significance of these figures in the
absence of comparable data. It is known, however, that inversion of
clauses was common at this time both in prose[4] and in verse.[5] And it is

---

[1] It would certainly be reasonable to consider as *inversions* all those cases where the interpolated clause precedes the governing *verb*. In practice, this is what Italian critics seem
to do. I have maintained the distinction, because interpolation—even in the simple
and common form of *ché, se* ..., *ma, se* ..., etc.—seems to create a *staccato* effect
(particularly when such an interpolation is limited to one short clause); whereas 'pure'
inversion serves to create a predominantly *legato* effect (cf. Terracini, *Stile e lingua*,
ch. 7, 'La *VN* e l'analisi dello stile legato', where he devotes several pages to inversion
at clause and word level (pp. 89–106).

It will be seen that a proleptic subordinate clause beginning with *e* (*e se, e quando*
etc.) has been taken as inversion (even though the *e* belongs—in logic—to the main
clause): but after *ma, perché, ché, così* etc., it is taken as an interpolation (for example in
Tre donne: 'però, se questo è danno' (65); 'ché, se noi siamo or punti' (70); 'onde, s'io
ebbi colpa' (88). There is one other exception to strict logic in classification: a proleptic relative clause qualifying a *pronominal* vocative (*voi*, che ... *tu*, che ...) has
been treated as an inversion.

[2] 'Manca uno studio sulla sintassi delle *Rime* di Dante; ad ogni modo è certo che il tipo
di costruzione prolettica, sebbene forse con frequenza minore in confronto a tipi di
altro genere, specialmente a forma di consecutiva, ... è tutt'altro che ignoto ai versi
della *Vita Nuova*', (*Stile e lingua*, p. 96).

[3] This is due in part to the higher proportion of brief relative clauses (usually interpolated after the main verb, for example 'Trova contraro tal (che lo distrugge)
l'umil pensero ...') in group I; and in part to the frequency of the type, 'ma, se ...'
'ché, se ...' 'onde, se ...' in groups J and M.

[4] Segre writes: 'Sull'ordine delle parole nelle lingue romanze, o nell'italiano, manca
purtroppo uno studio d'assieme da cui prendere le mosse' ('La sintassi', p. 101).
He himself does a good deal to remedy the situation concerning word-order (pp.

obvious that the presence of certain kinds of subordinate clause—especially the temporal and the hypothetic or concessive—implies the presence of inversion almost as surely as the presence of other clauses, such as the consecutive, make pure inversion impossible. Thus, in the fifth stanza of *Li occhi dolenti* the order is exceptional not in the second sentence, but in the first:[1]

> *Dannomi* angoscia li sospiri forte,
> quando 'l pensero ne la mente grave
> mi reca quella che m'ha 'l cor diviso   xxv, 43–5
> E quando 'l maginar mi ven ben fiso,
> *giugnemi* tanta pena d'ogne parte   ibid., 49–50

Nevertheless, we can at least get some idea of the possible range by studying the proportions in the various groups. In four of them (A, F, H, L), the proportion of complex sentences with some deviation from 'normal' clause-order exceeds 75 per cent: and in four other groups (B, C, D, G) that proportion is less than 45 per cent.

The distribution of these deviations at group level also shows some interesting variations on the general pattern with which we have become familiar.[2] Thus, the proportion of deviations in group A is extremely high, much higher than the average for the *VN* poems as a whole, to which the group conformed in earlier syntactic variables. The most complex passage comes perhaps in the *ballata*, and it can remind us that clause and word order in Guittone and the Tuscan school had been at

---

101–12); and he notes the frequent prolepsis of subordinates in the *Convivio* (pp. 174ff.), These are often of the type I have taken as interpolations: thus, '. . . l'uso di iniziare un periodo con una congiunzione, che viene distaccata dalla principale di cui fa parte da una secondaria proalettica, per lo più causale, e.g. (*Con.*, IV, viii, 10) "Ma però che, dinanzi da l'avversario se ragiona, lo rettorico dee molta cautela usare nel suo sermone, acciò che l'avversario quindi non prenda materia di turbare la veritade, io, che al volto di tanti avversarii parlo in questo trattato, *non posso brievemente parlare*" ' (ibid., p. 178).

5 Terracini, *Stile e lingua*, p. 97 ff. In his view, the prose of the *Vita Nuova* uses inversions (of clause) more frequently than poetic texts of the age: he speaks of '. . . la sua stessa *singolare* frequenza, che ne fa il tono dominante di questa prosa'.

1 The first word in stanzas 2, 3 and 4 of this poem is a finite verb.

2 As before, the frequencies have been calculated in terms of the number of complex sentences. Thus the fall in the number of deviations in the central groups of the *VN* poems is not simply the result of the lower number of complex sentences.

times extremely involved:[1]

> Madonna, quelli che mi manda a vui,
> quando vi piaccia, vole,
> sed elli ha scusa, che la m'intendiate.
> Amore è qui, che per vostra bieltate
> lo face, come vol, vista cangiare:
> dunque, perché li fece altra guardare,
> pensatel voi, da che non mutò 'l core.   IX, 18–24

The expected fall in groups B–D is followed by an unusually steep rise in the poems of lamentation (group F), and then, more surprisingly, by a drop to the lowest level in the four sonnets of the 'gentile donna' group (G). A passage from one of these sonnets will give some impression of the feel of 'normal' clause-order:[2]

Groups	Inversions				Interpolations			Total instances	No. of complex sentences	Frequency
	1	*2*	*3*	*4*	*1*	*2*	*3*			
A	12	1	–	–	10	4	–	27	35	77%
B	5	–	–	–	2	1	–	8	19	42
C	4	1	–	–	4	–	1	10	26	39
D	9	–	1	–	4	2	–	16	36	44
E	6	4	1	–	12	1	–	24	43	56
F	2	1	1	–	6	1	–	11	14	78
G	–	–	–	–	3	–	–	3	16	19
H	1	1	–	–	6	2	–	10	13	77
VN poems	39	8	3	–	47	11	1	109	202	54%
I	8	–	2	–	21	4	–	35	60	58%
J	5	3	1	1	20	7	1	38	58	65
K	5	1	–	–	14	3	1	24	42	57
L	4	1	1	1	6	2	1	16	20	80
M	10	2	–	–	21	4	1	38	73	52
Later poems	32	7	4	2	82	20	4	151	253	59%

[1] In fact, the most difficult of Dante's poems from this point of view are certainly the correspondence sonnets addressed to Dante da Maiano. See the notes to those poems in Foster–Boyde, *Dante's Lyric Poetry*.

[2] 13 strophes have 'logical' clause-order throughout viz.: XXII; XXV st. 2; XXVII, st. 2; XXXI; XXXII; LXXX, st. 2; LXXXIII, st. 2, 3; C, st. 4, *congedo*; CIII, *congedo*; CVI, st. 2, *congedo*.

L'anima dice al cor: 'Chi è costui,
che vene a consolar la nostra mente,
ed è la sua vertù tanto possente,
ch'altro penser non lascia star con nui?'
Ei le risponde: 'Oi anima pensosa,
questi è uno spiritel novo d'amore,
che reca innanzi me li suoi desiri;
e la sua vita, e tutto 'l suo valore,
mosse de li occhi di quella pietosa
che si turbava de' nostri martiri.'   XXXIV, 5–14

Among the later groups, there are not the same divergences between groups I, J and K; but there is a general increase in the number of interpolations.[1] The highest proportion of complex sentences with deviations from normal clause-order will be found in group L, while the final group again shows a marked simplification.

In the study of Dante's *word*-order, it will be assumed that the following sequences constitute the logical norm: Subject—Verb—Complement; Subject—Verb—Object.[2] It is also assumed that qualifying,

---

Those with one deviation only are in all twenty: VI; X; XIII; XIV, st. 2, 4; XVI; XX, st. 4, 6; XXIII; XXV, st. 3; LXXIX, st. 2, 3, *congedo*; LXXX, st. 3; LXXXII, st. 1; C, st., 3, 5; CIII, st. 3; CIV, st. 1, 2.

[1] I have not attempted a full survey of the most common species of inversion or interpolation. The examples given above were, however, chosen with a view to illustrating the most characteristic. On the whole, the most common species are those one would expect. Relative, temporal and hypothetical clauses appear both in inversions and interpolations. Parentheses are more often interpolated (for example IX, 12; XXV, 63; LXXXII, 49; CIV, 62). Neither noun clauses nor causals are inverted so frequently, but examples are not wanting (IX, 23–4; XVIII, 11; XXV, 60, 69; LXXXII, 56; and XIV, 58–60; XXV, 7; XCVI, 1–2).

[2] It is clearly 'normal' for the verb to occupy the initial position, when, as so often, the subject is not expressed. Note that, with one exception ('lo perdonare se le fosse a noia', IX, 32), the position of a conjunction or relative pronoun in a subordinate clause does not vary, and it is therefore ignored. Thus, the following is *not* an example of an object preceding its verb: 'le oscure qualità *ch*'Amor mi dona, XIII, 2: 'le oscure qualità' belongs to the preceding clause, and the 'ch(e)' is ignored. Cf. further:
   'In omni constructione *anteponitur agens* qui nominativo vel vocativo profertur, *dehinc* vero illius *actus, postea* autem in quo fit *paciens*, ut: "Johannes percussit Petrum"', quoted by A. Marigo in his edition of *DVE* (3rd ed., Florence, 1957), p. 208.
   'Naturalis hic est ordo, quando nominativus precedit, et verbum cum suis determinationibus et attinentibus subsequitur,' Conrad of Mure, *Summa de arte prosandi*, ed. L. Rockinger, *Briefsteller und Formelbücher des eilften bis vierzehnten Jahrhunderts* (2 vols, Munich, 1863), vol. I, p. 441.

modifying and otherwise dependent phrases or words are placed *after* the word to which they refer, unless it would clearly be exceptional for them to do so.[1] The position of unemphatic pronouns has been ignored, and so have collocations of adjective and noun.[2]

Deviations from the logical norm are not necessarily deviations from the norm of everyday or literary usage (this last is precisely what we are seeking in part to determine). But a passage with frequent deviations will *ipso facto* be very different from one which closely follows the norm. Here are two extreme examples from Dante's mature poems in order to clinch this point. In each case there is only one complex sentence, and apart from the interpolated clauses, which are marked off by parentheses, the *clause*-order is normal. In the first sentence, there are nine clauses without one deviation from 'normal' word-order; in the second, there is a deviation in every clause except 'perché conosce'—where it is impossible!

> Io son venuto al punto de la rota
> che l'orizzonte, (quando il sol si corca),
> ci partorisce il geminato cielo,
> e la stella d'amor ci sta remota
> per lo raggio lucente che la 'nforca
> sì di traverso, che le si fa velo;
> e quel pianeta (che conforta il gelo)
> si mostra tutto a noi per lo grand'arco
> nel qual ciascun di sette fa poca ombra   c, 1–9

> I'ho veduto già *senza radice*
> legno ch'è *per omor* tanto gagliardo,
> che que' (che vide *nel fiume lombardo*

---

[1] For example certain adverbs (*molto, tanto* etc.) usually precede the adjective and will be taken as normal in that position (ch'è bella *tanto*', LXXXIII, 12, is therefore a deviation). Inversion is normal in an interrogative statement or in an exclamation (for example 'ah *com poca difesa* / mostra segnore', CVI 97–8). In general, if a word cannot be moved without alteration to the sense, then it cannot be considered as a deviation (for example '*Ben* ne li occhi di costei ...' LXXIX, 36). Note that when *chi* functions as the subject of two clauses, I have treated it as belonging only to the dependent clause (for example, 'Or apparisce / chi lo fa fuggire', LXXIX, 20).

[2] With regard to proclitic and enclitic pronouns, it has been shown that Dante observes the Tobler–Mussafia law: see Terracini, *Stile e Lingua*, p. 100. As for the use of adjectives with nouns, there are so many cases where it is impossible to decide which order should be regarded as normal, that it seemed wiser not to attempt to count them. See below p. 206.

cader suo figlio), *fronde fuor* n'elice;
ma frutto no, però che 'l *contradice*
natura, ch'*al difetto* fa riguardo,
perché conosce che *saria bugiardo*
sapor non fatto da vera notrice.   XCV, 1–8

Our first task, then, must be to establish how frequently Dante does depart from the logical norm. His average practice is, as one would expect, nearer the mean than the examples just quoted. Forty-four per cent of all the clauses analysed have at least one deviation. Predictably, the percentage is lower in the *VN* poems than in the later poems (39 per cent and 47 per cent respectively). The pattern of development from group to group is broadly similar to the familiar one, but there are some interesting variations. Thus, the proportion of clauses with deviations falls after the first group, but does not rise again until the didactic *canzoni* of group J where it shoots up from 32 per cent to 54 per cent. In the '*canzoni* petrose', however, it returns to a near average figure. The highest proportion is found in the correspondence sonnets, but in the last group it is still higher than the average for the later poems.[1]

1

Groups	No. of clauses with deviations	Total clauses	Percentage with deviations
A	58	128	45%
B	27	69	39
C	39	89	43·5
D	42	118	35·5
E	63	165	38
F	20	50	40
G	20	54	37
H	15	47	32
VN poems	284	720	39%
I	76	221	32
J	135	250	54
K	76	167	45·5
L	44	76	58
M	132	268	49
Later poems	463	982	47%

Before making a detailed grammatical analysis of the deviant clauses, it will be profitable to introduce a basic distinction between *simple* and *complex* deviations. In a simple deviation, the 'normal' order can be 'restored' by the movement of a single element, be it a word, phrase, or a number of phrases which are in the normal order with respect to one another.[1] It follows, therefore, that in a complex deviation two or more elements would have to be moved in order to reach the norm.[2] Some examples will make the distinction clear. For the simple deviations the single 'displaced' element is printed in italics:

SIMPLE

Videro li occhi miei quanta pietate	XXXI, 1
sì che *per vinti* son remasi omai	XXV, 3
che nulla invidia *a l'altre* ne procede	XXIII, 6
e *una nuvoletta* avean davanti	XX, 60
che *da le genti* vergogna mi parte	XXV, 53
sì come il saggio *in suo dittare* pone	XVI, 2
ché forse non è bon *sanʒa lui* gire	IX, 10
benignamente *d'umiltà* vestuta	XXII, 6

COMPLEX

E simil face in donna omo valente	XVI, 14
bagnar nel viso suo di pianto Amore	XVIII, 6
Ancor l'ha Dio per maggior grazia dato	XIV, 41
e poscia imaginando,	

---

[1] In this first class, one will find such schemes as B–A; A–C–B; B–C–A; even B–C–D–A. I have also preferred to consider as *simple* deviations the common pattern *Complement* (or *Adverbial Phrase*)—*Verb*—*Subject* (C—B—A), in which the first and third elements have, as it were, changed places, for example:

Allegro mi sembrava Amor ...	I, 9
tanto dolore intorno 'l cor m'assembra la dolorosa mente	XXVII, 4–5
Spesse fiate vegnonmi a la mente le oscure qualità ...	XIII, 1–2

[2] In the second class, the clause must have at least four elements, and the schemes will be: B–A–D–C; A–D–C–B–etc.

di caunoscenza e di verità fora,	
visi di donne m'apparver crucciati	XX, 39–41
s'elli è dolore alcun, quanto 'l mio, grave	V, 3
così leggiadro questi lo core have	V, 12
chi d'amor per innanzi si notrica	VII, 12
però che intorno a' suoi sempre si gira	
d'ogni crudelitate una pintura	LXXX, 7–8
ramo di foglia verde a noi s'asconde	C, 43
e la crudele spina	
però Amor di cor non la mi tragge	C, 49–50
mentre / che durerà del verno il grande assalto	C, 57–8
e io de la mia guerra	
non son però tornato un passo a retro	C, 62–3

This distinction is similar to that made in the *Rhetorica ad Herennium* between *perversio*, as in 'rege sub ipso', 'tempus ad illud', 'ea de causa', 'rebus in illis', and *transiectio*, as in 'dura creavit pestiferam fortuna famem' or 'letalis egenam gente fames spoliavit humum'[1]

The value of this distinction, as the examples will have shown, is that in most cases the complex deviation will not be mandatory, and that it will probably be distinctively literary in character, even if it is not exceptional by any absolute standard. Thus, if one knows the proportion of clauses in a passage which have *complex* deviations in word order, one has a useful indication of the kind and extent of the deviations to be found there.

[1] This simple two-fold classification of hyperbaton belongs to the *ad Herennium* and its beneficiaries, such as the *Poetria Nova*, from which the above examples were taken (lines, 1,054–7). The other tradition, represented by Donatus and Isidore, recognized five species: *anastrophe* (which is identical with *perversio*), *hysteron proteron*, *parenthesis*, *tmesis* and *synthesis* 'ubi ex omni parte confusa sunt verba' (*Et.*, I, xxxvii, 16–20).

The definitions in the *ad Herennium* (IV, xxxii, 44) are hardly very precise, but it would seem that two distinct principles are involved: inversion and separation. In a *perversio* a word and its dependent are simply inverted (B–A). In a *transiectio* a word is separated from its dependent by a third element (A–X–B; B–X–A). I found it impractical to work with two different principles of classification, and it will be seen that all deviations have been analysed as inversions, or, better, as 'abnormal precedences'. Thus, the sequence A–X–B is described as X precedes B, *not* as X separates A from B. The sequence B–X–A would be a complex deviation, and would be analysed as *two* simple deviations: B precedes A, and X precedes A.

In Dante's poems, these complex deviations occur in approximately
1 in 17 of all clauses. The average figure is the same both for the *VN*
poems and the later poems.[1] They are proportionately most numerous
in the first group, in the 'canzoni petrose', and in the correspondence
sonnets,[2] where the proportion rises to 1 in 11. There is the predictable
drop in group D, but the poems with the lowest proportion of complex deviations (1 in 55 clauses) are the allegorical *canzoni* and the
ballata of group I.[3]

Perhaps the most coherent way of classifying the common deviations
will be to relate them to their effect on the position of the verb. By
definition, the verb is the only part of speech present in every clause,
and, more often than not it will be displaced if there is any deviation
from the 'normal' order. Since it is 'normally' the second element, it
may be moved either to the head of the clause or towards the end.
And to these two basic categories we may add a third, to cover the
transposition of verbal elements—gerunds, infinitives, participles and
auxiliaries—among themselves.

[1] 43 in 720 in the *VN* poems: 58 in 982 in the later poems.
[2] There is clearly some relation between the difficulty of the rhyme-sounds and the
kind of deviation.
[3] Here is the full distribution:

Groups	No. of complex deviations	No. of clauses	
A	12	128	1 in 11
B	3	69	1 in 23
C	7	89	1 in 13
D	4	118	1 in 29
E	11	165	1 in 15
F	1	50	1 in 50
G	4	54	1 in 13
H	1	47	1 in 47
VN poems	43	720	1 in 17
I	4	221	1 in 55
J	16	250	1 in 15
K	15	167	1 in 11
L	7	76	1 in 11
M	16	268	1 in 17
Later poems	58	982	1 in 17

Inversion of verb and subject, bringing the verb to the initial position in the clause, was common both in prose and verse in the Duecento,[1] and it is certainly one of the most common deviations in Dante's poems. It occurs in 9 per cent of all clauses in the *VN* poems, and in 6 per cent of those in the later poems.[2] The most common species to occur in a pure, relatively unvaried form is, naturally enough, the inversion of finite verb and subject in a subordinate clause (44 instances) for example:

quando m'*apparve* Amor subitamente	I, 7
là 've non *pote* alcun mirarla fiso	XIV, 56
fa' che li *annunzi* un bel sembiante pace	IX, 42
dopo la qual *gridavan* tutti: 'Osanna'	XX, 61
(le fronde) che *trasse* fuor la vertù d'Ariete	C, 40–1

But inversions which bring the finite verb to the head of the *main* clause are collectively more numerous (63 examples). This naturally strong placing becomes more emphatic when the main clause opens the sentence, when it is not coordinated, when the verb is followed by an enclitic pronoun, when past participle and auxiliary are inverted, when the subject is delayed yet further behind an object or adverbial phrase, and, most of all, when the verb appears at the beginning of a stanza or of a poem, for example:

(E quando 'l maginar mi ven ben fiso), *giugnemi* tanta pena d'ogne parte	XXV, 49–50
ed *è* la sua vertù tanto possente	XXXIV, 7
Videro li occhi miei quanta pietate	XXXI, 1
Versan le vene le fummifere acque	C, 53
Fenno i sospiri Amore un poco tardo	CIV, 55
Dannomi angoscia li sospiri forte	XXV, 43
Ita n'è Beatrice in l'alto cielo	XXV, 15

[1] See Terracini, *Stile e lingua*, p. 106; Segre, 'La sintassi', p. 106 ('... il verbo ... sovente, e non a capriccio, si trovava invece davanti al soggetto, inserendosi così nella ricchissima categoria delle inversioni'.)

[2] 68 and 62 examples respectively. Note that complex deviations have been analysed as a combination of two or even three simple deviations, and that each of these is added to the total for the relevant species.

Aspects of sentence structure

> *Partissi* de la sua bella persona
> piena di grazia l'anima gentile   XXV, 29–30

Inversion of verb and subject may also occur where the verbal element is not finite, and there are 17 examples of this pattern. Then as now, it is particularly common in a 'far fare' construction, for example:

> che face *consentir* lo core in lui   XXXIV, 4
>
> farei parlando *innamorar* la gente   XIV, 8
>
> E poco *stando* meco il mio segnore   XXI, 7

We also find inversion of verb and subject in another group, where, however, the verb remains in the second position, because a complement, adverb or adverbial phrase has been moved into the initial position. This also was common in the Duecento,[1] and one finds more than 50 examples in these poems—the majority being in the later poems.[2] Here are some characteristic examples:

> *allor sente* la frale anima mia   XXIV, 7
>
> Ché *più* mi *triema* il cor …   CIII, 27
>
> nel cor mi *si comincia* uno tremoto   XIII, 13
>
> di fonte *nasce* il Nilo picciol fiume   CIV, 46
>
> Per grazia de la mia nota soave
> *reman* tu qui con lei   IX, 38–9
>
> Allegro mi *sembrava* Amor …   I, 9
>
> Tanto gentile e tanto onesta *pare*
> la donna mia …   XXII, 1–2

On the other hand, Dante makes very little use of the potentially

---

[1] Cf. Segre, 'La sintassi', pp. 102–3, 111; and Terracini, *Stile e lingua*, p. 98 ('L'iniziare una proposizione con un complemento che precede e verbo e soggetto è uso comunissimo nella sintassi italiana e romanza'), and pp. 105–6, where he states that 'l'inversione del soggetto all'inizio della proposizione, o quando questa si inizi con un complemento, avverbio ecc.', is a characteristic of Duecento prose in general.

[2] This compensates for the slight fall in 'pure' verb-subject inversions in the later poems. The totals are 19 and 33 respectively. Note that I have counted the half-dozen examples like the following in this group:

> Morta è la donna tua …   XX, 56
>
> ch'entrar no i puote spirito benegno   XXV, 34

There are a further three examples of the type *Anticipatory pronoun—Verb—Adv. phrase—Subject*, for example, 'Elli era tale a veder mio colore', XX, 21. See also XXVII, 14; CIII, 35.

ambiguous order, Object—Verb—Subject, although Segre finds it to be common in Guittone's prose.[1] I can find only the following undisputed examples:

> sì che la scusa mia ...
> ragioni poi con lei lo mio segnore   IX, 3–4
>
> tanto dolore intorno 'l cor m'assembra
> la dolorosa mente   XXVII, 4–5

while two more leave room for genuine doubt:[2]

> la quale ognora impetra
> maggior durezza e più natura cruda   CIII, 3–4
>
> ciò è che 'l pensier bruca
> la lor vertù, sì che n'allenta l'opra.   ibid., 33–4

Inversion of verbal element among themselves tends to move the finite verb towards the end of the clause. There are 80 examples of this kind, the most common species being that in which an infinitive precedes the verb on which it depends.[3] Next in importance comes the inversion of participle and auxiliary,[4] followed by prolepsis of the gerund. Prolepsis of the complement in clauses where the subject is not expressed is uncommon, but not unknown.[5]

Most common of all are those deviations in which adverbs or adverbial phrases precede the verb they modify. Of these there are no less than 262. The resultant displacement of the verb is insignificant in the case of the most common species, in which only one adverb is

[1] 'La sintassi', p. 102.
[2] Attempts have also been made to interpret the following lines in this way: CIV, 47; CVI, 1, 63.
[3] Cf. Segre, 'La sintassi', p. 108: 'Frequentissimo fu nella lingua antica l'uso di anteporre l'infinito al verbo servile da cui dipende ... Costruzioni del genere si trovano in ogni tipo di proposizione, ma particolarmente nelle secondarie.'
There are 37 examples, for example: (lingua non è) che dicer lo sapesse, XXV, 62; ma lagrimar dinanzi a voi non sanno, XXXII, 14; ... che perder lei s'attende, XIV, 26. The total includes 5 of this type: per non usar (vedete) son turbate, CIV, 62; ch'Amor per consumarmi increspa e dora, CIII, 64. Note one in a *rima composta* ... la tua caccia non seguer de', XCV, 14.
[4] Cf. Terracini, *Stile e lingua*, p. 107. There are 17 'pure' examples, and another 5 which I have considered above (for example: Fuggito è ogne augel, C, 27). There is one rather striking example in rhyme in VI, 13: ove l'alma gentil già locata era.
[5] For example: e quando trova alcun che *degno* sia, XIV, 37 ... qual vuol *gentil donna* parere, XIV, 31. In all there are 36 examples.

involved and the subject is not expressed,[1] but it becomes increasingly noticeable when adjectives are used with adverbial force,[2] when there are adverbial phrases,[3] when the phrase is placed between auxiliary and participle or between governing verb and infinitive,[4] and especially in the sequences Subject—Adverbial Phrase—Verb[5] or Adverbial Phrase—Subject—Verb.[6]

Here is a representative list of examples arranged in the 'ascending' order just described.

però che *spesso* ricorda Beatrice	XXXVII, 13
(Peccato face) chi *allora* mi vide	XII, 9
e *sol* s'accordano in cherer pietate	X, 7
lietamente esce da le belle porte	CVI, 32
li quai *disconsolati* vanno via	XXVI, 3
e *'n ciascuna sua parola* ridia	XXI, 6
che *nel suo pianto* l'udimmo parlare	XIX, 11
Io mi credea *del tutto* esser partito	CXIV, 1
poi che tu se' *ne la mia donna* stata	XX, 75
e fella *di qua giù a sé* venire	XXV, 26
che vede *in sua persona perfettamente* star ...	LXXXII, 117–18
Lo suo parlar *sì dolcemente* sona	LXXXI, 5
quando 'l pensero *ne la mente grave* mi reca quella ...	XXV, 44
onde cammino *al bel giorno* mi piacque	C, 56
per essemplo di lei bieltà si prova	XIV, 50
... che *per lo suo splendore* lo peregrino spirito la mira	XXXV, 7–8
ché *rado sotto benda* parola oscura giugne ad intelletto	CVI, 57–8

[1] 25 in the *VN* poems; 65 in the later poems.
[2] For example: 'Deh peregrini che *pensosi* andate, XXXVI, 1; 'Lascia piangere noi e *triste* andare', XIX, 9. A small class with only 11 examples, of which 9 are in the *VN* poems.
[3] 19 in *VN* poems; 35 in the later poems.
[4] 6 in *VN* poems; 18 in the later poems. Terracini, *Stile e lingua*, p. 108, is inclined to see rhetorical influence on this type in the prose of the *VN*.
[5] 18 in *VN* poems; 47 in the later poems.
[6] 9 in *VN* poems; 9 in the later poems.

Lasso, *per forza di molti sospiri,*
(che nascon de' penser che son nel core),
li occhi son vinti ...   XXXV, 1–3.

Prolepsis of adverbial elements is more common in the later poems than
in those of the *Vita Nuova* (176 and 86 respectively: the gains being
chiefly in the first and fifth classes distinguished above). It is difficult
to generalize as to the effect of this increase, but I think there is a new
tendency to use such prolepses for greater emphasis, or to bring out the
structure of an argument.

Here are two fairly extreme examples:

... ma *poco* vale,
ché *sempre* fugge l'esca.
Poi che girato l'ha chiamando molto,
gitta 'l pasto ver lui, *tanto* glien cale;
ma quei non v'apre l'ale:
e se *pur* vene quand'ell'è partita,
tanto par che li 'ncresca   CVI, 109–15

Chi diffinisce: 'Omo è legno animato',
prima dice non vero,
e, *dopo 'l falso,* parla non intero;
ma *più forse* non vede.
Similemente fu chi tenne impero
in diffinire errato,
ché *prima* puose 'l falso e, d'*altro lato,*
con difetto procede   LXXXII, 41–8

Another very important group of deviations which delay the verb
are those in which the *object* precedes the verb. There are 34 examples
in the *VN* poems, and 72 in the later poems.[1] In most cases the object
is a noun, the verb is finite, and the subject is either in its 'normal'
position, or, more commonly, not expressed.[2] But there is a small
group in which the object is a pronoun (other than a personal pro-

---

[1] Included in this total are 8 examples with what I took as 'object-equivalents', for
example: 'che parla Dio, che *di madonna* intende', XIV, 23; '*di lei e del dolor* fece
dimanda', CIV, 30.

[2] 17 in *VN* poems; 40 in later poems. See Segre, 'La sintassi', p. 110. 'Non si può
negare l'influsso latino nelle proposizioni principali con l'ordine Soggetto + Oggetto +
Verbo: esse non sono rare nel periodo delle origini ...'.

noun)[1], and another where the verb is in the infinitive or gerund.[2] There are even examples in which the object precedes the subject.[3] The following list exemplifies these categories:

Sola Pietà *nostra parte* difende	XIV, 22
ch'*altro penser* non lascia star con nui	XXXIV, 8
che *tal detto* rivolse, e *l'ultima particula* ne tolse	LXXXII, 26–7
chi *la mia donna* tra le donne vede	XXIII, 2
e qual donna gentil *questo* non crede	LXXXI, 39
... quand'ella *altrui* saluta	XXII, 2
(né di calore) come l'*altre* face	XXV, 19
per *prova* fare a le parole conte	CXIII, 13
Questi mi face *una donna* guardare	LXXIX, 23
(Amore, a cui io grido) *merʒé* chiamando ...	CIII, 37–8
Bianca, Giovanna, Contessa chiamando	CVI, 153
camera di perdon savio uom non serra	CIV, 106
e passan sì, che 'l *cor* ciascun retrova[4]	XIV, 54

We may now turn to some deviations which do not necessarily affect the position of the verb. There are two deviations in which a word or phrase introduced by a *preposition* precedes the word it qualifies. They are particularly important as they are probably more restricted to verse, or to rhythmic prose, than are any of the types we have considered hitherto. The simplest species consists of Preposition

---

[1] 5 in *VN* poems; 10 in the later poems.

[2] 6 in *VN* poems; 10 in the later poems. 'Di uso frequentissimo, in francese, in provenzale, in italiano, sia in prosa che in poesia, fu la posposizione dell'infinito al suo oggetto, specialmente trattandosi di infinito preposizionale ... e alquanto meno frequente la posposizione del gerundio ... Va ... notato che effettivamente la posposizione del gerundio è in Guittone assai più frequente che negli altri scrittori contemporanei, alternandosi essa circa in pari proporzione con la posizione ora normale' (Segre, 'La sintassi', p. 107). As will be seen, neither usage is at all common in these poems, and only two involve the gerund.

[3] 1 in *VN* poems; 7 in the later poems.

[4] The frequency of these prolepses of adverb and object bear out what Segre writes about word order in early Italian: 'Eppure il verbo in fondo era in certi casi quasi di regola, o comunque frequentissimo anche in prose di carattere piuttosto dimesso; in altri casi si alternava con la posizione ora normale' ('La sintassi', p. 106).

+Pronoun. These occur quite frequently in the chosen poems (54 instances), and their effect is out of all proportion to their simplicity and brevity, for example:

e ha lasciato Amor *meco* dolente	XXV, 14
ché forse non è bon *sanƷa lui* gire	IX, 10
ma ciascuna *per lei* riceve onore	XXIII, 11
ché la beltà ch'Amore *in voi* consente	CVI, 7
Allora presi *di lui* sì gran parte	VIII, 13
che fai *di te* pietà venire altrui	XIX, 6

Equally numerous (64 examples) are those proleptic phrases composed of Preposition+Noun, used to qualify either adjectives or nouns.[1] The most common preposition is 'di', for example:

s'io son *d'ogni tormento* ostale e chiave	V, 6
che *di tristiƷia* saettavan foco	XX, 48
Io divenia *nel dolor* sì umile	XX, 71
… son *d'amor* disciolti	C, 34
I'ho veduto già *senƷa radice* / legno	XCV, 1–2

Such deviations can seem decidedly harsh, and they are almost certainly meant to be so in the sonnet, *Morte villana*:

Morte villana, *di pietà* nemica,
di dolor madre antica,
. . . .
(*di te blasmar* la lingua s'affatica).
E s'io *di graƷia* ti vòi far mendica,
. . . .
lo tuo fallar *d'onni torto* tortoso,
(non però ch'*a la gente* sia nascoso),
. . . .
chi *d'amor* per innanzi si notrica.   VII, 1–2, 6–7, 9–10, 12

But they are by no means necessarily harsh, as the following lines show:

[1] To these we may add a further 22 examples in which a proleptic prepositional phrase introduced by 'a' serves as the indirect object of a verb, for example: 'che nulla invidia *a l'altre* ne procede', XXIII, 6; 'ch'*al prenƷe de le stelle* s'assimiglia', LXXXIII, 114.

di lei e del dolor fece dimanda.
'Oh *di pochi* vivanda',
rispose in voce *con sospiri* mista,
'nostra natura qui *a te* ci manda'[1]   CIV, 30–3

For reasons given earlier, I have not attempted to count the cases
in which adjectives are placed abnormally with respect to the nouns
they qualify. The following short list will, however, illustrate some of
the more interesting patterns, especially those involving adjective and
possessive pronoun, or two adjectives.

Non è *pura* vertù la disviata	LXXXIII, 77
ma vertù *pura* in ciascuno sta bene	LXXXIII, 88
che le saprà contar mia ragion *bona*	IX, 37
ch'io vi rassembri sì figura *nova*	XI, 3
Gentil ballata mia ...	IX, 43
... *diletta* mia novella	LXXIX, 60
... e sfida / la *debole* mia vita ...	CIII, 40–1
ma conoscete il *vil* vostro disire	CVI, 6
la segna d'*eccellente* sua famiglia	CVI, 30
del *lungo* e del *noioso* tacer mio	XCVI, 6
come *soave e dolce* mio riposo	XXVII, 11
Ahi *angosciosa e dispietata* lima	CIII, 22
ed omo apparve *scolorito e fioco*	XX, 54
e lo intelletto loro *alto, sottile*	XXVII, 25
divenne *spirital* bellezza *grande*	XXVII, 22
... ne l'altro / *dolce* tempo *novello* ...	C, 66–7
O *cara* ancella e *pura*	CVI, 39
cieco avaro *disfatto*	CVI, 76
sì è *novo* miracolo e *gentile*	XVII, 14
O *falsi* cavalier, *malvagi e rei*	LXXXIII, 112

---

[1] The two passages just quoted are indicative of a minor tendency for a number of
similar deviations to occur in the space of a few lines. Other examples include:
LXXXI, 23–7, 77–9; LXXXII, 42–8; C, 55–61; CVI, 32–6; CXI, 6–13 (all adverbial); C,
lines 15, 19, 23, 27, 35, 36 (objects); XXVII, 14–26 (complement—verb—subject). In
Donne ch'avete, the deviations often share the scheme A—C—B. See lines 2, 3, 6, 8,
10; 20, 22, 23, 26; 30, 31, 33, 37, 40, 41; 45, 47, 49, 52, 53, 54.

Summary

With this, our survey of word-order in Dante's poems is complete, because the other kinds of deviation are not sufficiently important to warrant close description.[1] And with this, too, we have taken the study of Dante's syntax as far as seems profitable in the present circumstances. We have seen, in passing, that almost all the syntactic features described are to be found—in some unspecified degree—in Dante's predecessors and contemporaries. And further light on Dante's syntax in his poems will be derived from comparable studies of *their* works, and not from a further multiplication of variables, or a further refinement of the information here presented. We have seen, also, that the differences between some of the groups are so immense that it is not really worthwhile to attempt any summary description of Dante's syntax. On the other hand, the picture is not chaotic. In many variables —those which permit a classification of alternatives as a progression from simple to more complex structures—we noted a broadly similar pattern of development. Structures of average complexity were first drastically simplified, then elaborated to obtain a degree of organization far superior to that of the first poems, and, finally, they were somewhat simplified to approach a near average level again. That pattern is however far from constant. And this means that although there is a loose correlation between the different variables, with changes in one being matched by corresponding changes in the others, there is still room for significant variations. The syntax of the poems in the last group is about as 'complex' as that in the first group, but it is in no sense merely a return to it. And taken as a whole, I suggest, the findings justify both the quantitative method and the reasonably wide range of variables studied.

[1] These are those in which an adverbial phrase precedes the complement (3 examples), or object (33 examples), and those in which adverbial elements seem abnormally placed with respect to each other. Here are two examples of each:

s'io fosse *dal mio lato* sì fellone	XXXIII, 6
Tu risomigli *a la voce* ben lui	XIX, 3
non preser mai *così mirabilmente* viso di donna ...	XXXII, 2–3
e li altri han posto *a le lor voci* triegue	C, 30
ch'*a la mia donna* ne li occhi dimora	LXXXII, 19
Ancor che ciel *con cielo* in punto sia	LXXXIII, 58

I append a table summarizing all the results given in the preceding pages. Note that the totals are for the number of deviations, and not the number of clauses with deviations, because, as explained earlier, complex deviations have here been resolved into their constituent elements.

	VN poems	*Later poems*	*Total*
Adverbs precede verbs	86	176	262
Dependent phrases precede 'governor' (inc. indirect objects)	60	87	147
Verbs precede subjects	68	62	130
Objects precede verbs	34	72	106
Verb precedes finite verb	32	43	75
Adverbs precede complements, objects, or *inter se.*	22	32	54
Adv. / Comp. + Verb + Subject	19	33	52
Complement precedes verb	11	23	34
	332	528	860

CHAPTER 5

THE HENDECASYLLABLE

In the *Convivio* Dante praises the beauty of his *canzone*, *Voi che 'ntendendo* under three heads corresponding to three of the liberal arts, grammar, rhetoric and music: 'la sua bellezza ... è grande sì per construzione, la quale si pertiene a li *gramatici*, sì per l'ordine del sermone, che si pertiene a li *rettorici*, sì per *lo numero de le sue parti*, che si pertiene a li *musici*' (*Con.*, II, xi, 9).

The 'odd man out' here is music, both because it belonged with the arts of number in the *quadrivium* rather than with the arts of language in the *trivium*, and also because Dante is clearly thinking of music in an extended sense. He is not here referring to a musical setting of his poem, such as Casella provided for *Amor che ne la mente* in the famous episode in *Purgatorio* II, but to the organization of the words themselves into harmonious structures by the use of metre and rhyme. And it is clear from other passages in his prose works[1] that music, so defined, was for Dante the distinctive element in poetry. It is 'music' that distinguishes poetry from artistic prose, just as this is set above ordinary correct speech by its rhetoric. The poet's special task is to bind words together, tempering their rough and smooth qualities, and bringing them into an aural harmony founded on number and proportion. The poet's 'bond' is not something extraneous like string, glue or mortar: the words must be so arranged that they support themselves. The 'legame' is the 'bella relazione' which in turn is the 'armonia' which we perceive as 'dolcezza'.[2] It is this musical bond which makes a poem

---

[1] See *Con.*, I, x, 12–13; *DVE*, II, i, i; iv, 2; vi, 2–5. An important new study of Dante's conception of music and metric has appeared since I wrote this chapter: M. Pazzaglia, *Il verso e l'arte della canzone nel 'De Vulgari Eloquentia'* (Florence, 1967).

[2] See *Con.*, II, xiii, 23–4. The key-words in the *De vulgari eloquentia* are *fascio, ligo, vieo; compago, contextus, fascis*. And Dante wholeheartedly accepts the derivation of *auctor* from the rare verb *auieo*, which not only *means* 'I bind', but is symbolically appropriate, in that it is formed exclusively of the five vowels, which are the 'soul and bond of every word': moreover, the very movements of the pen required in writing the verb suggest the act of binding: *Con.*, IV, vi, 3–4.

untranslatable.[1] It is to *musica* that Dante devotes the greater part of the second book of the *De vulgari eloquentia*, where *grammatica* is taken for granted, and *rhetorica* is dispatched in two chapters.

There are therefore compelling theoretical reasons for studying some of the 'musical' aspects of Dante's poems at this point before we return to features proper to the art of rhetoric. And there are excellent practical reasons also. For it is Dante's use of verse and rhyme which most distinguishes his utterances from a hypothetical style-less base. And the demands of metre and rhyme were both a curb and a spur to his expression at every moment.

I shall not describe Dante's experiments with the *canzone*-stanza; nor, with regret, shall I attempt to analyse his growing mastery in the handling of rhyme, although in some of the later poems, rhyme has become what it is in certain cantos of the *Comedy*, the germ of Dante's inspiration.[2] Instead, I shall limit myself to a close description of his use of the hendecasyllable. This means that once again it will not be possible to conduct the analysis in terms drawn from Dante's own theoretical works. For he concerns himself almost exclusively with the *stanza* (the '*room* in which the whole art of the canzone resides'),[3] and with *rhyme* as a formal element. Of the hendecasyllable he tells us little more than that it is superior to all other Italian lines in that it holds more words, and therefore more complex syntactic structures, and therefore a greater thought content.[4]

---

[1] 'E però sappia ciascuno che nulla cosa per *legame musaico armonizzata* si può de la sua loquela in altra transmutare sanza rompere tutta sua dolcezza e armonia' (*Con.*, I, vii, 14).

[2] For Dante's handling of the *canzone*-stanza, see Kenelm Foster and Patrick Boyde, *Dante's Lyric Poetry* (Oxford, 1967), vol. I, pp. xliv–xlix, and the index in vol. II, *s.v. canzone*. Also: A. Marigo's edition of the *De vulgari eloquentia* (3rd ed., Florence, 1957), introduzione, pp. cxxxv–clvi. K. Bartsch, 'Dantes Poetik' in *Jahrbuch der Deutschen Dante Gesellschaft*, III (1871), 303–67. F. D'Ovidio, 'La metrica della canzone secondo Dante', in *Versificazione romanza. Poetica e poesia medievale* (3 vols, Naples, 1932), vol. III, pp. 147–67.

On his use of rhyme, the fundamental study is still that by E. G. Parodi, 'La rima e i vocaboli in rima nella *Divina Commedia*', now in *Lingua e letteratura*, ed. G. Folena (2 vols, Venice, 1957), vol. II, pp. 203–84.

There are also some excellent observations in M. Fubini, *Metrica e poesia. Lezioni sulle forme metriche italiane*: vol. I, *Dal 200 al Petrarca* (Milan, 1962); and in G. Contini's introduction to his edition of Dante's *Rime* (2nd ed., Turin, 1946).

[3] *DVE*, II, ix, 2.

[4] 'Quorum omnium endecasillabum videtur esse superbius, tam temporis occupatione, quam capacitate sentenzie, constructionis et vocabulorum' (*DVE*, II, v, 3).

The object of study, then, will be the rhythm of Dante's hendecasyllables, and the main aim will be to provide the evidence about the relative frequency of certain rhythmic schemes, which is necessary for the proper evaluation of particular rhythms in particular poems.[1] This same evidence may also make it possible to distinguish certain aspects of Dante's rhythm from those of his near contemporaries—although this is problematical.[2] What the evidence will not reveal of course, are the secrets of Dante's 'armonia'. But once this has been made clear, it must also be said that the 'abstractable' rhythm of a line is an important factor in the total aural harmony; and we shall see that there are certain measurable differences in rhythm between poems that are usually felt to be 'soavi' or 'dolci', and those which are felt to be 'aspre'.

In what terms, then, are we to describe Dante's rhythm? Unlikely as it may seem, there is no obvious answer, for there is no universal agreement on the method of analysis. Thus, the number of possible schemes for the hendecasyllable has been variously computed as 3, 4, 6, 12, 48, 87, 261, 432 and 828.[3] And it must be emphasized that all

[1] One still meets quite unfounded claims for the inherent expressive force of certain schemes, which must in themselves be neutral simply because they are so common.

[2] There is little doubt that this kind of evidence would be more than adequate to distinguish Dante's rhythms from those of poets as remote as the Sicilians or Petrarch.

[3] For 3 schemes, see B. Migliorini and F. Chiappelli, *Elementi di stilistica*, 9th ed. (Florence, 1960), pp. 195–7. For 4 schemes, see L. Fiorentino and O. Locatelli, *Tesoretto* (Milan, 1954), p. 538. For 6 schemes, see the *Enciclopedia Italiana s.v.* None of the above profess to be exhaustive. For 12 schemes, see U. Sesini, 'Il verso neolatino nella ritmica musicale', in *Convivium*, x (1938), 481–502; and 'L'endecasillabo: struttura e peculiarità,' ibid., xi (1939), 545–70. For 87 schemes, see G. Fraccaroli, *D'una teoria razionale di metrica italiana* (Turin, 1887), pp. 104–19. For 432 schemes, see M. Serretta, *Endecasillabi crescenti nella poesia italiana delle origini e nel canzoniere di Petrarca* (Milan, 1938), p. 63. For 828 schemes, see A. Levi, 'Della versificazione italiana', in *Archivum Romanicum*, xiv (1930) 449 ff. In the latest Italian treatise to appear, R. Spongano writes: 'Sono 48 le sue varietà formali dipendenti dagli accenti, giungono a 87 con quelle dipendenti dalle combinazioni all'incontro degli emistichi e dalle sedi che può prendere la cesura, e salgono a 261 se si tien conto della mobilità delle sue uscite, che possono essere ... tronche o piane o sdrucciole', *Nozioni ed esempi di metrica italiana* (Bologna, 1966), p. 20.

By far the best account of Italian metric now available is Professor W. Th. Elwert's *Italienische Metrik* (Munich, 1968), which appeared too late for me to use it in preparing this chapter. Professor Elwert is particularly thorough, clear and persuasive in his discussion of the problems I have considered on pages 214–21. See the brief postscript at the end of this chapter.

For a general introduction and bibliography in Italian, see V. Pernicone, 'Storia e svolgimento della metrica', in *Tecnica e teoria letteraria* (vol. coll.) (Milan, 1948),

these schemes have been manufactured from the same raw materials. They are simply the different patterns formed by different sequences of stressed and unstressed syllables in the words which form actual hendecasyllables. In the more generous estimates, the totals have been inflated by consideration of the position and the type of caesura; but none of the prosodists responsible have attempted to describe or regulate the distribution of particular phonemes, or of monosyllabic and polysyllabic words, or of oxytones, paroxytones and proparoxytones, although there is no doubt that variables such as these have a considerable effect on the rhythm. Nor have the theorists multiplied their schemes by paying attention to the number of syllables a hendecasyllable may in fact contain if one ignores the metrical elision of vowels between words, or the metrical coalescence of vowels within words, although this variable too has important consequences. Contrast the movement of the following lines, each pair of which has an identical rhythmic scheme:

Aiutatemi donne farle onore	12 syllables
poi che hai data matera al cor doglioso	15 syllables
a donne assai quand'io t'avrò avanzata	15 syllables
venite voi da sì lontana gente	12 syllables
e par che sia una cosa venuta	12 syllables
ma qual ch'io sia la mia donna il si vede[1]	15 syllables

---

pp. 237–77. One of the best, non-legislative accounts of the hendecasyllable I have seen is in M. Amrein–Widmer, *Rhythmus als Ausdruck inneren Erlebens in Dantes 'Divina Commedia'* (Zürich, 1932), pp. 11–77.

[1] Confining analysis to the 634 hendecasyllables in the *VN* poems, one finds that the number of syllables ranges from 11 to 15. Here is the distribution.

No. of syllables	No. of hendecasyllables in *VN*	
11	180	29%
12	260	40·5
13	149	23
14	42	7
15	3	0·5
	634	100%

Note that these figures represent Barbi's text faithfully. They do not include Dante's aphaereses, syncopes or apocopes (e.g. 'ntelletto, spirto, amor), nor any of the editorial apostrophes.

Even more important still, they have not acknowledged the existence—metrically speaking—of a third class of syllables bearing what may be called an 'intermediate' or 'light' stress. If these were recognized as a distinct, metrically relevant class, the number of possible schemes would run into thousands or tens of thousands. But to this problem we shall return below.

Behind such differing estimates as those I have just quoted there must clearly be differences in aim and method. But it should be noted that the metricians in question show no disagreement on basic principles. We are dealing neither with the crude normative approach, anxious to reduce all hendecasyllables to their 'proper' scansion and quick to condemn 'faults', nor again with the extreme reaction to that approach, which would analyse the rhythm of each verse as though it were an isolated passage of prose, and without reference to some kind of pattern or 'yardstick' existing in the mind of the poet and his immediate audience. All the metricians would agree that hendecasyllables have certain common properties by virtue of which they are hendecasyllables and not just sequences of eleven syllables. All would accept, on the other hand, that there may be real and highly desirable variations in rhythm between one actual hendecasyllable and another. Metrical analysis must focus on the interplay between the norm and the variations. A metrician, as such, may be more concerned to define the common elements, just as the literary critic may be more concerned with the individual variations; but there is no question now of an opposition. The two aims are rightly seen as complementary.[1] The 'norm' or 'pattern' has no absolute existence, but it is not possible to make a proper description of a particular line of verse without a prior understanding of that pattern.

The disagreements between the metricians are to be found in their approach to the definition of the norm; and it is on this point that I find them all, much as I have learnt from them, in some respects unsatisfactory. Sesini, for example, assumed that simple rhythms are either binary or ternary. By definition, therefore, there cannot be two successive strong beats without an intervening weak beat or an equivalent rest, and there cannot be more than two successive weak beats. On this view there are twelve patterns for the hendecasyllable, neither more nor less, since that is the number of possible combinations of

[1] See the postscript to this chapter.

binary and ternary groups within its confines. Fraccaroli's approach had been similar in essence, in that his aim was to define all the possible correct forms of the hendecasyllable. However, since he was not a musicologist like Sesini, he had been ready to admit the possibility of a sequence of three or more unstressed syllables or of two stressed syllables, and as a result he recognized 87 patterns as normal. But although he was able to find examples of all but two of these patterns in the *Comedy*, his whole approach was misguided both because of its *a priori* character, and also because by this test virtually all hendecasyllables are normal, and one has thus sacrificed the fruitful opposition between norm and variation, or between fixed and free elements. On the whole, then, those who content themselves with three or four basic schemes seem to me to err in the right direction.

In my view, a proper description of the 'normal rhythmic pattern' of the hendecasyllable should consist of two distinct parts; and both parts of the description should be recognized as valid only for the named poem or poet or period from which they have been derived: they may have wider validity, but this must not simply be taken for granted. We need to know: (a) which are the features common to *all* hendecasyllables in the sample analysed, or at least to an overwhelming majority of them; and (b) which are the most common actual schemes. This demands, in turn, that the rhythm of the hendecasyllables should be analysed *in the first place* as though each were an isolated phrase, clause or sentence of prose, that is, *without metrical expectation*. This may seem to contradict what was said above, but, obviously, we must not prejudge the issue of what constitutes the norm. The norm must be derived from the poems themselves, not be imposed on them. It is therefore most important to stress that, with the specific exceptions to be explained below, every scansion quoted in this chapter is a schematic description of the rhythm of the metrically relevant syllables in a particular hendecasyllable, as it would be heard in a 'prose' reading made with due attention to the sense and as objectively as possible.

Objectivity is made easy in one important respect just because all the hendecasyllables in the chosen poems—at least, as they appear in Barbi's text—do have eleven metrically relevant syllables,[1] when due

---

[1] The only apparent exception is LXXXIII, 33 (in rhyme with a heptasyllable), which has twelve syllables: but this is a 'verso sdrucciolo'. There are no 'versi tronchi' in the poems analysed.

allowance has been made for regular coalescence and elision.[1] Thus, there are always eleven 'positions' to be occupied by stressed or unstressed syllables, and this makes possible a description that is both economical and non-committal. All that need be done is to determine where the linguistic stresses fall, ascertain which positions they occupy, and write these as cardinal numbers; for example, if the stressed syllables fall in the second, sixth and tenth positions, the rhythmic scheme may be written 2—6—10. It is easy to compare schemes written in this way, and there is no prejudgement as to the regularity or irregularity of a verse, or as to its coincidence or non-coincidence with any predetermined scheme.

Absolute objectivity, in the sense of the possibility of complete agreement between all analysts on the scansion of all lines, founders on the problem of what I will call the 'intermediate' or 'light' stress. Italian prosody, like all other systems,[2] assumes that syllables may be divided into two classes, and not more than two. In the case of Italian, these are 'stressed' and 'unstressed'. More often than not, there is no difficulty in assigning a syllable to one or other of these classes. Broadly speaking, there is one stressed syllable in every noun, adjec-

---

[1] The earliest description of 'sinalefe' and 'sinerisi' in Italian metric may be of interest:
  'Sic ergo si in versu sonetti vel rithimi vulgaris excepto motu confecto inveniatur una vocalis ante alteram vocalem, quia una dictio finiret in vocalem, et sequens inciperet a vocali, nunquam reputarentur illae duae vocales nisi pro una syllaba, ut in hoc exemplo huius proximi versus vulgaris:
        "Chi porge al pover, giamai non gli manca."
  Nam illa vocalis litera *e*, quae est in fine illius dictionis *porge*, habetur pro non adiecta quantum ad numerum syllabarum.'
  'Si vero *in eadem dictione* vocalis veniat ante vocalem, saepissime et regulariter abjicitur una vocalis, licet non sit in metris grammaticalibus et poëticis, et maxime abjicitur in dictionibus bisyllabis, ut in his dictionibus *dio*, *mio* et *tuo*, *mai* et *hai* et similibus; quamlibet penes grammaticos sint bisyllabae, tamen in hac arte rithimici vulgaris tantum monosyllabae reputantur ... *nisi praedictae dictiones apponantur in rithimo in fine versus, quia tunc non abjicitur aliqua vocalis,* sicut patebit infra in exemplis.' Antonio da Tempo, *Summa artis rytmici vulgaris dictaminis*, ed. G. Grion (Bologna, 1869), p. 75.
[2] See J. Lotz, 'Metric Typology', in *Style in Language*, ed. T. A. Sebeok (New York–London, 1960), pp. 135–48. 'It is interesting to note that the phonological elements are grouped into only two base classes, never into more, although in principle much finer gradations would be possible. For example, in English, more than two stress levels could be utilised ...' (p. 141). For two very relevant, interesting and sensitive discussions of the problems in English metric, see J. Thompson, *The Founding of English Metre* (London, 1961), esp. pp. 1–14; and Marie Borroff, *Sir Gawain and the Green Knight. A Stylistic and Metrical Study* (New Haven and London, 1962), esp. pp. 144–91.

tive or verb which contains two or more syllables. Other syllables in these words, and those in articles, monosyllabic conjunctions and prepositions are unstressed. But difficulties do arise with other monosyllabic words. To which class must one assign pronouns like 'io', 'te', nouns like 're', verbs like 'ho', 'sei', adverbs like 'poi', 'qui', 'non', and interjections like 'ah'? And to which class does the more prominent syllable belong in bisyllabic pronouns like 'vostro', 'questo', or in adverbs like 'bene', 'quando', 'però', or in conjunctions like 'perché'? And how are we to treat the secondary stress in words with four or more syllables, such as 'smarriménto', 'oblieréste', 'corteseménte'? Italian metricians never seem to tackle this problem at a theoretical level, and they vary greatly in their practice. In general, one may suspect a tendency to *promote* all these ambiguous cases, where the analyst sees the hendecasyllable as a predominantly iambic metre, and a tendency to *demote* them where the analyst prefers to work with three or four simple schemes.[1] There is of course no straightforward answer to the questions just raised, simply because the perceptible levels of 'stress' or 'intensity' in Italian are not two but many. This is why scansion must remain to some extent subjective. But this is also why an analyst should show his awareness that a problem exists, state the principles he has tried to apply, and indicate his scansion of some of the more controversial verses in order that the reader may form his own opinion of the reliability of the findings.

My own empirical solution has been to recognize one 'intermediate' level of stress which covers all doubtful cases such as those exemplified above, and then to resolve at a later stage, and as a separate issue, the metrical status of these intermediate stresses, defining as closely as possible the circumstances in which they should be treated as stressed, and those in which they should be treated as unstressed, since metrical analysis cannot admit any third category. Thus, in the first 'diagnostic' analysis of the rhythm of a given hendecasyllable, any such intermediate stress was distinguished by the compound symbol ⌣; and its presence and position was indicated by a cardinal number in brackets, placed *after* the numerical notation described above, showing the posi-

---

[1] For example, both Chiappelli and the *Enciclopedia Italiana* quote the opening line of the *Comedy*. For the former it exemplifies the scheme 2—6—10; for the latter 2—6—8—10.

tion of the stressed syllables. For example, the following similar lines
would be distinguished as follows:

˘ ˘ ˘ ´ ˘ ˘ ´ ˘ ˘ ´ ˘ che nel suo pianto l'udimmo parlare[1]	4—7—10
˘ ´ ´ ´ ´ tu risomigli a la voce ben lui	4—7—10 (1)
˘ ´ ´ ´ ´ che non sospiri in dolcezza d'amore	4—7—10 (2)
´ ´ ´ ´ angelo clama in divino intelletto	1—4—7—10
´ ´ ´ ´ cader li augelli volando per l'are	2—4—7—10

It is at this point that one must take the fateful decision. Are the
second and third of these examples to be classified with the first, or are
they to be classified with the fourth and fifth respectively? It is a
difficult choice; but on the whole my experience suggests that the first
alternative is to be preferred. And this means that, as a general rule, a
syllable bearing an intermediate stress should be treated as an unstressed syllable. But only *as a general rule*: and we must now consider
the exceptions.

Intermediate stresses may rank as strong stresses on either of two
distinct grounds, which we may call 'syntactic' and 'metrical'. In the
first place, then, an intermediate stress may be 'promoted' if the sense of
the context demands that the syllable be given an emphatic stress. Such
promotion will not be awarded arbitrarily (although it is here that
subjectivity must enter[2]), but will follow indications in Dante's syntax.
The word in which the syllable occurs must be placed in an unnatural
position, or be followed by a marked 'pause' necessitated by a dislocation of word-order elsewhere in the clause or phrase; alternatively,
the word must be contrasted with another word in its own class, or it
must be repeated in a symmetrical position. The following examples
will make this clear (only the 'promoted' stresses are marked):

˘ ´ ˘
non vi saprei io dir ben quel ch'io sono

---

[1] In another syntactic or metrical context *suo* might well carry a 'promoted' strong
stress, in the sense to be described below. But where, as in this case, there is no
possible doubt as to the metrical status, I have not recorded an intermediate stress.

[2] Thus, to return to a matter broached in the note to p. 216, I would scan the first line
of the *Comedy* as 2—6—10 (8), and *not* as 2—6—8—10. There are some general
reasons for awarding an emphatic stress to 'nostra', but there is no specific justification
in the syntax—no displacement, no following 'pause', no opposition, no repetition.

nó la ci tolse qualità di gelo

di léi e del dolor fece dimanda

Só ío che parla di quella gentile

chí la mia donna tra le donne vede

peró quando mi tolle sí 'l valore

e pói vidi venir da lungi Amore

tál volta poca e tál lunga stagione

ógne dolcezza, ógne pensero umile

⎧ áltro sperando m'apporta dolzore
⎨
⎩ áltro pianger mi fa spesse fiate

⎧ (che sí com'elli m'era forte in pria)
⎨
⎩ cosí mi sta soave ora nel core

piú non vói discovrir quál donna sia

Before I can explain the *metrical* grounds which justify the promotion of certain intermediate stresses, we must examine part of the evidence concerning the *rhythmic norm* in the hendecasyllables analysed. We must proceed in fact to the first of the two necessary descriptions of that norm, and establish which are the common features shared by the great majority of rhythmically unambiguous lines.

The only elements to be held absolutely in common may be set down as follows: (a) all the hendecasyllables have eleven metrically relevant syllables; (b) there is always a stressed syllable in the tenth position. Analysed as prose, we could describe the hendecasyllables as *isocola* with an identical rudimentary *cursus* ($|$ $\smile$).

In the majority of cases, one of the stressed syllables in the first nine positions is metrically more important than the others. It achieves this dominant status by virtue of its near central position, and because the word in which this syllable appears is usually followed immediately by the caesura.[1] Some lines have no caesura; while others have two;[2] and

---

[1] There have been many conflicting attempts to define the term 'caesura'. The most satisfying I have yet seen is to be found in a paper by S. Chatman, 'Comparing

in some lines it is difficult to decide which of two 'rival' stressed syllables should be regarded as dominant. But for the great majority of lines, the following propositions hold true: (c) the hendecasyllables have a dominant stress in addition to the fixed stress; (d) this dominant stress falls either in the fourth or the sixth position.

As one would expect from the nature of the language, sequences of three unstressed syllables occur quite frequently, but a sequence of five unstressed syllables would be extremely rare. And this explains the last feature of the norm: (e) there is a third stressed syllable falling between the beginning of the line and the sixth position when this has the dominant stress, or between the fourth position and the tenth when the dominant stress falls in the fourth position. There may of course be more than three stressed syllables in the line, but the norm requires a *minimum* of three, distributed in the way just described.

We may now return to the intermediate stresses and describe the metrical grounds which require their promotion to the rank of stressed syllables. Such promotion will occur: (a) if the intermediate stress falls in the tenth position; (b) if it falls in the fourth or sixth positions when the other has no stressed syllable; (c) if it occurs as one of a sequence of five unstressed syllables in the longer part of the line.

Some examples will make this clear:

> (a) chiamando il nome de la donna mía
>
> che face consentir lo core in lui
>
> (b) Amore è qui che per vostra bieltate

Metrical Styles', in *Style in Language*, ed. Sebeok, pp. 149–72: 'The caesura is ... a perceptible break in the performance of a line, properly described as an *intralinear terminal juncture*' (p. 167).

'Junctures may be briefly defined as the boundary phenomena which signal important structural splits in utterances. Thus the two utterances "He came quickly, dispersing gifts" and "He came, quickly dispersing gifts" are distinguished by having the juncture in different positions ... These junctures may be of 4 sorts: a downward movement of the voice, an upward movement, an even movement with delay or suspension of some sort, and an even movement without delay (the difference between "a name" and "an aim", "that stuff" and "that's tough"). Absence of juncture is called smooth transition' (p. 158 note).

2 For example: io presi tanto smarrimento allora

e tolsimi   dinanzi a voi   sentendo

madonna   involta in un drappo   dormendo

che sì com'elli m'era forte in pria

sarebbe innanzi léi piangendo morta

che luce de la súa umilitate

(c)   sì che la vita quási m'abbandona

perché 'l piacere de la súa bieltate

e sì cóme la mente mi ridice[1]

If the line has a caesura, this is of vital importance in determining which is the dominant stress, and it may also create some anomalies. Thus, an intermediate stress in the fourth or sixth positions is *not* promoted in lines like the following, where the caesura follows a dominant stress in an abnormal position, for example:

per grázia de la mia nóta soave

a voler ch'è di veritáte amico

onde l'ánimo ch'è dritto e verace.

And, conversely, the intermediate stress may be promoted if the word in which it occurs is followed by the caesura, even though there is a natural stressed syllable in the other normal position.

levava li occhi miei	bagnati in pianti
bagnar nel viso súo	di pianto Amore
lingua non è	che dicer lo sapesse
dentro la quál	dormendo si riposa

Exposition of these procedural details has taken up a good deal of space, but I hope it has also justified its own length. It should be clear by now why assertions about the frequency of certain schemes are worthless, unless one knows how the analyst has approached the study of rhythm and metre, and, in particular, how he has dealt with those ambivalent syllables which have been classified as bearing an 'inter-

[1] Usually there are additional emphatic grounds for the promotion, for example:

ed è la sua vertù tanto possente

sì com'io credo, è ver di mé adirata

mediate' stress. Comparison of results is not possible unless these have been produced by the same methods; and this is why I have been unable to draw on Sesini's findings for Petrarch's *Canzoniere*.[1] To sum up: in the following survey all analysis of rhythm is based on a 'prose' reading in which nothing is assumed *a priori* to be impossible. Scansion is influenced by 'metrical expectation' only in the case of certain syllables bearing an 'intermediate' stress, and the norm on which this expectation depends is derived not from textbooks but from the poems themselves.

As our first variable we may consider the position of the dominant stress. How many lines do *not* have the dominant stress in one of the two 'normal' positions, the fourth or the sixth? Which if either of these two positions is more common?

We have seen that the concept of 'dominant stress' is intimately

[1] Sesini's approach is eminently sane and consistent, but is radically different from that adopted here. One should scan, he writes,

'facendo corrispondere, in linea di massima, gli accenti tonici e gli accenti secondari delle parole alle tesi ritmiche dei membri binari o ternari. In linea di massima, giacché la non corrispondenza tra tesi e accento è talora necessaria, e fino ad un certo grado tollerabile. Quindi non si confonda tesi ritmica con accento grammaticale ... L'accento deve cadere su tesi ritmica, e infatti nella assoluta maggioranza dei casi vi cade; per l'opposto la tesi ritmica può trovarsi benissimo su sillaba atona' (p. 151).

In some cases the systems of scansion coincide, for example (the examples and scansion are all Sesini's):

lassar il velo o per sole o per ombra

Et punire in un dì ben mille offese

Spezza a tristi nocchier governi e sarte.

But his system leads him to ignore linguistic stresses, as in:

E 'l giorno andrà pien di minute stelle;

to promote unstressed syllables without syntactic justification:

e col mondo, e con mia cieca fortuna;

to promote the wrong syllable:

nudo se non quanto vergogna il vela;

to promote intermediate stresses unnecessarily:

movesi il vecchierel canuto e bianco;

or to displace a linguistic accent:

onde questa gentil donna si parte.

See also the postscript to this chapter.

connected with that of 'caesura'. If we insist that the two concepts are interdependent, and that in a line where we recognize a caesura the dominant syllable must be in the word which precedes that caesura, then some 3 per cent of Dante's hendecasyllables depart from the norm,[1] for example:

distrutta hai l'amorosa leggiadria	(3)
che fa li miei spiriti gir parlando	(5)
quand'i' vegno a veder voi bella gioia	(7)
o voi che per la via d'Amor passate	(8)
e 'n ciascuna parola sua ridia	(8)

If, on the other hand, we allow our expectation of the normal pattern to influence the scansion, then we may choose to regard a stressed syllable (not a promoted stress) falling in the fourth or sixth positions as dominant, even though the word in which it occurs does not immediately precede the caesura. Thus in the first and in the last three examples the stressed syllables in 'amorosa', 'veder', 'via' and 'parola' would be dominant.

If we adopt this criterion (as has been done in all that follows), then only about 1 per cent of the hendecasyllables *cannot* be scanned as normal.[2] These are:

IX, 38	per grazia de la mia nota soave	2—7—10
XXII, 12	e par che de la sua labbia si mova	2—7—10
XXXII, 6	vedetevi la mia labbia dolente	2—7—10
LXXXII, 59	onde l'animo ch'è dritto e verace	3—7—10 (1)
LXXXII, 119	che seme di felicità sia costa	2—8—9—10 (5)
LXXXIII, 82	o in abito che di scïenza tiene	2—8—10
LXXXIII, 83	dunque s'ell' è in cavalier lodata	1—8—10 (4)

---

[1] Some 20 in the *VN* poems; between 30 and 40 in the later poems.

In the *VN* poems there are 3 out of a total of 634. In the later poems there are 10 in 697.

CIII, 15	né lòco che dal suo vìso m'ascónda	2—7—10
CIII, 45	e 'l sàngue ch'è per le véne dispérso	2—7—10
CVI, 44	si fà chi da cotal sérva si scòsta	2—7—10 (3, 6)
CVI, 56	più lìeve sì che men gràve s'intènda	2—7—10 (6)
CVI, 132	in ciascùn è di ciascùn vìzio assémbro	3—7—8—10
CVI, 2	a volér ch'è di veritáte amíco[1]	3—8—10

In the *VN* poems, 55 per cent of the hendecasyllables have the dominant stress in the fourth position, or, to put it in traditional terminology, 55 per cent are of the type called *a minore*.[2] In the later poems, the *a maiore* type, with dominant stress in the sixth position, become slightly more frequent, but the *a minore* lines still retain a narrow majority (52 per cent and 47 per cent respectively). In general, one finds something like these proportions in each poem, and even within each strophe. But of course, there are exceptions. Among the sonnets in the *Vita Nuova*, for example, *Deh peregrini* has thirteen *a minore* lines, whilst *Io mi senti' svegliar* has only two. There is also some evidence that the rhythmically harsher poems have a higher than average proportion of *a maiore* lines. In group M, for example, the harsh *Doglia mi reca* has 48 per cent *a maiore* hendecasyllables, 48 per cent *a minore* and 4 per cent 'abnormal'; whereas in *Tre donne* there are 63 per cent *a minore* and 37 per cent *a maiore*, with no exceptions. In group K, *Io son venuto* has the average proportions of 53 per cent and 47 per cent, but the harsher *Così nel mio parlar* has only 38 per cent *a minore* and 60 per cent *a maiore* lines.

---

[1] Professor Grayson writes that he would scan 'felicità' as 'felícita' in the fifth example (as 'pietà' becomes 'piéta' in five lines in the *DC*). He regards the seventh example as normal (i.e. he would promote—in my terminology—the intermediate stress on 'è').

For the penultimate example he would suggest a 4—8—10 scansion: 'in ciascun è di ciascùn vìzio assémbro'; and he remains dubious about the last example.

[2] They are called *a minore* because they 'begin with' the *shorter* hemistich. My use of this convenient terminology must not be taken to imply that every line does have a caesura 'cutting' or 'articulating' it into two unequal parts, or to imply that there is not a marked caesura elsewhere in the line, either in addition to the central one, or in its stead.

We have seen that every hendecasyllable has at least three stressed syllables (of which one may well be a promoted 'intermediate' stress). One is fixed, one is dominant, and the other falls in the longer hemistich. We may therefore take the position of the third, 'free' stress as our next variable, and distinguish various families within the two principal species. Since the fifth position is only rarely occupied by a stressed syllable, and even in those cases it is never the only stress in the hemistich, we find eight families, four in each species. Thus, among the *a minore* hendecasyllables, we find the basic schemes 4—6—10, 4—7—10, 4—8—10, 4—9—10, as in the following examples:

4—6—10   quando guardaste li atti e la statura

che fa de' polsi l'anima partire

4—7—10   che da le genti vergogna mi parte

che qual l'avesse voluta mirare

4—8—10   e ascoltando le parole vane

che mi tramuta lo color nel viso

4—9—10   di caunoscenza e di verità fora

e teme ancora sì che mi par fero[1]

In the species *a maiore* the basic schemes are 1—6—10, 2—6—10, 3—6—10, 4—6—10, for example:

1—6—10   priego che con vertù il correggiate

piacemi di prestare un pocolino

2—6—10   natura ch' al difetto fa riguardo

del prun che con sospir si medicina

[1] Professor Grayson is once again sceptical of my scansion of these two lines. He suggests that, like 'felicità', 'verità' might then have been read as 'vérita'; and he would not take 'par' as a stressed syllable. These are the only two examples of their kind in the chosen poems.

3—6—10   ma vólgibile cór ven disvicína

            salutò le germáne sconsoláte

4—6—10   ló mio pénser di fúor sì che si scópra

            che m' ha férito il córe e che m'invóla

It is both possible and convenient to allocate all *a minore* and *a maiore* hendecasyllables to one of these eight families, even when they have four or five stresses. The only difficulties in classification arise with those lines that have two or even three 'free' stresses in the longer hemistich. For example, the following line has the scheme: 2—4—6—8—10,

            ché più mi triéma il cór qualóra io pénso

It is clearly *a maiore* because the caesura falls after the sixth position. But it would be reasonable to classify it either with the 2—6—10 family or with the 4—6—10 family. The solution adopted here embodies the principle: 'to him that hath shall be given'. Thus, among verses with only three stresses, the 2—6—10 pattern is far more common than the 4—6—10. Accordingly, any *a maiore* line with a stress falling in the second position is considered to belong to the 2—6—10 family. The order of preference for each species (determined by the relative frequency of the verses with three stresses) is: *a minore* 8, 7, 6, 9; *a maiore* 2, 3, 4, 1.

The most common family is the 4—8—10, to which 28 per cent of all the hendecasyllables belong. This is followed fairly closely by the 2—6—10 family (24 per cent), and then at greater intervals by those with the schemes 4—7—10 (16 per cent), 3—6—10 (11 per cent), 4—6—10 (*a maiore*) (9 per cent), 4—6—10 (*a minore*) (8·5 per cent). There are only 29 examples (in 1331) of the family 1—6—10, and only 2 of the family 4—9—10.[1]

---

[1] The figures are 'weighted' by the principle used in classification, as described above. It must not be assumed that a stress in the first position is in any way unusual (see the survey of *incipits* below).

The distribution is remarkably constant in both the *VN* and the later poems. The only significant differences are a rise in the 2—6—10 family (there is a general rise in the number of *a maiore* lines), offset by a fall in the 4—7—10 family.

The evidence we have examined so far all relates to the first of the two accounts of Dante's norm—the description of the elements and features common to all his hendecasyllables. We must now move on to the second—the description of the actual rhythmic schemes[1] which recur most frequently.

Some 15 schemes may be called 'common', in that each is used more than twenty times in either the *VN* poems, or the later poems, or both.[2] Taken together they account for nearly two-thirds (64 per cent) of all the hendecasyllables.

Here are the totals and percentages:

	VN poems			*Later poems*	
'*Family*'	Total	Percentage		Percentage	Total
4—8—10	182	28·5		28	198
2—6—10	138	21·5		25	174
4—7—10	114	18·5		15	104
3—6—10	72	11		10·5	75
4—6—10	62	9·5		8·5	59
4—6—10	51	8·5		8·5	58
1—6—10	11	2		2·5	18
Others (inc. 4–9)	4	0·5		2	11
Total hendecasyllables	634				697

[1] From this point, all verses which are said to share one scheme are *exactly* alike with regard to the distribution of their stressed syllables (although 'promoted' stresses are not distinguished from 'natural' stresses). They may differ from one another in the number and distribution of 'intermediate' stresses; in the presence or absence of a caesura, and also in its position (although usually it falls immediately after the word bearing the dominant stress); and finally in the type of word ('tronca', 'piana' or 'sdrucciola') which precedes the caesura.

[2] Here are the totals for each scheme (the position of the dominant stress is shown by the italicized numeral):

					No. of examples	
Scheme				*VN poems*	*Later poems*	*Total*
2	*4*		8	10	48	57	105
	4		8	10	56	43	99
2		*6*		10	41	49	90
2		*6*	8	10	28	42	70

Since they are in every sense characteristic, I will give two examples
of each type, starting with the most common:

2—4—8—10	Ne li òcchi pórta la mia dònna Amóre	XVII, 1
	de' stár colùi che le mie pári ancíde	LXXIX, 37
2—6—10	fu pósta da l'altíssimo signóre	XXX, 3
	d'un'angela che 'n cíelo è coronàta	LXXIX, 29
4—8—10	che di tristízia saettàvan fóco	XX, 48
	ove una dònna gloriàr vedía	LXXIX, 17
2—6—8—10	si mòsse con paùra a piànger fórte	XX, 6
	un spírito da cíel che réca féde	LXXXI, 42
4—7—10	io divenía nel dolór sì umíle	XX, 71
	elle sovérchian lo nóstro intellétto	LXXXI, 59
2—4—7—10	passò li cíeli con tánta vertúte	XXV, 22
	ma prègia il sénno e li génti coràggi	LXXXIII, 38

Scheme (cont.)					VN poems	Later poems	Total
	4	7		10	33	30	63
2	4	7		10	32	31	63
	4		8	10	34	24	58
	4	7		10	23	25	48
2	4 6		8	10	25	(16)	41
2	4 6		8	10	(15)	25	40
3	6			10	(17)	23	40
3	6		8	10	(17)	20	37
2	6	7		10	22	(17)	39
	4 6			10	(13)	23	36
2	4 6			10	(7)	22	29
					411	447	858

1—4—8—10	dànnomi angòscia li sospìri fòrte	XXV, 43
	piéna d'amòre e di cortése lóde	LXXXII, 130
1—4—7—10	éscono spìrti d'amòre inflammàti	XIV, 52
	óltre 'l dimàndo di nòstra natùra	LXXXI, 29
2—4—6—8—10	colór di pérle ha quàsi in fòrma quàle	XIV, 47
	ancór che cièl con cièlo in pùnto sìa	LXXXIII, 58
2—4—6—8—10[1]	bieltàte appàre in sàggia dònna pùi	XVI, 9
	colór che vìvon fànno tùtti còntra	LXXXIII, 133
3—6—10	cavalcàndo l'altr'ièr per un cammìno	VIII, 1
	per lo ràggio lucénte che la 'nfòrca	C, 5
3—6—8—10	e dicéva a' sospìri andàte fòre	XXX, 7
	che m'infiàmmano il còr ch'ìo pòrto ancìso	CIII, 75
2—6—7—10	e d'ònne consolàr l'ànima spòglia	XXV, 40
	con èsse passeréi véspero e squìlle	CIII, 69
4—6—10	che si movéan le làgrime dal còre	XXXI, 10
	per non usàr vedéte son turbàte	CIV, 62
2—4—6—10	ch'ìo sólo intèsi il nòme nel mìo còre	XX, 17
	paròla oscùra giùgne ad intèlletto	CVI, 58

A further 18 per cent of Dante's hendecasyllables conform to one of twelve schemes, which we may term 'less common'. For admission to this *ad hoc* category, the scheme must appear between 5 and 20 times

---

[1] These two schemes are identical except for the position of the caesura. This is often difficult to place, and sometimes a decision one way or the other is quite arbitrary. Taken together, the 2—4—6—8—10 schemes would be the third most frequent. Similar problems are presented by those with the schemes 4—6—10 and 4—6—10, etc.

in *both* the *VN* poems and the later poems: thus, each scheme accounts for between 1 per cent and 3 per cent of the total number of hendecasyllables. Three points should be noted about this group.[1] All but one have a stressed syllable in both the fourth and sixth positions, whereas only 4 of the 'common' schemes had stresses in both positions. Two pairs of schemes are identical except for the position of the caesura; and if each pair were taken as one scheme, both the resultant schemes would be regarded as 'common' (there are 41 examples of 1—4—6—

[1] Less common schemes:

							No. in	
		Scheme				VN	Later poems	Total
(a)	2		4	6		10	17	19	36
(b)			4	6	8	10	9	19	28
(c)	1		4	6		10	15	9	24
(d)	1		4	6	8	10	10	14	24
(e)			4	6		10	12	12	24
(f)	2		4	6	7	10	11	11	22
(g)			4	6	8	10	9	11	20
(h)		3		6	7	10	6	12	18
(i)	1		4	6	8	10	10	7	17
(j)			4	6	7	10	11	6	17
(k)	1		4	6	7	10	9	5	14
							119	125	244

Examples (one of each, in the order given above):

(a)	trovai Amore in mezzo de la via	VIII, 3
(b)	sì che bassando il viso tutto smore	XVII, 5
(c)	piena di grazia l'anima gentile	XXV, 30
(d)	tanto gentile e tanto onesta pare	XXII, 1
(e)	lo peregrino spirito la mira	XXXVII, 8
(f)	veggendo li occhi miei pien di pietate	XX, 4
(g)	che la mia donna andò nel secol novo	XXV, 61
(h)	e vedea che parean pioggia di manna	XX, 58
(i)	fugge dinanzi a lei superbia ed ira	XVII, 7
(j)	e lo intelletto loro alto sottile	XXVII, 25
(k)	videro li occhi miei quanta pietate	XXXI, 1

8—10, and 48 examples of 4—6—8—10). Four of the schemes have a 'clash' between stressed syllables, that is they have stresses falling in adjacent positions, whereas among the 'common' schemes only one had such a clash. Like that common scheme (2—6—7—10), the 'clash' is limited to the sixth and seventh positions: 108 hendecasyllables with 'common' and 'less common' schemes have this kind of 'clash'.

It is possible to isolate another eight schemes, which occur more than five times in either the *VN* poems or the later poems, but *not* in both. These—accounting for 5 per cent of the total—we may call 'uncommon.'[1] The remaining schemes, which account for 13 per cent of all hendecasyllables, may be called 'rare'. Four of these 'uncommon' schemes have 'clashes' between stressed syllables (in the positions 6—7, 2—3, 3—4, 9—10).

[1] Uncommon schemes:

Scheme									No. in		
									VN poems	*Later poems*	*Total*
(a) 1 6 10									1	14	15
(b) 1 4 6 10									3	7	10
(c) 3 4 8 10									–	9	9
(d) 2 3 6 8 10									7	2	9
(e) 1 4 6 7 10									3	5	8
(f) 1 3 6 8 10									5	3	8
(g) 2 6 9 10									–	6	6
(h) 1 6 8 10									5	1	6
									24	47	71

Examples:

(a)	cóme con dismisúra si raúna (così con ...)	CVI, 85
(b)	Cóntra-li-errànti mía tu te n'andrái	LXXXII, 141
(c)	e 'l parlár nòstro che non ha valóre	LXXXI, 17
(d)	cosí vànno a pigliár villàn dilétto	LXXXIII, 54
(e)	écco l'ancélla túa; fà' che ti piàce	LXXIX, 52
(f)	cuì è scórto 'l cammíno e póscia l'érra	LXXXII, 39
(g)	è tàl che non potrébbe adequár ríma	CIII, 21
(h)	díce uno spirìtel d'amór gentíle	LXXIX, 42

It will not be profitable to study separately the 'rare' schemes found in 158 hendecasyllables. Of these all but the 13 listed earlier do have a stressed syllable in the fourth or sixth position, and, with the exception of some 50 lines, where the evidence of the caesura or caesurae had to be set aside, it was not difficult to assign them to one of the 'families' within the main species. Indeed, one can explain many of these patterns as a 'common' or 'less common' scheme, with an extra stress in an unusual position. Most of them have four or five stressed syllables (only 10 have six), and almost all have some clashes between stressed syllables.[1]

[1] As examples of 'rare' schemes, and to allow the reader to form an opinion of the system of scansion, I will quote the 18 lines in which I have recognized a stress in the *fifth* position (said to be impossible in many manuals of versification). It should be noted that I have recognized a stress in the equally 'impossible' *ninth* position in 43 lines (17 in the *VN* poems, 26 in the later poems).

	(e quando trova alcun che degno sia)	
3—4—5—6—10	di veder lei quei prova sua vertúte	XIV, 38
1—4—5—7—10	sola Pietà nostra parte difénde	XIV, 22
2—4—5—7—10	vedeste voi nostra donna gentíle	XVIII, 5
2—4—5—8—10	tu dei omai esser cosa gentíle	XX, 74
1—4—5—8—10	ogne dolcezza ogne pensero umíle	XVII, 9
2—4—5—8—10	veggendo in lei tanta umiltà formáta	XX, 72
4—5—8—10 (2)	*che fa li miei spiriti gir parlándo*	XXIV, 10
4—5—6—7—8—10	*non vi saprei io dir ben quel ch'io sóno*	XXV, 64
2—5—6—9—10	ma quei che n'uscian for con maggior péna	XXX, 12
4—5—6—8—10	ch'io mi sentia dir dietro spesse fíate	V, 10
2—4—5—8—10	tu sai che 'l ciel sempr' è lucente e chiáro	LXXXI, 77
4—5—7—10 (1)	chi diffinisce: omo è legno animáto	LXXXII, 41
2—4—5—8—10	vedete omai quanti son l'ingannáti	LXXXII, 140
2—5—6—10	causata di più cose; per che quésta	LXXXII, 85
2—4—5—6—10	ché 'l saggio non pregia om per vestiménta	LXXXIII, 36
	...	
	(ma pregia)	
2—5—6—8—10	però, se leggier cor così vi vólve	CXIV, 12
3—5—6—9—10	disvelato v'ho, donne, in alcun mémbro	CVI, 127
2—4—5—6—10	e crede amor fuor d'orto di ragióne	CVI, 147

To conclude this survey of the different schemes used by Dante, it will be useful to look at the material already presented from two different points of view: first, to note the number of stressed syllables in each line; second, to consider the favoured *incipits* and cadences.

When scanned according to the principles described above,[1] 28 per cent of Dante's hendecasyllables have only three strong stresses in the line, 51 per cent have four stresses, and 20 per cent have five stresses. The proportions are remarkably constant in both early and late poems.[2]

We have already noted that all Dante's hendecasyllables have the same rudimentary cursus (/ –). If we extend our gaze back along the line, and consider the disposition of the stressed syllables in the preceding positions, we find that all but about 6 per cent of the lines share three fundamental *cursus*:[3]

> 45 per cent have two trochees (/ – / –);[4]
> 28·5 per cent have a dactyl and a trochee (/ – – / –);[5]
> 21·9 per cent have a paeon and a trochee (/ – – – / –).[6]

If we study the *incipits* without reference to how the verse develops after the fourth syllable, we find that 92 per cent conform to one of

---

1 This breakdown could serve as a rough guide to the analyst's practice with respect to the 'intermediate' stresses. Thus, in Sesini's system, all hendecasyllables have at least 4 *tesi*; and according to him, the two schemes which are far and away the most common in Petrarch (1—4—6—8—10 and 2—4—6—8—10) both have five.

2

	VN poems		*Later poems*		*Overall*	
	Total	%	%	Total	Total	%
3 stresses	178	28	29	199	377	28
4 stresses	308	48	53	368	676	51
5 stresses	140	22	18	128	268	20
6 stresses	8	1	—	2	10	1
	634			697	1331	

3 These, and the figures for the *incipits*, have been obtained from all the hendecasyllables —common and rare—in the *VN* poems. The distribution of all prosodic variables is so similar in the *VN* and later poems that the overall figure would be very close.

4 285 out of 634. Of these, 143 have three trochees (/ – / – / –).

5 181. Of these, 80 have the cursus / / — — / — (ionic major and trochee).

6 136. In prose terms, the dactyl and trochee form the *cursus planus*; whilst the paeon and trochee is the Ciceronian favourite, the *cursus trispondaicus*, as in 'esse videatur'.

five patterns.[1] The most common (27·5 per cent) is formed by two iambs (– / – /). The others are: – – – / (25 per cent); / – – / (17 per cent); – / – – (15 per cent); – – / – (7 per cent).

I have deliberately refrained from identifying *incipits* and cadences with *quinari* and *settenari* as several Italian metricians do,[2] even though, as Spongano writes, 'questi si presentano a volte individuati nel suo stesso interno, in forza della rimalmezzo'.[3] In the first place it tends to perpetuate the view, now definitively rejected, that the hendecasyllable was originally created by the fusion of these two lines.[4] Second, it tends to draw attention away from the rhythmic unity of the line. Third, it implies that all hendecasyllables do have a clear 'terminal juncture' or 'sense pause' where the two verses join. Fourth, it creates more schemes than are analytically useful as the number of schemes obtained from analysis of the stressed syllables alone has to be multiplied by three.

However, the centre of the line is clearly as important as the beginning or the end, and the caesura is an important variable. In particular, the movement of a hendecasyllable is much influenced by the kind of word—'tronca', 'piana' or 'sdrucciola'—in which the dominant stress falls, and which therefore precedes the caesura.[5] Consider the following examples, of which the first four all have the scheme 4—8—10, the second four all have the scheme 3—6—10.

e sol s'accordano   in cherer pietate   x, 7

s'era svegliato   nel destrutto core   xxx, 6

---

[1] The actual totals in the *VN* poems for each incipit are:

– / – /	174
– – – /	157
/ – – /	111
– / – –	97
– – / –	43

582 out of 634 = 92%

[2] For example, Fraccaroli, Serretta, Chiappelli, Spongano.

[3] *Nozioni ed esempi*, p. 21.

[4] See ibid., p. 21, and D'Arco S. Avalle, *Preistoria dell'endecasillabo* (Milan–Naples), 1963.

[5] Italian metricians describe the caesura itself as 'tronca', 'piana', or 'sdrucciola'. Note that the findings refer to the word bearing the dominant stress in *every* hendecasyllable, whether or not it would be followed, in performance, by a 'terminal juncture'.

i' vo' con vói   de la mia donna dire[1]   XIV, 2

la qualità   de la mia vita oscura   XXXI, 6

in persona de l'ánima   dolente   XXVI, 13

maraviglia ne l'átto   che procede   XIV, 17

a respetto di léi   leggeramente   XIV, 12

e ragiona d'amór   sì dolcemente   XXXIV, 3

Taking all hendecasyllables together, the kind of word most used before the caesura is the 'parola piana'. This in itself is of little or no interest. What is of interest is that in the species *a maiore*, a 'parola tronca' is more common in this dominant position than a 'parola piana'.[2] In a majority of cases, therefore, the line is 'cut' into two nearly equal parts, either 5+6 or 6+5.

The hendecasyllable permits a splendid variety of rhythms, even when one considers the relatively simple variables that have been described above. A strophe of 14 lines will generally have at least 10 different schemes, even without taking the caesurae into account. It is

---

1 It is useful to distinguish true oxytones from metrical oxytones, i.e. those in which there is synaeresis in the stressed syllable.

2 Here is a full table. The 13 lines listed earlier which do not belong to either of the two main species have been omitted.

Kind of word at caesura	VN poems	Later poems	Total	%
A Minore				
Sdrucciola	1	—	1	—
Piana	254	277	531	75
Tronca	42	62	104	15
Tronca/Sineresi	51	22	73	10
	348	361	709	
A Maiore				
Sdrucciola	8	6	14	2
Piana	109	142	251	41·5
Tronca	126	127	253	41·5
Tronca/Sineresi	40	51	91	15
	283	326	609	

rare for lines with an identical scheme to follow one another, and comparatively rare for more than three or four of one *species* to be juxtaposed. And even where this does occur, as in *Deh peregrini*, Dante still varies *incipits* and cadences to avoid monotony.

It is in the study of individual poems that the findings presented in this chapter will be most immediately useful: their significance for the characterization of Dante's style will remain latent, until comparable figures are produced for other authors. In the meantime, they are at least a step towards the 'studio non disutile' envisaged by Fraccaroli:

Anche sarebbe uno studio non disutile certo, secondo i vari autori e più secondo le varie epoche e secondo l'intonazione della poesia, esaminare quale delle tante forme possibili più prevalesse o prevalga, e qual meno, vedere la differenza che corre in proposito tra la letteratura popolare (che in generale si attiene di più al ritmo giambico puro) e quella dei dotti.[1]

POSTSCRIPT

I should like to add a few more words concerning the different aims of the metrician and literary critic (see above, p. 213). Thanks in particular to Professor Elwert, I have come to see the merits of the system of scansion advocated by Sesini more clearly than when I first worked on the rhythm of Dante's hendecasyllables. Putting all technicalities aside, the moderate position they adopt is very close to that of F. L. Lucas, which he summarized in the following persuasive passage:

Some prosodists seem to me too lawless; to find as many as seven stresses in some decasyllabic lines, and as few as three in others, brings mere anarchy. Others seem too rigid; it is clearly ridiculous to scan in mechanical sing-song—

> While SMOOTH ADONiS FROM his NATiVE ROCK
> RAN PURple TO the SEA.

For 'from' and 'to' are syllables less prominent, or stressed, than the un-stressed 'While' or 'Ran'. But the fallacy lies in taking all the stressed syllables in a verse line to be more strongly stressed than all its unstressed syllables. Stress is only relative, not absolute—relative to the syllable before and the

[1] *D'una teoria razionale*, p. 118. According to his system of classification, set out with examples from the *Comedy* on pp. 113–17, the 15 'common' schemes would be (in order of frequency): aC; Gc; cC; Ga; cF; aF; bC; bF; Aa; aA; Fc; Fa; Gb; cG; Ac.

syllable after ('from', helped by the metrical pattern, is more strongly stressed than 'is' before it, or 'his' after it; 'to' than '-ple' or 'the').

In short, an iambic or trochaic line undulates like a telegraph-wire on a rolling plain, where the crests of some undulations are actually lower than the troughs of others; but, none the less, the undulations remain.

F. L. Lucas, Style (1955), ch. 10, p. 192n.

There would thus be no difference, from the *metrical* point of view, between the line from *Paradise Lost* quoted by Lucas, and such other Miltonic lines as:

> Or sight of vernal bloom, or summer's rose
>
> Of Man's first disobedience, and the fruit
>
> Those thoughts that wander through eternity
>
> Dusk faces with white silken turbans wreath'd.

But although the iambic pulse is not displaced in any of these lines, their rhythms are very different one from another. And these differences are no less important to the analyst of style than the kind of 'displacement' which will lead the metrician to recognize a distinct scheme, for example when a trochee is used instead of an iamb in the first foot of

> Bitter constraint and sad occasion dear.

These are the differences to which I have tried to do justice.

Perhaps it will be necessary in future to maintain a sharper distinction between the rhythm and the metrical structure of each hendecasyllable—a distinction which I have tended to minimize or even eliminate. Two distinct analyses could then be prepared, one following criteria similar to those I have adopted in this chapter, the other following the principles set out by Sesini and Professor Elwert. It would be extremely instructive to know how often and in what ways the two analyses produced different schemes.

CHAPTER 6

REPETITION AND ANTITHESIS

In this chapter we shall study the role of repetition in Dante's poems, taking this in its widest sense to include the repetition of mere letters, the repetition of words or word-roots, and the repetition of concepts, either by use of synonyms or by negation of the opposite concept. In other words, we shall consider all forms of repetition except rhythm and rhyme.

It is, of course, a far cry from alliteration to antithesis; and it is not suggested that all the following usages should be reduced to one simple variable: '*v*ersan le *v*ene', 'd'onni *tort*o *tort*oso', 'a scorza a scorza', 'malvagia e croia', 'omo no, mala bestia . . . ' There is first and foremost a basic distinction to be made between *conceptual* repetition on the one hand, and, on the other, *verbal* or phonetic repetition, in which the repeated element could be heard, or seen on the page, even by someone ignorant of the language. Nevertheless each of the examples just given does embody some form of repetition; and the variables are related not only in the mind of the linguist but in practice. For, although each species may occur in isolation, it is more common for one to occur in conjunction with others, and, in particular, for conceptual repetitions and antitheses to be pointed and reinforced by verbal repetitions, as in the following:

tanto la parli *faticosa e forte*	LXXIX, 55
e non responde / il lor *frutto a le fronde*	LXXXIII, 104–5
Come *con dismisura si* rauna, così *con dismisura si* distringe	CVI, 85–6

There is a further obvious distinction to be drawn between repetitions that are merely casual or even inevitable, and repetitions that have been introduced or retained to achieve some deliberate effect. The dividing line will not always be clear, of course; and we must beware of getting involved in any dispute as to an author's intentions. But the distinction must be made; and it usually can be made by looking for evidence of organization. Deliberate repetitions will declare themselves either by their insistency (as in Mark Antony's 'honourable men' speech), or by their symmetrical or otherwised contrived placing in the sentence or paragraph.

Clearly, it was only *organized* repetition, constituting as it does a departure from the norm, which could interest the rhetoricians. And interest them it did! The earliest figures to be consciously used and taught—the so-called Gorgianic figures—were all figures of repetition; and more than a quarter of the 65 figures given in the *Rhetorica ad Herennium* involve repetition at one of the five levels exemplified above.[1] Indeed organized repetition is so characteristic of the rhetorical style, both in theory and in practice, that wherever we find it, and especially where repetition *in verbis* sharpens repetition *in sententiis*, we may reasonably suspect a strong rhetorical influence on the text, whether at first or second hand.

If we limit our investigation to the species of organized repetition which were recognized as figures in the rhetorical manuals, then the story of repetition in Dante's poems is easily told. In the *VN* poems such figures are used little if at all: in the later poems they become more and more frequent. But this does not mean that we can simply pass over the role of repetition in the *VN* poems, because it plays an important part there in a more diffuse way and at a less obvious level. Repetition of this kind will not permit any description couched in numerical terms; but we may still avail ourselves of medieval literary theory by taking as our points of departure the figure *expolitio* of the Latin *artes*, and the 'coblas capfinidas' of the Provençal tradition.

The 'coblas', that is the stanzas, of a Provençal 'vers' or 'canso' were said to be 'capfinidas' when the last word in each stanza was repeated as the first word in the next, thus creating a verbal link between the 'cap' or 'head' of the new stanza and the 'fin' of its predecessor.[2] The

---

[1] 14 of the 35 *figurae verborum*, and 4 of the 19 *figurae sententiarum*, still excluding *isocolon*, *homoeoteleuton* and *homoeoptoton*. The very first figure is *repetitio*.

[2] '*Anadiplosis* est, quando ab eodem verbo quo prior versus finivit, sequens versus incipit, ut est illud (*Eclogues* VIII, 55):

> Certent et cygnis ululae, sit Tityrus *Orpheus*,
> *Orpheus* in silvis, inter delphinas Arion,'

Et., I, xxxvi, 7. See also Capella, V, 533, Matthew of Vendôme, III, 7.

artifice is not always encountered in this pure form, however: it may be loosened to a point where a word anywhere in the last line of a stanza is repeated, or even merely echoed by another word formed from the same root, somewhere in the first line of the next stanza. In its pure or looser forms this concatenation of stanzas was not uncommon among the troubadours,[1] and it was among the many stylistic features taken over by the Sicilian School. In Italy, however, it was not destined to find lasting favour, and although it occurs in a loose form in two of Guinizzelli's most important *canzoni*, it seems to have become a rarity by the end of the thirteenth century.

In *all* Dante's *canzoni* the artifice is to be found in its pure form only in one place. The second and third stanzas of *E' m'incresce di me* (LXVII) are linked by a copy-book repetition of the word 'innamorata':

st. 2, 'fin' e partir la convene *innamorata.*
st. 3, 'cap' *Innamorata* se ne va piangendo   28–9

It is true that the first and second stanzas of the same poem, with the repetition of 'pace' in the middle of the new first line, are clearly meant to be 'capfinidas'. And there are certainly a number of similar repetitions in other poems which, taken in themselves, could certainly be classed as cases of loose concatenation.[2] But since they occur in isolation they are no more significant than the cases where a verbal repetition links *frons* and *sirima* .[3] On the whole, then, it is reasonable and significant to say that Dante's *canzoni* do not have 'coblas capfinidas'.

On the other hand, there are a number of Dante's *canzoni*,[4] in which the 'joins' between all the stanzas are made through some form of conceptual repetition, and where this conceptual link is thrown into relief by at least one rhetorically unclassifiable verbal repetition. Here for example are the 'points of contact' in *Li occhi dolenti* (XXV):

[1] R. Dragonetti, *La technique poétique des trouvères dans la chanson courtoise. Contribution à l'étude de la rhétorique médiévale* (Bruges, 1960), p. 453, says that the device is characteristic of the epic and that 'on ne la rencontre que par exception dans la tradition lyrique'. But the trouvères as a whole were a good deal less virtuoso in all aspects of their technique (cf. ibid., p. 457).

[2] For example IX, 24, 25; L, 12, 14; LXVIII, 14, 15. The *ballate* are considered separately below.

[3] For example, XIV, 8–9; XXII, 8–9; XXV, 6–7; XXXVII, 8–9.

[4] Notably XXV; XCI; CIII.

I 'fin'   che si n'è *gita* in *ciel* subitamente,
          e ha *lasciato* Amor meco dolente.

II 'cap'   *Ita* n'è Beatrice in l'alto *cielo*,
           nel reame ove li angeli hanno pace,
           e sta con loro, e voi, donne, ha *lassate*:

II 'fin'   e fella di qua giù a sé venire,
           perché vedea ch'esta vita noiosa
           non era *degna* di sì *gentil* cosa.

III 'cap'   Partissi della sua bella persona
            piena di grazia l'anima *gentile*,
            ed èssi gloriosa in loco *degno*.

III 'fin'   ma ven tristizia e voglia
            di *sospirare* e di morir di pianto,
            e d'onne consolar l'anima spoglia
            chi vede nel *pensero* alcuna volta
            quale ella fue, e com'ella n'è tolta.

IV 'cap'   Dannomi angoscia li *sospiri* forte,
           quando 'l *pensero* ne la mente grave

IV 'fin'   poscia *piangendo*, *sol* nel mio lamento
           chiamo Beatrice, e dico: 'Or se' tu morta?'
           e mentre ch'io la chiamo, me conforta.

V 'cap'   *Pianger* di doglia e sospirar d'angoscia
          mi strugge 'l core ovunque *sol* mi trovo

Clearly, these are not 'coblas capfinidas' even in the loosest sense of the term; and, equally clearly, the two phenomena are not unrelated. But what is the nature of that relationship? Was Dante unconsciously influenced by the traditional artifice? Was he deliberately alluding to it, while reworking it in a less rigorous way? Or was there a deeper and more general common cause?

That the artifice had some influence on the structure of this poem can hardly be denied, but I would be inclined to posit a common cause for both phenomena in a widespread attitude to composition. If the 'joins' between the stanzas are examined more closely, it will be seen that they are of two kinds: either the close of the first stanza introduces the theme to be developed in the next; or the opening of the new stanza summarizes the matter of the preceding stanza before proceeding to a new subject. In other words, the verbal and conceptual repetitions are there because the poet has given either a *preview* or a *summary* of what he has to say.

Now this use of a preview or a summary is significant in several ways. It can remind us, in the most forcible way, that the matter of a typical stanza its often such that its substance can be conveyed in a very few words. And it demonstrates that the poet himself, in the act of composition, saw his task as the elaboration of a *thema*. As we have seen time and again, this was the normal approach to composition in the manuals of rhetoric; and it is worth noting that the actual introduction of such 'signposts' or 'milestones' as the preview or summary was also in accordance with rhetorical precept, and was indeed characteristic of all branches of medieval pedagogy. Finally, the use of preview and summary not only makes the poem easier to grasp for the listener, but it provides in itself a simple and (within narrow limits) a satisfying formal scheme.

Previews and summaries of this sort occur frequently in Dante's poems. Sometimes they declare themselves quite openly as in *Voi che 'ntendendo:*

> Io vi dirò del cor la novitate,
> come l'anima trista piange in lui,
> e come un spirto contra lei favella,
> che vien pe' raggi de la vostra stella. LXXIX, 10–13

or

> Madonna è disiata in sommo cielo:
> or vòi di sua virtù farvi savere. XIV, 29–30

or

> e io così per falsi li riprovo,
> e da lor mi rimovo;
> e dicer voglio omai, sì com'io sento,
> che cosa è gentilezza, e da che vene,
> e dirò i segni che 'l gentile uom tene. LXXXII, 76–80

But more often their presence is not so immediately obvious, and, as a result, it is easy to mistake what is either elaboration or summary, for the introduction of a new and distinct idea or subject. For example, from a careless reading of *Sì lungiamente* (XXIV), especially if one were misled by the modern senses of 'però' and 'poi', one might deduce,

241

that the second *pes* and the *sirima* are descriptions of successive states:

Sì lungiamente m'ha tenuto Amore
e costumato a la sua segnoria,
che sì com'elli m'era forte in pria,
così mi sta soave ora nel core.

Però quando mi tolle sì 'l valore,
che li spiriti par che fuggan via,
allor sente la frale anima mia
tanta dolcezza, che 'l viso ne smore,

poi prende Amore in me tanta vertute,
che fa li miei spiriti gir parlando,
ed escon for chiamando
la donna mia, per darmi più salute.
Questo m'avvene ovunque ella mi vede,
e sì è cosa umil, che nol si crede.

In fact 'però' and 'poi', mean *not* 'however' and 'then', but 'hence' and 'because'; and under the guise of giving an explanation, they merely re-state and elaborate the sense of line 4. If a new idea does appear after line 4, it comes not in line 5, but in lines 11–12.

Once we have become aware of the technique of composition and the simple structures it creates, we are in a position to appreciate certain simple but effective refinements to it. For example, in some of the early sonnets the summary may come not in the last line, but in the eleventh or twelfth; and the closing lines function as a 'coda' which introduces a new idea, or at least some new twist to what has gone before, and carries us for the first time beyond the point stated in the opening preview. Being unpredicted, the close is all the more effective, whether it moves towards a paradoxical climax as in *Tutti li miei penser* (x),[1] where the poet calls on his *enemy* to defend him, or whether

---

[1] No. x may be analysed as follows:

THEME 1–2	Tutti li miei penser parlan d'Amore;
	e hanno in lor sì gran varietate,
ELABORATION 3–8	ch'altro mi fa voler ... etc.
DEVELOPMENT 9–10	Ond' io non so da qual matera prenda;
	e vorrei dire, e non so ch'io mi dica:
SUMMARY 11	così mi trovo in amorosa erranza!
'POINT' 12–14	E se con tutti vòi fare accordanza,
	convenemi chiamar la mia *nemica*,
	madonna la Pietà, che mi *difenda*.

it subsides in a dying fall as in the following sonnet, *Con l'altre donne* (XI):[1]

> ma non sì ch'io non senta bene allore
> li guai de li scacciati tormentosi.

This technique of the climactic 'coda' will be used to excellent effect and with unprecedented subtlety in the *congedi* to the mature *canzoni*, and especially in those to the 'canzoni petrose'.[2]

In the later poems as a whole, the mode of composition we have just considered is not so all-pervasive. In particular, the four ethical *canzoni* in groups J and M are built on different principles and on a very different scale; and, as a result, they show only a few traces of a verbal or conceptual concatenation of stanzas.[3] But in the 'canzoni petrose', repetition enters into the structure with great ingenuity and virtuosity. In the *sestina* (CI) and the *canzone-sestina* (CII), repetition of key-words is transformed into a structural principle, usurping the function normally held by rhyme. In *Io son venuto* (C) of which we shall speak more fully in chapter 8, each stanza has exactly the same *materia*. And in *Così nel mio parlar* (CIII), every stanza is linked in a way that recalls *Li occhi dolenti*.[4]

---

[1] In no. XI the theme is stated in lines 2–3 ('e non pensate, donna, *onde*, si mova / ch'io vi rassembri *sì figura nova*'), and is re-stated in almost the same words in line 12 (*ond'*io mi cangio in *figura d'altrui*) before the poem moves on to its 'coda' quoted in the text.

[2] See the analyses in the notes to the poems in Kenelm Foster and Patrick Boyde, *Dante's Lyric Poetry* (Oxford, 1967), vol. II.

[3] In *Le dolci rime*, there is a general preview of the whole poem in lines 12–17, and a second preview of the last three stanzas (quoted above) in lines 78–80: but none of the stanzas are linked in the way shown in *Li occhi dolenti*. In *Poscia ch'Amor* only the last three stanzas are in any way linked, and here again one cannot usefully speak of repetition. In *Tre donne* the first line of the third stanza recapitulates the second; in *Doglia mi reca* there is antithetical 'join' between the first and second stanzas, whilst the fifth stanza begins with a double repetition—but that is all.

[4] The second stanza begins with a summary of the first, with one verbal repetition ('Non trovo scudo ch'ella non mi *spezzi* / né loco che dal suo viso m'asconda'). The third opens with an 'explanation' of the close of the second—again with one repetition ('sì di rodermi il *core* . . . Ché più mi triema il *cor*'). The fourth develops what had been announced at the beginning of the preceding *sirima* ('E' m'ha percosso in terra, e stammi sopra / con quella spada . . . Egli alza ad ora ad or la mano . . .'). The fifth begins with an antithesis to the close of the fourth ('Morte *m*'avrà chiuso / prima che 'l colpo sia disceso giuso. / Così vedess' io lui fender per mezzo / lo core *a la crudele*'). The sixth opens with a development, including synonymic repetition, from the close of the fifth ('ne' *biondi capelli* / ch'Amor *per consumarmi* increspa e dora / *metterei* mano . . . S'io avessi le *belle trecce prese*, / che fatte son per me *scudiscio e ferza*').

243

In the *ballata*-form, the use of preview and elaboration is not optional but statutory. The *ripresa* should state the theme of the whole poem; and it is normally linked to the opening of the first stanza by a verbal repetition, for example:

> 'I' mi son pargoletta bella e nova,
> che son venuta per mostrare altrui
> de le bellezze del loco ond'*io fui*.
>
> *I' fui* del cielo ...'   LXXXVII, 1–4

But to understand the thematic structure of a typical *ballata* it is better to start from the figure, or rather the rhetorical exercise, known as *expolitio*. There could hardly be a better description of the early poems of praise than the definition of this figure in the *Rhetorica ad Herennium*: 'expolitio est cum in eodem loco manemus et aliud atque aliud dicere videmur'.[1] The author in fact recognized two distinct forms of the figure. The first he calls 'eandem rem dic*ere* ... sed commutate'— a description which would certainly fit *Io son venuto*, although this was hardly what the author had in mind. The second he calls 'de eadem rem dic*ere*'; and for this he prescribes a definite sequence of operations. One should state the proposition, and give a reason to support it; then re-cast the proposition in a different form of words, and add another reason if desirable; then argue from the contrary proposition; then bring up a comparison and an *exemplum*, and finally present the proposition once more in the form of a syllogism or enthymeme.[2]

One will not find a complete formal *expolitio* in any of Dante's poems,[3] nor indeed is there any poem which closely resembles the

---

[1] See *Ad Her.*, IV, xlii, 54–xliv, 58. It is the author's version of the preliminary exercise or *progymnasma* known in Greek as the *Chreía*, and translated by Priscian as *Usus*— see in C. Halm (ed.), *Rhetores Latini Minores* (Leipzig, 1863), p. 552. In the Middle Ages it became the first source of *amplificatio*: see *PN*, 220–5, 1,301–44; *Documentum*, II, ii, 45–70 (essential reading); *Laborintus*, 309–12; John of Garland, p. 916. For a fuller discussion, see E. Faral, *Les arts poétiques du XII*e *et du XIII*e *siècle* (Paris, 1923, reprinted 1958), pp. 63–7; R. Baehr, 'Studien zur Rhetorik in den Rime Guittones von Arezzo', *ZRP*, LXXIII (1957), 212–14 and 220–3; Dragonetti, *La technique poétique*, pp. 289 ff.

[2] 'Sed de eadem re cum dicemus, plurimis utemur commutationibus. Nam cum rem simpliciter pronuntiarimus, rationem poterimus subicere; deinde dupliciter vel sine rationibus vel cum rationibus pronuntiare; deinde adferre contrarium ...; deinde simile et exemplum ...; deinde conclusionem'. (*Ad. Her.*, xliii, 56).

[3] Baehr has analysed two *canzoni* by Guittone (nos. I and XXXVII) in the light of the *expolitio*, and concludes 'wohl aber kann man sagen, dass das *System der expolitio* B'

figure. But it is easy to find quite a number of passages which conform
to its spirit and its general outline. Perhaps the best way to approach
these poems will be through Dante's own gloss to the sonnet, *Ne li
occhi porta*. In chapter xxi of the *Vita Nuova* he writes:

Questo sonetto si ha tre parti: ne la prima dico sì come questa donna riduce
questa potenzia in atto secondo la nobilissima parte de li suoi occhi; e ne la
terza dico *questo medesimo* secondo la nobilissima parte de la sua bocca ...
Poscia quando dico 'Ogne dolcezza', dico *quello medesimo che detto è ne la
prima parte*, secondo *due atti* de la sua bocca; l'uno de li quali è lo suo dol-
cissimo parlare, e l'altro lo suo mirabile riso...   *VN*, xxi, 5, 8

Critics who write on the *Vita Nuova* as a whole often react with
condescending pity or even hostility to passages like this. But in my
view it is quite wrong to dismiss them as pedantic afterthoughts. They
offer us a reasonably accurate guide to the way in which such a poem
was composed. For nearly all the poems in praise are built up by this
kind of repetition,[1] obtained by moving from the lady's 'anima' to
her 'corpo' (and hence from 'gentilezza' to her 'bieltà'), or from her
eyes to her mouth; or from the poet's sight to his hearing, from the
present to the past or future, from 'sospiri' to 'pianti', from 'spiriti' to
'pensieri', or from 'io' to 'ogn'om'; and it is through this kind of
unobtrusive repetition that the poems achieve form. Take, for
example, the third strophe of *Amor che ne la mente:*

> In lei discende la virtù divina
> sì come face in angelo che 'l vede;
> e qual donna gentil questo non crede,
> vada con lei e miri li atti sui.
>
> Quivi dov'ella parla, si dichina
> un spirito da ciel, che reca fede
> come l'alto valor ch'ella possiede
> è oltre quel che si conviene a nui.
>
> Li atti soavi ch'ella mostra altrui
> vanno chiamando Amor ciascuno a prova
> in quella voce che lo fa sentire.

(i.e. *de eadem re dicere*) 'fast in allen Gedichten mehr oder weniger wirksam ist',
'Studien zur Rhetorik' (1957), p. 223.
[1] On 'variations ornementales' in the lyrics of the 'trouvères', see Dragonetti, *La
technique poétique*, pp. 294–303.

> Di costei si può dire:
> gentile è in donna ciò che in lei si trova,
> e bello è tanto quanto lei simiglia.
> E puossi dir che 'l suo aspetto giova
> a consentir ciò che par maraviglia;
> onde la nostra fede è aiutata:
> però fu tal da etterno ordinata.   LXXXI, 37–54

It will be seen that the second *pes* repeats the substance of the first (which begins with a summary of the *sirima* in the preceding stanza), by substituting the sense of hearing for that of sight. The *sirima* opens with a consequence, drawn from what has just been said, which is expressed in a metaphor that effectively combines the two senses used in the *pedes* ('li *atti* . . . vanno *chiamando* . . . in quella *voce*'). Then the lady's transcendental nature is re-affirmed in lines which seem composed for an inscription, and which turn on the duality of 'anima' and 'corpo'. The last lines return more explicitly to the lady's 'virtù *divina*', and carry the theme forward to a powerful climax.[1] 'Aspetto' in line 51 will be echoed in the opening of the next stanza:

> Cose appariscon ne lo suo *aspetto*
> che mostran de' piacer di Paradiso   ibid., 55–6

The thematic structure of a typical *ballata* (to return now to our point of departure) may be compared to a seventeenth-century chaconne, or an eighteenth-century theme and variations, for each stanza presents what can be a quite independent elaboration of the theme, which, as we noted, is stated at the outset in the *ripresa*. Thus, the argument need not be drawn out from one stanza to the next, and the stanzas may stand in closer relationship to the *ripresa* than to each other. But again many variations are possible; and the last lines of the poem may well introduce a new motif to provide an effective conclusion, just as we saw in some of the sonnets. For example, in *Ballata, i' voi* (IX) the four stanzas elaborate in due order the commands given in the *ripresa*,[2] with the result that the poem reads more connectedly

---

[1] The syntax throws the repetitions into relief far more than is common in Dante's early verse ('virtù divina . . . discende—spirito da ciel . . . si dichina': 'di costei is può dire —e puossi dir': 'gentile è—e bello è').

[2]   *Ballata i' vòi che tu ritrovi Amore,*
      e con lui vade a *madonna* davante

246

than do other *ballate*. But the fourth stanza also introduces a request for a gesture of reconciliation on the lady's part, of which, most appropriately, there had been no hint in the *ripresa*. In *I' mi son pargoletta* (LXXXVII), as we saw above, Dante speaks in the *persona* of the 'pargoletta' herself. The first two stanzas are regular elaborations of the *ripresa*, but in the third Dante abruptly abandons the first-person presentation with the words 'queste parole si leggon nel viso / d'un'angioletta che ci è apparita' (lines 18–19), and passes on to the new theme of the love-wound he has received. In *Voi che savete* (LXXX), the theme of the lady's *disdegno* is elaborated in the *mutazioni* of each stanza from three differing standpoints, successively those of the stilnovist 'qualunque', the lady herself, and the poet. But whereas the *volte* of stanzas 1 and 2 pass on to the contrasted theme of the lady's *valore*, the poem is bought to a powerful conclusion in the *volta* of the last stanza, with the unexpected affirmation of the poet's power to triumph over the lady's disdain by his own unaided efforts.

It is against this background of frequent but asymmetrical repetition of words, and persistent but unclassifiable repetition of sense, that we must examine the relatively infrequent uses of the rhetorical figures involving repetition.

Alliteration need not detain us long.[1] There is only one example which could possibly be classed as paromoeon in these poems,[2] and

------

is the theme of the first stanza. The second and third stanzas elaborate line 3:

sì che la *scusa* mia, la qual tu *cante*,

whilst the fourth stanza re-expresses line 4:

ragioni poi con lei lo *mio segnore*.

(The words italicized are repeated, or otherwise implied (e.g. '*canti*' ... 'con dolze sono'; '*mio segnore*' ... 'del tuo servo'), later in the poem.)

[1] The term *alliteratio* is said to have been first used by Pontano in the fifteenth century.

[2] 'dissi, donne, dicerollo', XX, 28. This figure is the nearest equivalent in rhetoric. The terms are strict:

'*Paromoeon est multitudo* verborum ex una littera inchoantium, quale est apud Ennius (*Ann.*, 109):

"O Tite tute Tati tibi tanta tyranne tulisti."

Sed bene hoc temperat Virgilius, dum non toto versu utitur hanc figuram, ut Ennius, sed nunc in principio versus tantum, ut est illud:

"Saeva sedens super arma" (*Aen.*, I, 295);

nunc autem in fine, ut

only half a dozen examples of what modern critics call 'strict' alliteration:[1]

vita ... e ... valore (XXXIV, 12); vita e vertù (LXXXIII, 100); frutto ... fronde (LXXXIII, 105 and XCV, 4, 5); servo ... signor (CVI, 43, 48 etc.); faticosa e (forte LXXIX, 55).

Loose alliteration, as in the following examples, is more common:

a capo chino (VIII, 8); fermata fede (IX, 26); penser parlan (X, 1); vista vergognosa (XX, 18); divenia nel dolor (XX, 71); di pianger pronta (CIV, 41); toglie a la terra (CIV, 48); cerchio ne cinge (CVI, 93); coMandi per Messo ch'eo Moia (IX, 33); Vòi di sua Virtù farVi saVere (XIV, 30); Pien di Pietate, / e ascoltando le Parole vane, / si mosse con Paura a Pianger forte (XX, 4–6).

But it is always difficult to decide when one should recognize a case of loose alliteration, and an objective classification is impossible. Adopting a flexible, but conservative approach, I recognized between two and four cases[2] in most stanzas, which means that such alliteration is not usually obtrusive. There are a number of stanzas, however, in which alliteration is sufficiently frequent to thrust itself on our attention.[3] It certainly reinforces the play of the rhyme-sounds, and prepares the ground for the repetitions ('tornato—tornar'; 'dolce—dolce'), and the paranomasia ('*martiro—morte*') in the close of the last stanza of *Io son venuto*:

> *V*ersan le *v*ene le fummifere acque
> per li *v*apor che la terra ha nel *v*entre,

"Sola mihi tales casus Cassandra canebat" (*Aen.*, III, 183)',
Et., I, xxxvi, 14.

Matthew of Vendôme is even more precise:

'*Paranomeon* est per principia trium dictionum *immediate* positarum eiusdem litterae vel syllabae repetita prolatio ... Quod si ternarius numerus excedatur, non erit scema, sed scemati contrarium' (III, 10 and 16). The line from Ennius is cited by nearly everyone: e.g. *Ad Her.*, IV, xii, 18; *PN*, 1,928–30; Matthew, III, 10 and 16.

[1] Strict alliteration refers to the 'binding or contrasting by means of the same initial sound, of similar parts of speech syntactically coordinated, as the English expression "gather and gain"'. R. L. Taylor *Alliteration in Italian* (New Haven, Connecticut, 1900), p. 8. It is more frequent in the *Comedy* (Taylor lists 104 examples, or 1 in 128 lines p. 63); but even there it is only half as frequent as in Petrarch (1 in 71 lines), in whom it is more frequent than in any of the twenty major Italian authors studied by Taylor.

[2] Taking two, three or four words linked by one common letter as one case.

[3] See also XIX; XX, st. 3; XXVII, st. 1; LXXXI, st. 4; CIV, st. 3.

che d'abisso li tira suso in alto;
....
la terra fa un *s*uol che par di *s*malto,
e l'acqua morta si con*v*erte in *v*etro
per la *f*reddura che di *f*uor la serra:
e io de la mia guerra
non son però tornato un passo a retro,
nè vo' tornar; ché, se 'l martiro è dolce,
la morte de' passare ogni altro dolce.   c, 53–5, 59–65.

As I have already indicated, there is little symmetrical repetition of words. There are no examples of *gradatio*, or *conversio*, or *complexio*,[1] and only three examples of *conduplicatio*:[2] 'moia, moia;' (XII, 8); 'morra'ti, morra'ti' (XX, 42); 'che fai, che fai' (CVI, 90). Similarly, there are only three examples of *epanalepsis*[3]

> *Vede* perfettamente onne salute
> chi la mia donna tra le donne *vede*   XXIII, 1–2

> *veggendo* rider cosa
> che lo 'ntelletto cieco non la *vede*   LXXXIII, 43–4

> *Servo* non di signor, ma di vil *servo*   CVI, 43

---

[1] For *gradatio* (= *climax*) see *Ad Her.*, IV, xxv, 34; *Et.*, II, xxi, 4; Capella, V, 536. For *complexio* (= exoche, symplokè), see *Ad Her.*, IV, xiv, 20; *Et.*, II, xxi, 12; Capella, V, 534.

'*Conversio* est per quam *non*, ut ante, *primum* repetimus verbum, *sed ad postremum* continenter revertimur, hoc modo: "Poenos populus Romanus iustitia vicit, armis vicit, liberalitate vicit" ' (*Ad Her.*, IV, xiii, 19).

See Capella, V, 534 (*antistrophè*). One might conceivably classify the 'rime identiche' or 'rime equivoche' in the final couplets of the stanzas in *Io son venuto* under this head.

[2] '*Conduplicatio* est cum ratione amplificationis aut commiserationis eiusdem unius aut plurium verborum iteratio' (*Ad Her.*, IV, xxviii, 38).

'*Epiζeuxis* in uno sensu congeminatio verbi, ut (*Aen.*, IV, 660): "Sic sic iuvat ire per umbras" ', *Et.*, I, xxxvi, 10.

It is called *pallilogía* in Capella, V, 532. Cf. also the adverbial phrases: xxv, 5 'a poco a poco'; CIII, 25, 'a scorza a scorza'; ibid., 40, 'ad ora ad or.'

[3] '*Epanalempsis* est sermonis in principio versus positi eiusdem in fine replicatio, ut est illud (Juvenal, 14, 139):

"Crescit amor nummi quantum ipsa pecunia crescit" ',

Et., I, xxxvi, 11. See also Matthew of Vendôme, III, 6. It is called *Prosapódosis* in Capella, V, 533.

Strict anaphora (*repetitio*)[1] is also limited to four examples, and all of these are in the exilic *canzoni*.

> *Canzone*, uccella con le bianche penne;
> *canzone*, caccia con li neri veltri   CIV, 101–2

> *Omo* da sé vertù fatto ha lontana;
> *omo* no, mala bestia ch'*om* simiglia   CVI, 22–3

> *lietamente* esce da le belle porte,
> ....
> *lieta* va e soggiorna,
> *lietamente* ovra suo gran vassallaggio   ibid., 32, 34–5

> *Maladetta* tua culla,
> ....
> *Maladetto* lo tuo perduto pane   ibid., 78, 80

Even similar forms, in which the repeated word is a pronoun, adverb or conjunction, amount to scarcely twenty.[2]

The remaining word repetitions may be divided into two main classes, which we may link with the rhetorical figures *traductio*[3] and

---

[1] '*Repetitio* est cum continenter ab uno atque eodem verbo in rebus similibus et diversis principia sumuntur ...' *Ad Her.*, IV, xiii, 19.

'*Anaphora* est repetitio eiusdem verbi per principia versuum plurimorum, ut (*Aen.*, III, 157): "*Nos* te Dardania incensa tuaque arma secuti /, *nos* tumidum sub te permensi classibus aequor" ', *Et.*, I, xxxvi, 8.

[2] Cf. x, 3–6, ch'*altro* ... / *altro* ... / *altro* ... / *altro* ...; (XIII, 1, 3, Spesse fiate *vegnonmi* ... e *venmene* ...); (XVI, 8, *tal* volta poca e *tal* lunga stagione); XVII, 9, *ogne* dolcezza, *ogne* pensero ...; XVIII, 12–13, *veggio* li occhi ... / e *veggio*vi tornar ...; XX, 11–12, *qual dicea* ... e *qual dicea*; (XXI, 9, *monna* Vanna e *monna* Bice); XXI, 13, 14, *quell*'è Primavera, e *quell*'ha nome Amor; XXII, 1, *Tanto* gentile e *tanto* onesta ...; (XXV, 37–8, però no li *ven* ... ma *ven*); XXXI, 13, Ben è con *quella* donna *quello* Amore ...; LXXIX, 11–12, *come* l'anima trista piange ... e *come* un spirto ...; (LXXIX, 40, non *se*' ... ma *se*'); (LXXII, 42, 47, *prima* dice ... ché *prima* puose); (LXXII, 61–2, *Né* voglion che *vil* uom ... *né* di *vil* padre ...); (LXXII, 101, 103, è gentilezza *dovunqu*' è ... sì com' è 'l cielo *dovunqu*' è ...); (CIII, 44, 50, *allor*,... *allor* ..., both initial); (CIII, 40, 48, 50, *Egli* ... *Elli* ... S'*elli*, all initial); CXI, 3–4, *com*' egli affrena e *come* sprona, e *come* sotto lui; CXIII, 10, *quando* scende e *quando* poia; CIV, 5, *Tanto* son belle e di *tanta* vertute; CVI, 28, *lui* obedisce e *lui* acquista onore; CVI, 41–2, *tu* sola fai ... che *tu* se' ...; CVI, 119–20, *chi con* tardare, e *chi con* vana vista, *chi con* sembianza trista ...; CVI, 155, 156, *prima* ... *prima* ...; CVI, 157, *quel* che tu se' e *quel* per ch'io ti mando.

[3] '*Traductio* est quae facit uti, cum idem verbum crebrius ponatur, non modo non offendat animum, sed etiam concinniorem orationem reddat, hoc pacto: "Qui nihil habet in *vita* jucundius *vita*, is cum virtute *vitam* non potest colere" ', *Ad Her.*, IV, xiv, 20.

polyptoton.[1] In both cases the repetitions do not have to be placed symmetrically in any way, the difference being that in the second group the word is repeated in a different flectional form (for example, 'donna, donne;' 'dico, dire, dirò'). This second class may sometimes merge imperceptibly into another where the repetitions are not of a word but of a common root (for example, 'amore, amare, innamorata'), and we may group all examples of this type around the figure *replicatio.*[2] There are very few examples in the chosen poems which fit the rhetorical definitions exactly, but there are a great many that approximate to them in varying degrees, and these are certainly characteristic of Dante's style at all stages. It is very difficult to assess just how significant they are in the absence of comparable data; and comparisons will always be difficult, because the examples are too heterogeneous to permit a survey expressed in numerical form. Fortunately, in a sample of some 1,600 lines, it is still practicable to prepare complete lists of such repetitions, just as was done for the tropes, and these will be found at the end of the chapter. Here I will only call attention to the more important species in each of the three groups.

It is quite common for a whole strophe to be dominated by one word, or by words drawn from one root. This is perhaps only natural in the doctrinal *canzoni*, in which the strophe, or even the whole poem, is an attempt to define that word: so, for example, 'gentile' and 'gentilezza' dominate the fourth stanza of *Le dolci rime*, 'vertù' dominates lines 72–88 of *Poscia ch'Amor*, and the first stanza of *Doglia mi reca* revolves around 'amore' (and derivatives), 'vertù' and 'beltà'. But such repetition may be considered an *ornatus* where there is no such logical motivation, as is not uncommon in the early poems. *Se' tu colui* (XIX) has 'piangi', 'pianger', 'piangere', 'pianto', 'piangendo' in the space of ten lines. In lines 41–54 of *Donna pietosa* there are five forms drawn from 'parere' and 'apparire'; and there are six forms of 'vedere' between lines 64 and 83 in the same poem. Most striking of all perhaps are the uses of 'morte' and derivatives in *Ciò che m'incontra* (XII): 'more', 'tramortendo', 'moia moia', 'morta', 'morte'.

---

[1] '*Polyptoton* est, cum diversis casibus sententia variatur, ut (Pers. 3, 84): "Ex nihilo nihilum, ad nihilum nil posse reverti" ', *Et.*, I, xxxvi, 17.

[2] Following the *Leys d'Amor* with Contini. Curtius calls them *adnominationes*, but, as defined in the *Ad Her.* (IV, xxi, 29), this requires like sounds from *different* roots, or a contrast of *sense* in words from the same root, or both.

In the early poems particularly, it is not uncommon to find three or more repetitions in the space of three lines, for example:

> Io *veggio* li occhi vostri c'hanno pianto,
> e *veggiovi* tornar sì sfigurate,
> che 'l cor mi triema di *vederne* tanto.   XVIII, 12–14

> ... sì *parla* sottile
> al cor dolente, che lo fa *parlare*.
> So io che *parla* ...[1]   XXXVII, 10–12

> ... per non parer queta e *umile*,
> miri costei ch'è essemplo d'*umiltate*!
> Questa è colei ch'*umilia* ...[2]   LXXXI, 69–71

> ... ond'io vo sì *dolente*,
> tanto *dolore* intorno 'l cor m'assembra
> la *dolorosa* mente ...[3]   XXVII, 3–5

Another species to occur in the early poems is the use of two forms of a common verb in the same line, for example:

> *Dite*lmi, donne, ché 'l mi *dice* il core   XVIII, 7

> *vada* con lei, che quando *va* per via   XIV, 32

> *Piangete*, amanti, poi che *piange* Amore   VI, 1

It is not easy to generalize about the differences between groups, or between early and late poems: but, broadly speaking, the repetitions in the later groups tend to involve fewer terms, and they are deployed more forcefully, and are more clearly deliberate, for example:

> In *ciascun* è di *ciascun* vizio assembro   CVI, 132

> dimmi, che hai tu *fatto*,
> cieco avaro *disfatto*?   CVI, 75–6

> Maladetto lo tuo *perduto* pane,
> che non si *perde* al cane!   CVI, 80–1

Developments in the use of *conceptual* repetition are, however, much more sharply defined. As the looser or more diffuse kinds of conceptual

---

[1] For 'parlare', see also XIV, 8–9; XXV, 6, 7, 10.
[2] For 'umile', see also XX, 69, 71–2.
[3] For 'dolore', see also XXX, 8, 11.

repetition become less common in the later poems, with the change from amorous to ethical themes, so there is a compensating rise in the frequency of classifiable forms of *synonymia*,[1] especially in the form of pairs of related nouns, verbs, or adjectives, for example 'scudiscio e ferza', 'chiude e salda', 'vile e noioso'.

These 'iterazioni sinonimiche' of 'Synonymendopplungen' have recently been the subject of a number of studies.[2] And although much work remains to be done on individual authors, we now have a general picture, in outline at least, of their use and significance in medieval literature. For our purposes it will be sufficient to note the following points. The free use of such pairs, or 'binomials' as I shall call them, is one of the most characteristic features of courtly verse whether in Provence,[3] Northern France[4] or Italy. They are to be found in abundance in the Sicilians, in Guittone,[5] and again in Petrarch.[6] It must be added, however, that they are in no way restricted to the courtly register: they occur frequently in the *Chanson de Roland*,[7] for example.

[1] '*Synonymia* est, quotiens in conexa oratione pluribus verbis unam rem significamus, ut ait Cicero (*Catil.* I, 8): "nihil agis, nihil moliris, nihil cogitas". Et item: (*Catil.* I, 10); "non feram, non patiar, non sinam" ', *Et.*, II, xxi, 6.

'*Synonymia* est communio nominis, quotiens uno verbo non satis dignitatem rei aut magnitudinem demonstramus, ideoque ad eandem significationem plura conferimus', Capella, v, 535.

It is called *interpretatio* in *Ad Her.*, IV, xxviii, 38 and its descendants.

[2] Apart from those cited in the notes following: S. Pellegrini, 'Iterazioni sinonimiche nella canzone di Rolando', *SMV*, I (1953), 155 ff. Giovanna Marconi, 'Annominazioni e iterazioni sinonimiche in Juan Manuel', *SMV*, II (1954), 7 ff. V. Bertolucci-Pizzorusso, 'L'iterazione sinonimica in testi prosastici mediolatini', *SMV*, V (1957), 7 ff. On their use in Ariosto, see E. Turolla, 'Dittologia e enjambement nell'elaborazione dell'*Orlando Furioso*', *Lettere Italiane*, X (1958), 1–20. A. M. Carini, 'L'iterazione aggettivale nell'*Orlando Furioso*', *Convivium*, XXXI, N.S. (1963), 19–34.

[3] W. Th. Elwert, 'La dittologia sinonimica nella poesia lirica romanza delle origini e nella scuola poetica italiana', *Bollettino del Centro di studi filologici e linguistici siciliani*, II (1954), 152–77; 'Zur Synonymendopplung vom Typ "planh e sospir", "chan e plor" ', *Archiv für das Studium der neueren Sprachen*, CXCIII (1956), 40–2; and 'Formale Satire bei Peire Cardenal', in *Syntactica und Stilistica. Festschrift für E. Gamillscheg* (Tübingen, 1957), pp. 111–19.

[4] Dragonetti, *La technique poétique*, pp. 289–91. P. M. Schon, *Studien zum Stil der frühen französischen Prosa (Analecta Romanica* series, vol. VIII) (Frankfurt am Main, 1960), pp. 164–85—an excellent summary with much new material.

[5] Baehr, 'Studien zur Rhetorik' (1957), pp. 212–16, 362–80, 393–7.

[6] D. Alonso, 'La poesia del Petrarca e il Petrarchismo. Mondo estetico della pluralità', *Lettere italiane*, XI (1959), 279–319.

[7] Schon would correct Pellegrini's figure of 1 in 21 lines to 1 in 10 (*Studien zum Stil der frühen französischen Prosa*, p. 165).

And in the epic decasyllabic line, no less than it its lyric descendant, it was common for the binomials to occupy a whole hemistich—a fact which no doubt contributed to their popularity. Nor were they limited to poetic texts: they were used with comparable frequency in old French translations, sermons and chronicles.[1] It is also well known that such binomials have arisen quite independently in other languages, and that they are not uncommon in Christian Latin writers. Nevertheless, it is now apparent that the binomials were nowhere used so insistently as in the Romance texts just indicated, and that they are *not* to be attributed to the influence of rhetoric: they belong to the indigenous literary tradition.[2]

In all the poems of the *Vita Nuova* and of the allegorical group combined (855 lines) there are between twenty and twenty-five examples of *synonymia*, which means that it occurs approximately once in every 40 lines.[3] Now this is a *low* figure, and a *significantly* low figure, as we have just noted: it can only be interpreted as evidence of a deliberate rejection of the binomial, or at least of a conscious effort to curb its abuse. And so these figures reveal yet one more aspect of that process of purification and simplification of the language and style of

[1] See the lists and discussion in Schon (*Studien zum Stil der frühen französischen Prosa*, pp. 167–73).

[2] 'Somit ist die Synonymendopplung eine Satzfigur, die als Mittel zur affektischen Aussage und zur Verdeutlichung in allen Sprachen vorkommt, die ferner den rhetorischen Theorien des lateinischen Altertums und Mittelalters bekannt war, und die schliesslich durch die Technik der Predigt, der Übersetzung und der Versdichtung im französischen Mittelalter zur Manier wurde' (Schon, ibid., p. 185).

[3] It is impossible to be more precise: I have collected some 30 here, but only about 15 are 'pure' examples.
Apart from those in no. v, quoted in text, they are:
Nouns: XI, 8, prende baldanza e tanta securtate; XVII, 7, superbia ed ira; XXIII, 8, di gentilezza, d'amore e di fede; XXV, 38–9, tristizia e voglia di sospirare e di morir di pianto; XXV, 57, Pianger di doglia e sospirar d'angoscia; XXXII, 1, Color d'amore e di pietà sembianti; XXXII, 4, occhi gentili o dolorosi pianti; XXXIV, 12, e la sua vita, e tutto 'l suo valore.
Verbs: XI, 10, e quale ancide, e qual pinge di fore; XIV, 34, agghiaccia e pere; XIX, 9, Lascia piangere noi e triste andare; XXV, 42, quale ella fue, e com'ella n'è tolta; XXXIII, 9–10 ... mi fa pensare, e spaventami sì; LXXX, 25, nasconda e guardi.
Adjectives: (VIII, 7 ... sospirando pensoso venia); XIV, 44, sì adorna e sì pura; XIV, 60, giovane e piana; XX, 15–16, sì dolorosa e rotta sì; XX, 54, scolorito e fioco; XXV, 33, malvagio e vile; XXVII, 11, soave e dolce mio riposo; LXXIX, 55, faticosa e forte; LXXXI, 76, fera e disdegnosa; LXXXI, 77, lucente e chiaro.
It should be noted that there are only four pairs in group I.

courtly love poetry, as this was practised by Guittone and his followers.[1] It is relevant to note that in the early double-sonnet *O voi che per la via d'Amor passate*, which like the other poems in group A is still close to Guittonian models, there are no less than four binomials: 'attendete e guardate' (2); 'ostale e chiave' (6); 'dolce e soave' (9); 'struggo e ploro' (20).

In the last four groups the binomials are three times more frequent than in the first nine, and this is a characteristic sign of that extension of Dante's stylistic range which marks the end of his purist phase.[2] It is further characteristic that these—like the other stylistic devices which now reappear—are used with discretion. In no poem are they more frequent than 1 in 10 lines, and they never create an effect that would recall a Guittone or anticipate a Petrarch. But at this modest level they have become one of the distinctive features in the later poems: and they are particularly prominent in the two poems which have been most

[1] Baehr found more than 450 examples of *congeries* in Guittone (a term which, following Arbusow, he uses as 'Oberbegriff für alle Figuren die der Worthäufung dienen'), 'Studien zur Rhetorik' (1957), p. 362. He gives extensive lists of the binomials on pp. 362–9; and he introduces finer distinctions than are profitable for Dante: for example, verbal pairs are divided into tautologous ('che rechesta e pregata ho'), climactic ('m'ingegno e m'assotiglio') and heteronymous ('sento e veo').

[2] Nouns: (LXXXII, 130, piena d'amore e di cortese lode); LXXXIII, 100, vita e vertù; LXXXIII, 109, co' bei sembianti e co' begli atti novi; (C, 21, di fredda neve ed in noiosa pioggia); C, 44, se non se in lauro, in pino o in abete; (CIII, 14–15, Non trovo scudo ... né loco); CIII, 67, scudiscio e ferza; CIII, 69, vespero e squille; CXI, 5, ragione o virtù; CVI, 103, per colli e per paludi.
Verbs: LXXXII, 135, udire e ragionar; LXXXIII, 125–6, caro è tenuto e disiato; C, 19, chiude tutto e salda; C, 20, si solve, e cade; C, 22, s'attrista tutto e piagne; (CIII, 9, 10, si chiuda, né si dilunghi); (CIII, 12, giungono altrui e spezzan ...); (CIII, 13, non so da lei né posso atarme); (CIII, 80, che m'ha ferito il core e che m'invola); CXIII, 10, quando scende e quando poia); CVI, 28, lui obedisce e lui acquista onore; CVI, 83, hai raunato e stretto.
Adjectives: LXXXII, 5, atti disdegnosi e feri; LXXXII, 14, rima aspr'e sottile; LXXXII, 15, giudicio falso e vile; (LXXXII, 56, Che siano vili appare ed imperfette); LXXXII, 59, dritto e verace; (LXXXII, 125, 129, 133); LXXXIII, 10, vile e noioso; LXXXIII, 84–5, mischiata, causata di più cose; LXXXIII, 112, falsi cavalier, malvagi e rei; LXXXIII, 124, leggiadre e belle; C, 46, forte ed acerba; (C, 67, dolce tempo novello); CIII, 22, angosciosa e dispietata; CIII, 58, micidiale e latra; CIII, 70, pietoso né cortese; CIII, 76, presso e fiso; XCVI, 6, del lungo e del noioso tacer mio; CXIII, 2, dolce e latina; CXIII, 11, malvagia e croia; CVI, 39, O cara ancella e pura; CVI, 62, ch'abbiate a vil ... e a dispetto; CVI, 150, bella, saggia e cortese; CVI, 154, chiusa ed onesta.
Note that Dante uses a group of three adjectives only twice (LXXXIII, 112 and CVI, 150), whereas three and more are not uncommon in Guittone.

admired—*Così nel mio parlar* and *Tre donne*. No small part of the dignity
and poise of the latter poem is due to its binomials:

Ciascuna par *dolente e sbigottita*,	
come persona *discacciata e stanca*	9–10
e cui *vertute né beltà* non vale	12
or sono a tutti *in ira ed in non cale*	15
discinta e scalza, e sol di sé par donna	26
egli, *pietoso e fello*,	
di lei e del dolor fece dimanda	29–30
povera, vedi, *a panni ed a cintura*.	
Poi che fatta si fu *palese e conta*,	
doglia e vergogna prese	36–8
piangano gli *occhi* e dolgasi la *bocca*	66
ché, se *giudizio* o *forza* di destino	77
già consumato sì *l'ossa e la polpa*[1]	86

Both in its background, and in its role in Dante's poems, the story of
antithesis is broadly similar to that we have just outlined for *synonymia*.
Antithesis is clearly a universal phenomenon. It is not limited to any
one language or register; and the presence of antithetical constructions
is not *per se* a pointer to the influence of literary models or of a rhetorical education. On the other hand (and, in this, unlike the binomials),
the *deliberate* use of antithesis, revealed in contrived word placing, in
repetition and word-play, and above all in a rhythmically balanced
sentence structure, is certainly one of the most constant features of a
rhetorically influenced style.[2] And antithesis is extremely common

---

[1] In the latter part of the poem, *synonymiae* give way to antitheses. See below.

[2] In both rhetorical traditions antithesis was recognized as a figure of speech *and* as a
figure of thought. Definitions of the former should suffice:
    '*Contentio* est cum ex contrariis rebus oratio conficitur, hoc pacto: "Habet adsentatio
jucunda principia, eadem exitus amarissimos adfert." Item: "Inimicis te placabilem,
amicis inexorabilem praebes" ' (*Ad Her.*, IV, xv, 21).
    '*Antitheton*, ubi contraria contrariis opponuntur et sententiae pulchritudinem
reddunt, ut illud (*Met.*, I, 19):
        "Frigida pugnabant calidis, humentia siccis;
        mollia cum duris; sine pondere habentia pondus" '
(*Et.*, I, xxxvi, 21).

among the troubadours and their heirs or descendants in other lands: in Guittone's poems it is almost literally omnipresent.[1]

In the poems of the early groups, there are a few scattered examples of antithetical constructions which recall those to be found in Dante's predecessors.[2] In particular, one notes three variations on a solemn formula with 'non perché ... ma':[3]

Amor, non già per mia poca bontate,	
ma per sua nobiltate	v, 7–8
non però ch'a la gente sia nascoso,	
ma per farne cruccioso	VII, 10–11
non perch'io creda sua laude finire,	
ma ragionar per isfogar la mente.	XIV, 3–4

But apart from the opening of *Sì lungiamente, Vede perfettamente,* and the third stanza of *Li occhi dolenti,* antithesis is virtually absent in the poems of the 'stil novo' proper (groups C–I inclusive). And again there seems to be little doubt that this absence is another consequence of the minor revolution in the style of love poetry described above and elsewhere.

Development comes once again with the two doctrinal *canʒoni* in group J, where the free, diffuse and often unclassifiable use of conceptual repetition is replaced by a comparable use of antithesis. This is not the inevitable consequence of a shift from love poetry to moral poetry. It arises rather because Dante, like Guittone before him, writes with

---

See also Capella, v, 531, and Matthew of Vendôme (III, 25–9). The latter distinguishes four species: *per constructiones* (i.e. the figure of thought), *per nomina adjectiva, per nomina sustantiva, per verba.*

[1] 'Die zweite Figur, die in ähnlich beherrschender und durchgängiger Weise wie die *congeries* den Stil der Rime prägt, ist die Antithese ... mehr noch als ein blosses Stilmittel, geradezu eine Denkform, die gelegentlich entscheidenden Einfluss sogar auf die Komposition ganzer Strophen oder Strophenteile nehmen kann', Baehr, 'Studien zur Rhetorik' (1957), p. 376. Baehr counts more than 300 examples in Guittone's *Rime.*

[2] Cf. also: v, 19–20, *di fuor* mostro *allegranʒa,* e *dentro* da lo core struggo e *ploro;* v, 14–15, tesoro ... pover; VI, 5, *villana* Morte in *gentil* core; VII, 1–2, di pietà nemica, di dolor madre antica; IX, 5 ff., Tu vai sì ... che *sanʒa compagnia* ... ma ... se tu di lui *non* fossi accompagnata; x, 2 ff., varietate (fa voler—folle ragiona; dolzore—pianger), s'accordano. But these are all early poems.

[3] The same formula occurs in the 'proemio' of LXXXII: 'non perch'io non speri ... ma perché li atti ...'.

257

polemical intent. The poems are not calm discourses on the central values of the courtly system, but stinging attacks on false and harmful perversions of them. Only after the false notions have been refuted and derided does Dante expound the true nature of 'gentilezza' and 'leggiadria'. And this is why antithesis shapes the whole course of both poems. As a typical example we may examine the second stanza of *Poscia ch' Amor*. It will be seen that the second *pes* answers the first with a loosely organized double antithesis—'not only do they fail to do right, they do themselves additional harm'—and that the *sirima* condenses the argument, and spices it with contempt, by using simile, rhetorical question and a tauter, more symmetrically expressed antithesis:

> Sono che per *gittar via* loro avere
> credon *potere*
> capere là dove li *boni* stanno,
> che dopo morte fanno
> riparo ne la mente
> a quei cotanti *c'hanno canoscenza.*
>   Ma lor messione a' *bon non pò* piacere;
> per che *tenere*
> savere fora, *e* fuggiriano il danno,
> che si aggiugne a lo 'nganno
> di loro e de la gente
> *c'hanno falso iudicio in lor sentenza.*
>   Qual non dirà fallenza
> divorar cibo ed a lussuria intendere?
> ornarsi, come vendere
> si dovesse al mercato di *non saggi?*
> ché 'l *saggio non pregia* om per vestimenta,
> ch'altrui sono ornamenta,
> *ma pregia* il senno e li genti coraggi.   LXXXIII, 20–38

And in this poem, unlike *Le dolci rime*, antithesis is maintained even in the concluding stanza:

> *Dona* e *riceve* l'om cui questa vole,
> mai *non sen dole;*
> né 'l sole per *donar* luce a le stelle,
> né per *prender* da elle
> nel suo effetto aiuto;
> ma l'uno e l'altro in ciò *diletto tragge.*

Già non s'induce a ira per parole,
ma quelle sole
ricole che son bone, e sue novelle
sono leggiadre e belle;
per sé caro è tenuto
e disïato da *persone sagge,*
    ché de l'altre *selvagge*
cotanto *laude* quanto *biasmo* prezza;
per nessuna grandezza
monta in *orgoglio, ma* quando gl'incontra
che sua *franchezza* li conven mostrare,
quivi si fa laudare.
Color che vivon fanno tutti contra.   LXXXIII, 115–33

After the experience of the doctrinal *canzoni*, antithesis becomes more important in Dante's style—both *in sententiis* and *in verbis*. This is shown by the fact that antithesis is introduced even where it is not dictated by the matter or purpose of the poem. Thus, in the new love-poetry, it provides the framework of *Io son venuto*, and to a lesser extent of *Così nel mio parlar*; and this poem also has a most elaborate series of verbal antitheses in its first stanza.[1] The five correspondence sonnets all have two or three instances of antithesis.[2]

When Dante returns to ethical themes in the final group, antithesis is even more insistent, at all levels, than in the earlier ones. And, what is perhaps more important, the expression is now far more emphatic than before, because the contrasted words are placed more effectively, for example:

Omo da sé vertù fatto ha lontana;   CVI, 22–3
omo no, mala bestia ...

Corro l'avaro, ma più fugge pace   CVI, 69

---

[1] See analysis in chapter 3, p. 144.

[2] XCV, 4–5, *fronde* ... ma *frutto* no; XCV, 7–8, saria *bugiardo* / sapor non fatto da *vera* notrice; XCV, 10–11, *dentro* è gita ... la *partita*; XCVI, 7–8, il loco ... è sì *rio* / che 'l *ben* ...; XCVI, 13–14, a *danno* nostro ... da po' che 'l *ben*; (XCVI, 5–7, null'altra cosa ... se non il loco ...); CXI, 3–4, affrena e ... sprona, ... si ride e geme; (CXI, 12–14, *nuovi* spron ... se l'*altro* ...); CXIII, 1–3, Degno fa voi *trovare* ... ma volgibile cor ven *disvicina*; (CXIII, 1–4, 5–7, voi ... io, ... non fé foro—trafitto sono; ... *pur* trovo ...); CXIII, 9–11, Non è colpa del sol ... *ma* de la condizion; (CXIII, 10, quando scende e quando poia); CXIII, 12–13, *occhi* ... *parole*. CXIV, 1–8, Io mi credea ... ma perch'i' ho ...piacemi ...; CXIV, 10, sé lega e dissolve; CXIV, 14, sì che s'accordi i *fatti* a' dolci *detti*.

che *da sera e da mane*
hai raunato e stretto ad ambo mano
ciò che sì *tosto si rifà lontano.*   CVI, 82–4

We shall return to the antithesis of this poem in the final chapter, and so, as our final examples of the new formal mastery of antithesis, we may quote from *Tre donne*:

e seggonsi di *fore;*
ché *dentro* siede Amore   2–3

Tempo fu già nel quale,
secondo il lor parlar, furon *dilette;*
or sono a tutti *in ira* ed in *non cale.*   13–15

generai io *costei* che m'è *da lato*
....
generò *questa* che m'è *più lontana.*   50, 54

ecco l'armi ch'io volli;
per non usar, vedete, son *turbate.*
   ... e pur tornerà gente
che questo dardo farà star *lucente*   61–2, 71–2

piangano gli occhi e dolgasi la bocca
de li *uomini* ...
non *noi* ...
ché, se noi siamo *or* punti,
noi *pur saremo,* e *pur* tornerà gente   66–7, 69–71

E *io,* che ascolto nel parlar divino
consolarsi e *dolersi*
così alti *dispersi,*
l'*essilio* che m'è dato, *onor* mi tegno   73–6

vuol pur che il mondo versi
i *bianchi* fiori in *persi,*
cader co' buoni è pur di *lode degno.*   78–80

lieve mi conterei ciò che m'è *grave.*   84

(E se non che ...)
che *m'have* in *foco* miso,
....
Ma questo *foco* m'have
già consumato ...   81, 83, 85–6

   ... e 'l fior, ch'è bel di *fori,*
fa' disïar ne li amorosi *cori.*   99–100

Summary

Canzone, uccella con le *bianche* penne;
canzone, caccia con li *neri* veltri,
che fuggir mi convenne,
ma far mi poterian di pace dono.
Però nol *fan* ...   101–5

As far as antithesis is concerned, it is this *canzone* and the correspondence sonnets which we should regard as typical of Dante's late practice; and although we must recognize how much more frequent, and how much more assured, the use of antithesis has become, comparison with the work of either his predecessors or successors would show that he uses it comparatively sparingly.

And so we may sum up: for some years after Dante came under the influence of Cavalcanti, he tended to avoid nearly all the forms of repetition known to rhetoric, and popular among his predecessors, although the poems of this period make extensive use of 'loose' verbal and conceptual repetition. But in the doctrinal *canzoni*, and in ever-increasing measure thereafter, Dante began to exploit many of the simpler forms of repetition: the most important being antithesis, then *synonymia*, then the symmetrical repetition of words. However, he did not make use of the more elaborate figures such as *gradatio*, or of the more 'artificial' figures like strict alliteration, *figurae etymologicae*[1] or oxymoron; and even in his last lyric poems, he uses the simpler figures more discreetly than his predecessors, and a good deal less than he was to do himself in the *Comedy*.

APPENDIX

There follow complete lists of the asymmetrical repetitions in the selected poems, grouped, as explained in the text, around the figures *Traductio, Polyptoton, Replicatio*. The fact that a word is used twice in one strophe does not mean that it will necessarily appear in these

---

[1] The only example occurs in a pre-'stilnovo' poem: VII, 9 'd'onni torto tortoso'.

Paranomasia (the use of similar-sounding words, usually from different roots, usually in different senses), is absent in the *VN* poems, and used only very discreetly in the later poems. See: (XVIII, 3–4, venite ... divenuto); LXXIX, 40, Tu non se' *morta*, ma se' *ismarrita*; (LXXX, 27–8, *disiri, disdegno*); LXXXI, 55, appariscon, aspetto; (LXXXII, 114, 116, *dei, Iddio*); LXXXIII, 31–2, falso, fallenza; (C, 34, 35, amor, ammorta); C, 64–5, martiro, morte; (CIV, 91, 95, *ponga... mano, ... man piega*); CIV, 99, fior, fori; CVI, 62–3, *dispetto, diletto*; CVI, 67, come l'*avaro* seguitando *avere* (the most striking).

lists. The repetition must be reasonably close, or there must be more than casual connexion. Doubtful cases are placed in parentheses.

TRADUCTIO (50 examples)

XIV, 43–4, 46, *Cosa* mortale / come esser pò . . . di far *cosa* nova; XIV, 51, 53, De li occhi suoi . . . che feron li occhi; XIX, 1, 3, 5, 7, 7, *tu* . . .; XXXIII, 1, 3, L'amaro *lagrimar* . . . facea *lagrimar* . . .; (XXXIII, 11, 13, d'una donna . . ., la vostra donna); (XXXVII, 10, 14, io no lo intendo . . . io lo 'ntendo ben); (LXXIX, 1, 4, ciel . . . ciel); (LXXIX, 33, 36, occhi . . . occhi); LXXXI, 8, 10, dir *quel ch'odo* de la donna mia, . . . trattar di *quel ch'odo* di lei; ibid., 11, 16, 18, ciò che, di ciò, tutto ciò; ibid., 22, 26, Amor mi face, . . . Amor fa; ibid., 48, 51, Di costei si può dire . . . E puossi dir; ibid., 70–2, costei, colei, costei; ibid., 76, 80, 81, ella la chiama . . . li nostri occhi . . . chiaman la stella . . . ella la chiama . . .; ibid., 82–3, non . . . *secondo* il vero, ma pur *secondo* quel; LXXXII, 51, 56, però che *vili* son . . . Che siano *vili* appare; ibid., 61, 63, 67, 70, 79, 80, gentil, gentile, gentilezza, ibid., 81, 83, *Dico* ch'ogni *vertù* . . . *vertute, dico*; ibid., 89–91, Dico che nobiltate . . . *importa sempre* ben . . . come viltate *importa sempre* male . . .; ibid., 98, ma se l'una *val* ciò che l'altra *vale*; ibid., 101–2, è gentilezza dovunqu' è *vertute*, / ma non *vertute* ov'ella; (ibid., 121, 127, l'anima cui adorna . . . sua persona adorna . . .); (LXXXIII, 22, 26, li boni . . . a' bon); LXXXIII, 36, 38, ché 'l saggio non pregia . . . ma pregia; ibid., 58, Ancor che ciel con cielo; ibid., 76, 77, 79, 88, Sarà *vertù* o con *vertù* s'annoda. / Non è *pura vertù* . . ., là 'v' è più *vertù* richesta . . ., ma *vertù pura* . . .; ibid., 85–6, 89, per che questa / *conven* che . . . Sollazzo è che *convene*; (ibid., 90, 95, perfetta . . . perfetta; ibid., 99, 109, co li *bei* raggi . . ., co' *bei* sembianti e co' *begli* atti novi; C, 64–7, se 'l martiro è *dolce*, / la morte de' passare ogni *altro dolce* . . . che sarà di me ne *l'altro dolce* tempo; ibid., 67–70, *quando* piove / *amore* in terra . . . *quando* per questi geli / *amore* è . . .; CIII, 25–7, rodermi il core . . ., mi triema il cor; ibid., 30, 33, penser, pensier; (CIV, 1, 17, mi son venute . . ., venute son) (ibid., 8, 14, parlar); ibid., 20, 24, la man . . . l'altra man; ibid., 22, 30, di *dolor* colonna . . ., di lei e del *dolor*; ibid., 34–5 *son* la più trista, / *son* suora . . . e *son* Drittura; ibid., 50, 54, generai . . . generò; ibid., 69–71, non *noi* . . . ché, se *noi* . . . *noi* pur saremo, e *pur* tornerà gente; ibid., 83, 85, m'have in foco . . ., foco m'have . . .; ibid., 88, 90, s'io ebbi colpa . . . se colpa muore; ibid., 91, 95, non ponga uom mano . . ., per cui ciascun man piega; CVI, 3, 11, 18–19, dico, dico, dicer, dico; ibid., 8, 12, 17, vertù, vertute, vertù; ibid., 7, 13, 16, 21, beltà, beltà, biltà, beltà; ibid., 85–6, Come *con dismisura* si rauna, / così *con dismisura* si distringe; ibid., 132, In ciascun è di ciascun vizio . . .; ibid., 135, di radice di *ben* altro *ben* tira;

POLYPTOTON (43 examples)

VI, 1, *Piangete*, amanti, poi che *piange* Amore; X, 10, e vorrei *dire*, e non so ch'io mi *dica*; XI, 1–2, Con l'altre *donne* mia vista gabbate, / e non pensate, *donna* ...; XIV, 1–2, *Donne* ch'avete ... i' vo' con voi de la mia *donna* dire; ibid., 8–9 (14), farei *parlando* ... E io non vo' *parlar* ... (cosa da *parlarne* altrui); ibid., 19–20 ... che non *have* altro difetto / che d'*aver* lei; ibid., 32, *vada* con lei, che quando *va* ...; (ibid., 35, 38 ... starla a *vedere* ... di *veder* lei); XVIII, 7, Ditelmi, donne, ché 'l mi dice il core; ibid., 5, 8, 12–14, *Vedeste* voi ... vi *veggio* andar ... Io *veggio* li occhi vostri ... e *veggiovi* tornar sì sfigurate, / che 'l cor mi triema di *vederne* tanto (XIX, 5, 7, 9, 11, 14, piangi, pianger, piangere, pianto, piangendo); XX, 28, io *dissi*: Donne, *dicerollo*; ibid., 62, s'altro avesser *detto*, a voi *dire'lo*; ibid., 41, 45, 49, 50, 54, m'apparver, parea, parve, apparir, apparve; ibid., 64, 66, 68, 72, 77, 83, veder, veder, vedea, veggendo, vedi, vede; ibid., 77, 79 ... vegno ... Vieni; XXI, 12–13 ... mente mi *ridice*, / Amor mi *disse* ...; XXII, 8–9 ... miracol *mostrare*. / *Mostra*si sì piacente ...; XXIII, 2, chi la mia *donna* tra le *donne* vede; XXV, 6, 7, 10 convenemi *parlar* ..., me ricorda ch'io *parlai* ..., non vòi *parlare* altrui; ibid., 8, 9, 11, la mia *donna* ... *donne* gentili ... in *donna* sia; ibid., 62, 64, che *dicer* lo sapesse ..., non vi *saprei* io *dir* ...; XXVI, 7–8, di *pianger* sì la donna mia, / che sfogasser lo cor, *piangendo* lei; (XXXIII, 5, 13 (both final), obliereste, obliare); XXXVII, 10, 11, 12 ... sì *parla* sottile / al cor dolente, che lo fa *parlare*. / So io che *parla* ...; (LXXIX, 15, 19, se ne *gìa* ... men vo' *gire*); (ibid., 17, 23, donna); ibid., 31, 33, 36, dice, dice, dicea; LXXX, 14, 17, 22, guardi, guardi, guardare; LXXXII, 75, 78, 80, 81, 83, 85, 89, 100, diri, dicer voglio, dirò, dico, dico, dice, dico, dett'ho; ibid., 95, 96, convegnono, convien ...; LXXXIII, 35–6 ... al mercato di non *saggi*? / ché 'l *saggio* ...; ibid., 108, 115, 117, donar ... dona, ... donar; (C, 38, 39, né mi son dati ..., ma donna li mi *dà*); (ibid., 40–1, 50, le fronde / che *trasse* fuor ..., non la mi *tragge*); ibid., 63–4, non son però *tornato* ... né vo' *tornar*; CIII, 12, 14, spezzan ... spezzi; XCVI, 13, a danno *nostro* e de li *nostri* diri; CIV, 2, 3, seggonsi ... siede; ibid., 104–5, ma *far* mi poterian ... Però nol *fan* ...; CVI, 83, 85, 86, hai *raunato* e *stretto* ... si *rauna*, ... si *distringe*; (ibid., 118, 123, I' *vo*' che ciascun m'*oda* ... *Volete udire*); ibid., 151, 153, la *chiaman* tutti ... Contessa *chiamando*.

REPLICATIO (56 examples)

(VI, 1, Piangete, *amanti*, poi che piange *Amore*); VII, 9, d'onni torto tortoso; (IX, 27, 34, 40, servir, servidore, servo); (IX, 6, 13, compagnia, accompagnata); (ibid., 31–2, 41, preghero ... perdonare, prego ... perdona); (X, 7, 12, s'accordano, fare accordanza); XII, 1, 6, 8, 13, 14 ne la mente *more* ... tra-*mortendo* ... *moia, moia* ... ne la vista *morta* / de li occhi c'hanno di lor *morte* voglia; (XIII, 6, 7 ... *vita* quasi m'abbandona: campami un spirto *vivo*); (XIV, 6, 8, 13, *Amor* sì dolce ..., farei ... *innamorar* la gente ... donzelle *amorose*); XVI, 4, alma *razional* sanza *ragione*; XVI, 5, 6, quand'è *amorosa,/Amor* per sire ...; XVIII, 3–4, onde *venite* che 'l vostro colore / par *divenuto*; XVIII, 5, 6, *Vedeste* voi ... bagnar nel *viso* suo ...; XX, 18–19, 21, ... la *vista* vergognosa, / ch'era nel *viso* mio ... Elli era tale a *veder* mio colore; ibid., 32, 35, l'anima mia fu sì *smarrita* ... Io presi tanto *smarrimento*; ibid., 69, 71–2 ... avea seco *umiltà* verace ... Io divenia nel dolor sì *umile*, / veggendo in lei tanta *umiltà* formata; (XXV, 1, 4, 14, dolenti, dolore, dolente); XXV, 72, donne e le donzelle; XXVII, 3, 4, 5, dolente ... dolore ... dolorosa; XXVII, 20, 22, bieltate, bellezza; (XXX, 8, 11, dolente, dogliose); XXXII, 3, *viso* di donna, per *veder* sovente; XXXII, 12–13 ... crescete sì lor *volontate*, / che de la *voglia* ...; XXXIII, 12–13 ... se non per *morte,/*la vostra donna, ch'è *morta* ...; XXXV, 6, 11, 12, dolore ... dole ... dolorosi; (LXXIX, 3, 10, novo, novitate); LXXXI, 69–71 ... queta e *umile*, / miri costei ch'è essemplo d'*umiltate*. Questa è colei ch'*umilia*; (LXXXII, 13, 16, gentile ... gentilezza); (LXXXIII, 1–2, 19, *Amor* ... m'ha lasciato, / non per mio *grato* ..., *Amor* di sé mi farà *grazia* ancora); ibid., 49, 52, 55, donna, ... donneare ..., donne; ibid., 48–9, non sono *innamorati* / mai di donna *amorosa*; ibid., 39, 43, per esser *ridenti* ... veggendo *rider* cosa; ibid., 45, 50, E' *parlan* ... ne' *parlamenti* lor; (ibid., 59–60, 77, leggiadria / disvia ... la disviata); ibid., 96, 104, 107, 109, 114, è ... simigliante, sembiante, simili, sembianti, s'assimiglia; C, 43, 45, ramo di foglia *verde* ... che sua *verdura* serba; (CIII, 24, 29, non ti *ritemi* ... per *tema*); ibid., 27, 30, qualora io *penso* ... lo mio *penser*; ibid., 67, 72, *ferza* ... me ne *sferza*; ibid., 73, 77, 83, vendicherei, vendicar, vendetta; CXIV, 11–12, ch'Amor *leggermente* il saetti. / Però se *leggier* cor; (CIV, 5, 12, Tanto son *belle* e di tanta *vertute* ... cui *vertute* né *beltà* non vale); ibid., 19, 22, *Dolesi* ... di *dolor* colonna; ibid., 106, 107, camera di *perdon* ... ché 'l *perdonare* ... CVI, 7, 11, 15 *Amore* in voi consente ... voi che siete *innamorate* ... non dovreste *amare*; ibid., 43–4, *Servo* non di signor, ma di vil *servo* / si fa chi da cotal *serva*; ibid., 49–52, occhi ... adocchia; ibid., 58–9 *parola* oscura giugne ad intelletto; / per che *parlar*; ibid., 64, 67, seguace ... seguitando; ibid., 65, 68, segnore ... segnoreggia; ibid., 75, 76, che hai tu *fatto*, / cieco avaro dis*fatto*; ibid., 80–1, lo tuo *perduto* pane, / che non si *perde* ... (ibid., 88, 97, difende ... difesa); ibid., 133, 134, 140, 143, 147, amistà, amorose, amata, amore, amor.

CHAPTER 7

THE RHETORICAL SITUATION
AND ITS FIGURES

The great majority of the stylistic procedures described and recommended by the rhetoricians can of course be employed on almost any occasion where circumstances demand that the language should be in some way heightened and raised above its normal, everyday level as a vehicle of informal, spoken communication. Had this not been so, rhetoric could never have exerted so enduring an influence on all branches of literary composition. However, all that the rhetoricians originally set out to teach was the art of public speaking. And so it is only natural that some of their figures and devices should be virtually restricted to what we may call a 'rhetorical situation'. These figures might seem to lie outside our field of interest, for, whatever else Dante's poems may be, they are clearly not the transcripts of speeches made in public. But, in fact, we shall find that the 'rhetorical situation' is necessarily a very elastic concept, and that a large number of Dante's poems will have to be accommodated within its confines.

In the narrow sense of the word, it will be agreed, there cannot be a 'rhetorical situation', unless there is an orator addressing an audience which is physically present before him. In the narrowest sense, it would imply that the place was the assembly or the law court, and that the purpose of the speaker was to *persuade* his hearers that one course of action was better than another, or that an accused person was or was not guilty. Such political and legal situations were of course the archetypes, and they remained influential in the teaching of rhetoric.[1] But even in the ultra-conservative and unreal world of the textbooks of rhetoric, it was recognized that neither law court nor assembly was indispensable, and that the aim of the speaker might well be entertain-

---

[1] The sections dealing with *inventio* are primarily legal. Thus, in the second book of Cicero's *De inventione* (the *Rethorica vetus*), paragraphs 14–153 deal with the *genus iudiciale*. The *genus demonstrativum* (epideictic) gets only two paragraphs. Most of the examples or illustrations are from political or forensic speeches. The exercises for advanced pupils were the *suasoriae* (political) and *controversiae* (legal).

ment and not persuasion.[1] In practice, the most common 'rhetorical situation' in later antiquity resembled nothing more than the popular lecture or *conferenza*.[2]

With the spread of Christianity, there arose another kind of 'live' rhetorical situation—that in which a minister preached to a congregation. It was the ex-rhetor St Augustine who saw most clearly the similarity between oratory and preaching and who did most to defend the study of pagan rhetoric as beneficial to the cause of Christianity;[3] and it was he also, who handed down to the Middle Ages the most influential and widely applicable classification of the orator's aims: 'ut doceat, ut delectet, ut flectat'.[4] Certainly, the sermon was one of the most flourishing branches of rhetoric in medieval times.[5]

But there is in fact no need for an audience to be physically present before a 'genuine' or 'live' rhetorical situation can come into being. In Dante's own words, rhetoric has two aspects: first, 'quando *dinanzi al viso de l'uditore* lo rettorico parla'; second, 'quando *da lettera*, per la parte remota, si parla per lo rettorico'.[6] Secular medieval rhetoric was almost exclusively the rhetoric of the epistle. And the pupil who followed a course in the *ars dictaminis* would have been expected to assume the role of a prelate *writing* to the pope, or of a duke *writing*

---

1 Cf. Votienus Montanus, quoted with approval by the elder Seneca:
'Qui declamationem parat, scribit non ut vincat sed ut placeat, omnia itaque lenocinia conquirit; argumentationes, quia molestae sunt et minimum habent floris, relinquit; sententiis, explicationibus audientes delenire contentus est; cupit enim se approbare, non causam.' *Controversiae*, IX, praef. I: quoted by F. J. E. Raby in *A History of Secular Latin Poetry in the Middle Ages* (Oxford, 1934), ch. I.

2 Cf. H. Marrou on the decline in importance of political and legal rhetoric. 'Seul subsiste, florissant, le troisième genre, l'éloquence "épidictique" ou d'apparat: disons, en meilleur français, l'art du conférencier', *Histoire de l'éducation dans l'antiquité*, 4th ed. (Paris, 1958), p. 270.

3 In the *De doctrina christiana*, esp. II, xxxvi, 132, in W. M. Green (ed.), *Corpus Scriptorum Ecclesiasticorum latinorum*, vol. LXXX (Vienna, 1963).

4 Ibid., IV, xii–xiv, xvii–xxvi. He drew on the following passage in Cicero's *Orator*: 'Erit igitur eloquens ... is qui in foro causisque civilibus ita dicet, *ut probet, ut delectet, ut flectat*. Probare necessitatis est, delectare suavitatis, flectere victoriae; nam id unum ex omnibus ad obtinendas causas potest plurimum', XXI, 69–70.

5 See Th.-M. Charland, *Artes Praedicandi. Contribution à l'histoire de la rhétorique au Moyen Age* (Paris–Ottawa, 1936); G. R. Owst, *Preaching in Medieval England* (Cambridge, 1926); and *Literature and Pulpit in Medieval England* (Cambridge, 1933); A. C. Spearing, *Criticism and Medieval Poetry* (London, 1964), ch. 4, 'The Art of Preaching and Piers Plowman'.

6 The passage forms part of an ingenious comparison between rhetoric and the planet Venus, which appears '*or* da mane *or* da sera ... cioè retro' (*Con.*, II, xiii, 13–14).

to the emperor, and no longer that of a general haranguing his troops, or of an advocate pleading a cause.

Thus, to take the term in the widest sense in which it is still applicable to rhetorical practice and theory, a 'rhetorical situation' comes into being whenever a work is composed as a *formal* address to a *specific* audience (who may on occasion be a single person). That audience will be named or otherwise indicated in the opening of the work, and, typically, it will be addressed at intervals in the second person. And the customs, culture and status of the particular audience will obviously affect the presentation and tone of the composition at every point. Provided these conditions are satisfied, it does not greatly matter whether the 'rhetorical discourse'—to use a neutral term—is intended for its author to declaim, or for the recipient to peruse. The situation and the discourse become more specifically rhetorical, however, if the author is seeking to gain some specific and non-aesthetic end—for example to obtain a favour for himself or for some third party, to instruct, to persuade or convert.

But what kind of relationship exists between a rhetorical discourse and a work of literature? Clearly, a work of fiction, whether narrative or dramatic, can enact a *fictitious* rhetorical situation; but can a work of literature ever be a *genuine* rhetorical discourse, or can a genuine rhetorical discourse ever be a work of literature? In the past, such questions have been answered with an unqualified 'yes' or 'no'. But today this is no longer possible. On the one hand, we can see that rhetorical discourses of such unimpeachable purity and even historical importance as Cicero's orations against Catiline were almost certainly composed (and were certainly revised) with an eye to posterity, and may be read in some sense as literature. On the other, we remember that for centuries after the diffusion of the printed book, novelists would persist in addressing themselves directly to their 'gentle reader' or 'venticinque lettori' and thereby perpetuate, if only in a vestigial form, the original 'story-telling situation' which is in many respects identical to the 'rhetorical situation' as described above. Or again, we may cite Dante's *Comedy* as the supreme example of the many works of literature which have been written with a view to persuading an immediate audience to take a certain course of action (typically, private or public reform), even though the works are not cast in the form of a second-person address. At present, however, we need do no more than remind ourselves of the existence of these wider problems. For our purposes, it will be enough to establish a few simple points about the 'rhetorical situation' as it affects lyric poetry in general and the courtly love-lyric in particular.

In the first place, then, a lyric poem of any period and any culture will take on the form of a rhetorical discourse whenever it is addressed to some specific person or persons. It is indeed quite likely that such a poem would actually be sent in the first instance to the person designated; and it may well be intended to secure some definite, non-literary goal. In other words, a poem of this kind might be in some sense a *genuine* rhetorical discourse. However, there is no need to try and discriminate between the genuine and the fictitious. When reading poems of this kind we do not have the impression that we are invading another's privacy, or prying into personal correspondence. We know or we assume, that the poem was written to be circulated; and we treat the rhetorical situation as fictitious, as part of the total strategy by which the poem makes its impact on *us*.

As is well known, the majority of courtly lyrics—and especially the love-lyrics—are fictitious rhetorical discourses of the kind we have just described. But they are further limited and defined in three important respects. First, they come closer than do other lyrics to the condition of being rhetorical discourses enacted in the course of a work of fiction. They may be compared in some respects to letters contained in a work of narrative fiction, or as Valency aptly suggests,[1] to arias in an opera. Of course the narrative framework in which they are set is not usually stated explicitly (the *Vita Nuova* remains an exceptional work). But—and this is the second point—it does not need to be stated, because in broad outline that framework remains quite remarkably constant. In writing a love-lyric, the thirteenth-century poet laid aside his individuality and assumed the stance, sentiments and language of the archetypal courtly lover as these had been evolved and codified in the twelfth century. He composed 'rhetorical discourses' which would fit more or less predetermined 'rhetorical situations'. Finally, it must be remembered that in the most common of these situations, the lover is pleading for the lady to requite his love, and that his discourse is therefore rhetorical in the special sense that it is designed to persuade and move. Thus, this fictitious rhetorical situation corresponded in

[1] M. Valency, *In Praise of Love* (New York, 1958), p. 117.

many ways to the genuine rhetorical situations recognized in the *artes rhetoricae*. So much so that Brunetto Latini could write:

Cosìe usatamente adviene che due persone si tramettono lettere l'uno all'altro o in latino o in proxa o *in rima* o in volgare o inn altro, nelle quali *contendono* d'alcuna cosa, e così *fanno tencione*. Altressì *uno amante chiamando merzé alla sua donna* dice parole e ragioni molte et ella si difende in suo dire et inforza le sue ragioni et indebolisce quelle del pregatore.[1]

And, as a result, the lover can deploy all the resources of rhetoric, including those which belong exclusively to the 'rhetorical situation'.

The stylistic devices which are relevant only to such situations fall into certain fairly obvious groups. Omnipresent, but scarcely to be considered as a figure, will be the use of direct address and particularly of the vocative. Where the aim is to move or stir, use will be made of the related *affective* figures: exclamation, the rhetorical question, apostrophe and prosopopoeia. Where the aim is to prove or instruct, use may be made of the *dialectic* figures, which are really logical procedures adapted to suit the needs of rhetoric. Where the audience is hostile, or likely to take offence, the author must turn to *dissimulation* and insinuation.[2] We shall find examples of all these procedures in Dante's poems, but before we examine them, a few words must be said about the rhetorical situations in which they occur.

Some of the poems are, in Dante's own technical phrase, 'a indiffinita persona';[3] but about two-thirds of them are 'rhetorical discourses' in one or other of the senses which we have just given to the term. As a first step, we might divide the implied rhetorical *situations* into two

---

[1] *La rettorica italiana di Brunetto Latini*, ed. F. Maggini (Florence, 1915), p. 105, quoted by M. Corti, 'Il linguaggio poetico di Cino da Pistoia', *CN*, XII (1952), p. 207; and D. De Robertis, 'Nascita della coscienza letteraria italiana', *L'approdo letterario*, XXXI (sett. 1965), 3–32, p. 25.

[2] 'Species causarum sunt quinque: honestum, admirabile, humile, anceps, obscurum ... *Anceps* est, in quo aut iudicatio dubia est, aut causa honestatis et turpitudinis particeps, ut benivolentiam pariat et offensam' (*Et.*, II, viii, 1–2).

'Sin turpe causae genus erit, *insinuatione* utendum est ... Inter insinuationem et principium hoc interest. Principium eiusmodi debet esse ut statim apertis rationibus quibus praescripsimus aut benivolum, aut adtentum aut docilem faciamus auditorem; at *insinuatio* eiusmodi debet esse ut *occulte, per dissimulationem* eadem illa omnia conficiamus, ut ad eandem commoditatem in dicendi opere venire possimus' (*Ad Her.* I, iv, 6 and I, vii, 11).

[3] For example nos VIII, X, XVI, XXI–XXIV, XXVII, XXXV, LXXXI, C, CIV. The phrase is used in *VN*, viii, 12 and xxiii, 29.

main classes: the verisimilistic and the improbable. Into the first go the correspondence sonnets which are addressed to individual poets,[1] and which were actually dispatched to them, as we know from their extant replies. And we may also assign to this class the poems addressed to 'madonna' herself (of which there are significantly few[2]), those addressed to his fellow poets in general—the 'fedeli d'amore'[3]—and those addressed to an apparently specific group of 'donne e donzelle'.[4] In all these cases we may readily 'suspend our disbelief' in the fictitious character of the situation. Into the second category go those poems in which Dante addresses his own eyes, or Death, or Love, or the angelic intelligences of the planet Venus, or the poem itself.[5] And perhaps we might set up a third intermediate class to accommodate the two sonnets[6] in which Dante hails a group of pilgrims or grief-stricken young ladies, and also the *canzone, Donna pietosa*,[7] with its narrative within a narrative. But however many degrees of verisimilitude we choose to recognize in our classification of these situations, we must never lose sight of the fact that the real audience of these poems are *we ourselves*, as representatives of the reading public at large. In fact, it is hardly too much to say that the use of a fictitious or nominal audience in Dante's poems should always be treated as a 'figura' in itself—sometimes an affective figure, and sometimes a figure of dissimulation. To establish this important point, let us begin by examining the case which admits least doubt, and where we may draw on Dante's explicit testimony in the prose of the *Convivio*.

It had long been customary for a poet to conclude a *canzone* with a 'tornata' (better known as a *congedo* or 'envoi') in which he addressed the poem itself. It was a traditional decorative element in Dante's view,[8]

---

[1] For example nos XL ff., LII, LXXIII ff., XCV, XCVI, XCIX, CXI, CXIII, CXIV.

[2] In the *Vita Nuova* only six—nos XI–XIII; XXXI, XXXII, XXXIV.

[3] For example nos I, V, VI, XXVI, LXXX.

[4] For example nos XIV, XVII, XXV; CVI.

[5] Respectively, nos XXXIII; VII; XC, CII, CXVI; LXXIX; IX.

[6] Respectively, nos XXXVI; XVIII.

[7] 'Questa canzone ha due parti: ne la prima dico, parlando *a indiffinita persona*, come io fui levato d'una vana fantasia da certe donne, e come promisi loro di dirla; ne la seconda dico come *io dissi* a *loro*', *VN*, xxiii, 29.

[8] '... la quale per tornata di questa canzone fatta fu ad alcuno *adornamento* ... E qui primamente si vuole sapere che ciascuno buono fabricatore, ne la fine del suo lavoro, quello nobilitare e *abbellire* dee in quanto puote, acciò che più celebre e più prezioso da lui si parta' (*Con.*, IV, xxx, 1–2).

and sometimes he used it as conventionally as many of his predecessors and contemporaries. More often, as he expressly says,[1] it is there to some purpose, and Dante turns the convention to new ends. One cannot better the account he himself gives:

Ma però che molte fiate avviene che l'ammonire pare presuntuoso, per certe condizioni suole lo rettorico *indirettamente parlare* altrui, dirizzando le sue parole non a quello per cui dice, ma verso un altro. E questo modo si tiene qui veramente; ché *a la canzone vanno le parole, e a li uomini la 'ntenzione*[2] (*Con.*, II, xi, 6).

A study of these 'tornate' reveals Dante's ever-increasing originality. Those in the *Vita Nuova* and in the early *canzoni* are effective but conventional. In *Voi che 'ntendendo*, and in the first *congedo* of *Tre Donne*, the 'tornata' serves as a defence of Dante's poetic, and in particular of the use of allegory. In *Amor che ne la mente*, to which the passage just quoted refers, the 'tornata' is used to forestall any misunderstandings in his audience concerning the interpretation of the poem. But in *Io son venuto*, the *congedo* is an organic part of the poem and gives the final twist to the conceit on which the poem is built.[3] Then there are two variations on the established pattern. In *Poscia ch'Amor* there is no 'tornata', and this is probably not fortuitous, because all the other *canzoni* with formal 'proemi'[4] have one. Rather, it is

---

[1] '... dico che prima si chiama in ciascuna canzone 'tornata', però che li dicitori che prima usaro di farla, fenno quella perché, cantata la canzone, con certa parte del canto ad essa si ritornasse. *Ma io rade volte a quella intenzione la feci*, e acciò che *altri se n'accorgesse*, rade volte la puosi con l'ordine de la canzone...; ma fecila quando alcuna cosa in adornamento de la canzone *era mestiero* a dire, fuori de la sua sentenza ...' (*Con.*, II, xi, 2–3).

[2] Cf. 'E questa cotale figura in rettorica è molto laudabile, e anco necessaria, cioè quando le parole sono a una persona e la 'ntenzione è a un'altra; però che l'ammonire è sempre laudabile e necessario, e non sempre sta convenevolemente ne la bocca di ciascuno. ... questa figura è bellissima e utilissima, e puotesi chiamare "*dissimulazione*" ' (*Con.*, III, x, 6–7).

Dante is always careful to specify that these apostrophes are *figurative*, for example: 'io mi rivolgo con *la faccia* del mio sermone a la canzone medesima' (II, xi, 1); 'E però mi volgo a la canzone, e *sotto colore* d'insegnare a lei come scusare la conviene, *scuso quella*: ed è una *figura* questa, quando a le cose inanimate si parla, che si chiama da li rettorici prosopopeia; e usanla molto spesso li poeti' (III, ix, 2). For the term *dissimulatio* compare the passage from the *Ad Her.* quoted in the note to p. 269.

[3] Cf. ch. 8, p. 299.

[4] Nos. XIV, XXV, LXXIX, LXXXI, LXXXII, CVI. The technical term is again that used by Dante (e.g. *VN*, xix, 15; xxxi, 3).

meant to intensify the 'point' made in the poem, that Dante has no specific audience,[1] which in its turn is an oblique attack on the degeneracy of the times, which is precisely the theme of the whole poem. In *Così nel mio parlar*, the *canzone* is despatched—as usual—to the lady: however, its task is not to plead for the poet, but to stab the lady through the heart as an act of revenge! And, finally, there are the two 'tornate' which have had the greatest interest for readers of the *Comedy*: those to *Tre donne* and *Amor, da che convien*, in which the exile sends his *canzoni* to Florence, and indirectly makes a plea to be allowed to return. Here, indeed, 'a la canzone vanno le parole, e a li uomini la 'intenzione'; and here one hears the personal voice, so rare in the lyric poetry.

> O montanina mia canzon, tu vai:
> forse vedrai Fiorenza, la mia terra   CXVI, 76–7

However, although the figurative element is seen most clearly in the least plausible rhetorical situations, it is no less important in the verisimilistic. Again, we may call the poet in evidence. He tells us, for example (*VN*, xl, 5), that the sonnet *Deh peregrini* was deliberately cast into the form of direct address 'acciò che più paresse pietoso'. And earlier in the same work he tells us that the inspiration for the famous opening line 'Donne ch'avete intelletto d'amore', which his tongue pronounced as though moved by its own accord, came to him when, having hit upon a 'new and more noble matter', he was meditating as to which audience he might address:

> a me giunse tanta volontade di dire, che io cominciai a *pensare lo modo* ch'io tenesse; e pensai che parlare di lei non *si convenia* che io facesse, se io non *parlasse a donne in seconda persona*, e non ad ogni donna, ma solamente a coloro che sono gentili e che non sono pure femmine.   *VN*, xix, 1

As a last example, let us take the correspondence sonnet *Guido, i' vorrei*. As the extant reply proves, this was clearly written for Cavalcanti to read; and thus the 'rhetorical situation' is not wholly fictitious. But, equally clearly, the sonnet was written for a wider, unspecified audience. Nor is there any contradiction in this. Indeed, it can be argued that the fact of its being addressed to Guido 'in seconda persona' is essential to *our* enjoyment of the poem, and essential also to the poem's unity and meaning. Even on a superficial reading, we can sense that the daydream

---

[1] 'tratterò il ver di lei, *ma non so cui*', LXXXIII, 69.

or fantasy which it puts into words is so delicate and etherial that it could be expressed only as a kind of thinking aloud, in the presence, or in the imagined presence, of an intimate friend. If the world at large is ever to participate in such feelings, then it must not *hear* them, but *over*hear them. But the direct address is not simply a frame to the central image of the magical voyage in a magic boat. For that image might well have been experienced—as visions of this kind usually are —as a tantalizing mirage, or a mere escape into fantasy from the delusions and bleakness of real life. In fact, the tone of spontaneity and relaxed intimacy, created immediately by the opening vocative, 'Guido', turns the whole fourteen lines into a celebration of a friendship which truly exists. The magic voyage is an image of a friendship which is already 'magical' in its own right.

So far we have concentrated on the rhetorical situations implied by any poem taken as a whole. But a rhetorical situation in miniature can be introduced at any time, into any discourse, whatever its nature, by the use of the figures *sermocinatio* and *prosopopoeia*. And since they provide further opportunities for the use of question, exclamation and the like, it will be convenient to treat them here. Both these figures[1] consist in the use of a passage in direct speech attributed to a third party;

[1] '*Sermocinatio* est cum *alicui personae sermo adtribuitur* et is exponitur cum ratione dignitatis' ... (*Ad Her.*, IV, lii, 65).
    'En alium florem, personae quando loquenti
    Sermo coaptatur redoletque loquela loquentem' *PN* 1,265–6
Examples are given ibid., 1,305–24 and 1,392–410. See also *Laborintus*, 553–8.
    '*Prosopoeia* est, cum *inanimalium et persona et sermo* fingitur. Cicero in Catilina (I, 27): "Etenim si mecum patria mea, quae mihi vita mea multo est carior, loqueretur, dicens", et cetera. Sic et *montes* et *flumina* vel *arbores* loquentes inducimus, personam inponentes rei quae non habet naturam loquendi; quod et tragoedis usitatum et in orationibus frequentissime invenitur' (*Et.*, II, xiii, 1–2).
    '*Conformatio* est cum aliqua quae non adest persona confingitur quasi adsit, aut cum *res muta aut informis* fit eloquens, et *forma ei et oratio adtribuitur* ad dignitatem adcommodata ... Haec conformatio licet in plures res, in mutas atque inanimas transferatur. Proficit plurimum in amplificationis partibus et commiseratione' (*Ad Her.*, IV, liii, 66).
    The figure is one of the eight sources of 'amplification' in the *Poetria Nova* and descendants. See *PN* 461–526; 1,267–9; 1,411–15. *Laborintus*, 321–4, 559–60. John of Garland, p. 914–15.
    It is interesting that Dante does not distinguish between apostrophes addressed to inanimate objects, and prosopopoeia in the traditional sense. See *VN*, xxv, 8–9, *Con.*, III, ix, 2 (quoted above, p. 271n).

the difference being that in the first, the words are put into the mouth of a human being, whereas in the second, the 'speaker' is an inanimate object. This distinction is normally important, for the second involves greater licence, and implies a much higher level of style. However, in the *Vita Nuova*, there is little or nothing to distinguish the utterances of *Amore*, on the one hand, and an *omo*, on the other; and in what follows I shall treat most of the *prosopopoeiae* on the same footing as the *sermocinationes*.

Taken together in this way, they are certainly one of the most typical features of Dante's style in the *VN* poems. For the most part they are extremely brief, often hardly more than an exclamation. But they are always placed in prominent positions to form the climax of a period. Sometimes, as in the first two examples, the sentence or period continues after the climax, and the tension is eased gradually under full authorial control; at other times the tension is left deliberately unresolved.[1]

> sì mi fa travagliar l'acerba vita;
> la quale è sì 'nvilita,
> ch'ogn'om par che mi dica: '*Io t'abbandono*',
> veggendo la mia labbia tramortita.   XXV, 65–8

> Poscia piangendo, sol nel mio lamento
> chiamo Beatrice, e dico: '*Or se' tu morta?*'
> e mentre ch'io la chiamo, me conforta.   XXV, 54–6

> e quand'io vi son presso, i' sento Amore
> che dice: '*Fuggi, se 'l perir t'è noia*'.   XII, 3–4

> e per la ebrïetà del gran tremore
> le pietre par che gridin: '*Moia, moia*'.   XII, 7–8

---

[1] Note that the second example is a 'pseudo'-*sermocinatio*, in that the speaker is 'io'; and note the common attenuative use of 'e par che' in the first, fourth and fifth examples.

Here is a complete list of those in the *VN* poems, classified by 'speaker'. There are 32 in all.

Sermocinatio: (a) (*la gente*) *ogn'om*: V, 11–12; XXV, 67. (b) *omo*: XX, 55–6. (c) *donne*: XX, 11–12, 23, 26, 42. (d) *io*: XIII, 4; XX, 28, 73; XXV, 55; XXVII, 6, 12; XXXI, 13–14. Prosopopeia: (a) *Amore*: VIII, 10–12; XII, 4; XIV, 43–4; XX, 63–4; XXI, 5, 13–14; XXX, 7. (b) *Spirito*: XXII, 14; XXX, 13–14; (c) *Pietre*: XII, 8. (d) *Angelo*: XIV, 16–18; (XX, 61). (e) *Dio*: XIV, 24–8. (f) *Madonna morta*: XX, 70. (g) *Words to be spoken by the composition*: IX, 18–24, 25–8, 38–42; XIV, 62–3.

One might also include the whole of XIX (the reply spoken by certain 'donne' to the questions put to them in XVIII); the words addressed to 'anima' by 'core' in XXXIII, 1–13; and the proper dialogue between 'anima' and 'core' in XXXIV, 5–14.

ed omo apparve scolorito e fioco,
dicendomi: '*Che fai? non sai novella?*
Morta è la donna tua, ch'era sì bella.'   XX, 55–6
e par che de la sua labbia si mova
un spirito soave pien d'amore,
che va dicendo a l'anima: '*Sospira*'   XXII, 12–14

The origin of the device is not in doubt: although the free use of direct speech is one of the characteristics of Duecento narrative prose,[1] as it had been of the Old French epic and the French chroniclers,[2] the immediate source is clearly Cavalcanti, in whose work it is equally frequent and important, and in whom one finds the same types, the same formulae, the same placings, even the same 'speakers'.[3]

Their close association with the themes and poetic of the 'stil novo' is confirmed by their decline in the later poems. Having reached their peak in *Voi che 'ntendendo* (LXXIX), they are infrequent in LXXXII and CIII and absent in LXXXIII, C, and in the correspondence sonnets.[4] In

---

[1] 'La frequenza dei discorsi diretti si presenta come un aspetto tipico del volgare dei secoli XIII e XIV, soprattutto della prosa narrativa, e si lega alla tendenza duplice del volgare verso l'uso della coordinazione in luogo della subordinazione propria dello stile letterario latino, e verso la sostituzione dell'indicativo al congiuntivo e all'infinito nei dipendenti.' M. Corti, 'La fisionomia stilistica di Guido Cavalcanti', *RAL*, ser. VIII, V (1950), 541. She further notes the contrast between the 'popularity' of the device and the highly literary, rarefied atmosphere of the 'stil novo.'

[2] See P. M. Schon, *Studien zum Stil der frühen französischen Prosa* (*Analecta Romanica* series, vol. VIII) (Frankfurt am Main, 1960), pp. 185–96. The figures which he gives for the percentage of whole works to be cast in the form of direct speech are of considerable interest: *Chanson de Roland*, 43.6 per cent; *La vie de Saint Alexis*, 29·8 per cent; *Le Couronnement Louis*, 52 per cent; *Erec et Enide*, 34 per cent; *Cliges* 27 per cent. The chroniclers of the fourth crusade have: Clari 10·5 per cent; Villehardouin, 9 per cent; Valenciennes 27 per cent. The figure for the *VN* poems, taking all the examples listed in the notes to p. 274 (98 lines in 676), would be 14 per cent.

[3] See Corti, 'La fisionomia stilistica', pp. 541–5. The 'speakers' are: the composition; Love; 'una voce interiore', 'un pensero'; and 'la gente'. Miss Corti also notes their use as a dramatic climax in consecutive periods, and the frequency of the introductory *par che* ('uno degli attacchi più comuni e quasi convenzionali dello stil novo', p. 543).
It is interesting to note that there are no prosopopeiae in the works of Guittone, even though *apostrophes* abound. 'Bei Guittone jedoch fehlt dieses Stilmittel völlig. ... Wohl werden bei Guittone alle möglichen Gegenstände und Abstracta, besonders natürlich *Amore*, die Tugenden und die Laster, angesprochen, *aber sie bleiben alle stumm*', R. Baehr, 'Studien zur Rhetorik in den Rime Guittones von Arezzo,' *ZRP*, LXXIII (1957), 234–5.

[4] For LXXIX, see below. There are words to be spoken by the composition in LXXXI, 89–90 and LXXXII, 146. There are interjections by the *anima* in LXXX, 10 and LXXXI, 7–8. There is a solitary 'par ch'ella dica ...' in LXXX, 13–16. In LXXXII there are three

Tre donne they appear in strength, but in an entirely new context—that of an allegorical masque played out by Love and the three ladies.[1] In *Doglia mi reca* there is only one brief example ('Se vol dire "I' son presa", / ah com poca difesa ...,' (lines 96–7), unless we understand lines 74–84 as the words spoken by Death, thus:

> Ecco giunta colei che ne pareggia:
> 'Dimmi, che hai tu fatto,
> cieco avaro disfatto?' etc.

This would then constitute a pure example of prosopopeia, used in precisely the kind of context envisaged by the rhetorical manuals.

Not all the interventions are as short as those we have just examined. For example, the dialogue between 'core' and 'anima' in *Gentil pensero* (XXXIV) is developed in *Voi che 'ntendendo* into a full-scale *contentio* between the 'anima' which is striving to remain faithful to the memory of the dead Beatrice, and a 'spirito' who eventually carries the day in favour of the 'donna gentile'.[2] And there had been an earlier *contentio* in the second stanza of *Donne ch'avete*, where we may read first the speech for the plaintiff ('Angelo clama in divino intelletto / e dice ...'), then a summary of the defence ('Sola Pietà nostra parte difende'), and finally the judgement given in the words of God. But the most complex situation of all is to be found in an even earlier poem, *Ballata, i' vòi*. It would take too long here[3] to show how and why the poem is 'quasi un mezzo' (*VN*, xii, 8), through which Dante contrives to address his irate lady, since he cannot do so 'immediatamente'. It must be sufficient to recall that the whole poem is an address to itself ('la ballata non è

---

brief phrases attributed to hypothetical speakers: 34–5, l'uom chiama colui / omo gentil che può dicere: ...; 112–13, Però nessun si vanti / dicendo: ...; 41, Chi diffinisce: ...

[1] CIV, 31, 33–6, 44, 45–54 (the ladies); 60–72 (Amore). In this poem one is struck more by the way Dante *avoids* direct speech. Thus 13–14, 'Tempo fu già nel quale, / *secondo il lor parlar*, furon dilette;' 30, 'di lei e del dolor *fece dimanda*'; 39–40, e *chiese* / chi fosser l'altre due ch'eran con lei'; 58, '*salutò* le germane sconsolate.' The result is that 'Amore' speaks only once.

[2] Direct speech becomes increasingly prominent in each successive stanza, until the fourth stanza is given over completely to the triumphant speech by the 'spirito'—a little masterpiece of persuasion. See lines 19, 24–6, 31–2, 34–9 (including self quotation in 36–7), 40–1, 43–52, 61.

[3] See Kenelm Foster and Patrick Boyde, *Dante's Lyric Poetry* (Oxford, 1967), vol. II, p. 68.

altro che queste parole ched io parlo' (*VN*, xii, 17)). The poem tells itself to deliver speeches and to request Love to deliver speeches on its behalf, and it is thus one of the most elaborate exercises in 'indirection' or 'dissimulazione' that Dante ever composed.

We have now considered all the various species of rhetorical situation to be found in Dante's poems, and so we are in a position to examine the figures which may be used in these situations. Let us begin with the affective figures.

The use of a noun in the vocative is not in itself a figure, but we cannot pass over the usage in silence, as it is so characteristic of Dante's style, especially in the early poems.[1] The first poem in the *Vita Nuova* begins with what is a vocative in spirit, and the last poem ends with one:

A ciascun'alma presa e gentil core	I, I
sì ch'io lo 'ntendo ben, donne mie care	XXXVII, 14

The vocative forms a favourite opening move, and it can establish a poetic atmosphere almost in one stroke,[2] for example:

Piangete, amanti, poi che piange Amore	VI, I
Donne ch'avete intelletto d'amore	XIV, I
Deh peregrini che pensosi andate	XXXVI, I

Nor are they limited to one tone: they can be abrupt and harsh, elegiac, or intimate and almost caressing, as in the following examples:

Morte villana, di pietà nemica	VII, I

[1] There are 31 in the *Vita Nuova* poems, *excluding* pronominal vocatives like 'O voi che per la via d'Amor passate', V, I. Grammatically they fall into the following categories:
(a) 'Outside syntax', for example '*Sire*, nel mondo si vede', XIV, 16. See XIV, 27; XXXIV, 9; XXXVII, 14.
(b) As subject, or in apposition to subject pronoun, for example, 'e non pensate, *donna*, onde si mova', XI, 2; 'Tu vai, *ballata*, sì cortesemente', IX, 5. See IX, I; IX, 43; XIV, 57; XXV, 71; VI, I; XXVI, 1–2; XIV, 24; XXXVI, I; XXXIII, 1–2; XXVII, 6; XXX, 13; XVII, 8; XVIII, 7.
(c) In apposition to object pronoun, or to a pronoun following preposition, for example 'Donne, dicerollo a vui', XX, 28; 'Morte, assai dolce ti tegno', XX, 73. See XIV, 1–2; XIV, 11–13; XXV, 9; XXV, 63–4; XXV, 17; IX, 18; IX, 25–7; VII, I and 6; XII, 2; XX, 83.
[2] Cf. also nos VII, IX, XI, XII, XXVI, XXXIII; and, with pronominal vocatives, nos V, XVIII, XIX. The first line of a poem had great importance for Dante, as we know from the account of the genesis of *Donne ch'avete*; and on purely practical grounds, an arresting opening line must have been as important as a good title is for a modern novel.
E. Auerbach (*Dante, Poet of the Secular World*, trans. R. Manheim (Chicago, 1961), pp. 36–8) devotes three pages to the use of the vocative in Dante.

dimmi, che hai tu fatto,
cieco avaro disfatto   CVI, 75–6

Pietosa mia canzone, or va' piangendo   XXV, 71

Oh, messer Cin, come 'l tempo è rivolto   XCVI, 12

Guido, i' vorrei che tu e Lapo ed io   LII, 1

dicendo lor, *diletta mia novella*   LXXIX, 60

Gentil ballata mia, quando ti piace   IX, 43

The vocatives are indisputably figures when they are used as apostrophes, that is, when the speaker feigns to 'turn aside'[1] from his nominal audience, and to call on some absent person or inanimate object.[2] This was one of the favourite devices of the medieval high style.[3] In the poems, the only pure examples[4] are the 'tornate' discussed above.[5] There is one example each in *Poscia ch'Amor* and in *Così nel mio parlar*;[6] but it is only in *Doglia mi reca* that apostrophes appear in their true glory. This poem, as we shall see in more detail in the last chapter, is a 'rhetorical discourse' in the fullest sense of the term. Dante's primary aim here is not instruction (*ut doceat*), but *persuasion* (*ut flectat*), and so he gives free rein to the affective figures traditionally suited to his purpose.[7] And since he keeps his nominal

---

[1] The term means literally '*aversus* a iudice sermo' (Quintilian, IX, ii, 38).

[2] '*Exclamatio* est quae conficit significationem doloris aut indignationis alicuius per *hominis* aut *urbis* aut *loci* aut *rei cuiuspiam conpellationem*, hoc modo: "Te nunc adloquor, Africane, cuius mortui quoque nomen splendori ac decori est civitati. Tui clarissimi nepotes suo sanguine aluerunt inimicorum crudelitatem!"... Hac exclamatione si loco utemur, raro, et cum *rei magnitudo* postulare videbitur, *ad quam volemus indignationem animum auditoris adducemus*' (*Ad Her.*, IV, xv, 22).

[3] It is one of the sources of *amplificatio* in Geoffrey's system. In the *Poetria Nova* he manages to spin out his examples for nearly 200 hexameters! (264–460). There he calls it *apostropha*, in the *Documentum* II, ii, 24–8 it is *apostrophatio*. Dante's more passionate letters abound with them.

[4] In another sense of the term, all the poems addressed to *insentient* audiences—see above p. 270—are apostrophes (Dante called them *prosopopoeiae*).

[5] Very probably as part of the reaction against Guittone: cf. Baehr, 'Die Apostrophe ... ist, zusammen mit ihren exornationes, *ein durchgängiges Stilprinzip bei Guittone* ... est ist kaum eines [Gedicht] dabei, das keine Apostrophe enthielte; die meisten sind in Du-Form abgefasst', 'Studien zur Rhetorik' (1957), p. 231.

[6] 'Oh falsi cavalier, malvagi e rei', LXXXIII, 112 ff.; and 'Ahi angosciosa e dispietata lima', CIII, 22ff.

[7] Cf. St Augustine: '... si *docendi* sunt qui audiunt, narratione faciendum est ... documentis adhibitis ratiocinandum est. Si vero qui audiunt *movendi* sunt potius quam docendi, ... maioribus dicendi viribus opus est. Ibi obsecrationes et increpationes, concitationes et coercitiones et quaecumque alia valent ad commovendos animos sunt necessaria' (*De doctrina christiana*, IV, iv, 15).

audience of 'donne' steadily in view throughout the poem, the 'turning away' achieves its maximum effect:

O cara ancella e pura,	
colt' hai nel ciel misura	CVI, 39 ff.
oh mente cieca, che non pò vedere	ibid., 70 ff.
Morte, che fai? che fai, fera Fortuna	ibid., 90 ff.
falsi animali, a voi ed altrui crudi	ibid., 101 ff.

Closely linked with the apostrophe, and indeed often part of it,[1] is the exclamation. The simplest forms are the interjection and the command, as in the following examples:

Lasso, per forza di molti sospiri	XXXV, 1
Omè, perché non latra	CIII, 59
Deh, consoliam costui	XX, 23
Beato, anima bella, chi te vede	XX, 83
ch'a l'anima gentil fa dir: 'Merzede'	LXXX, 10
dopo la qual gridavan tutti: *Osanna*[2]	XX, 61
che mi dicean pur: 'Morra'ti, morra'ti'.	XX, 42
Ponete mente almen com'io son bella	LXXIX, 61
Oh cotal donna pera	CVI, 144

But Dante uses these forms with comparative and significant discretion.[3]

---

[1] For Geoffrey of Vinsauf, it is one of the four *exornationes* associated (*quae incidunt*) with the apostrophe: *Documentum,* II, ii, 24–5.

[2] Cf. Isidore's definition: 'Interiectio vocata, quia sermonibus interiecta, id est interposita, *affectum commoti animi* exprimit ... Quae voces quarumcumque linguarum propriae sunt, *nec in aliam linguam facile transferuntur*' (*Et.,* I, xiv).

[3] Thus 'lasso' appears only seven times in the poems analysed: XIII, 4; XXVI, 7; XXVII, 1; XXXV, 1; LXXIX, 31; LXXXI, 7; CVI, 18. Contrast what M. Corti says of Cino: 'A questo proposito colpisce l'uso enorme che egli fa della esclamazione, una delle figure più consigliate dai trattati del tempo: ... vi è in primo luogo il solito tipo di esclamativa che ricorre in tutti i poeti del tempo con tale frequenza da renderne veramente faticosa la nostra digestione letteraria; voglio dire l'inciso esclamativo *lasso!, me lasso! o lasso* ecc.', 'Il linguaggio poetico', p. 219.

She gives 27 examples in Cino (pp. 219–20), and continues: 'Dall'esame dell'uso non solo ciniano si può dedurre che questo inciso ha perso sia la funzione grammaticale, sia la sua originaria intensità ... In Guittone d'Arezzo, in Chiaro Davanzati, per non citare che due tra i poeti che più hanno abusato di *lasso,* l'espressione ha gli stessi aspetti' (p. 220).

See further R. Dragonetti, *La technique poétique des trouvères dans la chanson courtoise. Contribution à l'étude de la rhétorique médiévale* (Bruges, 1960), p. 151, for trouvère poems which open with the exclamation 'Las'.

More interesting, and more characteristic of Dante, are those climactic exclamations which both summarize and complete the lines that precede them,[1] for example:

> Ond'io non so da qual matera prenda;
> e vorrei dire, e non so ch'io mi dica:
> *così mi trovo in amorosa erranza!*　　　　　　　X, 9–11

> e quale è stata la mia vita, poscia
> che la mia donna andò nel secol novo,
> *lingua non è che dicer lo sapesse*[2]　　　　　XXV, 60–2

> Omo da sé vertù fatto ha lontana;
> omo no, mala bestia ch'om simiglia.
> O Deo, qual maraviglia
> voler cadere in servo di signore,
> o ver di vita in morte!　　　　　　　　　　CVI, 22–6

They can even 'sum up' an entire poem:

> Oh, messer Cin, come 'l tempo è rivolto
> a danno nostro e de li nostri diri,
> da po' che 'l ben è sì poco ricolto!　　　　XCVI, 12–14

> Vedete omai quanti son l'ingannati!　　　　LXXXII, 140

> Color che vivon fanno tutti contra.　　　　LXXXIII, 133

The rhetorical question was one of the most favoured of all figures in the Middle Ages. It was always closely associated with the exclamation both in theory[3] and in practice. Indeed Segre has shown that they

---

[1] These correspond exactly to the figure *epiphonema* as defined by Rufinianus and Quintilian:

'*Epiphonema*. Hac sententia in fine expositae rei cum affectu enuntiatur. Cicero in Verrinis: "Non vitam liberum, sed mortis celeritatem precabantur" '. Rufinianus, I, 29, in C. Halm (ed.), *Rhetores Latini Minores* (Leipzig, 1863), p. 45.

'Est enim *epiphonema* rei narratae vel probatae summa acclamatio:

　　"Tantae molis erat Romanam condere gentem!" '　　　　(*Aen.*, I, 33)

Quintilian, VIII, v, 11 (repeated in C. J. Victor, ch. 22, in Halm (ed.), *Rhetores Latini Minores*, p. 437).

[2] There are a number of this type in which the exclamatory element is not so obvious, for example:

sì è novo miracolo e gentile, XVII, 14. And cf. XXI, 14; XXVI, 4; XXVII, 26; LXXIX, 45; LXXX, 23; LXXXII, 28, 73; LXXXIII, 57; C, 10, 23, 36, etc. CXIII, 14; CVI, 126.

[3] In the *Ad Her.*, and thus in most medieval manuals, the forms of the question are treated immediately after the exclamation.

'*Interrogatio* non omnis gravis est neque concinna, sed haec quae, cum enumerata sunt

---

are often grammatically indistinguishable from affirmations in the letters of Guittone, where they abound.[1] Possibly as part of the reaction against Guittone, Dante uses such common coinage very rarely, and as a result of this restraint, his more ambitious *interrogationes* have lost none of their purchasing power. The most remarkable is certainly the *frons* of *Deh peregrini* ('Venite voi da sì lontana gente ... che non piangete ...' etc.), where the implications of the question are so far-reaching that they almost defy analysis.[2] But the interrogative form also adds considerably to the poetic effect of the following lines:

> Dice di lei Amor: 'Cosa mortale
> come esser pò sì adorna o sì pura?'   XIV, 43–4
>
> chiamo Beatrice, e dico: 'Or se' tu morta?'   XXV, 55

In the later poems, the questions are equally infrequent, but tend to be more elaborate and more obviously rhetorical.[3] This change in technique may be seen particularly clearly in *Doglia mi reca* where we encounter not only the simple *interrogatio*, but the related *ratiocinatio*[4]

---

ea quae obsunt causae adversariorum, confirmat superiorem orationem, hoc pacto: "Cum igitur haec omnia faceres, diceres, administrares, utrum animos sociorum ab re publica removebas et abalienabas, an non? et utrum aliquem exornari oportuit qui istaec prohiberet ac fieri non sineret, an non?" ' (*Ad Her.*, IV, xv, 22).

On the use of question and exclamation in the trouvères, see Dragonetti, *La technique poétique* pp. 41–5.

[1] '... la forma interrogativa non è ormai altro che una maniera di rendere più sonora ed enfatica un'affermazione', C. Segre, 'La sintassi del periodo nei primi prosatori italiani', *RAL*, ser. VIII, IV (1952), 64. This is proved by the fact that they can be co-ordinated with non-interrogative forms, or followed by constructions with *ché*, *per che*, *unde*, *dunque*. See also pp. 94–5 of his article.

[2] In a Greek distinction, preserved by Capella, the question here is a *pýsma* ('quaesitum') and not an *erôtema* ('interrogatio'): '*pýsma* est quaesitum, quae figura a superiore [sc. erotema] eo differt, quod *interrogato una voce* tantum responderi potest, *quaesito* autem *nisi pluribus* responderi non potest ...' Capella, V, 524.

[3] For example: Qual non dirà fallenza / divorar cibo ed a lussuria intendere? / ornarsi, come vendere / si dovesse al mercato di non saggi? LXXXIII, 32–5. Ahi angosciosa e dispietata lima, / ... / perché non ti ritemi / sì di rodermi il core a scorza a scorza, / com'io di dire altrui chi ti dà forza? CIII, 22–6. (And cf. CIII, 59–60.)

[4] '*Peusis*, id est soliloquium, cum ad interrogata ipsi nobis respondemus' (*Et.*, II, xxi, 47).

'*Ratiocinatio* est per quam ipsi a nobis rationem poscimus quare quidque dicamus, et crebro *nosmet a nobis petimus* cuiusque propositionis explanationem' (*Ad Her.*, IV, xvi, 23).

See *PN*, 1,109–16, and *Laborintus*, 455–6, where the example is conveniently brief: 'Cur misit? quia tempus erat. Quare? quia laesit Hostes. Cur? homini perniciosus erat.'

and *subiectio*,[1] which consist in the use of question and answer:

> Lasso, a che dicer vegno?
> Dico che bel disdegno
> sarebbe in donna, di ragion laudato,
> partir beltà da sé per suo commiato.   CVI, 18–21
>
> Volete udir se piaga?
> Tanto chi prende smaga,
> che 'l negar poscia non li pare amaro.   ibid., 123–5
>
> Morte, che fai? che fai, fera Fortuna,
> che non solvete quel che non si spende?
> se 'l fate, a cui si rende?
> Non so, poscia che tal cerchio ne cinge
> che di là su ne riga.   ibid., 90–4

This last example is at once a challenge to, and a justification of, the method I have adopted in the discussion of the 'affective' figures: a challenge, in that it may seem absurd to seek to distinguish vocative, apostrophe, *interrogatio* and *subiectio* when they can all appear in one passage; a justification, in that it is precisely the combination of all these elements[2] which distinguishes it from, or in medieval terms, sets it above all the other examples, in which there is only an apostrophe, or only an exclamation and a vocative.

It is particularly difficult to generalize concerning Dante's typical practice with respect to this group of figures precisely because there are so many possible combinations. But it is clear that his use of the

---

[1] '*Subiectio* est cum *interrogamus* adversarios aut *quaerimus* ipsi quid ab illis aut quid contra nos dici possit; *dein subicimus* id quod oportet dici aut non oportet, aut nobis adiumento futurum sit aut offuturum sit idem contrario' (*Ad Her.*, IV, xxiii, 33). The example in the *Poetria Nova* runs:

> Serpens invidiae nostraeque propaginis auctor,
> Cur cruce damnasti Christum? Meruitne? Sed expers
> Omnis erat maculae. Corpus fantasma putasti?
> Sed veram carnem sumpsit de virgine. Purum
> Credebas hominem? Sed de virtute probavit
> Esse Deum.   I,139–44

(See also *Documentum*, II, ii, 27; *Laborintus*, 279–84.)

[2] We would also have to take into account the chiasmus and the alliteration of line 90, and especially the *conduplicatio* ('fai ... fai ... non ... non'), which, like *subiectio*, is another of the *exornationes* which 'in apostrophatione incidunt', (*Documentum*, II, ii, 24–6).

interjection and the rhetorical question is very discreet, when compared with that of his contemporaries; that the exclamation is more commonly found in the more 'subtle' final position than elsewhere;[1] and that the most characteristic element is his use of the vocative, with the full range of effects illustrated above. The most 'elevated' examples occur in the first group of poems (especially in the double sonnets), and in the last (especially in *Doglia mi reca*).

As for those figures which are, in reality, nothing more than logical procedures, they are naturally rare in these poems, and restricted to the doctrinal *canzoni* of group J. For the rhetorician,[2] both *Le dolci rime* and *Poscia ch'Amor* might be considered as examples of *paradiastole*,[3] whilst their form is that of the *procatalepsis*,[4] in which the opponent's arguments are anticipated and refuted before he has had the opportunity to speak.

Only in *Le dolci rime* does Dante make open use of the definition.[5]

---

[1] Exclamations which interrupt the flow are rare; but there is a particularly good, motivated example in *Le dolci rime*:

> Ma vilissimo sembra, a chi 'l ver guata,
> cui è scorto 'l cammino e poscia l'erra,
> e tocca a tal, ch'è morto e va per terra!   38–40

which Dante glosses: 'Poi che la mala condizione di questa populare oppinione è narrata, *subitamente*, quasi come cosa orribile, quella percuoto *fuori di tutto l'ordine de la riprovagione*' (*Con.*, IV, vii, 5).

[2] Dante will certainly have derived these modes of argument from his study of *philosophia*, just as the overall structure (refutation-proof) is characteristic of scholastic argumentation. But it is not entirely misleading to consider them in this study, for they remind us that *rhetorica* and *dialectica* were closely associated, and that both these poems are still more rhetorical than logical.

[3] '*Paradiastole* est, quotiens id quod dicimus interpretatione *discernimus*: "cum te pro astuto sapientem appellas, pro inconsiderato fortem, pro inliberali diligentem"' (*Et.*, II, xxi, 9).

This example (also in Quintilian, IX, iii, 65) comes ultimately from Rutilius Lupus, whose definition is much clearer: 'Hoc schema plures res aut duas, *quae videntur unam vim habere, disjungit* et quantum distent docet, suam cuique propriam sententiam subiungendo', Lupus, I, 4, in Halm, ed. *Rhetores Latini Minores*, p. 5.

This seems a perfect description of *Poscia ch'Amor*. The *Ad Her.* (IV, xxv, 35) does not distinguish the figure, but gives unmistakeable examples under *definitio*, for instance: 'Non est ista diligentia, sed avaritia, ideo quod diligentia est adcurata conservatio suorum, avaritia iniuriosa appetitio alienorum.'

[4] '*Procatalempsis*, cum id, quod nobis obici poterat, ante praesumimus ad diluendum …' (*Et.*, II, xxi, 27).

[5] '*Definitio* est quae rei alicuius proprias amplectitur potestates breviter et absolute, hoc modo: "Maiestas rei publicae est in qua continetur dignitas et amplitudo civitatis"' (*Ad Her.*, IV, xxv, 35). A good definition gives the same pleasure as a *sententia*, as the

Here he begins by stating the definition of nobility ascribed to Frederick II, and the popular corruption of it (lines 21–37). Then he explains by analogy ('Chi diffinisce: "Omo è legno animato" ') the ways in which a definition can be defective (41–4), and demonstrates that the imperial and popular definitions are faulty in just these ways (45–73). The poem ends with Dante's own definition of nobility ('. . . seme di felicità . . . messo da Dio ne l'anima ben posta', 119–20), and his description of the outward signs of nobility. In *Poscia ch'Amor* the attack on the opposition is by ridicule and sarcasm, and there is no attempt to give alternative definitions of 'leggiadria', or to attack these on logical grounds. Dante's own definition ('sollazzo è che convene / con esso Amore e l'opera perfetta,' 89–90) is cryptic, and the positive 'proof' rests heavily on analogy.

Both poems use the rhetorical syllogism (*conclusio* or *enthymema*),[1] which is characterized by its highly elliptic form, for example:

> che siano vili *appare* ed imperfette,
> ché, quantunque collette,
> non posson quïetar, ma dan più cura;   LXXXII, 56–8

> che sanza ovrar vertute
> nessun pote acquistar verace loda:
> *dunque*, se questa mia matera è bona,
> come ciascun ragiona,
> sarà vertù o con vertù s'annoda.   LXXXIII, 72–6

These may have real rhetorical force as in the case of the lines which most openly parade a logical formula:

> Ancor, *segue di ciò che innanʒi ho messo,*

---

author notes. 'Haec ideo commoda putatur exornatio quod omnem rei cuiuspiam vim et potestatem ita dilucide proponit et breviter, ut neque pluribus verbis oportuisse dici videatur, neque brevius potuisse dici putetur' (ibid.).

1 '*Conclusio* est quae brevi argumentatione ex iis quae ante dicta sunt aut facta conficit quid necessario consequatur' (*Ad Her.*, IV, xxx, 41).
   The example in the *Laborintus* runs:
   > Non est certa dies mortis: re certior omni
   > Mors est. Erroris ergo relinque viam.   519–20

'*Enthymema* igitur Latine interpretatur mentis conceptio, quem *inperfectum syllogismum* solent artigraphi nuncupare. Nam in duabus partibus eius argumenti forma consistit, quando id, quod ad fidem pertinet faciendam, utitur, *syllogismorum lege praeterita*, ut est illud: "Si tempestas vitanda est, non est igitur navigandum". Ex sola enim propositione et conclusione constat esse perfectum, *unde magis rhetoribus quam dialecticis convenire iudicatum est*' (*Et.*, II, ix, 8).

che siam tutti gentili o ver villani,
o che non fosse ad uom cominciamento:
ma ciò io non consento,
ned ellino altressì, se son cristiani![1]   LXXXII, 69–73

In *Poscia ch' Amor*, however, the syllogistic section is limited to a mere twenty lines (72–93).

The most forbiddingly logical passage comes in the section of *Le dolci rime* where Dante distinguishes the concepts of 'gentilezza' and 'virtù'; and it is marked by the frequent repetition of 'dico' as Dante endeavours to make the stages in the argument clear. The nearest rhetorical figure in this case would be the *expeditio*.[2]

Of the rhetorical figures which involve some kind of simulation or dissimulation, Dante makes very little use.[3] In the chosen poems he does not pretend to doubt which of two terms he should employ, nor use one of them and ostentatiously correct himself; he does not give information in the very act of denying any intention to do so; he does not break off in mid-sentence, leaving his audience to complete the sense for themselves, nor does he want them to realize that his real

---

[1] This is in fact an example of the figure *divisio*, 'quae rem semovens ab re utramque absolvit ratione subiecta, hoc modo: "Cur ego nunc tibi quicquam obiciam? Si probus es, non meruisti; si inprobus non commovebere" ' (*Ad Her.*, IV, xl, 52).

[2] '*Expeditio* est cum, rationibus conpluribus enumeratis quibus aliqua res confieri potuerit, ceterae tolluntur, una relinquitur quam nos intendimus' (*Ad Her.*, IV, xxix, 40).

e.g.   'Simplex, vel stultus, vel sis insanus oportet.
     Non es simplex, nam sunt mala nota tibi;
    Non etiam stultus, quia nosti quo sit eundum:
    Quod sis insanus hac ratione patet.'   *Laborintus*, 511–14

The bones of Dante's argument may be exposed as follows:

per che in medesmo detto
convegnono ambedue, ch'en d'uno effetto.
Onde convien da l'altra *vegna* l'una,
o d'un terzo ciascuna;
ma se l'una val ciò che l'altra vale,
e ancor più, da lei *verrà* più tosto.
....
È gentilezza dovunqu'è vertute,
ma non vertute ov'ella;
....
Dunque verrà, come dal nero il perso,
ciascheduna vertute da costei,
o vero il gener lor...   LXXXII, 94–9, 101–2, 109–11

[3] But see above pp. 271–6.

meaning is very different, and possibly just the opposite, of what his words convey at their face value; he does not use the *double entendre*, nor the enigmatic proverb.[1] Only on one occasion does he pretend to throw himself on the mercy of his hearer;[2] and only on one occasion— in *Doglia mi reca*—does he seemingly break the cardinal rule of rhetoric by addressing harsh words to his audience.[3]

There are two usages which we may perhaps consider as examples of *emphasis*.[4] Dante has an increasing fondness for the use of an *if*-clause to express what is either a fact or patently absurd:

> però, donne, s'io dico
> parole quasi contra a tutta gente,   CVI, 3–4
>
> che se beltà tra i mali
> volemo annumerar, creder si pòne.[5]   ibid., 141–2

And he sometimes leaves the reader to supply for himself the phrase 'i.e., not at all', after a periphrasis or simile:

> ché de l'altre selvagge
> cotanto laude quanto biasmo prezza   LXXXIII, 127–8
>
> Cotanto del mio mal par che si prezzi
> quanto legno di mar che non lieva onda   CIII, 18–19

---

[1] The figures referred to are, in order: *dubitatio*, *Ad Her.*, IV, xxix, 40, or *apora*, *Et.*, II, xxi, 27; *correctio*, *Ad Her.*, IV, xxvi, 36; *occultatio*, *Ad Her.*, IV, xxvii, 37, or *paralipsis*, Capella, V, 523; *praecisio*, *Ad Her.*, IV, xxx, 41, or *abscisio*, ibid., liv, 67, or *aposiopesis*, *Et.*, II, xxi, 35; *ironia*, *Et.*, I, xxxvii, 23–30, and II, xxi, 41, Capella, V, 523; *significatio*, *Ad Her.*, IV, liii, 67; *ambiguum* (a species of the last), *Ad Her.*, IV, liii, 67; *paroemia Et.*, I, xxxvii, 28.

The whole of *Tutti li miei penser* (X) may be read as a *dubitatio*. There is an antithetical *correctio* in CVI, 22–3. As examples of *ironia* one might take LXXXII, 27–8 or LXXXIII, 45.

[2] Or, rather, he advises the *ballata* to tell Love to do so in the lines:
> ed a la fine falle umil preghero,
> lo perdonare se le fosse a noia,
> *che mi comandi per messo ch'eo moia,*
> e vedrassi ubidir ben servidore.   IX, 31–4

This is the figure *permissio* (*Ad Her.*, IV, xxix, 39), or *epitrope* (*Et.*, II, xxi, 30).

[3] The figure here is *licentia* (*Ad Her.*, IV, xxxvi, 48). This will be discussed in detail in the last chapter.

[4] 'At contra orationem extollit et exornat energia tum *emphasis*, quae plus quiddam quam dixerit intellegi facit; ut si dicas ... "Demissum lapsi per funem" (*Aen.*, II, 262). Cum enim dicit "lapsi", altitudinis imaginem suggerit' (*Et.*, II, xx, 4).

'*Significatio* est res quae plus in suspicione relinquit quam positum est in oratione' (*Ad Her.*, IV, liii, 67).

[5] Cf. CIV, 65, 70, 88; (C, 64; CIII, 72).,

e così esser l'un sanza l'altro osa
com'alma razional sanza ragione.[1]   XVI, 3–4

But if these minor, schematized and easily identifiable subterfuges are conspicuous by their absence, dissimulation in a broader and much more subtle form is wholly characteristic of Dante's poems. To do justice to this subject we should have to examine such matters as the protestations of his inability to praise his lady, which in itself 'risulta in grande loda di costei', as Dante observes (*Con.*, III, iv, 3); or again his characteristic praise of the lady's 'operazioni' rather than her person, that is, of the effects and not the cause.[2] And above all, we should have to consider in far greater detail his use of the fictitious rhetorical situation. But these lie outside the scope of the present study; and so perhaps we may conclude by quoting once again, without comment, two of Dante's own observations on the subject: ... 'questa figura è bellissima e utilissima, e puotesi chiamare "dissimulazione" '. '... ché a la canzone vanno le parole, e a li uomini la 'ntenzione'.[3]

---

[1] One might add the unexplained similes of xcv, 1–8, 'I' ho veduto già ...' etc. cxiii, 9–11, 'Non è colpa del sol ...' etc. or cxi, 5–8, 'Chi ragione o virtù contra gli sprieme, / fa come que' che 'n la tempesta sona ...' etc. Cf. *Paradiso*, x, 35, 'non m'accors' io, *se non com*'uom s'accorge, / anzi 'l primo pensier, del suo venire'; x, 90, '*se non com*' acqua ch'al mar non si cala'; xxxii, 52, 'Dentro a l'ampiezza di questo reame / casüal punto non puote aver sito, / *se non come* tristizia o sete o fame.'

[2] Cf. *Con.*, III, viii, 15: 'Onde è da sapere che di tutte quelle cose che lo 'ntelletto nostro vincono, sì che non può vedere quello che sono, *convenevolissimo trattare è per li loro effetti*: onde di Dio, e de le sustanze separate, e de la prima materia, così trattando, potemo avere alcuna conoscenza'.

[3] *Con.*, III, x, 7 and II, xi, 6.

CHAPTER 8

'DESCRIPTIO', 'SIMILE',
'SENTENTIA'

In this chapter we shall consider the rhetorical figures relating to three main procedures—description, comparison, and the general reflection. Obviously, these are very different one from another, but they are not simply the 'leftovers'. They have a number of common features which makes their association here more than casual. All are, or may be treated as, 'bravura' figures; which means that at times they can be taken and studied out of their context, without destroying either the amputated passage or the truncated body of the work. All are treated exhaustively in the manuals of rhetoric. All are characteristic of at least one branch of medieval literature.[1] Finally, they are all virtually absent in the poems of the *Vita Nuova*, but make some appearance in the chosen later poems. This last circumstance will permit us to treat three very large problems on quite a modest scale. All we shall have to do is examine the possible significance of the *absence* of these procedures in the *VN* poems (which will entail a brief exposition of the rhetorical theory, and of their use in the relevant vernacular genres), and then characterize the innovations, and assess their part in Dante's development.

In the *Rhetorica ad Herennium*, as in other manuals of the classical period, *description* is the specific element in four of the figures of thought; and the brief definitions of these figures together with the lengthy examples, already show most of the features we shall find in later works on the subject.[2] Thus, descriptions are said to be of two

---

[1] For the *descriptio* it is sufficient to cite the *roman*; for the simile we need think only of Dante's *Comedy*; the *sentenza* plays a prominent part in almost any work with a broadly moralistic or didactic aim.

[2] The most important of the four is the last, *demonstratio*: 'D. est cum ita verbis res exprimitur ut geri negotium et res ante oculos esse videatur' (IV, lv, 68). This corresponds to *energia* in Quintilian, VIII, iii, 61 and in Isidore, *Et.*, II, xxi, 33, or to *descriptio* in Priscian's translation of Hermogenes, c. 10, §29, in C. Halm (ed.), *Rhetores*

kinds—of events, or of people. In the latter case, the natural distinction between description of physical appearance and description of temperament or character is observed with a perhaps unnatural rigour. Any description must be subservient to a rhetorical goal, and is intended to excite pity or disgust, admiration or condemnation. We may therefore expect the horrific or the idyllic, virtue or depravity, but never a description in neutral terms. Then as now, an unsophisticated audience responds most readily to an appeal to its established prejudices and one which exploits the current stereotypes. And we must remember that in the cultural climate of the period, truth was felt to lie in what was typical, and therefore essential, and not in what was individual, and therefore incidental. Hence, since expediency and intellectual integrity were in alliance, it is hardly surprising that the descriptions in the *ad Herennium* are not only emotively charged, but are conventional and generic in their exaggerations.

But in the *ad Herennium*, the treatment is rather rudimentary, and the examples are chosen to illustrate political or legal situations. In fact, description was to find its true home in the third branch of oratory —epideictic or ceremonial oratory, especially in the formal panegyric —as also in poetry and the classroom exercise. In these cases it was no longer a passing ornament, but the 'raison d'être' of the whole work. And so, not surprisingly, description was later analysed and regulated in greater detail by the theorists. Priscian's translation of the *Progymnasmata* of Hermogenes provides an excellent key to the art of description as it was practised in the late Empire. Descriptions, he wrote, may be of people, of events (such as a battle by land or sea), of the seasons, of the states of peace and war, of places (such as the sea-shore, fields, mountains, towns or rivers), and of many other things.[1] We

---

Latini Minores (Leipzig, 1863), p. 558. In the *ad Herennium*, *descriptio* is limited to a description of the *future* consequences of a decision: 'D. nominatur quae *rerum consequentium* continet perspicuam et dilucidam cum gravitate expositionem' (IV, xxxix, 51). This corresponds closely to Isidore's *metathesis*, *Et.*, II, xxi, 34; see also Quintilian, IX, ii, 41.

Effictio is the description of a person's appearance, 'cum exprimitur atque effingitur verbis *corporis* cuiuspiam *forma* ...' (*Ad Her.*, IV, xlix, 63). This is Isidore's *characterismus* ('descriptio figurae'), *Et.*, II, xxi, 40. *Notatio* is the description of a person's character, 'cum alicuius *natura* certis describitur signis', *Ad Her.*, IV, l, 63; and it corresponds to *ethopoeia* in Quintilian, IX, ii, 58, or in Isidore, *Et.*, II, xiv, and ibid., xxi, 32.

[1] Priscian, *De praeexercitamine*, c. 10, § 29, in Halm (ed.), *Rhetores Latini Minores*, p. 558.

may note the significant addition of season, state and place. And in the section on *laus* in the same work we learn how it is to be done. For he provides an exhaustive and carefully ordered sequence of *topoi* or 'heads' which can be used in the praise or the description—the terms are virtually interchangeable at this point—of a hero or famous man. One can praise his countrymen, his city, his family. One can say if any portent accompanied his birth in dreams, or signs, or other harbingers of the man that was to be. One should then pass to his style of life (*victus*) and his education. Next one can praise, but under distinct heads, his moral and bodily attributes. Of his person you can say he was handsome, tall, fleet of foot and strong: of his moral qualities you can say he was just, self-disciplined, wise and energetic. After this one should consider his profession, laying the stress on what he *did*. You can also praise him for such adventitious features as his relatives, friends, wealth, household, and luck. Then one can find topics for praise or blame in the length of his life, whether short or long. From this one can pass to the manner of his death. Was he fighting for his country? Did anything extraordinary occur? Who killed him? Lastly, you must find out what happened after his death. Were there funeral games? Has his tomb become a shrine where oracles are delivered? Were his children famous? Hermogenes then shows how one may adapt these heads in order to compose a panegyric of animals, trees or cities, or activities such as hunting.[1]

The next significant statement of the theory of description is to be found in the *Ars versificatoria* of Matthew of Vendôme, written in the second half of the twelfth century. It is particularly interesting in that its precepts and methods are reflected not only in the Latin literature of the period but also in the vernacular *roman* and, to a lesser extent, in the courtly lyric. Matthew contributes little that is strictly new, but several features of his account deserve our attention. More than a third of the whole *ars* (33 pages out of 84) is given over to description, a fact which we may reasonably interpret, with Faral, as a sign that Matthew considers it 'l'objet suprême de la poésie' (p. 76). He discusses

---

[1] Ibid., c. 7, §§20–4, ed. Halm, p. 556. The main heads in the Latin are: gens, civitas, genus; quid in nascendo evenit mirum, ut ex somniis vel signis vel huiuscemodi quibusdam praenuntiationibus; natura animi corporisque ... per divisionem; a professionibus (... in omnibus autem est exquisitissimum de gestis dicere); extrinsecus, id est a cognatis, amicis, divitiis, familia, fortuna et similibus; a tempore, quantum vixit; a qualitate mortis; quae secuta sunt post mortem.

and exemplifies the description of season and place, but the description of *people* takes absolute priority. In accordance with tradition, these are divided sharply into *superficiales* and *intrinsecae*. They are always *ad laudem* or *ad vituperium* (1, 74); and may be introduced only when they serve some specific purpose (1, 38, 110). Matthew provides an exhaustive list of topics, which are drawn not from a work such as Priscian's, but from Cicero's *De inventione*, 'crossed' with the relevant lines from Horace's *Ars poetica*. And, partly no doubt as a result of his reliance on these texts, and on an overliteral interpretation of them, he is one of the most explicit and most extreme advocates of portraiture by type. He insists that every feature of the description must be derived not from mere personal experience but, as we would say, from codified notions of what is universally appropriate to the sex, age, profession, standing, temperament or passion of the personage to be described. Finally, and perhaps most important, all his lengthy descriptions of physical appearance conform to the enumerative scheme in which description proceeds item by item, cliché by cliché, from the crown of the head to the sole of the foot—*a summo capitis . . . ad ipsam radicem* as Geoffrey of Vinsauf puts it (*PN* 598–9). This is a technique which may be observed in many of the setpiece descriptions in the contemporary *roman*, and which has been traced back to the *Progymnasmata* of Aphthonius, probably before the end of the fourth century A.D.[1]

The other medieval theorists do not enter into anything like this detail. Indeed Geoffrey, writing a generation later, speaks of descriptions of appearance as hackneyed (*cum sit formae descriptio quasi trita / et vetus*, *PN* 622–3). But he still makes it one of the sources of *amplificatio*—in which he will be followed by John of Garland[2] and Brunetto Latini—[3] and his examples extend to more than 110 hexameters.[4]

Before turning to Dante's poems we must briefly examine the place of descriptions in the Romance vernacular lyric before *c.* 1280. How

---

[1] Cf. R. R. Bolgar, *The Classical Heritage* (Cambridge, 1954), p. 38.

[2] p. 915.

[3] Brunetto gives a long description of the beauty of Isolt as Tristan might have described her: the features listed are, in order: hair, forehead, eyebrows, nose, eyes, complexion, mouth, lips, teeth, chin, neck, shoulders, hands, fingers, fingernails, breasts and waist. *Li livres dou Tresor*, (ed. F. J. Carmody, Berkeley and Los Angeles, 1948), pp. 331–2.

[4] *PN* 554–667.

frequent were they in the relevant genres? How extended were they? How closely did they adhere to Latin exemplars?

Jeanroy,[1] Dragonetti[2] and Baehr[3] make it clear that virtually the only descriptions of *persons* (we will deal with *seasons* below) to be found in the courtly 'song' are encomiastic descriptions of the lady. In *spirit*, these are certainly similar to those of the rhetorical tradition. Praise of beauty and praise of virtue are kept distinct. The technique is enumerative, generic and conventional, and the descriptions are pieced together from a very limited stock of epithets and attributes.[4] However, the actual terms used are quite independent of Latin models, and proper *descriptiones superficiales* are rare:[5] they cannot be compared with those in Matthew or in some of the *romans*. Jeanroy and Dragonetti can produce nothing longer than the following:

> Del sieu *belh cors graile* e *sotil,*
> *blanc* e *gras, suau, len* e *dos*
> volgr'ieu retraire sas *faissos*
> . . . .
> Sa *saura crin* pus que aur esmeratz
> e son *blanc front,* els *cils voutʒ* e *delguatʒ,*
> els *huelhs* el *nas* e la *boca riʒen.*[6]

> Uns *gens cors lons, grailles, cras,*
> *chief blont, col blant* come lis,
> *biau front, vairs ex, plaisans ris,*
> *blans dens,* rengiez par conpas,
> les *mains droites,* li *lonc bras.*[7]

Nor can Chiaro Davanzati go beyond them:

> li suoi *cavei dorati*
> e li *cigli neretti*
> e vòlti com'archetti,
> con due *occhi morati,*

[1] A. Jeanroy, *La poésie lyrique des troubadours* (Toulouse–Paris, 1934), vol. II, pp. 106–7.
[2] R. Dragonetti, *La technique poétique des trouvères dans la chanson courtoise* (Bruges, 1960), pp. 248–72.
[3] R. Baehr, 'Studien zur Rhetorik in den Rime Guittones von Arezzo', *ZRP*, LXXIII (1957), 238–52.
[4] Dragonetti provides an excellent catalogue, *La technique poétique*, pp. 253–4.
[5] Jeanroy, *La poesie lyrique*, p. 107n.   [6] Ibid.
[7] Moniot d'Arras, quoted by Dragonetti, *La technique poétique*, p. 259.

li *denti minotetti*
di perle son serrati;
labbra vermiglia, li *color' rosati*:
cui mira, par che tutte gioie saetti.[1]

And even these passages, I repeat, are quite exceptional in the lyric. Enumerations of the lady's moral perfections were perhaps more common, but these are usually concentrated into two or three lines and rarely exceed half a dozen.[2] The following is a characteristic specimen:

> e ave più *valere* e *'nsegnamento*
> che non ebbe Morgana né Tisbia;
> da voi surge la *gioia* e 'l *compimento*:
> dunque ben posso dire che 'n voi sia
> *pregio* ed *onore* e tutto *valimento*.[3]

Dante was certainly familiar with the traditional sharp distinction between outward appearance and moral character, for he exploits it as an element of structure in the poems *Donne ch'avete* and *Amor che ne la mente*. Analysing the latter poem, he writes: '... ne la prima parte io commendo questa donna *interamente e comunemente*, sì ne *l'anima* come nel *corpo*; ne la seconda discendo a laude speziale de *l'anima*; ne la terza a laude speziale del *corpo*.'[4] But even in these two poems which are explicitly given over to the praise of ladies—Beatrice and the 'donna gentile'—there is nothing at all which remotely resembles a rhetorical *descriptio*. Of Beatrice's 'corpo' or 'persona', we learn only that she had a pearl-like complexion—'color di perle ha quasi' (xiv, 47). And this, as Dante later explains[5] is the colour of love. Otherwise Dante *suggests* his lady's beauty through the protestation of ineffability,

---

[1] Chiaro Davanzati, *La gioia e l'alegranza*, 25–32. Text from *C.D., Rime*, ed. A. Menichetti (Bologna, 1965), p. 137.

[2] Guittone d'Arezzo was already untypical of the Provençal–Sicilian tradition. Baehr affirms that, 'absolut gesehen jedoch sind Guittones Frauenbeschreibungen sowohl der Zahl als auch der Qualität nach sehr kärglich', 'Studien zur Rhetorik' (1957), p. 245. The same could be said of Guittone's *descriptiones intrinsecae* quoted by Baehr ibid., pp. 247–8. Accumulated descriptions come only in his religious and moral poetry.

[3] Chiaro Davanzati, *Rime*, xxxix (*Madonna, lungiamente aggio portato*) lines 7–11, ed. Menichetti, p. 141.

[4] *Con.*, iii, v, 1; cf. *VN*, xix, 18–20.

[5] The 'gentile donna' took on a 'vista pietosa e d'un *colore palido quasi come d'amore*; onde molte fiate mi ricordava de la mia nobilissima donna, che di *simile colore si mostrava* tuttavia', *VN*, xxxvi, 1.

or through an abstraction, such as:

per essemplo di lei bieltà si prova	XIV, 50
voi le vedete Amor pinto nel viso	XIV, 55
Vede perfettamente onne salute	
chi la mia donna tra le donne vede[1]	XXIII, 1–2

Or, more characteristically, her beauty is perceived as an active principle:

De li occhi suoi, come ch'ella li mova,	
escono spirti d'amore inflammati	XIV, 51–2
La vista sua *fa* onne cosa umile	XXIII, 9
Sua bieltà *piove* fiammelle di foco	LXXXI, 63

Praise of the lady's *smile* does not seem to have been cultivated among the troubadours, nor by their heirs in Northern France and at the Sicilian court.[2] But it is Beatrice's smile, in the poems, as later in the *Paradiso*, which sets her apart:

Quel ch'ella par quando un poco sorride,	
non si pò dicer né tenere a mente,	
sì è novo miracolo e gentile.	XVII, 12–14

In other poems we catch glimpses of 'Amore … in abito leggier di peregrino' (VIII, 3–4), of 'madonna involta in un drappo dormendo' (I, II); but nothing else. We must create our own mental images of the pilgrims (XXXVI), or the young ladies (XVIII), or of Dante himself (XIX). In fact, only in one *canzone*, *Tre donne*, do we meet a passage in any way resembling a *descriptio superficialis*. There we are introduced to an allegorical lady in distress—an opportunity for fifty hexameters if ever there was one! But all we are given is an attitude sketched with three or four expressive strokes of the pen, the whole being focussed and synthesized in the memorable but unpictorial half-line 'sol di sé par donna':

Dolesi l'una con parole molto,

---

[1] These were the more traditional means. There are many close parallels to lines in Dante's poems in the passages from the trouvères quoted by Dragonetti, *La technique poétique*, pp. 260–3.

[2] Cf. Jeanroy, *La poésie lyrique*, p. 107. Among the Sicilians, the lady's smile is praised from time to time, as in Giacomo da Lentini, *Chi vide mai*, 1. 3. But 'riso' is commonly an inert synonym for 'gioco', 'gio' ', 'diporto'.

e 'n su la man si posa
come succisa rosa:
il nudo braccio, di dolor colonna,
sente l'oraggio che cade dal volto;
l'altra man tiene ascosa
la faccia lagrimosa:
discinta e scalza, e sol di sé par donna.   CIV, 19–26

In its concentration on revealing gesture and pregnant suggestion, this is already the technique of the *Comedy*. And perhaps we have here another reason for rejoicing that Dante served his literary apprenticeship as a lyric poet, and not in one of the established narrative genres.

The descriptions of Beatrice's 'anima' or 'vertù' in the *VN* poems are again totally unlike the typical *descriptio intrinseca*, for, as we have already seen, emphasis is laid on her 'mirabili *operazioni*' on the 'vertudi *effettive* che de la sua anima *procedeano*' (*VN*, xix, 18).[1] There are two passages, and two only, which may seem to approximate to the kind of catalogue recommended by a Matthew—the concluding stanzas of the two doctrinal *canzoni*. But here the motive sets them apart. Dante is not describing one person: he is seeking to define the characteristic external signs by which one may know that a person is truly 'leggiadro', or truly 'gentile'.

The most effective passage of personal description is neither of one person, nor 'in praise'. It is the highly slanted, remarkably acute, and very amusing vignette of the 'smart-set' of Dante's day:

E altri son che, per esser ridenti,
d'intendimenti
correnti voglion esser iudicati
. . . .
E' parlan con vocaboli eccellenti;
vanno spiacenti,
contenti che da lunga sian mirati   LXXXIII, 39 ff.

---

[1] Indeed, the prose of the *Convivio* stresses that the beauty of the 'donna gentile' is simply an *effect* of her 'goodness': '... in quanto nel suo corpo, *per bontade de l'anima*, sensibile *bellezza* appare ...' (*Con.*, III, viii, 3) '... in qualunque parte *l'anima* più adopera del suo officio ... a quella più fissamente *intende ad adornare*' (ibid., 6) '... mostra quello per che potemo conoscere l'uomo nobile a li *segni apparenti*, che sono, di questa *bontade* divina, *operazione*' (IV, xxiii, 4). 'Intorno a la quale si vuole sapere che ciascuno *effetto*, in quanto effetto è, riceve la *similitudine* de la sua cagione, quanto è più possibile di ritenere' (ibid., 5).

The other main species of description to be associated with the courtly lyric before Dante was the description of the season, especially of the return of spring. This theme has been studied by a number of scholars in recent years,[1] and their main conclusions, as far as they concern us, will be summarized in what follows.

The association of spring, love and joy is universal and requires no explanation. It forms the argument of literally thousands of medieval lyrics, both in Latin and in the vernaculars. The first and most important point to establish, therefore, is that the theme is in no way restricted to the *courtly* love-lyric. Indeed we can go further. For, as Dragonetti points out, any celebration of love as a natural force, subject to the rhythms of nature, must be not only inessential but downright inimical to the troubadour conception of love.[2] All men should be superior to the natural order, and the man possessing a 'gentle heart' must rise above the rest of mankind. 'Fin' amors' cannot ebb and flow according to the time of year; and no service would be worthy of the name which was restricted to the rutting season.

This helps to explain why the description of spring in the courtly lyric is virtually confined to one function and one place. It is only and always a topic of the *exordium*, a mere prelude to the poem proper. This is why the troubadour likes to introduce it as a contrasting theme: 'the rest of the world is "amorous" and "gay", but he alone has no joy from love'. This, too, is why he is attracted to the *winter* opening: 'the rest of the world is frozen to love, but he alone burns in inextinguishable fire'. And this would also explain why the 'nature opening' suffered a marked decline in the thirteenth century, whether in Northern France,[3] in Sicily, or in Guittone.[4]

In content and expression, these descriptions tend to be as generic, conventional, enumerative and stereotyped as were the descriptions of the lady. And, not unnaturally, this gives them some affinity with the description of place and season exemplified in the *artes poeticae*,[5] or in

---

1 Jeanroy, *La poésie lyrique*, vol. II, pp. 128–30; E. R. Curtius, *European Literature and the Latin Middle Ages*, trans. W. Trask (London, 1953), pp. 183–202; Baehr, 'Studien zur Rhetorik' (1957), pp. 248–9; Dragonetti, *La technique poétique*, pp. 163–93.

2 Bernart de Ventadorn is the true lover: 'Lo tems vai e ven e vire / Per jorns, per mes e per ans, / Et eu, las! no·n sai que dire, / C'*ades* es *us* mos talens. / *Ades* es *us* e *no·s muda*, ...' etc.

3 Dragonetti, *La technique poétique*, p. 192.

4 Baehr, 'Studien zur Rhetorik', (1957), p. 248.

5 For example Matthew of Vendôme, I, 111; II, 3; Geoffrey, *Documentum*, II, 2, 19.

almost any representation of a *locus amoenus* in Latin poetry.[1] But in
their extreme brevity, and in their actual phraseology, they are probably closer to pre-courtly or non-courtly vernacular lyrics. In other
circumstances, we should have to insist on these differences, and we
should also have to show just how varied individual descriptions can
be within the framework of the courtly genre. But here it must suffice
to give four characteristic examples, two taken from troubadours and
two from trouvères. Note that in each pair, the trouvère is, not un-
typically, less inventive and nearer the mean; the descriptions by
Raimbaut and Arnaut may be fairly taken as representing the extreme
of linguistic elaboration before Dante's time.

> Kant li boscaige retentist
> Dou chant des oxillons en may,
> Et la roze el vergier florist
> En icel tens joious et gai:
> Lors chanterai de cuer verai . . .[2]

> Autet e bas entre ·ls prims fuoills,
> son nou de flors els rams li renc,
> > e no·i ten mut bec ni gola
> > nuills auzels, anz brai' e chanta
> > > cadahus
> > > en son us:
> > pel ioi q'ai d'els e del tems
> > chant . . .[3]

> Quant l'erbe muert, voi la fueille cheoir
> Que li vens fet jus des arbres descendre,
> Adonc convient les dous chanz remanoir
> Des oiseillonz, qui n'i poënt entendre;
> Lors me convient a Amours mon cuer rendre . . .[4]

> Ar resplan la flors enversa
> pels trencans rancx e pels tertres.
> Cals flors? Neus, gels e conglapis,
> que cotz e destrenh e trenca,
> don vey morz quils, critz, brays, siscles
> en fuelhs, en rams e en giscles,
> mas mi ten vert e jauzen joys . . .[5]

---

[1] Curtius, *European Literature*, pp. 195–200.
[2] Jehan de Neuville, quoted by Dragonetti, *La technique poétique*, p. 173.
[3] Arnaut Daniel, text from *A. D. Canzoni*, ed. G. Toja (Florence, 1961), p. 221.
[4] Gace Brulé, quoted by Dragonetti, *La technique poétique*, p. 177.

(*For footnote 5 see p. 298.*)

What we would expect to find in Dante's poems, written as they are at the very end of the thirteenth century, is no *descriptio temporis* at all. And with one exception our expectations are justified: it is almost impossible to imagine a spring opening in the *Vita Nuova*! But the one exception, the *canzone, Io son venuto,* is surely the most brilliant and sustained working out of the winter opening to be found anywhere in medieval literature. The *canzone* is so well known that it is scarcely necessary to describe it here, but it may be relevant to indicate briefly just what is derived and what is original in the poem, both in the elements of which it is compounded, and in the mode of their synthesis. We have seen that the winter opening in itself is not new, nor is its use as a contrasting theme. It is not new, as such, to make a *whole* poem out of an extended description of winter, followed by the contrasted description of the lover's state: a well known Latin poem of the twelfth century, *De ramis cadunt folia,* contains in miniature nearly all the elements of Dante's poem.[1] But the structure of the poem is nevertheless quite original, for Dante gives us not *one* extended description of winter but *five*: each stanza is a 'winter opening' and contrast, apparently complete in itself. Winter is not just the prelude, but the theme of the whole poem. On the other hand, the fact that the matter is ostentatiously the same in each stanza does not mean that there are five independent poems instead of one. Unity is ensured, first of all, by the symmetry of the syntax in each stanza: in each case, the description is presented in three phrases each occupying three hendecasyllables, whilst the contrast is introduced by an adversative *e* at the beginning of the tenth line, which is the only heptasyllable.[2] Then, there is an unobtrusive but perfectly acceptable 'narrative' ordering of the stanzas: the first establishes the time (and also the year); the second describes the coming of wintry conditions, and the following stanzas describe the effects of those conditions on the earth and its plants and

---

[5] Raimbaut d'Aurenga, text from W. T. Pattison, *The Life and Works of the Troubadour Raimbaut d'Orange* (Minneapolis, 1952), p. 199.

---

[1] Thus: St. 1 (in Dante), 'nam signa caeli ultima sol petiit'. St. 2, 'est inde dies niveus, nox frigida'. St. 3, 'et avis bruma laeditur, et philomena ceteris conqueritur ...' St. 4 'nec prata virent herbida'. St. 5, 'modo frigescit quicquid est', and for the refrain, 'sed solus ego caleo'. The poem can be found in almost any anthology, for example *The Oxford Book of Medieval Latin Verse*, ed. F. J. E. Raby, p. 353.

[2] The second, third, fourth and fifth stanzas all begin with a finite verb.

creatures. On reflexion, one can also see that each description is couched in terms of a different science, and that these are arranged in a carefully ordered sequence of descent from the incorporeal influences of the planets down to inorganic matter by way of the atmosphere, animal life and plant life. Finally, all the stanzas are united by their relationship to the *congedo*, in which the thought of the poem at long last moves forward to reach a striking conclusion. In retrospect, we realize that each stanza, although differently 'orchestrated', had the same 'harmonic structure'; and this structure is revealed as something akin to a dominant seventh chord demanding that the poem should move forward onto the chord of the 'tonic', represented by the *congedo*.

The content of the descriptions in the third and fourth stanzas—the silence of the birds, the fall of the leaves, the death of the flowers—is clearly derived from tradition,[1] although the length of the treatment is in each case unusual, and the actual expression is remarkably free from cliché. There are precedents, too, in the poems of Raimbaut of Orange and Arnaut Daniel, for the harsh sound-effects which render the wintry landscape in the brilliant fifth stanza, although here too the resemblance is a very generic one, and the models, if such they were, were hardly conventional. But for the astronomic periphrasis of the first stanza, and the account of the passage of the wind in the second stanza, there is no precedent at all in the vernacular lyric.

Like description, *comparison* enters as the specific element into more than one of the rhetorical figures of thought. The various authorities are not in perfect accord as to the terminology, nor as to the criteria which distinguish one species from another; and perhaps because of this uncertainty their analysis of the subject is deeper and more penetrating than in other fields. However, since our inquiry will be strictly limited in scope, we may confine ourselves to the *Rhetorica ad Herennium*, which offers more than enough material for our purposes. Its author recognizes three species, which are distinguished by the nature of that term in the comparison with which we are assumed to be familiar. If this is an allusion to a historical event or person, the figure is *exemplum*;[2] if it introduces an animate being, as when a man is com-

---

[1] See Dragonetti, *La technique poétique*, pp. 176–7, 181.

[2] '*Exemplum* est alicuius facti aut dicti praeteriti cum certi auctoris nomine propositio' (*Ad Her.*, IV, xlix, 62).

pared to a bull, lion or serpent, the figure is *imago*.[1] In all other cases it is a *similitudo*;[2] and this is also the general term covering all species of comparison.[3] Comparisons are further subdivided according to their *purpose* and their *form*. They may serve to enliven or to adorn a passage, or at a more utilitarian level, they may be intended to clarify a point or to clinch an argument.[4] And with regard to form, the two parts of the comparison may be presented either concurrently, *coniuncte et confuse* in the author's phrase, or else successively and distinctly.[5] It is this second class, often although not necessarily signposted by the familiar 'quale ... tale', that readers of the *Iliad*, *Aeneid* or the *Comedy* will call most readily to mind. It was precisely this type, however, which drew a rather hostile reaction from the medieval rhetoricians, and underwent a certain decline in some branches of medieval literature. Matthew of Vendôme (IV, 3) and the *Laborintus* (lines 313–17) both urge modern writers to be sparing in the use of similes, while Geoffrey of Vinsauf explicitly prefers the first type, *quae fit in occulto* as he says (*PN*, 247), that is without grammatical signposts. This may seem rather odd, as the simile is introduced as one of the sources of *amplificatio*; but in fact Geoffrey spins out a series of these 'hidden' similes for fifteen hexameters in the course of extolling the virtues of the device (lines 249–63). Faral, who was the first scholar to call attention to this hostility on the part of the theoreticians, also asserts that the

---

'*Paradigma* vero est exemplum dicti vel facti alicuius aut ex simili aut ex dissimili genere conveniens eius, quam proponimus, rei' (*Et.*, I, xxxvii, 34).

[1] '*Imago* est formae cum forma cum quadam similitudine conlatio ...' (*Ad Her.*, IV, xlix, 62). '*Icon* est imago, cum figuram rei ex simili genere conamur exprimere ...' (*Et.*, I, xxxvii, 32). *Per imaginem* simile fit, cum ex simili specie vultus vultibus comparamus ...' (Victorinus, on *De inventione*, I, xxviii, ed. Halm, *Rhetores Latini Minores*, p. 228).

[2] '*Similitudo* est oratio traducens ad rem quampiam aliquid ex re dispari simile ...' (*Ad Her.*, IV, xlv, 59). '*Parabola* [est] conparatio ex dissimilibus rebus...' (*Et.*, I, xxxvii, 33). 'Per *conlationem* simile faciamus cum rerum diversarum conferimus et copulamus *non speciem, sed naturam* ...' (Victorinus, on *De inventione*, I, xxviii, ed. (Halm, *Rhetores Latini Minores*, p. 228).

[3] 'Homoeosis est, quae Latine interpretatur *similitudo*, per quam minus notae rei per similitudinem eius, quae magis nota est, panditur demonstratio. Huius *species* sunt tres: icon, parabolae, paradigma, id est imago, conparatio, exemplum' (*Et.*, I, xxxvii, 31).

[4] 'Similitudo ... sumitur aut *ornandi* causa aut *probandi* aut *apertius dicendi* aut *ante oculos ponendi*' (*Ad Her.*, IV, xlv, 59; see also ibid., xlix, 62).

[5] The two modes are described as *per brevitatem* and *per conlationem* respectively (*Ad Her.*, IV, lxv, 59). Geoffrey of Vinsauf will use the terms *occulte* and *aperte* (*PN*, 242).

two-part simile or *similitude par parallèle* as he calls it, had indeed fallen into disfavour from the eleventh century onward; and it is particularly significant that the authors of the courtly adaptations of the *Aeneid* and the *Thebaid* suppressed the epic similes which they found in the originals.[1] In this respect we may recall that the extended simile was not a feature of the Old French epic, just as it was not characteristic of the epic literature of the Germanic peoples.

In the courtly lyric there is no evidence of such a reaction: extended similes are extremely common, and are indeed characteristic of the genre. But as in any well-established genre, be it epic or lyric, the similes tend to be generic and conventional in character. They do not come from the Book of Life—just from books. Many of them are brief *exempla*, which usually take the form of a stereotyped reference to Paris and Helen, or Tristan and Isolt.[2] And the true similes are drawn from a severely limited field. The lady's beauty is compared to precious stones, or flowers, or the morning star. Her conquest of the lover calls forth images of warfare and hunting. The lover, once conquered, becomes the storm-tossed ship or the helpless child; and the contradictions of his life-in-death and death-in-life are expressed through images of fire, water and ice. Particularly popular were similes drawn from the marvels known to contemporary science—the irresistible power of the magnet, for example, or the formation and properties of the crystal, or the remarkable customs of the animals described in the bestiaries.[3] Such similes are prominent in the work of the Sicilian poets, and although they are less common in Guittone,[4] they are still to be found in abundance in Guinizzelli. Indeed, his *Al cor gentil* may be read together with the anonymous *Mare Amoroso* as one of the most densely packed repertories of the courtly simile. The following short list exemplifies some of the more common species:

> De mon penser aim meuz la compaignie
> C'onques *Tristan* ne fist d'*Iseut* s'amie[5]

---

[1] See E. Faral, *Les arts poétiques du XIIe et du XIIIe siècle* (Paris, 1923), pp. 69–70; L. Arbusow, *Colores rhetorici* (Göttingen, 1948), p. 24; Baehr, 'Studien zur Rhetorik' (1957), pp. 226–7.   [2] See Dragonetti, *La technique poétique*, pp. 199–205.

[3] These last were associated in particular with the thirteenth-century troubadour, Rigaut de Berbezilh, and with Dante's older contemporary, Chiaro Davanzati. There is a very useful account of the similes used by the trouvères in Dragonetti, *La technique poétique* pp. 205–25.   [4] See Baehr, 'Studien zur Rhetorik' (1957), pp. 225–9.

[5] Raoul de Soissons, quoted by Dragonetti, *La technique poétique*, p. 199.

E di valor portate maggior pregio
che non fa il buon *rubin* fra l'altre pietre ...

la bocca, piccioletta e colorita,
vermiglia come *rosa* di giardino ...
e ben parete dea d'amare, e meglio
che la chiarita *stella de la dia*.[1]

Domna, *aissi* com us *chasteus*
Qu'es *assetjatz* per fortz senhors,
Can la peirer' abat las tors
E·ls chalabres e·ls manganeus
    Et es tan greus
La *guerra* devas totas partz ...[2]

Ele resamble a celui qui braiete,
Par quoi *il prent les oisselés* petiz;
Par son chanter le deçoit et aguete,
Et quant les tient, adont si les ocist.
Aussi ma dame ...[3]

Ben mi menò follia
di *fantin* veramente,
che crede fermamente
pigliar lo sol ne l'agua splendiente,
e stringere si crede lo splendore
de la candela ardente,
ond'ello immantenente
si parte e piange, sentendo l'ardore.[4]

Lo vostr'amor che m'ave
in *mare tempestoso*,
è si como la *nave*
c'a la *fortuna* getta ogni pesanti,
e campan per lo getto
di loco periglioso.
Similemente eo getto
a voi, bella, li mei sospiri e pianti[5]

---

[1] *Il Mare Amoroso*, lines 140–1, 98–9, 134–5; text from *Poeti del Duecento*, ed. G. Contini (Milan–Naples, 1960), vol. I, pp. 491–2.

[2] Guiraut de Bornelh, *Can lo glatz*, lines 40 ff.; text from R. T. Hill and T. G. Bergin, *Anthology of the Provençal Troubadours* (New Haven, 1941), p. 59.

[3] Anon., quoted by Dragonetti, *La technique poétique*, p. 212.

[4] Mazzeo di Ricco, *Sei anni ho travagliato*, lines 11–18; text from *Poeti del Duecento*, ed. Contini, vol. i, p. 150.

[5] Giacomo da Lentini, *Madonna, dir vo voglio*, lines 49–56, text ibid., p. 53.

Ancor che l'*aigua* per lo *foco* lassi
la sua grande freddura,
non cangerea natura
s'alcun vasello in mezzo non vi stasse,

. . . .

Cusì, gentil criatura,
in me ha mostrato Amore
l'ardente suo valore,

. . . .

ch'eo fora consumato
se voi, donna sovrana,
non fustici mezzana
infra l'Amore e meve,
che fa lo *foco* nascere di *neve*.[1]

e serete sicura
che la vostra bellezze mi ci 'nvita
per forza, come fa la *calamita*
quando l'*aguglia* tira per natura.

ch'io non mi credo già mai snamorare;
ché lo *cristallo*, poi ch'è ben gelato,
non pòi avere speranza
ch'ello potesse neve ritornare.[2]

Come lo *lunicorno*, che si prende
a la donzella per verginitate,
e va a la morte, già non si contende
da·llei, poi che no gli usa veritate;
quando l'ha preso al cacciator lo rende
ed el ne face la sua volontate:
così Amor . . .[3]

In the poems of the *Vita Nuova* there are just six similes; and of these, only two conform to the traditional schemes:

Ne la sembianza mi parea meschino,
come avesse perduto segnoria   VIII, 5–6

e *così* esser l'un sanza l'altro osa
com'alma razional sanza ragione.   XVI, 3–4

[1] Guido delle Colonne, *Ancor che l'aigua*, lines 1–4, 9–11, 15–19. Text, ibid., p. 107.
[2] Mazzeo di Ricco, *Lo gran valore*, lines 27–30, 43–6. Text, ibid., p. 154.
[3] Chiaro Davanzati, *Rime*, 27, 1–7 ed. Menichetti, p. 245.

Of the remainder, two are introduced by 'e par che', and two may be classified as *pseudo*-similes ('pseudo' in that the comparison does not really involve two distinct terms: everything that is said of the one could be said literally of the other):

e par che sia una cosa venuta da cielo in terra a miracol mostrare	XXII, 7–8
e par che de la sua labbia si mova un spirito soave pien d'amore	XXII, 12–13
Sì che volendo far come coloro che per vergogna celan lor mancanza	V, 17–18
come quelle persone che nëente par che 'ntendesser la sua gravitate	XXXVI, 7–8

All of them are brief; none of them are drawn from the familiar fields we have just described and exemplified. And so, although we still await a close, quantitative study of the simile in the work of Dante's predecessors and contemporaries, there seems little doubt that the virtual *absence* of the simile in the *VN* poems is significant. And it seems likely that the absence is to be interpreted as yet another aspect of Dante's negative reaction to the modes prevailing in his youth.

In the later groups there are perhaps twenty comparisons, which means that they are proportionately about twice as frequent as in the *VN* poems.[1] But, as we shall see, Dante still uses them guardedly and almost grudgingly. Let us consider first those which are introduced *apertius dicendi causa* or *probandi causa*. Only six out of thirteen are of the type *per conlationem*, and only three of these have the straightforward form—STATEMENT + *sì come* + COMPARISON, for example:

È gentilezza dovunqu'è vertute, ma non vertute ov'ella; sì com'è 'l cielo dovunqu'è la stella, ma ciò non e converso.[2]	LXXXII, 101–4

In the other cases, the comparisons precede the proposition which they are intended to clarify; and in two of these there is no grammatical

---

[1] They are found principally in the doctrinal poems, *Le dolci rime*, *Poscia ch'Amor* and *Doglia mi reca*, and towards the end of *Amor che ne la mente*. It is worth recalling that in Guittone similes are twice as frequent in the moral and religious poetry as in the love poetry (Baehr, 'Studien zur Rhetorik' 1957, p. 228).

[2] See also LXXX, 19–20; LXXXIII, 93–5.

forewarning. We discover that the lines in question function as a simile only when we are arrested by the following 'così' or 'similemente'.[1] In the sixth, there is a detailed comparison between the quality 'leggiadria' and the sun; but the grammatical articulation is neither conventional nor clear, and no attempt is made to highlight the various correspondences by repetitions or syntactic parallelism:

> Al gran pianeto è tutta *simigliante*
> che, dal levante
> avante infino a tanto che s'asconde,
> co li bei raggi infonde
> vita e vertù qua giuso
> ne la matera sì com'è disposta:
> *e questa* ...
> ....
> simili beni al cor gentile accosta   LXXXIII, 96–102, 107

The other seven similes of this explicative kind are *per brevitatem*, and are all slipped in as unobtrusively as possible. In three of them, there is no grammatical signal at all: *nullo veniunt indice signo* as Geoffrey of Vinsauf puts it:

> poi chi pinge figura,
> se non può esser lei, non la può porre   LXXXII, 52–3
> né la diritta torre
> fa piegar rivo che da lungi corre.   ibid., 54–5
> Dona e riceve l'om cui questa vole
> mai non sen dole;
> né 'l sole per donar luce a le stelle,
> né per prender da elle
> nel suo effetto aiuto[2]   LXXXIII, 115–19

All the nine similes of a more poetic character (used, that is, *ornandi causa* or *ante oculos ponendi causa*) are of the *per brevitatem*[3] type. In four of them, which we have already mentioned when discussing dissimulation, we are given only the comparison, and we have to deduce its relevance to the theme.[4] The others are extremely brief and

---

[1] LXXXI, 77 ff., 'Tu sai che... Così...'; LXXXII, 41 ff., 'Chi diffinisce... Similemente...' (See also CII, 25 ff.)

[2] The remainder are LXXXI, 59–60; LXXXII, 109; CVI, 64; ibid., 69.

[3] There is one implied *exemplum* in CIII, 36, 'con quella spada ond'elli ancise *Dido*'.

[4] XCV, 1–8; CIII, 18–19; CXI, 6–8; CXIII, 9–11.

trite,[1] with the possible exception of:

> Qual non dirà fallenza
> divorar cibo ed a lussuria intendere?
> ornarsi, *come vendere*
> si dovesse al mercato di non saggi? LXXXIII, 32–5

> e non sarei pietoso né cortese,
> anzi farei *com'orso quando scherza* CIII, 70–1

But the bear is no newcomer to the Romance lyric,[2] and a reference to the Fools' Fair is not as such exceptional.

There is evidence, then, of a slight increase in the use of the simile in the chosen later poems. But they are deployed in the least obtrusive forms, and the level remains low: it is almost certainly lower than in a typical poet of the earlier courtly tradition. In the *Comedy* there are 597 similes in 14,233 lines;[3] and whether we consider the length, variety, source, purpose, form or originality of the similes, the gulf between even the later poems and the *Comedy* is immense.

Of the many acceptations of the word *sententia* in the Middle Ages, we need concern ourselves only with two. It may mean, first, an authoritative pronouncement on some general issue, in the form of a duly acknowledged quotation from a recognized *auctor*, who may be a poet, a jurist, a philosopher, or a Father of the Church, according to the circumstances. And the importance of these sentences in every branch and at all levels of medieval intellectual life is well known and can hardly be exaggerated.[4] Alternatively, *sententia* may mean a

---

[1] See also CIII, 62 ff.; CIV, 9–10; CIV, 21.

[2] See Chiaro Davanzati, *Rime*, ed. Menichetti, p. lv.

[3] The figure is given by L. Venturi. Every analyst will find a different total, depending on his criteria; but the differences would not be vital.

[4] Suffice it to recall the *Book of Proverbs*, the *Disticha Catonis*, the *Digest*, Gratian's *Decretum*, Peter Lombard's *Sententiae*, or the numerous collections of *sententiae* and *exempla* compiled for use in sermons and similar writings. See C. H. Haskins, *The Renaissance of the Twelfth Century* (New York, 1927), chs VII and XI: G. Paré, A. Brunet, P. Tremblay, *La renaissance du XIIᵉ siècle* (Paris–Ottawa, 1933), ch. VI (pp. 240–74); G. Paré, *Les idées et les lettres au XIIIᵉ siècle, Le Roman de la Rose* (Montreal, 1947), pp. 23–7; M. D. Chenu, *Introduction à l'étude de S. Thomas d'Aquin* (Paris, 1950), pp. 106–25; Curtius, *European Literature*, pp. 57–61; F. Di Capua, 'Sentenze e proverbi nella tecnica oratoria e loro influenza sull'arte del periodare', in *Scritti minori* (2 vols, Rome, 1959), vol. I, pp. 41–189.

'pointed, terse saying, embodying a general truth in a few words'.[1] And in this, the earlier sense, it was one of the recommended figures of thought in all manuals of rhetoric from the time of Aristotle.[2] The content and manner of expression vary a good deal. It may be what we would now call a platitude (whence the current meaning of 'sententious'); and this is certainly how Matthew of Vendôme understood the term: '... generale proverbium, id est communis sententia, cui *consuetudo* fidem attribuit, *opinio communis* assensum accomodat, incorruptae veritatis integritas adquiescit' (1, 16). It may be a set phrase, or the wording of the common-place idea may be original. It may be proverbial in the strict sense (in which case the expression will probably be figurative), or again it may not. Strictly speaking, as Aristotle, the *Rhetorica ad Herennium* and Priscian all agree, it should embody not just any general truth, but a general truth about human life and conduct, about ethics or politics.[3] Depending on the context, then, *sententia* may be variously translated as platitude, truism, dictum, proverb, maxim, adage, apophthegm, gnome, or aphorism. But it should always possess certain formal properties: it should be brief, pointed, memorable and quotable; it should have the qualities of a good slogan or motto. And this being so, it is hardly surprising that the term was sometimes extended to take in any pithy utterance, or any epigrammatic turn of phrase whatever its content.[4] The works of Ovid are perhaps the richest quarry for such near *sententiae*; and Pope's famous couplet,

> True wit is nature to advantage dressed,
> What oft was thought but ne'er so well expressed,

[1] This is the *O.E.D.* definition of 'apophthegm'.

[2] *Rhetoric*, II, xxi. This remains one of the best general discussions of the *sententia* and its use in oratory.

[3] 'Est autem sententia enuntiatio, non tamen de singularibus, ut qualis Iphicrates, sed *de universalibus*; neque de omnibus universalibus, ut rectum curvo contrarium esse, sed *de iis, quorum actiones sunt*, et ea quae eligimus aut fugimus ad agendum' (Aristotle, *Rhetoric*, II, xxi, 2; in the literal Latin version by A. Riccobono).

'Sententia est oratio sumpta de vita quae aut quid sit aut quid esse oporteat in vita breviter ostendit' (*Ad Her.*, IV, xvii, 24).

'Sententia est oratio generalem pronuntiationem habens, hortans ad aliquam rem vel dehortans, vel demonstrans quale sit aliquid' (Priscian, *Praeexercitamina*, iii, 11; ed. Halm, p. 553).

[4] 'Sed consuetudo iam tenuit, ut mente concepta "sensus" vocaremus, *lumina* autem praecipueque *in clausulis posita* "sententias"' (Quintilian, VIII, v, 2).

is not only a perfect definition of the traditional *sententia*, but a *sententia* in this extended sense. At this point we must emphasize, however, that the various acceptations of the word, although distinct, are not necessarily incompatible. A tag taken from Ovid may be very different from a paragraph taken from St Gregory; but a 'sentence' from Seneca, such as may be found on almost any page of almost any moralistic work in the Middle Ages, was probably composed by its author as a *sententia* in the rhetorical sense of the word.

A sententia may be introduced at any appropriate point, of course, but the medieval theorists[1] recommend it in particular as an opening or conclusion to a work, which is thus presented as a particular instance of the general law ('et illud quod datur per generalem sententiam "docetur", "probatur", "perhibetur" per aliud speciale, quod subjungitur', *Documentum*, II, i, 5). And it is well known that a great many medieval works, both of fiction and of non-fiction, do begin or end with a *sententia* in just this way. For the student of Dante it is enough to refer to the opening of the fifth, seventh and eleventh of his Latin letters, the first and fourth books of the *Convivio*, and all three books of the *Monarchia*.

So far we have spoken of the *sententia* as just one rhetorical figure among many; and perhaps this might be sufficient for our limited purposes. But it must also be remembered that there have been writers whose every utterance seems to 'aspire to the condition' of the *sententia*. And in writers such as these—one thinks in particular of the Silver Latin writers like Seneca, Juvenal and Lucan, whose works were so congenial to the Christian Fathers and to the medieval intellectual— one could not begin to study the *sententiae* without seeking to determine the underlying cultural and psychological causes of their profusion, or without exploring the other stylistic consequences of the pursuit of this ideal. For the constant pursuit of the *sententia* must inevitably affect an author's style at every level—in the use of figures, in rhythm, and above all in sentence structure. Cicero and Seneca were both moralists who used their powers of persuasive speech to influence their fellow men. But their works embody, and early came to symbolize, two radically different conceptions of the ideal prose style.

Now, it might easily be assumed that the *sententia* has no place in

---

[1] Matthew of Vendôme, I, 16–29; *PN*, 126–41; *Documentum*, II, i, 5–8; John of Garland, *Poetria*, pp. 889–92.

the love-lyric, except perhaps as a device used to secure a passing contrast of tone. But, whether or not such an assumption would be justified in general, it so happens that the *sententia* is totally characteristic of *courtly* love-song, at least in its maturity. And, as with the Silver Latin writers (although in a very different way), the *sententia* is *not* simply one ornament chosen among many. It is *not* something extraneous; it arises from the very nature of the fictions which underly and govern the genre. Accordingly, it is these fictions which we must briefly pass in review if we are to understand the role of the *sententia* in the courtly lyric.

For our purpose, the most convenient way to present these fictions is to compare them in their totality to the 'cult' of a minority religious sect or of a self-styled 'chosen' people. The comparison is a traditional one,[1] of course, and hence we need do no more than rehearse some of the more important similarities. The deity is Love. And Love requires both worship and service from his elect. But this worship and service cannot be accorded to him directly. They can be shown only to a lady; and in fact, for much of the time, the poet speaks of her as his god. She is the term of his desire, the fount of his joy, the pattern of all human perfections. But she herself is more than human: she is incommensurable and cannot be constrained. Her favour is given, *if* it is given, only out of her uncovenanted bounty and grace. It must be deserved, but it cannot be won as of right. When the lover 'complains' of her aloofness, as he so often does, he is guilty simultaneously of two kinds of heresy: first, he is treating the lady herself as the deity (but that is almost orthodoxy); and second, he is assuming that the relationship of the deity to the faithful is identical to that which binds the liege-lord to his vassals. But the true lover will understand, at least in his lucid moments, that in serving the lady he is really serving love, and that this service is its own reward.[2] Since his service of the lady requires a

---

[1] It has also led some scholars into excess. But it need do no harm if it is remembered that the comparison is not intended to hold at every point, nor to be equally applicable to every poet or every poem. And one must also keep in mind that the 'cult' of *fin'amors* is a *fiction*: a fiction which had roots in reality, and which had repercussions in real life, but was still a fiction. For a very different approach to the religion of love worship, see P. Dronke, *Medieval Latin and the Rise of European Love-Lyric* (2 vols, Oxford, 1966).

[2] Cf. *Io sento sì d'Amor la gran possança*, l. 56: 'si fa 'l servir merzé d'altrui bontate'. Many details in this sketch have been suggested by this poem and its predecessor, *Amor, che movi tua vertù da cielo*.

constant attempt to live up to the standards which she embodies, it brings about in him a process of moral and spiritual refinement, through which the lover rises nearer and nearer to the ideal, and higher and higher above the profane, the 'villani', the common herd. In so far as he serves a particular lady, the lover must observe discretion and secrecy. But in so far as his service is of Love, he must declare it to the world in his deportment and conduct. He must show 'onestà', 'franchezza', 'leggiadria'—in a word 'cortesia'. He must associate with those who worship and serve the same deity. His acts of courtliness are precisely the observances required of him by his 'religion'. And the court is his church, both in that it is the place where the rituals are performed, and also in that those who belong to the court form the body of the 'church spiritual'.

It is in this kind of sense—and the details could be multiplied— that the ruling fictions of the courtly lyric may be compared to a 'religion' or 'cult'. And this is familiar ground. But once this has been established, we find that there is another and equally illuminating side to the comparison, and it is this which is directly relevant to our inquiry.

All the different aspects of this fiction are to be found, either explicitly or implicitly, *in the courtly love-lyrics themselves*. One may indeed seek confirmation or qualification from other sources: but these are not necessary, and may be positively misleading.[1] The only witnesses we need to examine are the lyric poets. And the reason why their testimony is so abundant is this: the poet does not speak simply as a worshipper, or a member of the congregation. He does this, it is true; but he is also and primarily the *celebrant* of the rite—not a mere participant. The true participants in the rites are those who hear or read the poems; for the poems constitute the liturgy. To participate is to enter imaginatively into a fiction which was created by poets, and is maintained and yet modified by each poet in turn. We must dream the dream in the manner which he dictates. Or to revert to our guiding image, one must recognize that the poet's voice is the voice of the initiate, the priest, the voice of authority. The poet is almost always conscious of his quasi-sacerdotal position, and this consciousness informs his every utterance. It may be detected even when he praises,

---

[1] I am thinking on the one hand of the courtly *romans*, and on the other hand of a work like Andreas Capellanus's *De Amore*.

upbraids or pleads to the 'deity', or to his surrogate, the lady; for even then he is not speaking as a private individual. He is enacting a ritual of which the main outlines and the recurrent formulae are all known in advance. But the note of authority is naturally heard more clearly when the poet leaves the altar rail, as it were, and ascends the pulpit, as when he gives instruction in the 'faith', or in the courtly way of life, or admonishes those who have transgressed in word or deed. And it is most pronounced when he presides in the 'ecclesiastical court' and gives judgement in the 'quistioni d'amore' which are brought before him. Thus, the poet is not only the trembling suppliant, but priest, preacher, arbiter, defender of the faith, and Chairman of the Watch Committtee: and in all these capacities, the *sententia* comes to his lips as naturally and as inevitably as leaves to the tree. There is in fact no clean division between the 'materia amorosa' and moral or didactic themes.[1]

Again, a few examples may help to convey the feel or flavour of this tone of authority:

> E no es bo qu'om sia trop senatz,
> que a sazos no sega son talen,
> e si no·i a de cascun mesclamen,
> non es bona sola l'una meitatz.[2]

> Bone amours est, dame, maistresse sage
> Ki vrais amans set saner et garir[3]

> Honis soit il ki en femme se fie
> Por bel semblant ne por simple resgairt.[4]

> Gioia gioiosa piagente,
> misura e ragione
> tutta stagione deggiasi trovare.[5]

> Li contrariosi tempi di fortuna,
> il soferire affanno malamente
> dimostrâr l'om saccente e vigoroso[6]

---

[1] This is contrary to the implications of *VN*, xxv, 6, but in perfect harmony with the 'proemi' of *Le dolci rime* and *Poscia ch'Amor*.

[2] Aimeric de Pegulhan, *Si cum l'albres*, lines 9–12; text from K. Bartsch, *Chrestomathie Provençale* (Elberfeld, 1875), p. 159.

[3] Jehan de Renti, quoted by Dragonetti, *La technique poétique*, p. 46.

[4] Anon., quoted by Dragonetti, ibid., p. 50. Dragonetti deals with *la diction sentencieuse* on pp. 45–55.

[5] Guittone d'Arezzo, *Rime*, xxii, 1–3. On the *sententia* in Guittone, see R. Baehr, 'Studien zur Rhetorik in den Rime Guittones von Arezzo', *ZRP*, lxxiv (1958), 165–7.   [6] Chiaro Davanzati, *Rime*, xxxv, 1–3; ed. Menichetti, p. 127.

Dunque aggiate voglienza
come l'amore congiunga,
ca per troppo tardare omo amarisce,
e gran pena patisce
chi non ha provedenza:
se 'n voi pregio s'agenza,
pietanza è quel ch'avanti lo norisce.[1]

ché buon signor già non ristringe freno
per soccorrer lo servo quando 'l chiama,
ché non pur lui, ma suo onor difende.

ché tutti incarchi sostenere a dosso
de' l'uomo infin al peso ch'è mortale,
prima che 'l suo maggiore amico provi,
poi non sa qual lo trovi[2]

certanamente a mia coscienza pare,
chi non è amato, s'elli è amadore,
che 'n cor porti dolor senza paraggio.

Amico (certo sonde, acciò ch'amato
per amore aggio), sacci ben, chi ama,
se non è amato, lo maggior dol porta[3]

The last examples are taken from poems written by Dante at much the same time as the first group of poems in the *Vita Nuova*, that is, almost certainly, when Dante was in his late teens or perhaps in his very early twenties. The fact that so young a poet should aspire to and achieve this complacent, portentous and dogmatic manner is the most convincing proof of just how widespread, acceptable and normal it must have been in the 1270s and 1280s.

But in all the poems included by Dante in the *Vita Nuova*, there is not one true *sententia*, and there are remarkably few lines in anything like a sententious vein.[4] And seen against the background which has just been sketched in, it should be apparent that this is a significant absence indeed. In this and earlier chapters, we have noted other significant omissions, other 'negative developments' as being characteristic of Dante's new style. But the absence of the *sententia* is arguably the

[1] Ibid., xiv, 54–60, p. 55.
[2] Dante, *Rime, La dispietata mente*, lines 17–19, 33–6.
[3] Ibid., xlii, 12–14, xliv, 9–11.
[4] Exception made for *Amore e 'l cor gentil* and perhaps for passages in *Donne ch'avete* (29–50), *Li occhi dolenti* (35–42).

most important of them all. For the other 'negative developments' all admit of an explanation framed solely in terms of taste and style: just as women's fashions undergo profound changes in silhouette, hemline, colours, materials and ornamentation, so there may be similar revolutions in fashion with regard to the '*vesta di figura*'. But if the frequency of the *sententia* in the courtly lyric is indeed to be attributed to the general causes outlined above, then their absence will point to some significant change at this deeper level—a change in what we called the 'ruling fictions', a renovation in the conception of love, and in the conception of the poet, his lady, and his audience.

Well, as everyone knows, just such a *renovatio* did take place, and it had the most profound consequences for Dante's poetry. We cannot possibly discuss its nature and scope adequately here, for this would entail a detailed discussion of the *Vita Nuova* as a whole, the work in which Dante himself describes and interprets the transformations of what we are calling the 'underlying fictions'. However, if we revert to the analogy obtaining between these fictions and the customs, practices and beliefs which constitute a religious cult, we can use the analogy once again to suggest something of the character of this transformation, and to highlight the reasons which made the use of the *sententia* almost impossible. In the poems of the 'new style',[1] then, we may say that Dante no longer speaks as the priest or preacher, and no longer addresses himself to the regular congregation. He speaks as the man 'overtaken by joy', the neophyte, the man who has had a mystical experience of such ecstasy that he is left profoundly dissatisfied by the routines of Sunday morning religion. The 'established Church' in its apparent complacency and neglect of the transcendental, cannot meet his devotional needs. The 'Church' is not rejected; and it still provides him with his cultural framework and the elements of his language. But the fixed prayers, responses and doxologies of public worship are abandoned for private devotions. The 'renewed' poet worships in his own words and in his own way: whether in meditation, re-enactment, or in praise, his language is simple, passionate, fervent and intimate. In such a mood, the earlier poets, and the earlier self who had written *La dispietata mente*, or the sonnet exchanges with Da Maiano, must come to resemble the 'hypocritae, qui amant in synagogis et in angulis

---

[1] That is, the poems in groups C–I inclusive, but, in particular the early ones: Dante too began to 'settle down' in his new system.

platearum stantes orare, *ut videantur ab hominibus'*; now he must retire
into his 'cubiculum', with the door closed.[1]

We may turn now to the later poems, and first of all to the doctrinal
canzoni, Le dolci rime and *Poscia ch'Amor*. In these two poems, Dante is
obviously speaking both formally and publicly, and as a moralist; but
the tone cannot be described as sententious, nor are there any real
sententiae.[2] Again this absence is not fortuitous, although the reasons
are of a different kind. In the first place, Dante is speaking not as an
orator, whose task it is to persuade and for whom the *sententia* is an
ideal weapon; he is speaking as a philosopher, whose aim it is to prove
and refute with logically cogent arguments. And in the second place,
he is not seeking to identify himself with the audience, or to speak as
one of them. He is in fact attacking just the kind of 'communis sententia
cui consuetudo fidem attribuit',[3] which another speaker might have
used on these subjects.

The first unmistakable *sententia* in the chosen poems appears as the
last line in *Così nel mio parlar*, that is, in just the position for which
the *sententia* was particularly recommended in the *artes poeticae*. But
there is nothing conventional here: in fact, the content and function
of the line make it a total surprise:

> Canzon, vattene dritto a quella donna
> ....
> e dàlle per lo cor d'una saetta:
> *ché bell'onor s'acquista in far vendetta.*   CIII, 79, 82–3

In the exilic *canzoni* we may discern a clear development. In *Doglia
mi reca*, a *sententia* is used to round off a stanza and an important stage
in the argument:

> *ché simiglianza fa nascer diletto.*   CVI, 63

In *Tre donne*, the second *congedo* ends with two successive *sententiae:*

> camera di perdon savio uom non serra,
> ché il perdonare è bel vincer di guerra[4]   CIV, 106–7

---

[1] Saint Matthew, vi, 5. The passage quoted continues: 'amen dico vobis, rece-
perunt *mercedem* suam. Tu autem cum oraveris, intra in *cubiculum* tuum, et *clauso ostio*,
ora Patrem tuum in abscondito'. Cf. *VN*, xii, 2: 'misimi ne la mia *camera*, là ov'io potea
lamentarmi *sanza essere udito*'; ibid., xiv, 9 '... mi ritornai ne la *camera* de le lagrime';
ibid., xxxi, 14 = *Rime*, xxv, 52–5 'e sì fatto divento, / che *da le genti* vergogna *mi
parte*. / Poscia piangendo, *sol* nel mio lamento / chiamo Beatrice ...'
[2] The only candidates are the two definitions quoted above, p. 284.   [3] See p. 307.
[4] It will be noticed that these final *sententiae* are all introduced by *ché*; they serve in fact

whilst another has been used in the course of the solemn final stanza:

> cader co' buoni è pur di lode degno.   ibid., 80

In this poem one is also struck by a number of lines which have all the formal requirements of a good *sententia*, without containing general reflections:

l'essilio che m'è dato, onor mi tegno	76
lieve mi conterei ciò che m'è grave	84
se colpa muore perché l'uom si penta	90

These half dozen examples may seem insignificant, but they are among the first indications of a major development in Dante's art, and especially in his conception of his art. Here, for the first time, we see Dante's power of compression, and his gift for the memorable phrase, that have made so many lines from the *Comedy* proverbial in Italian. And these *sententiae* may be taken as symbolic evidence that Dante was approaching full intellectual and moral maturity, and beginning to show the virtues proper to the age which he calls 'senettute'.[1] These virtues are prudence, justice, generosity and affability. They all have this in common that their exercise tends not so much to the perfection of the individual, as to the general good of mankind at large:

a la senettute [è data] la maturitade acciò che la dolcezza del suo frutto e a sé e ad *altrui* sia *profittabile*; ché, sì come Aristotile dice, l'uomo è animale civile, per che a lui si richiede non *pur a sé ma altrui essere utile*. Onde si legge di Catone che non a sé, ma a la patria e a tutto lo mondo nato esser credea.
(*Con.*, IV, xxvii, 3)

Practical wisdom is fruitless unless it is made available to men in the form of good advice:[2] good advice is useless unless it is persuasive,

---

as the major proposition of a two-part syllogism or enthymeme. Cf. Isidore: 'Enthymema igitur Latine interpretatur mentis conceptio, quem inperfectum syllogismum solent artigraphi nuncupare. Nam in duabus partibus eius argumenti forma consistit, quando id, quod ad fidem pertinet faciendam, utitur, syllogismorum lege praeterita ...' (*Et.*, II, ix, 8).

1 'Senettute', the third of man's four 'ages' runs from forty-five to seventy. Dante would have been nearly forty when he wrote the poems.

2 'Se bene si mira, da la prudenza vegnono li buoni consigli, li quali conducono sé e altri a buono fine ne le umane cose e operazioni; e questo è quello dono che Salomone, veggendosi al governo del populo essere posto, chiese a Dio ...' (ibid., xxvii, 6).

that is, unless men act on that advice. To be 'persuasive' means to be expressed in 'rhetorical form', and to a medieval, 'rhetorical' form was virtually synonymous with 'artistic' form. This was the essence of the new poetic that was taking shape in Dante's mind during the first years of his exile. It was to lead him eventually to abandon the traditional lyric forms, and to set his hand to the 'poema sacro': for the aim of the *Comedy* was primarily *removere viventes in hac vita de statu miserie et perducere ad statum felicitatis.*[1] Of course, the *Comedy* is persuasive at an utterly different level, and on an utterly different scale, but we may still regard the *sententia*, with its dual requirement of a general moral truth and persuasive form, as the first fruit and the emblem of the new poetic: and there is no more fitting note on which to close.

---

[1] *Epistolae*, XIII, [15], 39.

CHAPTER 9

STYLE AND STRUCTURE IN 'DOGLIA MI RECA'[1]

———

If unity of style implies consistency, continuity, stability, then there is no easily definable unity of style in Dante's poems taken as a whole. It is true that, if we agree to substitute a dynamic model for a static one, there is a kind of unity in *growth*. But that process of growth was not to be complete until the final cantos of the *Paradiso*. And within the narrower context of the poems themselves, it must be emphasized that there is no obvious coherency in Dante's stylistic development. The poems of the second decade are too unlike those of the first, and, above all, they are too unlike one another.

We have seen, however, that there is one remote and limited viewpoint from which the many different changes and developments do seem to arrange themselves in a simple and meaningful pattern. If we look at the poems with the blinkered eye of a rhetorician, and consider the degree of stylistic elaboration in each group of poems, then we can see a pattern of steady development in which there are two main phases. In the first phase, all the developments take the form of a *contraction* or *restriction* in the range of expressive means which Dante employs. In the second phase, the developments all represent an *expansion*. In rhetorical terms, there is a move towards the *humile genus dicendi*, followed by a move away from it. But the moves are so decisive that it is almost possible to see them as a virtual rejection of the rhetorical conception of good style followed by a qualified acceptance.

Dante's very earliest poems, and especially those which have been excluded from close study in this book, belong to a tradition which made bold but indiscriminate use of rhetorical *ornatus*. Poems of the period from *c.* 1260 to *c.* 1280 are often crabbed, congested and obscure as a result. At times indeed, they strike us as positively absurd in their

———

[1] The substance of this chapter appeared under the title 'Style and Structure in Dante's *canzone, Doglia mi reca*', in *Italian Studies*, XX (1965), 26–41.

pretentiousness and preciosity. They do not lack vitality or energy: but they do lack taste. It is hardly surprising, therefore, that a new generation, led by Cavalcanti and Dante, should have reacted fiercely and polemically against the prevailing modes, and carried through a revolution in the name of good taste, *discretio*.[1] They transformed the style of love poetry by rejecting the excesses of the Guittoniani. It is not at all easy to give a meaningful description of the new style except in *negative* terms: one must show that this kind of word, that syntactic link, this or that figure of thought or speech was common in earlier poets, whereas it is now used rarely, or in an attenuated form, or not at all. If we make exception for metre and rhyme (which are structural and not ornamental), the new style is sometimes closer to a *naturalis ratio dicendi* than to the lowest of the three levels of style.

In the hands of Cavalcanti and Dante, the results can be exquisite, perfect; but the perfection is that of the miniaturist, and the new style was adequate to express only its own very exclusive and very limited *materia*. And when, after the death of Beatrice, Dante's new interests led him to write 'sopra altra matera che amorosa', (*VN*, xxv, 6) he had perforce to expand his expressive range. Thus, in the later poems as a whole, the vocabulary becomes more concrete and particular, and drawn from a much wider field; metaphor is used a little more freely and with some originality; the syntax becomes more ambitious and more complex, the word-order more vigorous; rhyme is handled with ever greater freedom and virtuosity, the strophe becomes longer and more elaborate; antithesis and all forms of repetition become more frequent, as do the affective figures such as the exclamation and the rhetorical question; descriptions, *sententiae* and similes all begin to appear. In short, one finds ever more frequently all the banished sources of expressiveness, but used now by a master, with that *discretio* which the earlier poets, and the early Dante, so signally lacked. From the point of view of the literary merit of its immediate results, it is certainly possible to deplore Dante's new and more positive attitude to rhetoric. But it should also be remembered that without these *praeexercitamina* there could have been no *Comedy*: Dante's 'favella' would really have been 'corta', and his 'alta fantasia' would really have lacked 'possa'.

[1] On *discretio*, see F. Di Capua, 'Insegnamenti retorici e medievali e dottrine estetiche moderne nel *De Vulgari Eloquentia* di Dante', in his *Scritti minori* (2 vols, Rome, 1959): esp. vol. II, pp. 310–13.

From the rhetorician's point of view, the richest of all Dante's poems is certainly *Doglia mi reca*. And this is one reason why I have singled it out for discussion in this concluding chapter. It can be seen as crowning that process of expansion which I have just described, and it is thus the poem which comes nearest to the prodigious wealth and variety of style to be found in the *Comedy*. Now, this is not self-evident. Most people would feel that the mature poem which most resembles the *Comedy* is not *Doglia mi reca* but *Tre donne*. In many ways *Doglia mi reca* seems to look backward rather than forward; and it has not found many friends among modern critics. But there are two important aspects of its style and structure which are definitely *not* 'old-fashioned'. They are virtually without precedent in his earlier poetry, and they seem to me to represent a new and important step towards the *Comedy*. It is these which I now want to describe. And since they cannot be studied in isolation, we must examine the poem as a whole.

Doglia mi reca is probably the fourth and last of Dante's *canzoni* on ethical subjects; and its particular theme is liberality. The others are *Tre donne*, dealing with justice, and the two *canzoni* written before his exile, *Le dolci rime* and *Poscia ch' Amor*, which deal with 'gentilezza' and 'leggiadria' respectively. It is to these last that our poem is more closely related. It too comprises seven long stanzas; it too characterizes and praises a virtue intimately connected with traditional love-poetry, and attacks its opposite vice. But there the resemblances end. In the earlier poems Dante had been moved to write by the prevalence of certain wrong ideas about nobility and charm. He was content first to show that the opinions of the masses were false and then to establish a correct definition. Here he is attacking not venial misconceptions but mortal sin, and his intention is to move his audience to repent, to convert them from their vicious ways. Consequently, the poem no longer resembles a *quaestio*, but a sermon. His purpose in writing is no longer to please or to teach, but to 'move' (*ut flectat*). Or in Dante's own pregnant phrase, used in the passage of the *De vulgari eloquentia* where he cites this poem (II, ii, 8), his aim is *directio voluntatis*.

All the poem's vital characteristics derive from this new purpose. First and foremost it determines the tone. It is a fact of everyday experience (duly noted in the rhetorical manuals), that if a speaker is to rouse the emotions of his audience, he must be, or seem to be, moved himself. As Horace succinctly puts it:

319

si vis me flere, dolendum est
primum ipsi tibi;   *AP*, 102–3

So throughout the poem, the utterance is that of an angry man, violent, wilful, disdainful of the logical arguments and logical progression that characterize *Le dolci rime*. Contrast the carefully balanced, proleptic opening of that poem with the way in which Dante bursts into his subject here:

> Le dolci rime d'amor ch'i' solia
> cercar ne' miei pensieri,
> convien ch'io lasci; non perch'io non speri
> ad esse ritornare,
> ma perché ...   LXXXII, 1–5

> Doglia mi reca ne lo core ardire
> a voler ch'è di veritate amico;
> però, donne, s'io dico
> parole quasi contra a tutta gente,
> non vi maravigliate ...   CVI, 1–5

This kind of energetic, abrupt, staccato syntax is maintained throughout. It leads to climactic repetitions like these:

> *lietamente* esce da le belle porte,
> a la sua donna torna;
> *lieta* va e soggiorna,
> *lietamente* ovra suo gran vassallaggio;
> per lo corto vïaggio
> *conserva, adorna, accresce* ciò che trova   32–7

Or it can issue in dense antitheses and word-plays as in the following lines, where Dante is clearly playing on a presumed derivation of 'avaro' from 'avere', and seems to link 'servo' and 'segnore' both semantically and through alliteration with 'seguace' and 'seguitando':

> Chi è *servo* è come quello ch'è *seguace*
> ratto a *segnore*, e non sa dove vada,
> per dolorosa strada;
> come l'*avaro seguitando avere*,
> ch'a tutti *segnoreggia*   64–8

And it is most conspicuous in the unprecedented abundance of affective figures—exclamations, rhetorical questions, passages in question

320

and answer form, apostrophes and imprecations—which may combine
to give a passage like this:

> Morte, che fai? che fai, fera Fortuna,
> che non solvete quel che non si spende?
> se 'l fate, a cui si rende?
> Non so, poscia che tal cerchio ne cinge
> che di là su ne riga.   90–4

In relating the presence of these features to the nature of this particular poem, I am not suggesting that they are something new in
themselves. Quite the reverse in fact, for the rhetorical approach to
style is founded on the assumption that any language possesses a store
of objectively definable 'expressive means', which everyone can be
taught to discern and then consciously exploit. Nor, on the other hand,
am I suggesting that Dante had suddenly and belatedly 'discovered'
the affective figures from a formal study of Latin rhetoric (although he
certainly had an intimate knowledge of rhetorical theory by this time).
In part they arose naturally, given the emotive purpose of the poem.
In part they would have been taken over from sermons and moral
writings. In large part they were derived from Guittone d'Arezzo—
that is from the very poet whose language and style seem to have been
found intolerable by the young Dante and the mature Dante alike.[1]
Guittone had been the first Italian to write sonnets, *canzoni* and prose
letters on political, moral and religious themes. Avarice, in a very
broad sense, was one of his favourite topics.[2] Many of the words in
Dante's poem, its syntax, the predilection for repetition, antithesis and
the affective figures, are, as we have seen, among the hallmarks of
Guittone's style. Even the structure of the strophe is unlike that of the
early Dante, and very Guittonian, in its length, in the high proportion
of *settenari*, and in the succession of couplets in the *sirima*.[3] Compare
for example the tone and devices of the following passage with the

---

[1] For the young Dante one must judge from his writing; for the mature Dante, cf.
DVE, I, xiii, 1; II, vi, 8; *Purg.*, XXVI, 121–6.

[2] See *Lettere*, I, III, XXV, all available in *La Prosa del Duecento*, ed. C. Segre and M.
Marti (Milan–Naples, 1959), pp. 29–93.

[3] Rhyme-scheme: ABbCd; ACcBd: D,eeFfGHhh,GG. Compare this with Guittone,
Rime (ed. Egidi), XXVI: ABC; ABC: DEEFfGGHhIiD. Ib. XL: ABC; cAB: DEe-
FfggDHhIiiD. Typical of the earlier Dante would be *Li occhi dolenti* (*Rime*, XXV):
ABC: ABC: C,DEeDE,FF.

fifth stanza in Dante's poem, to which it is very close thematically:

> Ohi, lasso! Già vegg'io genere omano,
> che segnoril naturalmente è tanto,
> che 'l minor om talenta emperiare;
>   e ciò, più ch'altro, i piace, e più li è strano
> d'aver segnor; ché Dio volontier manto
> non vole già ciascun, sì come pare.
>   Come poi donque lo minore e 'l maggio
> sommette a vizio corpo ed alma e core?
> Ed è servaggio alcun, lasso, peggiore,
> od è mai segnoria perfetta alcona,
> che sua propia persona
> tenere l'omo ben sotto ragione?
> Ahi, che somm'è 'l campione
> che là, ov'onne segnor perde, è vincente,
> né poi d'altro è perdente;
> ché, loco u' la vertù de l'alma empera,
> non è nocente spera,
> né tema, né dolor, ned allegraggio.
>   O morti fatti noi de nostra vita,
> o stolti de vil nostro savere,
> o poveri di riccor, bassi d'altezza   *Rime*, XXVI, 19–39

And before we leave the subject of models and influence, we must not forget that the content of *Doglia mi reca* is also largely received. Avarice is seen as spiritual blindness (49–50), as death in life (26), as bestiality (23), and as the enslavement of reason (95–8). It has two aspects—hoarding and coveting (85–6). The miser is insatiable (70–3). The truly liberal man must give cheerfully and without waiting to be asked (119–26). These are its key images and ideas; and they are all commonplaces in writings on avarice, whether classical or medieval.[1] And it is these qualities which have given the poem its bad name.[2] What Jeanroy said of the troubadour moralists seems all too relevant:

Presque toute la poésie morale du moyen âge souffre d'un défaut qui a été maintes fois déploré, *l'excès de généralité*. Les troubadours n'y ont pas

---

[1] For example, Aristotle, *Nicom. Ethics*, IV, 1; St Thomas, *Summa Theol.*, IIa IIae, 117–18; Boethius, *Consolat. Philos.*, III, 3; Innocent III, *De miseria humanae conditionis*, II.

[2] For example, Peter Dronke writes of its 'arid fulminations and grandiose platitudes' in a review of *Dante's Lyric Poetry*, in *New Blackfriars* (1967), p. 383.

échappé: *ils sortent trop rarement des ces lieux communs*, qui par leur nature même, n'ont pas d'âge, et trop souvent ils les enveloppent de métaphores ou les chargent de personnifications qui enlèvent à leur style toute précision et toute sauveur. ... *La vertu dont l'éclipse leur est plus sensible, c'est Liberalité*, battue en brèche, mise à mal, *anéantie par Convoitise*, racine de tous maux.[1]

But to note these general and specific derivations is not to say that Dante's inspiration was not genuine or that his poem is quite 'un-original'. No one would want to apply Jeanroy's further remark that 'à tous ces moralistes d'occasion il manque cet accent que donne seule une indignation sincère' (p. 189). Guittone too had been deeply in-debted to his models—the troubadours and medieval Latin moralists:[2] but he has one of the most personal and distinctive voices in the whole of Italian literature. And Dante's poem could never be mistaken for one by Guittone, for both negative and positive reasons. It would be comparatively easy to show what features of Guittone's lexicon and style have *not* been taken over, and this selectiveness (*discretio*) on Dante's part is itself of great importance in the context of the general evolution of his style. But it will obviously be more significant to dwell on the two important features of *Doglia mi reca* which are not to be found in Guittone or in any of Dante's models: the firm but complex architecture, and the beginnings of a poetic use of metaphor.

Even Dante's earliest *canzoni* differ from those of many of his predecessors in that they are composed *as a whole*. To rearrange their stanzas, or to omit a stanza, as can be done in many troubadour poems, would be to destroy the poems completely. However, apart from such a rare concern for *dispositio*, for a logical and clearly articulated de-velopment of one theme, there is little remarkable in the structure of the pre-exilic *canzoni*. Guittone too can marshall an argument, even if the structure of one of his moral *canzoni* is never so rigorous or satisfying as those of *Le dolci rime* and *Poscia ch'Amor*. Here, for example, is a brief summary of *Altra fiata aggio già, donne, parlato* (*Rime*, XLIX), the

---

[1] A. Jeanroy, *La poésie lyrique des troubadours* (Toulouse–Paris, 1934), vol. II, pp. 187–8: my italics.

[2] 'Basta sfogliare qualcuno dei trattati morali del 200, ad esempio i trattati di Albertano da Brescia o quelli di Bono Giamboni per trovare frasi e affermazioni che riportano alla mente brani di Guittone: e soprattutto (ed è la testimonianza più interessante) una stessa intonazione e uno stesso gusto'. M. T. Cattaneo, 'Note sulla poesia di Guittone' (*GSLI*, cxxxvii (1960), 165–203; 325–67), p. 331.

structure of which is quite typical of Guittone and moreover bears a general resemblance to that of *Doglia mi reca*. In the *proemio* (st. I) Guittone promises his audience of women to make amends for his earlier love poetry by teaching them to avoid the kind of snares he had once set. The second stanza shows why women should hate vice and love virtue more than men. The third and fourth condemn vice and praise virtue, concluding with words strikingly similar to those of the equivalent section in *Doglia mi reca* (41–2):

> Vertù è *possession* d'onne riccore,
> lo qual *non perde alcun*, se non lui piace.

The fifth stanza passes to the particular theme, which is the praise of chastity (the transition is affected as in *Doglia mi reca*, 53–63, by a renewal of the direct address of women). Stanza 6 praises matrimonial fidelity, and begins the vituperation of unchastity which continues throughout stanza 7. The eighth warns against the falsity of men's promises and lamentations; the ninth adds that women ought also to be 'umili' and 'mansuete'; the tenth cautions them against adorning themselves, and it ends with a line that distantly anticipates the close of the first stanza in Dante's poem:

> covra onestà vostra bella fazone.

Up to and including the seventh stanza (Dante would never have allowed a poem to fizzle out as Guittone here does), the structure of this canzone is not unlike that of *Doglia mi reca*, inasmuch as it is addressed to women, and passes from vituperation of vice and praise of virtue in general to the praise of a particular virtue and the denunciation of a particular vice. But there the similarity ends, for in Dante's poem this clear outline is only the ground-plan for an edifice of considerable complexity. And that plan seems to be there only by accident and not by design.

This unique structure, like the syntax and the use of metaphor, was determined by the purpose of the poem. Dante wanted to attack and convert his listeners—those listeners being 'men' in general, and, in particular, the class of patrons on whom he was now dependent. His first task was to ensure that his assault would not fail by falling on deaf ears, as it surely would have done if mounted prematurely. So he addresses himself ostensibly to an audience of 'women', and he tries moreover to capture the *benevolentia* of the men, who are meant to 'overhear' his remarks, by apparently unleashing his attack on women.[1] The first stanza begins controversially as Dante promises to speak the truth and *therefore* to speak against nearly everybody; and by the sixth line he has applied one of the most offensive epithets in his vocabulary to his apparent audience:

> ma conoscete il *vil* vostro disire.

The first explanation of the charge (lines 7–10) seems only to strengthen it, and to bring it into line with thousands of lovers' complaints against the *orgoglio* and *disdegno* of womankind: they are sinning against Love's primeval decree. But then a flourish of logic (11–14) leads us to a totally unexpected conclusion (note how the poet feigns surprise at where his reasoning has brought him):

> voi non dovreste amare,
> ma coprir quanto di biltà v'è dato,
> poi che non c'è vertù, ch'era suo segno.
> Lasso! a che dicer vegno?[2]   15–18

The ladies may relax. They are being reproached for doing what they were usually reproached for *not* doing—being 'amiable'. And the reiterated plea for them to become disdainful, to conceal their beauty, even to pluck it out, is only an oblique approach to the real theme of the stanza: 'non c'è vertù'. *O tempora, o mores!*

The argument of the whole poem proceeds in a similarly unforeseeable way, and it was necessary that it should. At one level, Dante had to seem to speak with passion if he was to arouse emotion; at another level, he had to hold his audience's attention, against their will, by constant changes of direction. Thus, in the second stanza, Dante

---

[1] Cf. *Con.*, III, x, 7–8: '. . . questa figura è bellissima e utilissima, e puotesi chiamare "dissimulazione." Ed è simigliante a l'opera di quello savio guerrero che combatte lo castello da uno lato per levare la difesa da l'altro . . .'

[2] This mode too has its analogues. R. Dragonetti, *La technique poétique des trouvères dans la chanson courtoise* (Bruges, 1960), pp. 42–3, quotes these lines from Gautier d'Epinal, and Raoul de Soissons:

> *Dieus! qu'ai je dit?* Qui porroit deservir
> Le bien qui vient de loiaument amer?
> *Las! qu'ai je dit?* Son sens ne sa hautece
> Ne daigneroit a ma dolor partir.

restates the theme 'discovered' at the close of the first, and immediately bursts into invective:

> Omo da sé vertù fatto ha lontana;
> omo no, mala bestia ch'om simiglia.
> O Deo, qual maraviglia
> voler cadere in servo di signore,
> o ver di vita in morte!   22–6

But just as quickly he checks himself, seizes on the *servo-signore* image he has just introduced and develops it in a totally different way, to present an *allegoria* of the true service of the virtuous soul to God. A paradox at the close of this section (virtue is the *ancella* who alone can make man *segnore*) prepares the way for another, now sharpened by word-play, which opens the third stanza and leads us back to vituperation.

> *Servo* non di *signor*, ma di vil *servo*
> si fa chi da cotal *serva* si scosta.
> Vedete quanto costa   43–5

Again he breaks off almost at once. He returns to his nominal audience of 'donne', and promises to move from the general to the particular, and to speak more clearly. But having given himself and us this breathing space, he immediately returns to the same *servo-signore* image, which had presumably caused the obscurity which he has promised to avoid. He introduces a simile to elucidate it—and the simile turns out to be his true theme!

> come l'avaro seguitando avere,
> ch'a tutti segnoreggia.
> Corre l'avaro, ma più fugge pace   67–9

This theme too is developed in a similarly brilliant and surprising way, but there is no need to follow it through in detail. Indeed, to do so might be to obscure the vital point, that this structure is determined *arte* not *casu* (*DVE*, II, iv, I); that Dante achieves this spellbinding display of waywardness and passion without any sacrifice of the firm outline that the poem shares with Guittone's *Altra fiata aggio già*; that everything in the first part is directly relevant to the second (whereas in Guittone's poem the relation was rather tenuous), and that the poem is therefore a unified whole. Thus, the use of a 'fictitious audience of women' permitted an oblique approach to the subject, but is not limited to the fulfilment of that one aim. It also serves to create a perfectly symmetrical frame to the poem, since Dante returns to address them throughout the final stanza, having used a similar passage to mark the centre and turning-point of his poem. And it permits a contrast of tones—the relatively restrained language of these sections making the invective seem all the more violent. The dominant images in the second part are all introduced in the first, and some of the incidental images there are drawn from the miser's world of money and acquisition (for example lines 28, 37, 42, 45–6, 60), thus preparing the reader unobtrusively for the main theme. Similarly, the *allegoria* of virtue (lines 27–42) in fact suggests the specific virtue, liberality, which Dante is seeking to inculcate, and the metaphors are all drawn from the context most relevant to his situation.

We are shown an ideal court and the ideal relationship between lord and vassal: the vassal must first prove himself, but is then rewarded by being taken on as a close retainer with considerable freedom of movement. We are told of the joy which the vassal spreads in all his activities. And it is suggested that he is not an expense but an investment. In all these ways Dante is implicitly depicting his ideal patron, and advertising the kind of benefits that artists and scholars can confer. The structure is then of a kind quite new in Dante's poems, and in its complexity but perfect organization, in its apparent artlessness which is in fact 'rincalzato con più arte' (*Purg.*, IX, 71–72), it represents an important move towards the kind of structure we find in the *Comedy* as a whole and in many of its parts.

The other new, distinctive, and forward-looking feature of this poem is the use Dante here makes of metaphor. We saw that, in his earlier poems, metaphor is infrequent, unsustained and unoriginal. But in this *canzone* I have said that metaphor is no longer a trope, no longer something that can be analysed as an 'improper' term, used to replace a preexistent 'proper' term in a logically conceived and otherwise logically correct proposition, in order to make it more expressive. One feels for the first time that extensive sections of the poem were actually conceived in figurative language, and that the argument was influenced or even shaped by association and metaphor.[1] This is the claim I must now substantiate.

---

[1] See chapter 4, pp. 151–2.

The first point to notice is that the former clear distinction between proper and metaphorical modes of expression has become blurred. Thus, even in a passage of argumentation, Dante can pass swiftly and inadvertently from one mode to the other, and equally swiftly back again:

> per che amistà nel mondo si confonde:
> ché l'amorose *fronde*
> di *radice* di ben altro ben tira,
> poi sol simile è in grado.   133–6

And, more significantly, the 'plant' or 'cultivation' image which makes so brief an appearance in these lines, seems to have lingered in his mind and suggested the image of the 'garden of reason' (l. 147) with which the poem closes.

Another and more striking example of this osmosis between proper and metaphorical terms is to be found in the most original image of the poem, that of the falconer (virtue) trying to lure the sulky falcon (avarice). At first it seems a simple case of personification, and, characteristically in this poem, it is by no means clear *how* or *if* the image will develop:

> Fassi dinanzi da l'avaro volto
> vertù, che i suoi nimici a pace invita,
> con *matera pulita*,
> per *allettarlo* a sé   106–9

The metaphorical terms become more insistent and more specific until with *ale* we cannot mistake the image:

> ma poco vale,
> ché sempre fugge *l'esca.*
> Poi che *girato* l'ha *chiamando* molto,
> *gitta 'l pasto* ver lui, tanto glien cale;
> ma quei non *v'apre l'ale*:
> e se pur *vene* quand'ell'è *partita*   109–14

Then Dante suddenly abandons his *allegoria*, so abruptly as to do violence to the syntax:

> tanto par che li 'ncresca
> come ciò possa dar, sì che non esca
> dal benefizio loda.   115–17

It is this kind of interpenetration, whereby an image can be unmistakably present without actually declaring itself as such, that makes it possible for the bulk of the poem to consist of more or less disguised variations on three related image-clusters, all of which express the basic antithesis between virtue and vice. These three clusters we may call *life-death, man-brute* and *freedom-bondage*.

The *life-death* group first appears in the second stanza ('cadere ... di vita in morte', 25–6; 'per lo corto viaggio', 36; 'Morte repugna ...,' 38; and in the suggestion of *eternal* life: 'colt' hai *nel ciel* misura', 40; 'tu se' possession che *sempre* giova', 42). It is dominant in the fourth stanza, from the appearance of Death,

> Ecco giunta colei che ne pareggia   74

through the following ten lines which we can imagine as being actually spoken by Death. And it returns to bring the poem to its conclusion:

> Oh cotal donna *pera*
> che sua biltà dischiera
> da natural bontà per tal cagione,
> e crede amor fuor d'orto di ragione!   144–7

The *man-brute* antithesis is also introduced in the second stanza:

> *omo* no, mala bestia ch'om simiglia.   23

It reappears at the close of the fifth stanza ('*falsi animali*, a voi ed altrui crudi, che vedete *gir nudi*' ... etc., 101–5); and it dominates the sixth stanza in the falcon image which we have already examined. Finally, it heralds the return of the *life-death* theme at the close:

> chiamando amore appetito di *fera*.   143

From the second to the fifth stanza the dominant images come from the cluster centred on *freedom* and *bondage*. And here more than anywhere else, one feels that it was the many-sided image which dictated the argument and not vice versa. Dante cannot let it rest until he has exploited all its resources. Thus, in the fourth and fifth stanzas, the relevant aspects of the *signore-servo* relationship are those of 'leader and follower' (64–6), which sprang from a reminiscence of the Biblical image of the 'blind leading the blind' in lines 45–52, and in turn suggests that of 'enslaver and enslaved' in lines 87–98.[1] And in his use of the

---

[1] Lines 64–6 have been quoted above. The other passages run: 'Che gli *occhi* ch'a la mente lume fanno *Chiusi* per lui si stanno, Sì che *gir ne convene a colui posta*, Ch'*adoç-*

image in the second stanza Dante had been at his most inventive, dense and suggestive. He is inventive in the way that he draws from the image a whole chain of paradoxes, which we might paraphrase as follows: vice is bondage, but virtue is not freedom; for to be virtuous is to be an ever obedient servant—to God; in this service one finds freedom; to decline this service is to find not freedom but servitude; in such servitude one is not servant of a lord, but slave of a slave. He is dense and suggestive because he is constantly moving from one aspect of the lord–servant relationship to another. Thus we pass from a suggestion of the contrast between high estate and low estate (25), to the medieval liege-lord and vassal (30–5), to a hint of the master and good steward of the parable of the talents (37), to the handmaid of the Lord (39–40). There is nothing remotely resembling a passage like this in Dante's earlier work:

> Vertute, al suo fattor sempre sottana,
> lui obedisce e lui acquista onore,
> donne, tanto che Amore
> la segna d'eccellente sua famiglia
> ne la beata corte:
> lietamente esce da le belle porte,
> a la sua donna torna;
> lieta va e soggiorna,
> lietamente ovra suo gran vassallaggio;
> per lo corto vïaggio
> conserva, adorna, accresce ciò che trova;
> Morte repugna sì che lei non cura.
> O cara ancella e pura,
> colt'hai nel ciel misura;
> tu sola fai segnore, e quest'è prova
> che tu se' possession che sempre giova.   27–42

A diatribe against avarice is hardly likely to win a place in the *affection* of its readers, especially when it is set in a conventional framework now foreign to us, when neither the speaker nor his targets are in any way particularized, when the tone of indignation is not relieved by sarcasm, and when the style is wiry and taut, making no concessions to music or

---

chia pur follia', 49–52; 'Questo è quello che *pinge* Molti in *servaggio*; e s'alcun si *difende*, Non è sanza gran *briga* ... Colpa è de la ragion che nol *gastiga*. Se vol dire "I' son *presa*", Ah com poca *difesa* Mostra *segnore* a cui *servo sormonta*', 87–98.

song. We are more likely to turn to *Tre donne*, or *Convivio*, I, iii, or *Purgatorio*, XX, for a more attractive statement of the mood and themes of this poem. But *Doglia mi reca* certainly deserves to be much better known than it is, both because it is a rich, original, subtle and coherent poem, and because it occupies a unique place among Dante's 'preparations' for the *Comedy*.

SELECT BIBLIOGRAPHY

━━━

For a bibliography of more general studies on Dante's poems, the reader is referred to *Dante's Lyric Poetry*, ed. K. Foster and P. Boyde (Oxford, 1967), vol. II, pp. 363–71. A discussion of more recent articles will be found in the review article occasioned by our work, 'A New Edition of Dante's Lyric Poetry' by J. A. Scott, in *Romance Philology*, XXII (1969), 581–600. The abbreviations used here are listed on pp. xi–xii.

I: BIBLIOGRAPHIES OF STYLISTIC STUDIES

Bailey, R. W., and Burton, D. M. *English Stylistics: a Bibliography.* M.I.T., 1968.

Hatzfeld, H. A. *A Critical Bibliography of the New Stylistics applied to the Romance Literatures*, 1900–1965. 2 vols, Chapel Hill, 1953, 1966.

II: ARTES RHETORICAE ET GRAMMATICAE, ETC.

(A) CLASSICAL LATIN

(i) *Collections*

Halm, C. (ed.) *Rhetores Latini Minores.* Leipzig, 1863. It contains (among lesser works): P. Rutilius Lupus, *Schemata lexeos*; Aquila Romanus, *De figuris sententiarum et elocutionis*; Julius Rufinianus, *De figuris sententiarum et elocutionis*; Victorinus, Commentary on Cicero's *De inventione*; C. Julius Victor, *Ars rhetorica* (with much material from Quintilian); the rhetorical works of Capella, Cassiodorus, and St Isidore; Alcuin, *Dialogus de rhetorica*; Priscian, *Praeexercitamina* (trans. from Hermogenes); Bede, *Liber de schematibus et tropis*.

Keil, H. (ed.) *Grammatici Latini.* 8 vols, Leipzig, 1855–80. Vols II–IV contain the *artes* of Donatus and Priscian.

(ii) *Individual editions*

Augustine, St. *De doctrina christiana*, ed. W. M. Green, in *Corpus scriptorum ecclesiasticorum latinorum*, vol. LXXX. Vienna, 1963.

Capella, Martianus. *De nuptiis Mercurii et Philologiae* (Book v), ed. A. Dick. Leipzig, 1925.

Cassiodorus. *Institutiones* (Book II, i–ii), ed. R. A. B. Mynors. Oxford, 1937; reprinted 1961.

Cicero. *De inventione (Rethorica Vetus)*, ed. E. Stroebel. Leipzig, 1915.

Orator, ed. A. S. Wilkins. Oxford, 1903.

De oratore, ed. A. S. Wilkins. Oxford, 1903.

Donatus—*see* Keil above.

Horace. *Ars poetica*, ed. E. C. Wickham and H. W. Garrod. Oxford, 1912.

Isidore, St. *Etymologiae* (Books I and II), ed. W. M. Lindsay. Oxford, 1911; reprinted 1957.

Priscian—*see* Halm and Keil above.

Quintilian. *Institutio oratoria*, ed. L. Radermacher. 2 vols, Leipzig, 1907 and 1935.

Rhetorica ad Herennium (Rethorica nova), ed. H. Caplan. London, 1954.

(B) MEDIEVAL LATIN

(i) *Collections*

Faral, E. (ed.) *Les arts poétiques du XIIe et du XIIIe siècle*. Paris, 1923; reprinted 1958. It contains an excellent introduction and editions of: Matthew of Vendôme, *Ars versificatoria*; Geoffrey of Vinsauf, *Poetria Nova*, and *Documentum de modo et arte dictandi et versificandi*; Everard the German, *Laborintus*.

Rockinger, L. (ed.) *Briefsteller und Formelbücher des eilften bis vierzehnten Jahrhunderts*. 2 vols, Munich, 1863 (*Quellen zur bayerischen und deutschen Geschichte*, vol. IX). It contains (among lesser works) *artes dictaminis*, often abbreviated, by: Alberic of Monte Cassino; Hugo of Bologna; an anonymous *Summa dictaminis* from Orleans; Buoncompagno (*Cedrus, Rhetorica antiqua*); Guido Faba (*Incipit doctrina ad inveniendas, incipiendas et formandas materias, Doctrina privilegiorum*); a *Summa prosarum dictaminis* from Saxony; Ludolf of Hildesheim (*Summa dictaminum*); Conrad of Mure (*Summa de arte prosandi*); John of Garland (*Poetria*); Dominicus Dominici of Viseu (*Summa dictaminis*); Giovanni da Bologna (*Summa notarie ...*); Giovanni Bondi da Aquileia (*Practica dictaminis*).

(ii) *Individual editions*

Albericus Casinensis. *Flores Rhetorici*, ed. D. M. Inguanez and H. Willard, in *Misc. Cassinense*, XIV (1938).

Alexander of Villedieu. *Doctrinale*, ed. D. Reichling, in *Monumenta Germaniae Pedagogica*, XII. Berlin, 1893.

Antonio da Tempo. *Summa artis rytmici vulgaris dictaminis*, ed. G. Grion. Bologna, 1869.

Buoncompagno da Signa. *Rhetorica Novissima*, ed. A. Gaudenzi, in *Bibliotheca Juridica Medii Aevi, Scripta Anecdota Glossatorum*. Bologna, 1892, vol. II, pp. 251–97. (See also Rockinger, above.)

Francesco da Barberino. *De variis inveniendi et rimandi modis*, ed. O. Antognoni, in *Giornale di filologia romanza*, IV (1880), 93–8.

Dante. *De vulgari eloquentia*, ed. A. Marigo. 3rd ed., 'con appendice di aggiornamento a c. di P. G. Ricci', Florence, 1957.

DVE, ed. P. V. Mengaldo. 2 vols, Padua, 1968.

Gervais of Melkley. *Ars Poetica*, ed. H. J. Gräbener. Münster, 1965.

Giovanni del Virgilio. *Ars dictaminis*, ed. P. O. Kristeller, in *Italia medievale e umanistica*, IV (1961), 181–200.

Guido Faba. *Summa dictaminis*, ed. A. Gaudenzi, in *Il Propugnatore*, n.s. III (1890), 287–338, 345–93.

La gemma purpurea, ed. A. Monteverdi, in *Testi volgari dei primi secoli*. Modena, 1941, pp. 121. ff. (See also Rockinger, above.)

Jacques de Dinant. *Ars arengandi*, ed. A. Wilmart, in *Analecta Reginensia*. Rome, 1933, pp. 113–52.

John of Garland. *Poetria*, ed. G. Mari, in *Romanische Forschungen*, XIII (1902), 885–950.

Tommasino d'Armannino. *Il Microcosmo*, ed. G. Bertoni, in *Archivum Romanicum*, V (1921), 19–28.

(C) VERNACULAR

(i) *Provençal and Catalan*

Jaufré de Foxa. *Continuacion de Trobar*, ed. P. Meyer, in *Romania*, IX (1880), 51–70.

Las Leys d'Amors, ed. J. Anglade. 3 vols, Toulouse–Paris, 1919–20.

Terramagnino da Pisa. *Doctrina de cort*, ed. P. Meyer, in *Romania*, VIII (1879), 181–210.

Uc Faidit. *Donatz Proensals*, ed. J. H. Marshall. Oxford, 1969.

R. Vidal. *Doctrina de compondre dictats*, ed. P. Meyer, in *Romania*, VI (1877), 355–8.

Las reglas de trobar, ed. P. Meyer, in *Romania*, VI (1877), 344–53.

(ii) *Italian (Old French)*

Brunetto Latini. *La rettorica italiana*, ed. F. Maggini. Florence, 1915.

Li livres dou Tresor (Bk. III), ed. F. J. Carmody. Berkeley and Los Angeles, 1948, pp. 317–90.

III: GENERAL WORKS ON STYLE AND STYLISTICS

Albert, H. 'Stilistica e testi antichi' (trans. G. Giorgi), *Strumenti critici*, I (1966), 3–12.

Bally, Ch. *Traité de stylistique française*. Heidelberg, 1909; 3rd ed., Paris, 1951.

    Le langage et la vie. 3rd ed., Geneva, 1952.

Brooke-Rose, C. *A Grammar of Metaphor*. London, 1958.

Cressot, M. *Le style et ses techniques: précis d'analyse stylistique*. Paris, 1947.

Devoto, G. *Studi di stilistica*. Florence, 1950.

De Dieguez, M. *L'écrivain et son langage*. Paris, 1960.

Guiraud, P. *La stylistique*. Paris, 1954.

Hatzfeld, H. A. 'Recent Italian Stylistic Theory and Stylistic Criticism', *Studia Philologica et Litteraria in honorem L. Spitzer*. Berne, 1958, pp. 227–44.

Hough, G. *Style and Stylistics*. London, 1969.

Leed, J. (ed.) *The Computer and Literary Style*. Kent, Ohio, 1966.

Lodge, D. J. *Language of Fiction: Essays in Criticism and Verbal Analysis of the English Novel*. London, 1966.

Marouzeau, J. *Traité de stylistique appliquée au latin*. Paris, 1935.

    Précis de stylistique française. 2nd ed., Paris, 1946.

Meier, H. *Die Metapher: Versuch einer zusammenfassenden Betrachtung ihrer linguistischen Merkmale*. Winterthur, 1963.

Migliorini, B., and Chiappelli, F. *Elementi di stilistica*. 9th ed., Florence, 1960.

Muller, Ch., and Pottier, B. *Statistique et analyse linguistique*. Paris, 1966.

Munteano, B. 'Des "constantes" en littérature. Principes et structures rhétoriques', *Revue de littérature comparée*, XXXI (1957), 388–420.

Ohmann, R. 'Generative Grammars and the Concept of Literary Style', *Word*, XX (1964), 423–39.

    (ed.) *Style in Prose Fiction: English Institute Essays 1958*. New York, 1959.

Posner, R. 'The Use and Abuse of Stylistic Statistics', *Archivum Linguisticum*, XIV (1963), 111–39 (with useful bibliography).

Riffaterre, M. *Le Style des 'Pléiades' de Gobineau. Essai d'application d'une méthode stylistique*. Paris–Geneva, 1957.

    'Criteria for Style Analysis', *Word*, XV (1959), 154–74.

    'Stylistic Context', *Word*, XVI (1960), 207–18.

    'Vers la définition linguistique du style', *Word*, XVII (1961), 318–44.

    'Problèmes d'analyse du style littéraire', *Romance Philology*, XIV (1961), 216–27.

Sayce, R. A. *Style in French Prose: a Method of Analysis*. Oxford, 1953; reprinted with corrections, 1958.

Sebeok, T. A. (ed.) *Style in Language*. New York–London, 1960.

Spitzer, L. *Linguistics and Literary History*. Princeton, 1948.

Terracini, B. *Analisi stilistica; teoria, storia, problemi*. Milan, 1966.

Ullmann, S. *Style in the French Novel*. Cambridge, 1957.

Language and Style. Oxford, 1964.

Wellek, R., and Warren, A. *Theory of Literature*. Princeton, 1949; 3rd ed., 1962: esp. chs 13–15.

Yule, G. U. *The Statistical Study of Literary Vocabulary*. Cambridge, 1944.

Zumthor, P. *Langue et techniques poétiques à l'époque romane*. Paris, 1963.

IV: WORKS RELATING TO RHETORIC AND RHETORICAL ATTITUDES TO LITERATURE

Abrams, M. H. *The Mirror and the Lamp: Romantic Theory and the Critical Tradition*. Oxford, 1953.

Arbusow, L. *Colores rhetorici*. Göttingen, 1948; 2nd rev. ed., 1963.

Aston, S. C. 'The Troubadours and the Concept of Style', *Stil- und Formprobleme in der Literatur*. Heidelberg, 1959, pp. 142–7.

Auerbach, E. *Mimesis* (trans. W. Trask). Princeton, 1953.

Literary Language and its Public in Late Latin Antiquity and in the Middle Ages (trans. R. Manheim), London, 1965: German original, Berne, 1958.

Baehr, R. 'Studien zur Rhetorik in den Rime Guittones von Arezzo', *ZRP*, LXXIII (1957), 193–258, 357–413; LXXIV (1958), 163–211.

Baldwin, C. S. *Mediaeval Rhetoric and Poetic*. New York, 1927; reprinted Gloucester, Mass., 1959.

Barberi Squarotti, G. 'Le poetiche del trecento in Italia', *Momenti e problemi di storia dell'estetica*, vol. coll. Milan, 1959, vol. I, pp. 255–324.

Battaglia, S. *La coscienza letteraria del Medioevo*. Naples, 1965 (many valuable essays).

Bolgar, R. R. *The Classical Heritage*. Cambridge, 1954.

Brinkmann, H. *Zu Wesen und Form mittelalterlicher Dichtung*. Halle, 1928.

Buck, A. *Italienische Dichtungslehren vom Mittelalter bis zum Ausgang der Renaissance*. Tübingen, 1952.

'Gli studi sulla poetica e sulla retorica di Dante e del suo tempo', *Atti del Congresso Internazionale di Studi Danteschi*. Florence, 1965, vol. I, pp. 249–78.

Charland, Th.-M. *Artes Praedicandi. Contribution à l'histoire de la rhétorique au Moyen Age*. Paris–Ottawa, 1936.

Curtius, E. R. *European Literature and the Latin Middle Ages* (trans. W. Trask). London, 1953.

Gesammelte Aufsätze zur romanischen Philologie. Berne, 1960.

Davis, C. T. 'Education in Dante's Florence', *Speculum*, XL (1965), 415–35.

De Bruyne, E. *Études d'esthétique médiévale.* 3 vols, Bruges, 1946.

Di Capua, F. *Scritti minori.* 2 vols, Rome, 1959 (esp. 'Sentenze e proverbi nella tecnica oratoria e loro influenza sull'arte del periodare', vol. I, pp. 41–188; 'Per la storia del latino letterario medievale e del "cursus" ', vol. I, pp. 524–63; 'Insegnamenti retorici medievali e dottrine estetiche moderne nel *De Vulgari Eloquentia* di Dante', vol. II, pp. 252–355).

D'Ovidio, F. *Versificazione romanza. Poetica e poesia medioevale.* 3 vols, Naples, 1932 (most of the material had appeared in *Versificazione italiana e Arte poetica medioevale*, Milan, 1910).

Dragonetti, R. *See* section V.

Dronke, P. 'Medieval Rhetoric', *The Literature of the Western World*, ed. D. Daiches and A. K. Thorlby. London, 1971.

Faral, E. *See* section II.

Forti, F. 'La transumptio nei Dettatori bolognesi e in Dante', in vol. coll. *Bologna nei tempi di Dante.* Bologna, 1967, pp. 127–50.

Gilson, E. 'Michel Menot et la technique du sermon médiéval', *Les idées et les lettres* (Paris, 1932), pp. 93–154.

Gunn, A. M. F. *The Mirror of Love: A Reinterpretation of the 'Romance of the Rose'.* Texas, 2nd printing, 1952 (see especially pp. 509–22).

Hagendahl, H. 'Le manuel rhétorique d'Albericus Casinensis', *Classica et Medievalia*, XVII (1956), 63–70.

Haskins, C. H. *The Renaissance of the Twelfth Century.* New York, 1927.

Studies in Mediaeval Culture. Oxford, 1929.

Kelly, D. 'The Scope of the Treatment of Composition in the Twelfth- and Thirteenth-century Arts of Poetry', *Speculum*, XLI (1966), 261–78.

Lausberg, H. *Handbuch der literarischen Rhetorik.* 2 vols, Munich, 1960.

Elemente der literarischen Rhetorik. 2nd ed., Munich, 1963.

Mari, G. 'I trattati medievali di ritmica latina', *Memorie del Reale Istituto di scienze e lettere, classe di lett., scienze stor. e mor.*, vol. XX, ser. III, no. 11, Milan, 1899.

Marrou, H. I. *Histoire de l'éducation dans l'antiquité.* 4th ed., Paris, 1958.

Saint Augustin et la fin de la culture antique. 4th ed., Paris, 1958.

McKeon, R. 'Rhetoric in the Middle Ages', *Speculum*, XVII (1942), 1–32.

Morpurgo-Tagliabue, G. *Linguistica e stilistica di Aristotele.* Rome, 1968.

Murphy, J. J. 'Rhetoric in Fourteenth-century Oxford', *Medium Aevum*, XXXIV (1965), 1–20.

Norden, E., *Die antike Kunstprosa*. 2 vols, Leipzig, 1898; reprinted Stuttgart, 1958.

Owst, G. R. *Preaching in Medieval England*. Cambridge, 1926. *Literature and Pulpit in Medieval England*. Cambridge, 1933.

Paetow, L. J. *The Arts Course at Medieval Universities with special reference to Grammar and Rhetoric*. Champaign, Ill., 1910.

Paratore, E. 'Alcuni caratteri dello stile della cancelleria federiciana', *Atti del Convegno Internazionale di Studi Federiciani*. Palermo, 1952, pp. 283–314.

Paré, G., Brunet, A., Tremblay, P. *La renaissance du XIIe siècle, les écoles et l'enseignement*. Paris–Ottawa, 1933.

Polheim, K. *Die lateinische Reimprosa*. Berlin, 1925.

Quadlbauer, F. *Die antike Theorie der 'genera dicendi' im lateinischen Mittelalter*. Vienna, 1962.

Robins, R. H. *Ancient and Medieval Grammatical Theory in Europe, with particular reference to modern linguistic doctrine*. London, 1951.

Schiaffini, A. *Tradizione e poesia nella prosa d'arte italiana dalla latinità medievale al Boccaccio*. 2nd ed., Rome, 1943.

Schmale, F. J. 'Die Bologneser Schule der *Ars Dictandi*', *Deutsche Archiv für Erforschung des Mittelalters namens der Monumenta Germaniae Historica*, XIII (1957), fasc. I.

Stahl, W. H. 'To a better understanding of Martianus Capella', *Speculum*, XL (1965), 102–15.

Tateo, F. *Retorica e poetica fra Medioevo e Rinascimento*. Bari, 1960. 'La teoria degli stili e le poetiche umanistiche', *Convivium*, XXVIII (1960), 141–64.

Thurot, Ch. *Notices et extraits de divers manuscrits latins pour servir à l'histoire des doctrines grammaticales au Moyen Age (Notices et extraits de la Bibliothèque Impériale*, XXII, 2). Paris, 1868.

Volkmann, R. *Die Rhetorik der Griechen und Römer in systematischer Übersicht dargestellt*. Berlin, 1875; 2nd ed., Leipzig, 1885.

Wieruszowski, H. '*Ars Dictaminis* in the time of Dante', *Medievalia et Humanistica*, I (1943), 95–108.

Wilkinson, L. P. *Golden Latin Artistry*. Cambridge, 1963.

V: STUDIES OF PARTICULAR STYLISTIC VARIABLES IN MODERN ITALIAN OR RELEVANT NON-ITALIAN TEXTS, OR 'IN UNIVERSO'

Alisova, T. 'Studi di sintassi italiana', *Studi di filologia italiana*, XXV (1967), 223–313.

Select bibliography

Bertolucci-Pizzorusso, V. 'L'iterazione sinonimica in testi prosastici medio-latini', *SMV*, V (1957), 7–29.

Borroff, M. *Sir Gawain and the Green Knight. A Stylistic and Metrical Study.* New Haven and London, 1962.

Colby, A. M. *The Portrait in Twelfth-century French Literature.* Geneva, 1965.

Di Capua, F. *See* section IV.

Dragonetti, R. *La technique poétique des trouvères dans la chanson courtoise. Contribution à l'étude de la rhétorique médiévale.* Bruges, 1960.

Elwert, W. Th. 'Zur Synonymendopplung vom Typ "planh e sospir", "chan e plor"', *Archiv für das Studium der neueren Sprachen*, CXCIII (1956), 40–2.

'Formale Satire bei Peire Cardenal', *Syntactica und Stilistica. Festschrift für E. Gamillscheg.* Tübingen, 1957, pp. 111–19.

François, A. *La désinence '-ance' dans le vocabulaire français, une 'pédale' de la langue et du style.* Geneva, 1950.

Glasser, R. '*Abstractum agens* und Allegorie im älteren Französisch', *ZRP*, LXIX (1953), 43–122.

Hatcher, A. G. 'Consecutive clauses in Old French. A contribution to medieval syntax and psychology', *Revue des études indoeuropéennes*, II (1939), 30–66.

Heinimann, S. 'Zur stilgeschichtlichen Stellung Chrétiens', *Mélanges de linguistique et de littérature romanes à la mémoire d'István Frank.* Univ. of the Saar, 1957, pp. 235–49.

Das Abstraktum in der französischen Literatursprache des Mittelalters. Berne, 1963.

Herczeg, G. *Lo stile indiretto libero in italiano.* Florence, 1963.

Lo stile nominale in italiano. Florence, 1967.

Lindholm, G. *Studien zum mittellateinischen Prosarhythmus. Seine Entwicklung und sein Abklingen in der Briefliteratur Italiens.* Stockholm, 1963.

Lombard, A. *Les constructions nominales dans le français moderne.* Uppsala, 1930.

MacDonald, D. 'Proverbs, *Sententiae* and *Exempla* in Chaucer's Comic Tales: the Function of Comic Misapplication', *Speculum*, XLI (1966), 453–65.

Marconi, G. 'Annominazioni e iterazioni sinonimiche in Juan Manuel', *SMV*, II (1954), 57–70.

Miles, J. *Eras and Modes in English Poetry.* 2nd ed., Berkeley, 1964.

Pellegrini, S. *Studi Rolandiani e Trobadorici.* Bari, 1964.

Rajna, P. 'Per il cursus medievale e per Dante', *Studi di filologia italiana*, III (1932), 7–76.

Select bibliography

Rennert, A. 'Studien zur altfranzösischen Stilistik' (diss.) Göttingen, 1904.
Salverda de Grave, J. J. *Observations sur l'art lyrique de Giraut de Borneil.* Amsterdam, 1938.
Scheludko, D. 'Beiträge zur Entwicklungsgeschichte der altprovenzalischen Lyrik', *Archivum Romanicum*, XI (1927), 273–312; XII (1928), 30–127; XV (1931), 137–216.
Schon, P. M. *Studien zum Stil der frühen französischen Prosa* (*Analecta Romanica* series, vol. VIII), Frankfurt am Main, 1960.
Schwieder, A. *Le discours indirect dans Crestien de Troyes.* Berlin, 1890.
Stefenelli, A. *Der Synonymenreichtum der altfranzösischen Dichtersprache.* Graz, Vienna, Cologne, 1967.
Stempel, W.-D. *Untersuchungen zur Satzverknüpfung im Altfranzösischen.* Brunswick, 1964 (in series *Archiv für das Studium der neueren Sprachen*, special volume, 1).
Taylor, R. L. *Alliteration in Italian.* Newhaven, Conn., 1900.
Ullmann, S. *See* section III.
Valesio, P. *Struttura dell'allitterazione.* Bologna, 1967.
Zumthor, P. *See* section III.

VI: STUDIES ON STYLE IN EARLY ITALIAN, AND SOME STYLISTIC STUDIES OF MEDIEVAL AND RENAISSANCE ITALIAN AUTHORS

Ageno, F. *Il verbo nell'italiano antico. Ricerche di sintassi.* Milan–Naples, 1964.
'Annotazioni sintattiche sui più antichi testi siciliani', *Bollettino del Centro di Studi filologici e linguistici siciliani*, IX (1965), 26 ff.
Alonso, D. 'La poesia del Petrarca e il Petrarchismo. Mondo estetico della pluralità', *Lettere italiane*, XI (1959), 277–319.
Baehr, R. *See* section IV.
Baer, G. *Zur sprachlichen Einwirkung der altprovenzalischen Troubadourdichtung auf die Kunstsprache der frühen italienischen Lyriker.* Zürich, 1939.
Beccaria, G. L. *Ritmo e melodia nella prosa italiana. Studi e ricerche sulla prosa d'arte.* Florence, 1964.
Bezzola, R. R. *Abbozzo di una storia dei gallicismi italiani nei primi secoli* Zürich, 1924 (and Heidelberg, 1925).
Bigi, E. 'Alcuni aspetti dello stile del Canzoniere Petrarchesco', *Lingua Nostra*, XIII (1952), 17–22.
Branca, V. 'Tecnica e poesia nella prosa del Decameron', *Siculorum Gymnasium* (1951) pp. 21–58.
Carini, A. M. 'L'iterazione aggettivale nell'*Orlando Furioso*', *Convivium*, XXXI (1963), 19–34.

Cattaneo, M. T. 'Note sulla poesia di Guittone', *GSLI*, CXXXVII (1960), 165–203; 325–67.

Chiappelli, F. *Studi sul linguaggio di Machiavelli*. Florence, 1952.
Studi sul linguaggio del Tasso epico. Florence, 1957.

Contini, G. 'Preliminari sulla lingua del Petrarca', *Paragone*, II (1951), 3–26; reprinted as introduction to *F.P.*, *Il Canzoniere*, Turin, 1964, pp. vii–xxxviii.

Corti, M. 'La fisionomia stilistica di G. Cavalcanti', *RAL*, ser. VIII, V (1950), 530–52.
'Il linguaggio poetico di Cino da Pistoia', *CN*, XII (1952), 185–223.
'I suffissi dell'astratto "-or" e "-ura" nella lingua poetica delle origini', *RAL*, ser. VIII, VIII (1953), 294–312.
'Studi sulla sintassi della lingua poetica avanti lo stilnovo', *AMAT*, XVIII, n.s. IV (1953), 263–365.
'Contributi al lessico predantesco. Il tipo, "il turbato", "la perduta" ', *AGI*, XXXVIII (1953), 58–92.

Dardano, M. *Lingua e tecnica narrativa nel Duecento*. Rome, 1969.

Del Monte, A. *Studi sulla poesia ermetica medievale*. Naples, 1953.

Elwert, W. Th. 'Per una valutazione stilistica dell'elemento provenzale nel linguaggio della scuola poetica siciliana', *Homenaje a Fritz Krüger*. Mendoza, 1954, vol. II, pp. 85–111.
'La dittologia sinonimica nella poesia lirica romanza delle origini e nella scuola poetica italiana', *Bollettino del Centro di Studi filologici e linguistici siciliani*, II (1954), 152–77.

Favati, G. 'Tecnica ed arte nella poesia cavalcantiana', *Studi petrarcheschi*, III (1950), 117–41.

Ghinassi, G. *Il volgare letterario nel Quattrocento e le 'Stanze' del Poliziano*. Florence, 1957.

Langheinrich, B. 'Sprachliche Untersuchung zur Frage der Verfasserschaft Dantes am *Fiore*', *DDJ*, XIX (1937), 97–202.

Letizia Rizzo, P. M. 'Influssi provenzali e francesi sulla lingua della scuola poetica siciliana', *Convivium* (1949), 740–8.
'Elementi francesi nella lingua dei poeti siciliani della "Magna Curia" ', *Bollettino del Centro di Studi filologici e linguistici siciliani*, I (1953), 115–29; II (1954), 93–151.

Malagoli, L. *Motivi e forme dello stile del Duecento*. Pisa, 1960.
'Forme dello stile mediolatino e forme dello stile volgare', *Studi letterari. Miscellanea in onore di E. Santini*. Palermo, 1956, pp. 57–86.

Marti, M. 'Arte e poesia nelle rime di Guido Cavalcanti', *Convivium* (1949), 178–95.

Mengaldo, P. V. *La lingua del Boiardo lirico*. Florence, 1963.

Nencioni, G. 'Fra grammatica e retorica. Un caso di polimorfia della lingua letteraria dal secolo XIII al XVI', *AMAT*, IV (1953), 213–59.

Neuhofer, P. 'Zur Reihung der Epitheta bei Petrarca und in der älteren italienischen Literatur', *DDJ*, XLIV (1967), 190–211.

Ramaciotti, M. D. 'The Syntax of *Il Fiore* and of Dante's *Inferno* as Evidence in the Question of the Authorship of *Il Fiore*' (diss.). Washington, 1936.

Santangelo, S. *Il volgare illustre e la poesia siciliana del secolo XIII*. Palermo, 1924.

Schiaffini, A. *Tradizione e poesia*, etc.—see section IV.
Momenti di storia della lingua italiana. Rome, 1953.
'La lingua dei rimatori siciliani del Duecento' (typewritten). Rome, 1957.
I mille anni della lingua italiana. Milan, 1961.

Segre, C. 'La sintassi del periodo nei primi prosatori italiani', *RAL*, ser. VIII, IV (1952), 41–193; reprinted in his *Lingua, stile e società*. Milan, 1963, pp. 81–270.

Sorrento, L. *Sintassi romanza, ricerche e prospettive*. 2nd ed., Milan, 1951.

Taylor, R. L. *See* section V.

Terracini, B. *Pagine e appunti di linguistica storica*. Florence, 1957.

Tosi, G. 'Coordinazione e subordinazione nei *Fioretti*', *AGI*, XXVII (1935), 40–63.

Travi, E. 'Il linguaggio biblico nella letteratura di fine Duecento', *Lettere italiane*, X (1958), 189–92.

Turolla, E. 'Dittologia e enjambement nell'elaborazione dell'*Orlando Furioso*', *Lettere italiane*, X (1958), 1–20.

Volpi, G. 'Appunti sul lessico di Monte Andrea', *AGI*, XLVII (1962), 143–61.

VII: STUDIES OF ITALIAN METRIC

Avalle, D'Arco S. *Preistoria dell'endecasillabo*. Milan–Naples, 1963.

Biadene, L. *Il collegamento della stanza mediante la rima nella canzone italiana dei secoli XIII e XIV*. Florence, 1885.
'Morfologia del sonetto nei secoli XIII e XIV', *Studi di filologia romanza*, IV (1889), 1–234.

D'Ovidio, F. *See* section IV.

Elwert, W. Th., *Italienische Metrik*. Munich, 1968 (with good bibliography).

Flamini, F. *Notizia storica dei versi e metri italiani dal medioevo ai tempi nostri*. Livorno, 1919.

Fraccaroli, G. *D'una teoria razionale di metrica italiana*. Turin, 1887.

Fubini, M. *Metrica e poesia. Lezioni sulle forme metriche italiane*: vol. I, *Dal 200 al Petrarca*. Milan, 1962.

Guarnerio, P. E. *Manuale di versificazione italiana.* 3rd ed., Milan, 1913.

Leonetti, P. *Storia della tecnica del verso italiano.* 3 vols, Naples, 1933, 1934, 1938.

Levi, A. 'Della versificazione italiana', *Archivum Romanicum,* xiv (1930), 449 ff.

Lisio, G. S. *Studio sulla forma metrica della canzone italiana nel secolo XIII.* Imola, 1895.

Menichetti, A. 'Rime per l'occhio e ipometrie nella poesia romanza delle origini', *CN,* xxvi (1966), 5–95.

Mönch, W. *Das Sonett. Gestalt und Geschichte,* Heidelberg, 1955.

Mozzati, E. 'Gli elementi della versificazione volgare nel trattato di Antonio da Tempo e in *Las Leys d'Amors',* *Rendiconti dell'Istituto lombardo,* xcii (1958), 558–68; and cf. 929–45.

Pernicone, V. 'Storia e svolgimento della metrica', *Tecnica e teoria letteraria,* vol. coll., Milan, 1948, pp. 237–77.

Serretta, M. *Endecasillabi crescenti nella poesia italiana delle origini e nel Canzoniere di Petrarca.* Milan, 1938.

Sesini, U. 'Il verso neolatino nella ritmica musicale', *Convivium,* x (1938), 481–502.

'L'endecasillabo: struttura e peculiarità', *Convivium,* xi (1939), 545–70.

Spongano, R. *Nozioni ed esempi di metrica italiana.* Bologna, 1966.

Wilkins, E. H., *The Invention of the Sonnet and other Studies in Italian Literature.* Rome, 1959.

VIII: GENERAL STUDIES ON DANTE'S STYLE AND ON HIS VIEWS CONCERNING STYLE

Auerbach, E. *Dante als Dichter der irdischen Welt.* Berlin, 1929. Trans. R. Manheim as *Dante, Poet of the Secular World.* Chicago, 1961.

Bahner, W. 'Dantes Bemühungen um die Geltung und Formung der italieni- schen Literatursprache', *Sitzungsberichte der deutschen Akademie der Wissenschaften zu Berlin* (1966), pp. 1–39.

Bartsch, K. 'Dantes Poetik', *Jahrbuch der Deutschen Dante Gesellschaft,* iii (1871), 303–67.

Batard, Y. *Dante, Minerve et Apollon. Les images de la 'Divine Comédie'.* Paris, 1952.

De Robertis, D. 'Nascita della coscienza letteraria italiana', *L'approdo letterario,* xxxi (1965), 3–32. Reprinted in the second edition of his *Il libro della 'Vita Nuova'.* Florence, 1970, pp. 177–238.

Glunz, H. H. *Die Literarästhetik des europäischen Mittelalters: Wolfram,*

Rosenroman, Chaucer, Dante. Pöppinghaus, 1937; reprinted Frankfurt am Main, 1963.

Grayson, C. 'Dante e la prosa volgare', *Il Verri*, IX (1963), 6–26.

'*Nobilior est vulgaris*: Latin and Vernacular in Dante's Thought', *Centenary Essays on Dante* by members of the Oxford Dante Society. Oxford, 1965, pp. 54–76.

Groppi, F. *Dante traduttore*. 2nd ed., Rome, 1962.

Malagoli, L. *Linguaggio e poesia nella 'Divina Commedia'*. 2nd ed., Pisa, 1960.

'Medievalismo e modernità di Dante', *SMV*, IV (1957), 131–76.

'Il linguaggio del *Paradiso* e la crisi dello spirito cristiano medievale', *L'Alighieri*, VII (1966), 40–52.

Marti, M. *Realismo dantesco e altri studi*. Milan–Naples, 1961.

Mengaldo, P. V. 'L'elegia "umile" (*DVE*, II, iv, 5–6)', *GSLI*, CXLIII (1966), 177–98.

Nencioni, G. 'Dante e la retorica', in vol. coll. *Dante e Bologna nei tempi di Dante*. Bologna, 1967, pp. 91–112.

Noyer-Weidner, A. *Symmetrie und Steigerung als stilistisches Gesetz der 'Divina Commedia'*. Krefeld, 1961.

Pagliaro, A. *Ulisse. Ricerche semantiche sulla 'Divina Commedia'*. 2 vols, Milan–Florence, 1967. See especially the essays in the second volume: 'Dialetti e lingue nell'oltretomba'; 'Simbolo e allegoria'; 'Teoria e prassi linguistica'; 'Il linguaggio poetico'.

Paparelli, G. '*Fictio*: la definizione dantesca della poesia', *FR*, VII (1960), 1–83.

Paratore, E. *Tradizione e struttura in Dante*. Florence, 1968.

Pazzaglia, M. *Il verso e l'arte della canzone nel 'De Vulgari Eloquentia'*. Florence, 1967.

Santangelo, S. *Dante e i trovatori provenzali*. Catania, 1920; reprinted 1959.

Sapegno, N. 'Tecnica, poetica e poesia nelle opere giovanili di Dante' (typewritten). Rome, 1939.

Schiaffini, A. 'Dante, Retorica, Medioevo', *Atti del Congresso Internazionale di Studi Danteschi*, Florence, 1965, vol. II, pp. 155–86.

'Lettura del *De Vulgari Eloquentia* di Dante' (typewritten). Rome, 1959.

Staedler, E. 'Das rhetorische Element in Dantes *Divina Commedia*', *DDJ*, XXII (1940), 107–51 (mostly concerned with *Inf.*, VII, 1; XXXI, 67).

'Die Wendungen zur Einführung der direkten Rede in der *Divina Commedia* und ihre klassischen Vorbilder', *DDJ*, XXV (1943), 106–24.

Taddei, A. 'Dante traduttore nel *Convivio*', *CN*, XXII (1962), 141–59.

Vallone, A. *La prosa della 'Vita Nuova'*. Florence, 1963.

Studi su Dante medievale. Florence, 1965.

La prosa del 'Convivio'. Florence, 1967.

Ricerche dantesche. Lecce, 1967.

Vinay, G. 'Ricerche sul *De Vulgari Eloquentia*', *GSLI*, CXXXVI (1959), 236–74; 376–88.

IX: STUDIES ON PARTICULAR FEATURES OF DANTE'S STYLE

Alaerts, Y. 'Essai sur l'épithète dans la *Divine Comédie*', *Les lettres romanes*, VIII (1954), 3–18.

Amrein–Widmer, M. *Rhythmus als Ausdruck inneren Erlebens in Dantes 'Divina Commedia'*. Zürich, 1932 (cf. Casella's review in *Studi Danteschi*, XVIII (1934), 130–6).

Applewhite, J. 'Dante's Use of the Extended Simile in the *Inferno*', *Italica*, XLI (1954), 294–309.

Austin, H. D. 'Multiple Meanings and their Bearing on the Understanding of Dante's Metaphors', *Modern Philology*, XXX (1932), 129–40.

Blasucci, L. 'L'esperienza delle "petrose" e il linguaggio della *Divina Commedia*', Belfagor, XII (1957), 403–31.

Casella, M. 'Studi sul testo della *Divina Commedia*', *Studi Danteschi*, VIII (1924), 5–85 (25 ff. on 'dieresi' and 'dialefe').

Cernecca, D. 'L'inversione del soggetto nella prosa della *Vita Nuova*', *Atti del Congresso Internazionale di Studi Danteschi*. Florence, 1965, vol. II, pp. 187–212.

Ciafardini, E. 'Dierisi e sinerisi nella *Divina Commedia*', *Rivista d'Italia*, XIII (1910), 888–919.

'Dialefe e sinalefe nella *Divina Commedia*', *Rivista d'Italia*, XVII (1914), 465 ff.

Costanzo, L. *Il linguaggio di Dante nella 'Divina Commedia'*. Naples, 1969.

Curtius, E. R. 'Periphrase, Annominatio, Anaphora', *Gesammelte Aufsätze zur romanischen Philologie*. Berne, 1960.

Di Capua, F. 'Appunti sul "cursus" o ritmo prosaico nelle opere latine di Dante Alighieri', *Scritti minori*, 2 vols, Rome, 1959, vol. I, pp. 564–85.

Franciosi, G. *Dell'evidenza dantesca nelle metafore, nelle similitudini e nei simboli*. Modena, 1872; Parma, 1889.

Franz, A. 'Sinn und Rhythmus in Danteversen', *DDJ*, XXXVI (1958), 13–39.

Fubini, M. 'La terzina della *Commedia*', *DDJ*, XLIII (1965), 58–89.

Gloth, A. 'Der übertragene Gebrauch von Verwandtschaftsnamen bei Dante', *DDJ*, XV (1933), 1–60; XVI (1934), 132–87.

Gmelin, H. 'Konzentrierende Imitatio', *Syntactica und Stilistica. Festschrift für E. Gamillscheg*. Tübingen, 1957, pp. 171–81.

'Die dichterische Bedeutung der Latinismen in Dantes *Paradiso*', *Germanische-Romanische Monatsschrift*, VIII (1958), 35–46.

'Die Sprache des Transzendenten in Dantes *Paradiso*', *Stil- und Formprobleme in der Literatur*. Heidelberg, 1959, pp. 189–95.

Grana, G. 'Appunti sul linguaggio figurato nelle rime di Dante', *Convivium*, XXXIV (1966), 293–317.

Jakobson, R., and Valesio, P. '*Vocabulorum constructio* in "Se vedi li occhi miei" ', *Studi Danteschi*, XLIII (1966), 7–33.

Lewis, C. S. 'Dante's Similes', *Studies in Medieval and Renaissance Literature*. Cambridge, 1966, pp. 64–77.

'Imagery in the Last Eleven Cantos of Dante's *Comedy*', ibid., pp. 78–93.

Lisio, G. S. *L'arte del periodo nelle opere volgari di Dante Alighieri e del secolo XIII*. Bologna, 1902.

Mariotti, F. 'Dante e la statistica delle lingue', *RAL*, CCLXXVII (1879–80), 262–90.

Marzot, G. *Il linguaggio biblico nella 'Divina Commedia'*. Pisa, 1956.

Mazzali, E. 'Appunti sul ritmo e sui modi narrativi dell' *Inferno* (canti I–VIII), *Convivium*, XXXIV (1966), 184–209.

Natali, G. 'Versi brutti di Dante', *Italica*, XXXVI (1959), 17–27.

Oxilia, A. 'L'endecasillabo con accento sulla settima usato in coppia, nella *Commedia*', *Atti del Congresso Internazionale di Studi Danteschi*. Florence, 1965, vol. II, pp. 221–9.

Pagliaro, A. *See* section VIII.

Palgen, R. 'Due particolarità dello stile epico di Dante: la nomenclatura pseudoclassica e le metafore allusive', *Convivium*, XXXI (1963), 10–18.

Paratore, E. 'Analisi "retorica" del canto di Pier della Vigna', *Studi Danteschi*, XLII (1965), 281–338.

Parodi, E. G. 'La rima e i vocaboli in rima nella *Divina Commedia*', now in his *Lingua e letteratura. Studi di teoria linguistica e di storia dell'italiano antico*, ed. G. Folena. 2 vols, Venice, 1957, vol. II, pp. 203–84.

Review of G. S. Lisio, *L'arte del periodo nelle opere volgari di Dante Alighieri e del secolo XIII*, ibid., pp. 301–28.

Porcelli, B. 'Appunti sul linguaggio del *Paradiso*', *L'Alighieri*, IX (1968), 37–54.

Rabuse, G. 'Dantes Bilder und Vergleiche', *Orbis Litterarum*, XV (1960), 65–94.

St Clair, G. 'Dante viewed through his imagery', *The University of New Mexico Bulletin* (1935), pp. 1–77.

Sanguineti, E. 'Dante, *praesens historicum*', *Lettere Italiane*, X (1958), 263–87.

Scaglione, A. D. 'Periodic Syntax and Flexible Metre in the *Divine Comedy*', *Romance Philology*, XX (1967), 1–22.

Select bibliography

Schiaffini, A. 'Note sul colorito dialettale della *Divina Commedia*', *Studi Danteschi*, XIII (1928), 31–45.

Vazzana, S. 'Le similitudini nella *Divina Commedia*', *Ausonia*, XIII (1958), 3–10.

Venturi, L. *Le similitudini dantesche ordinate, illustrate e confrontate.* Florence, 1874.

Vezin, A. 'Die Periphrase in der *Göttlichen Kömodie*', *DDJ*, XXXIII (1954), 120–41.

Vincent, E. R. 'Dante's Choice of Words', *Italian Studies*, X (1955), 1–18.

Von Richthofen, E. 'Dantes Verwendung von gleichgerichteten und gegensätzlichen Sinnbildern', *DDJ*, XXXII (1953), 24–41.

Veltro und Diana. Dantes mittelalterliche und antike Gleichnisse nebst einer Darstellung ihrer Ausdrucksformen. Tübingen, 1956.

INDEX OF POEMS CITED

Index of Poems Cited